THE SOUL OF RECOVERY

THE SOUL *of* RECOVERY

Uncovering the Spiritual Dimension in the Treatment of Addictions

CHRISTOPHER D. RINGWALD

OXFORD
UNIVERSITY PRESS

2002

OXFORD
UNIVERSITY PRESS

Oxford New York
Auckland Bangkok Buenos Aires
Cape Town Chennai Dar es Salaam Delhi Hong Kong Istanbul
Karachi Kolkata Kuala Lumpur Madrid Melbourne Mexico City Mumbai
Nairobi São Paulo Shanghai Singapore Taipei Tokyo Toronto
and an associated company in Berlin

Published by Oxford University Press, Inc.,
198 Madison Avenue, New York, New York 10016

Oxford is a registered trademark of Oxford University Press

Library of Congress Cataloging-in-Publication Data is available
ISBN 0-19-514768-5

Book design by Adam B. Bohannon

1 3 5 7 9 8 6 4 2

Printed in the United States of America
on acid-free paper

"The Twelve Steps of Alcoholics Anonymous and excerpts from *Twelve Steps and Twelve Traditions* and *Alcoholics Anonymous* are reprinted with permission of Alcoholics Anonymous World Services, Inc. (AAWS) Permission to reprint this material does not means that AAWS has reviewed or approved the contents of this publication, or that AAWS necessarily agrees with the views expressed herein. AA is a program of recovery from alcoholism *only*—use of this material in connection with programs and activities are patterned after AA, but address other problems, or in any other non-AA context, does not imply otherwise."

Excerpts from the AA Preamble are reprinted with permission of the AA Grapevine Inc.

To Amy Jeanne Biancolli Ringwald,
my wife and best editor,
colleague and conversationalist,
who came late to religion but was always of God.

CONTENTS

PREFACE

The book reports on the role of spirituality in treating addictions. Many people who recover from an addiction to drugs or alcohol do so by developing a spiritual life. When I first learned of this, I was fascinated by the idea that spiritual beliefs and habits could have an immediate and daily function, that faith would make a concrete difference, that belief could save and improve an alcoholic's life. As a newspaper reporter, I wrote a series of articles about drug and alcohol treatment in New York State. The investigation concentrated on the costs and the results of care. It found that most programs, and the state, had little idea of their results with patients. The series led to a state Senate investigation and a new law requiring programs to track their outcomes.

During my reporting, administrators and officials spoke to me of methods and modalities and biopsychosocial models of care. The alcoholics and addicts themselves preferred to talk about why and how they were getting clean. Most mentioned spirituality or God. That, I decided, was the real action in the treatment and recovery of people addicted to drugs.

This book's premise, based on the evidence and dozens of personal accounts, is that many addicts recover by spiritual means. If their faith in God or some "high power" makes the difference, so be it. I am concerned with the results, not the validity, of such beliefs. Others are better equipped to debate the existence of a deity. Many people once dependent on drugs also recover with a spirituality devoid of a deity. My subject is how and why addicts develop spiritually, and the implications for them and society.

To avoid repetition, I use the word addicts, generally, to include alcoholics. Alcohol is a drug and most people who enter treatment have abused both. Treatment and recovery from either or both share basic elements. The book draws on interviews with about 300 alcoholics, addicts, experts, counselors, and family members; hundreds of studies and books; and visits to people, programs, and conferences in Arizona, California, Florida, Maine, Massachusetts, Minnesota, New Jersey, New York, Vermont, and Washington, D.C.

My reporting, research, and writing continued for several years. From it, I reached several broad conclusions, some obvious and others not, but all of interest and worth. Though others have seen more deeply or clearly into these subjects, I have collected their insights and mine into what I trust will be a fresh and useful synthesis.

The ten chapters progress from the general to the specific to the medical and scientific, then to contrasting specifics before looking at the broader picture and outside lessons. The book also serves as a travelogue through the world of treatment and recovery. Chapter I lays out the premise—that a significant portion of alcoholics and addicts recover through spiritual development—and the major reasons and issues. The next three chapters explore treatments based on spiritual methods. Chapter V looks at the science of addiction, the business of measuring results and the trickier matter of measuring spirituality. Chapter VI looks to the extremes—religious and secular—on either side. The next two chapters look at approaches with spiritual foundations of a different and evolving nature. Then I pull back to assess the recovery movement in Chapter IX. The last Chapter looks outside the field to see its implications for society and for the utility and legality of faith-based social programs. Nine of the chapters have two profiles of individual addicts and alcoholics—one man, one woman—whose recovery illustrates relevant themes.

Many people helped create this book and I thank them all, named and unnamed. My wife, Amy Biancolli Ringwald, gave her good humor, support, sharp mind, and superb editing. My children, Madeleine Margaret, Jeanne Annemarie, and Mitchell Furey, all cheered me on in their exuberant manner and tolerated many dinner-table conversations about neuro-chemistry, spirituality, and dead French sociologists.

The book could not have been written without the warm generosity of Jeanne Neff, president of The Sage Colleges, who gave me a room of my own in a scintillating atmosphere. Sally Lawrence arranged many practical details with aplomb and good cheer. I began my research while on a year-long fellowship from The Henry J. Kaiser Family Foundation, and I thank especially Penny Duckham, Tim Johnson, and Drew Altman. Near the end, the Anonymous Foundation and Walter Ludewig provided a crucial grant. Rex Smith at the (Albany N.Y.) *Times Union* gave invaluable recommendations.

At Oxford University Press, Cynthia Read saw the point of it all, bless her, and rescued the better part. Paula Cooper copyedited with finesse and insight. Theo Calderara and Ruth Mannes kept the wheels turning.

I thank the people I interviewed for this book, many of whom are named herein and even more whom are not, for their candor, time, and insight. I thank AA World Services for permission to quote generously from their literature. Colleagues, family, and friends helped immensely. Mike Virtanen scrutinized six chapters and held me to journalism's highest standard: a search for truth. Jane Gottlieb saw me through difficult periods. My siblings Tom, Anne, Carl, and Marie all kept asking about it. Liza Frenette, Jeanne Neff, Tim Johnson, Joanne Valenti, and Larry Hauptmann read and helped with various concepts and sections. Brad Warner, Victor Pagano, John Dwyer, and Fred Boehrer explained many points of treatment, spirituality, and theology to me.

I was blessed with fine colleagues in West Hall at the Sage Albany campus. Joan Maguire helped me hash out many ideas; Doreen Tiernan and Judy Waterman encouraged me daily; Jeff Soleau set me straight on points of philosophy, and Olivia Bertagnolli shared her book-writing wisdom. I thank many others at the Sage library, mailroom—where Deborah Dorsey tamed the copy machine—and various offices.

Finally, many thinkers and writers influenced me but I was most informed by those who took the effects of faith seriously, often despite their own doubts, notably Emile Durkheim, William James, Bill Wilson, Alfred Kazin, Edmund Wilson, Harold Bloom, Ernest Kurtz, Gerald G. May, and William R. Miller. Ultimately, the book was written thanks to the scores of addicts who found in their faith, spirituality, or religion the means to live and were willing to talk about it.

I was always in pain. The drugs stopped working and I was left with me.
John, recovered addict, New York City, New York

Addiction is a disease of death, really, so you need something strong to stop it.
Amy Denenberg, program director, Corning, New York

The believer who has communed with his god is not simply a man who sees new truths that the unbeliever knows not; he is a man who is stronger.
Emile Durkheim, *The Elementary Forms of Religious Life*

One day, they were talking about being set free. That really hit home with me.
Eric, addict in treatment, Rochester, New York.

THE SOUL OF RECOVERY

CHAPTER I

Addictions, Spiritual Solutions, and the Insights of Alcoholics Anonymous

Awakening to Recovery

It is an autumn day in 1993. Timothy H. Green stumbles down a street in Rochester, New York, his hometown. At 33, Green has been drinking alcoholically for at least a decade and shredding all the trappings of a middle-class existence. He has lost jobs, homes, family. This is his life: getting drunk, staggering, lying, and stealing, finding more to drink. On this day, a woman stops alongside and speaks with him. She invites him to a church meeting, the upstate conference of a non-denominational Christian group. Green walks there with her and enters. He hears singing, preaching, praising. Little sinks in. But his life changes. On some level, he is transformed such that, eventually, he will be able to stop drinking.

"At the conference, I just began to feel things. I realized that Satan was robbing me of things in my life. My knees rattled, I fell to the ground. I had a spiritual awakening, and I knew that whatever I was meant to receive from God would come through those people."[1]

Green tells this story four years later, in October 1997, sitting inside a screened porch on the second floor of Freedom House, a publicly funded Twelve-Step-style treatment program housed in a former rectory. Green's bass voice emanates in sure complete sentences. Unlike many recovered alcoholics, he insists on using his full name. He finds in his past no shame and in his redemption considerable but quiet joy and gratitude. Just over six feet tall, Green is thin and his manner hard. He has been sober now for the six months he has lived at Freedom House. He did not stay stopped after that afternoon in 1993, though the process of his recovery began that day. Looking back, Green casts that period in the vernacular of addiction rehabilitation.

"I tried to do it on my own, in 1995. Sixty, ninety days later I was back out, using." Later, he says, "I realized that relapse was not a requirement, that relapse was not an option." Nor is recovery guaranteed. "For some people, their bottom is meant to be death," Green adds. He says he later turned himself in to the authorities and served a one-year sentence in state prison for a previous conviction. After work release, he went through treatment, relapsed and then returned to Freedom House. He has remained sober these six months.

Daily, Green attends support groups and cultivates a network of ex-addicts and alcoholics who are leading a similar life. He also serves as an usher at his church. Prayer and help from others constitute the twin pillars of his new life. "I pray as much as I can. I sit down at the end of the day and reflect on my day to see what I did wrong. I have a group, I have my church, I have recovering people in my life. Some support, that's my problem. Before, I never had any support."

Spirituality Central to Most Treatments

Green's story differs in degree but not in nature from that of millions of alcoholics and addicts who have recovered. Yet much of the public, and private, discussion on addictions and treatment ignore the Timothy Greens. When politicians or commentators call for "treatment instead of jail" for drug-abusing offenders, they rarely add the caveat, "so they'll develop spiritually." And when people all around us—spouses, friends, colleagues, relatives—stop drinking or drugging by attending support group meetings, rarely do we learn that they are sober not only because of the solidarity they find there, but primarily because they have found some sort of "high power" by which to set their compass. Typically, they learn about it in treatment.

This means that most of the millions of Americans treated for substance abuse are encouraged to develop a spiritual life. Most of the more than 11,000 treatment programs in the country introduce their clients to some form of spirituality, usually based on the Twelve-Step program of Alcoholics Anonymous or Narcotics Anonymous, or dozens of similar fellowships. These fellowships, actually networks of autonomous groups, rightly emphasize that they are not treatment, are not affiliated with any outside enterprise, and take no positions on outside issues. But rehabs like what they have to offer. A survey of 450 treatment centers found that 93 percent used the Twelve-Step philosophy.[2] Other estimates put it lower, at 80 percent, but H. Wesley Clark, director of the federal Center for Substance Abuse Treatment, said that the figure was definitely in the range between the two.[3]

Depending on the length and intensity of treatment, addicts may be merely introduced to the workings of AA or NA or the Twelve Steps, or they may be fully immersed in these by the time they graduate. According to the 1996 Alcoholic Anonymous Membership Survey, treatment or counseling helped direct half of its members into the fellowship.

During the 1980s, treatment often consisted of 28-day, or longer, stays at a residential program. But with government cutbacks and managed care, bolstered by studies showing equivalent results, most treatment now occurs in outpatient settings. This can range from all-day, daily attendance at a center to some combination of weekly visits to a counselor and, perhaps, group therapy. Many of the interviews in later chapters were conducted at residential programs, since these offer an accessible and stable pool of subjects. Long-term care has also provided most elements of outpatient care. Further, much of the scientific research has been conducted among patients of long-term programs. But research also indicates that spiritual methods, primarily Twelve-Step facilitation, of residential programs may work even better in outpatient care. A review of 74 studies found that AA involvement was "modestly predictive of drinking reduction and psycho-social improvement," and that "AA participation and drinking outcomes were more strongly related in outpatient samples."[4]

The Twelve Steps lead an alcoholic or addict to admit the problem, turn to a higher power or "God as we understood him," take a moral personal inventory, make amends, pray, and meditate, and to live by these principles and help others. As *Twelve Steps and Twelve Traditions*, one of the group's major texts, describes it, "AA's Twelve Steps are a group of principles, spiritual in their nature, which, if practiced as a way of life, can expel the obsession to drink and enable the sufferer to become happily and usefully whole."[5] A minority of programs offers alternative spiritualities, such as yoga or Islam or native American religions or Christianity, or blends these practices with the AA approach. Some refer clients to support groups other than AA, such as Women for Sobriety, which also encourage members to develop spiritually or to follow their own religion. A small number of treatments eschew talk of the transcendent altogether.

So what is spirituality? The word derives from spirit, which in turn comes from the Latin words for breath or breathe. "Spirit" is used in the Bible to speak of God's power and presence. Today, spirituality is understood as a quest for ultimate reality, meaning, truth, or a deity. Webster's College Dictionary defines it as "pertaining to the spirit or the soul" especially the spirit or soul "as the seat of moral or physical nature."

Among AA members, the understanding is routinely generic, powerful, and flexible. "Spirituality boils down to truth; what is the truth for that individual?" said Larry Bonniwell, an addictions counselor in St. Paul.[6] The Twelve Steps mention God, but qualified by the phrase, "as we understood Him." This echoes a suggestion made by a friend to one of

AA's cofounders who was skeptical of religion: "Why don't you choose your own conception of God?"[7]

Spirituality can exist outside religion, and one religion may contain a range of spiritual methods. Speaking at a conference on addictions, Richard McGowan, a priest and professor at Boston College, defined spirituality in both realms. "For the religious person, quite simply, it is the way we express our longings to somehow touch and be touched by God. For the nonreligious, it is the search for a power, cause or being that is within our reach but beyond our grasp."[8]

Spirituality does not require belief in a God. As anthropologists, and the examples of Buddhism or Jainism attest, a deity is not even necessary for religion. And beliefs alone do not make for spirituality. What is necessary is for those beliefs to lead to values through personal verification, for one's philosophy of life to be "vitalized by emotion."[9] In contrast religion is "a set of beliefs about the cause, nature and purpose of the universe, especially when considered as the creation of a superhuman agency or agencies, usually involving devotional or ritual observances and often containing a moral code for the conduct of human behavior," according to Webster's. This reveals five basic ingredients: a set of beliefs; a deity, in most cases; rituals; a moral code, and, I would add, the fact that adherence readily identifies membership. The spirituality used in addiction treatment lacks most of those elements. Spirituality, as seen above, is basically a search for a deity or ultimate truth or reality on a personal and flexible basis. Or consider that religion consists of beliefs and rites. Spiritual approaches to addiction have both. But unlike religion, the beliefs are not mandatory and the rites, when these exist, are generic and not prescribed.

Perhaps no group is, informally, more responsible for popularizing this difference in the modern era than members of AA, NA, and the like. The popular mantra, "I'm spiritual but not religious," bears out a distinction held by the founders of AA and refined in blunter terms by later members. These embrace the flexible, tolerant, and practical elements of spirituality while often denigrating, or at least distancing themselves from what they call the rigidity and dogma of religion. As one recovered alcoholic put it, "Religion is the politics of spirituality." The distinction is not new. Yet some of the confusion may be, since many today are eager to push religion out of the way and apply the term spiritual to a whole galaxy of what were once known as religious sentiments, beliefs, and practices. The 1960s rebellion against institutions continues. Many people feel aggrieved at the idea of any authority in the realm of their deepest and loftiest instincts and beliefs. But the rift is barely a new one. Almost every religious reform (see Jesus) began with a rejection of the prevailing form of organized worship. At the same time, the distinction is a real one. Spiritually based treatments, such as meditation or Twelve-Step facilitation, suggest a program of action rather than a code of beliefs. These are methods, not doctrines—the very reason for their appeal, even for people who recover without formal treatment.

Profile: Ellen—Judaism and the Twelve Steps

In recovering from alcoholism, Ellen found common ground between her Jewish faith and heritage and the spiritual program of Alcoholics Anonymous. "Before, I never thought of God, I never turned to God in a crisis. Never! I had no concept of personal God." After sobering up, she said, "I started going to the synagogue, and all of this old stuff had new meaning. It was very calming." Alcoholics Anonymous, despite its Christian roots and remnants, led her that way. "The Lord's prayer, which they say at the end of [AA] meetings, it's Christian and I don't say it. I listen because I'm grateful for this group of primarily Christians that took me in and set me on the right track to a relationship with God. All the meetings are in churches, but I wanted to know so much how to do this."[10]

Ellen, 48, is both vivacious and serious. In conversation, she thinks, speaks, then pauses to consider her remark. She directs a New York statewide educational association and is a mother of two and a wife. Ellen grew up in an upstate town. Her father taught college and the family attended a small synagogue where she received her religious education. For her, being Jewish was "a cultural, racial, ethnic thing—it's the food, it's the everything." Most of all, Ellen learned the importance of education and benevolence.

Growing up, she saw people drink alcohol nonalcoholically. "If we had pizza, my father would ask, 'Who wants to split a beer?' " Nevertheless, her first real drink, at age 16 at her brother's bar mitzvah, hit her hard. "I thought, 'Wow! If one makes me feel this great then two will make me feel better. And if two make me feel better, three will make me feel even better. So I kept drinking. And everybody thought it was funny." Ellen paused. "For most of my life, I was enabled by friends who thought it was funny."

At age 29, she was married and had an infant. "The only time I had been able to stop drinking for more than nine days was when I was pregnant." Just weeks after the birth, Ellen had a glass of champagne on New Year's Eve. "Within two weeks, I was back at it worse than ever—sneaking it, drinking vodka from the bottle." It mystified her. "I knew what it was like to be not drinking. I was not miserable. I had a husband to live for, a beautiful baby girl, everything to live for. I was screwing up my life and it was so clear it was the alcohol."

About this time, Ellen drove a friend to a hospital detoxification unit and saw the person recover over the next few years. Later, Ellen started attending AA meetings at the same detox and reading AA literature, thinking those would suffice. "I was so sick, I didn't know I was sick. People started saying to me, 'Hey, there are other meetings you can attend.' Then I thought I'd stop trying to do this myself."As is customary in Twelve-Step groups, Ellen asked a more experienced woman to be her sponsor, a person who guides a newcomer through the Steps and the challenge of living sober. As it turns out, the woman was a devout Catholic who had been treated at a Twelve-Step-style facility near Pittsburgh founded by Rabbi Abraham J. Twerski, M.D., who has written and lectured extensively on the consistency between the Twelve Steps and Jewish tradition. The coincidence is not lost on Ellen, who eventually asked her sponsor about connecting with God.

"After about six months, I asked this woman, 'How do you pray?' It was obvious to me that it wasn't me keeping me sober." The woman wrote out a few prayers and suggested she start out slowly. Ellen and her family joined a synagogue, and she began integrating AA and Judaism, despite reservations. "My religion still drives me crazy—it's still a sexist religion, there's too much Hebrew. I love Hebrew too, but I don't need three hours of it." (When she told her rabbi of her distraction during Sabbath services, he suggested she bring something to read such as the AA monthly magazine, the *AA Grapevine*.)

"Spirituality is about belief. Religion is about ritual and how you get to God. Jews talk to God as an equal. We stand when the ark is open, where the Torah is stored, which tells us how to live. My rituals get me to God." She found company through Jewish Alcoholics, Chemically Dependent Persons, and Significant Others, or JACS, a New York City based support group and attended one of their retreats, in the Catskills. She heard Rabbi Twerski speak and enjoyed the company, especially since Jews are, by and large, greatly outnumbered in AA and NA. Meetings at the retreat ended with the Shema, the primary declaration of fidelity in Jewish liturgy. ("Hear, O Israel, the Lord is our God, the Lord is one.")

Attending two JACS-sponsored retreats furthered the connection between Ellen's spiritual and religious life. She leaned in toward the table at the restaurant where we spoke and dropped her voice for emphasis. "In Judaism, there is *denial* that there is alcoholism among Jews." This was one reason she and a friend started an AA discussion meeting, open to all, at a Jewish community center in Albany. Ellen also found similarity between the personal moral inventory, followed by amends, suggested in AA and the atonement for sins that is part of Rosh Hashanah and Yom Kippur.

A year later, I spoke with Ellen again. A monthly Jewish Twelve-Step-recovery group she had helped start was a year old. "We have about seven regular members from all different Twelve-Step groups. We do a step a month and use the book, 'Twelve Jewish Steps to Recovery.'" (Rabbi Kerry

M. Olitzky and Stuart A. Copans, M.D., Boston: Jewish Lights Publishing, 1992) "It shows how the steps really are in sync with our religion. Many in the group had gotten away from their religion or were turned off by it."

She reflected on the practical, inclusive nature of the spirituality she credits for her recovery. "I had a Catholic sponsor who taught me how to pray. She moved away and then I had a Jewish sponsor, who died, and now I have another Catholic sponsor. At our Jewish Twelve-Step group, we have people from AA, NA, Overeaters Anonymous, Gamblers Anonymous. You've got to take your tools out of the toolbox. And use them."

A Primer On Addiction and Treatment

Before exploring the function and utility of spirituality, consider some facts about addiction. Alcoholism and addiction are terms with numerous definitions. Common sense offers one. "We alcoholics are men and women who have lost the ability to control our drinking," as the book *Alcoholics Anonymous* puts it.[11] Science and medicine acknowledge two basic categories, dependence and abuse, as outlined in the standard reference, *The Diagnostic and Statistical Manual of Mental Disorders*. This defines dependence as "a cluster of cognitive, behavioral and physiological symptoms indicating that the individual continues use of the substance despite significant substance-related problems" and usually leading to "tolerance, withdrawal and compulsive drug-taking activity."[12] The definition corresponds to that used by the World Health Organization in its International Classification of Diseases.[13] Substance abuse, on the other hand, is characterized by "recurrent and significant adverse consequences related to the repeated use of substances," and does not include the "tolerance, withdrawal, or a pattern of compulsive use" of dependence.[14] As the manual notes, some persons abuse drugs or alcohol for a long time without developing dependence.

When most people say alcoholic or addict, they mean a person dependent on alcohol or drugs. I do the same in this book, for clarity and also since the people who enter treatment are usually the ones whose addiction is more severe.

How many are there? According to the 1999 National Household Survey on Drug Abuse, 3.6 million Americans, or 1.6 percent of the total population age 12 and older, were dependent on illicit drugs and 8.2 million Americans—3.7 percent of the population—were dependent on alcohol.[15] Of these, 1.5 million people were dependent on both. Overall, an estimated 10.3 million people were dependent on either alcohol or illicit drugs, which is 4.7 percent of the population. These are the addicts and constitute most of those who seek or need treatment.

Many go for help. In 1998, an estimated 963,000 had received treatment or counseling for their drug use and 1.7 million people reported receiving treatment or counseling for alcohol use.[16] H. Wesley Clark told me that, based on more recent and complete data, about 3 million people are treated annually.[17] On any given day, about 1 million Americans are being treated for substance abuse.[18]

Measuring Results: A Quick Look

So, does treatment work? "Whenever people ask me that, I always say, 'compared to what?'" A. Thomas McClellan, a leading researcher based at the University of Pennsylvania, said with some exasperation at a conference in 1998.[19] From the research emerge several basic themes. First, a sizeable proportion of alcoholics and addicts do recover after treatment. Unfortunately, many programs have overstated their success rates, which has added to public skepticism about treatment. "Not all treatment works," McClellan said in his talk. "Not all programs work." Second, proven results come in many areas—employment, family, health, and criminality.[20] Abstinence is not the only measure of success. Third, many relapse only to sober up again. Most of those who relapse, 60-80 percent, do so within three to four months, and many of those reenter treatment.[21] Others resume drinking or drug use with fewer problems, at least at first. Permanent sobriety on the first time out is rare. By one estimate, only about 20 percent of addicts will achieve a year of abstinence on the first try.[22] Few are cured immediately and forever. Fourth, the period of abstinence before a relapse counts as an improvement over their pretreatment days.

McClellan, who has studied outcomes for decades, and a group of other scientists reviewed hundreds of controlled studies and found that results of treatment for addictions was comparable, and sometimes better, to treatment of other chronic illnesses, namely adult-onset asthma, hypertension and insulin-dependent diabetes.[23] A year after treatment, 40-60 percent, of drug-dependent individuals were continuously abstinent. But among diabetics, asthmatics, and individuals with hypertension, less than 30 percent adhered to treatment, basically dietary or behavioral guidelines. McClellan and his colleagues noted that the role of behavior, personal responsibility, and genetics were similar for all four chronic diseases. But they emphasized the relative success of drug rehabilitation. "Our review of treatment response found more than 100 randomized controlled trials of addictions, most showing significant reductions in drug use, personal health, and reduced social pathology but not cure."

The federal government has funded several long-term, large-scale studies of addicts before, during, and after treatment. The Treatment Outcomes Prospective Study involved 11,000 drug abusers who entered various types of programs, 1979-1981 year abstinence rates averaged 40-60 percent.[24] From 1993 to 1995, the National Treatment Improvement Evaluation Study followed 5,388 clients in federally funded substance abuse programs and found that illicit drug use dropped by half in the 12 months after treatment.[25] Problems of health, crime, alcohol use, and homelessness all decreased significantly.

Finally, the National Institute on Drug Abuse reported in 1999 that, based on conservative estimates, every $1 spent on addiction treatment saved between $4 and $7 in crime and criminal justice costs alone.[26] Add in health care savings, the institute reports, and the savings can exceed treatment costs by $12 to $1. Federal studies showing the effectiveness of treatment are based on both residential and outpatient care, since "outpatient treatment has been the prevailing mode since the early to mid-1990s," said H. Wesley Clark.[27]

Project MATCH, an eight-year, $27 million federally funded effort, studied alcoholic patients in three types of out-patient care—Twelve-Step facilitation, cognitive behavioral therapy, and motivational enhancement therapy.[28] The study found comparable results with all three groups: 35 percent were abstinent a year later. Interestingly, large segments of each group attended AA, underscoring its role in successful recovery.[29]

Many addicts stop or cut back on their own. Some grow up, or encounter a crisis, or have a religious or spiritual conversion without formal treatment. A landmark analysis of returning Vietnam veterans found that 20 percent were addicted in Vietnam, but ten months later in the United States, only 1 percent were, a 95 percent remission rate that brought their addiction rate down to the level in the general population, leaving a hard core still in need of outside help.[30]

A federal epidemiologist, Deborah A. Dawson, analyzed a sample of 4,585 adults who had been classified as alcohol dependent at points ranging up to 20 years earlier. Half were now drinking without abuse or dependence. But these persons, by and large, had less severe or more acute and short-lived alcohol dependence. People with more severe alcoholism were much more likely to have been treated and, when contacted by the researchers, to be either abstinent or in trouble with their drinking. That makes sense.

Few people enter treatment unless they really need it. Those who don't, don't. Those who can drink moderately, do so. So how are the teetotalers doing it? One way is spiritual. "This study supported previous findings indicating that attendance at Alcoholics Anonymous was strongly predictive of abstinence."[31]

Hence the use of the Twelve-Step philosophy in treatment. Interestingly, however, it all started with a small group of alcoholics who figured out, with some outside help and in the dark of the Depression, a way to get sober with the help of God or something quite like God.

Spiritual Solutions: A Short History

Alcoholics Anonymous began on June 10, 1935 when its second member, Robert "Dr. Bob" Smith, of Akron, Ohio, stopped drinking with the help of Bill Wilson, a New York stock investigator. The story is told in the writings of AA, Ernest Kurtz, William L. White, and others, who also point out several historical antecedents.[32]

In 1810, physician Benjamin Rush formulated the modern concept of alcoholism as a progressive disease, characterized by loss of control and resolved by abstinence. His ideas sparked a fledgling temperance movement. Most notable was the Washingtonian Total Abstinence Society, founded in 1840 by six members of a drinking club. The Washingtonian message spread rapidly and offered heavy drinkers a route to sobriety through public confession and commitment, weekly meetings, and a complete social life. It grew to 600,000, then collapsed after 1847 due to internal divisions and "the lack of a sustainable recovery program."[33] The Washingtonians left several legacies for future mutual-aid groups, especially AA. Among these were the value of fellowship, confession, service, and a single-minded focus on alcoholism; the potential of religious or spiritual solutions; and the danger of personal fame and outside entanglements.[34] These lessons influenced the societies, reform clubs, and the asylums and institutions for inebriates that came and went through the late nineteenth and early twentieth centuries.

During the 1930s, some alcoholics sobered up through the Oxford Group, a Protestant evangelical group that sought to revive early Christian practices, notably public confession. One member, Rowland H., had previously sought help several times from Carl Jung, the Swiss psychiatrist. (Given the AA tradition of personal anonymity, members identify themselves by first name and last initial.) Jung finally told Rowland his case was near hopeless, that medicine and psychiatry were of no avail and that only a spiritual change or awakening might help. It did.

Back in New York, Rowland helped a man named Ebby T. achieve a period of sobriety. Ebby visited a still struggling Bill Wilson and told him of his conversion experience. Though skeptical, Wilson finally stopped drinking thanks to a dramatic spiritual experience and guided by the lessons of the Oxford Group. Paramount among these was the need to help other alcoholics. On a business trip to Ohio, Wilson sought to do so and was referred to Dr. Bob, an alcoholic who eventually stopped as well. They co-founded AA, and began working out the practices and principles of the program. Over time, AA members broke away from the Oxford Group, uneasy with its strict religious overtones and its emphasis on "absolute" honesty, purity, unselfishness, and love.[35]

Within a few years, AA had 100 members in New York and Akron.

These spelled out their experiences and ideas in their text, *Alcoholics Anonymous,* first published in 1939 and known to members as the "Big Book." The writing is marked by simple insights and plain speaking based on personal experiences. In it they promise, "to show other alcoholics *precisely how we recovered.*"[36] Most strikingly, the book depicts their alcoholism and recovery in spiritual terms. "If, when you honestly want to, you find you cannot quit entirely, or if when drinking, you have little control over the amount you take, you are probably alcoholic. If that be the case, you may be suffering from an illness which only a spiritual experience will conquer."[37]

If the solution is spiritual, so too was the malady, at least in part. They wrote that, "we have been not only mentally and physically ill, we have been spiritually sick."[38] Though defined in this tripartite way as a malady of the spirit, mind, and body, in the very next sentence they make clear that recovery began in one realm: "When the spiritual malady is overcome, we straighten out mentally and physically." Decades later an addiction expert refined the prognosis, saying that while alcohol cannot touch the spirit directly, it does "knock out the brain's ability to serve as the sensory instrument of the soul. The result is spiritual dysfunction or disease."[39] AA does not dwell on the cause of addiction so much as its solution.

If impaired spirituality and addiction go hand in hand, which comes first may never be fully established. For addicts, however, drugs become a counterfeit God. Rather than escaping, alcoholics are seeking, usually God or serenity or a spiritual life, a point made by Carl Jung, Bill Wilson, and other thinkers, as well as by numerous addicts I interviewed. Some spoke of trying to fill a "God-sized hole" with drugs or alcohol. Said Joseph Molea, a doctor who treats addicted physicians in Tampa, Florida, "Addicts discover the cure for their symptoms in substance abuse." [40] Research confirms "that most alcoholics do not drink to sedate psychological problems, but for the lift, the glow, the positive effects of alcohol. They are not looking for the sedation so much as for solace, trying to satisfy the hunger of the heart."[41]

In alcohol or drugs, they find such a superior force, alas, one that can kill them. Yet admitting this seems a hurdle for many alcoholics whose debility can be characterized by self-centeredness and delusions of omnipotence. This is overcome by admitting that they have lost control over their drinking and a greater force, or higher power, is needed to defeat this compulsion.

William James, the psychologist and philosopher, provided the founders of AA with insights into the utility of faith. Bill Wilson learned from James's 1902 work, *Varieties of Religious Experience,* that spiritual beliefs could have concrete results. The prerequisite, for many people, would be personal shipwreck—precisely the state of the hopeless alcoholic.[42] Given its practical bent, AA sailed a route that combined, as Ernest Kurtz explains in *Not-God: A History of Alcoholics Anonymous*, two currents of American religiosity: the Pietist/ Evangelical, emphasizing salvation from a power outside the self, and the Humanist/ Liberal, stressing human participation in salvation.[43] At the same time, the AA approach—then as now—embodies a deep wariness of organized religion and its dogmas, creeds, rituals, and hierarchies. In more than a hundred interviews I conducted with recovered addicts, dozens expressed a caution if not hostility toward religion in language that echoes AA's founders.

One of AA's central contributions was in disentangling morality from the debate. It basically determined, for its members, that while alcoholics were not necessarily to blame for their conditions, they were responsible for doing something about them. Powerful in the 1930s, when the condemnations of nineteenth-century reformers were still echoing over the land, this insight continues to liberate prospective members and patients in treatment from self-castigation.

The workings of AA have been discussed and examined in hundreds of books and are rehashed and refined daily by members. Its methods and suggestions inspired dozens of other mutual-aid fellowships and guide the work of rehabilitation centers. At AA's core is its spiritual program of recovery, the Twelve Steps as developed by its founding members and described in their main text.

"Here are the steps we took, which are suggested as a program of recovery:

1. We admitted we were powerless over alcohol, that our lives had become unmanageable.
2. Came to believe that a Power greater than ourselves could restore us to sanity.
3. Made a decision to turn our will and our lives over to the care of God *as we understood Him.*
4. Made a searching and fearless moral inventory of ourselves.
5. Admitted to God, to ourselves, and to another human being the exact nature of our wrongs.
6. Were entirely ready to have God remove all these defects of character.
7. Humbly asked Him to remove our shortcomings.
8. Made a list of all persons we had harmed, and became willing to make amends to them all.
9. Made direct amends to such people wherever possible, except when to do so would injure them or others.
10. Continued to take personal inventory and when we were wrong promptly admitted it.
11. Sought through prayer and meditation to improve our conscious

contact with God *as we understood Him,* praying only for knowledge of His will for us and the power to carry that out.

12. Having had a spiritual awakening as the result of these steps, we tried to carry this message to alcoholics, and to practice these principles in all our affairs."

AA, *Alcoholics Anonymous,* 59-60

These are aimed at fostering a spiritual awakening that will keep the alcoholic sober on a daily basis. Spirituality allows life without alcohol. One supplants the other. As Carl Jung wrote in a 1961 letter to Bill Wilson, the formula is *"spiritus contra spiritum."* Or "spirit against spirits."[44]

At meetings, of which there are endless varieties, members recount their drinking past and the benefits of sobriety and discuss how they live sober and useful lives. The book, *Alcoholics Anonymous,* serves as a kind of bible and excerpts are often read aloud. Senior members exercise some leadership, usually as sponsors to newer members. Helping others is paramount. Members find as much companionship, in and out of meetings, as suits their needs. "Sobriety is maintained through sharing experience, strength and hope at group meetings and through the suggested Twelve Steps for recovery from alcoholism."[45] This applies, generally, to other Twelve-Step fellowships.

AA reported two million members in January 2000, almost half of those outside the United States and Canada, and 99,000 groups in more than 150 countries.[46] Narcotics Anonymous, founded in 1953, reports 25,000 weekly meetings in more than 40 countries, which would suggest an estimated membership of 250,000.[47] Cocaine Anonymous, founded in 1982, reports an estimated 30,000 members in 2,000 groups, mostly in the United States, Canada, and Europe.[48]

AA works for people for whom it works, usually those who want it. Figures from AA surveys indicate that only 50 percent of those who come stay more than three months. For addicts coming out of treatment, often mandated to attend meetings, outside research show drop-out rates ranging up to 88 percent by one year after discharge.[49] In 1996, AA's survey of 7,200 members in the United States and Canada, found that the average period of sobriety was six years, with 45 percent of members sober more than five years, 28 percent one to five years and 27 percent less than one year.[50]

AA recognizes that its methods are not for everyone. "Upon therapy for the alcoholic himself, we surely have no monopoly," reads one of several such qualifiers in its main text.[51] But everyone can, potentially, find a home there, as have people across the globe. The AA survey reported an average age of 44, with 13 percent under age 30; 67 percent were men and 33 percent women; 86 percent were white, with the remainder equal parts black, Hispanics, and native American. Outside research indicates that race, income, education, severity of alcoholism, and other factors do not determine successful affiliation. The only apparent exception: those not desiring abstinence.[52]

Spirituality into Treatment

Today, simply put, AA and other Twelve-Step fellowships continue to view the lack or distortion of spirituality as the cause of addiction and an improved spiritual life as the solution. AA is a way of life, not a treatment. Only the first step mentions alcohol, the others concern spiritual process-es. Abstinence merely allows a journey toward wholeness to begin. But after the early successes of AA, medical and other facilities began incor-porating its methods into their treatment.

What became known as the Minnesota Model developed cooperatively among several institutions—Pioneer House, Willmar State Hospital, and Hazelden—during the 1940s and 1950s.[53] This approach treated the addiction rather than its causes, emphasized spirituality, used multidisci-plinary teams of doctors, nurses, social workers, and others, and recruited recovered alcoholics as counselors. Today the Minnesota Model continues most of these practices. It treats addiction as an involuntary disease for which abstinence is the cure and makes the patient responsible for recov-ery. Patients learn about and begin working on the Twelve Steps and attend AA, NA, or other meetings on-and off-site. Patients participate in group and personal therapy and attend classes on addiction, and receive medical, psychological, social, and pastoral care. Exercise, nutrition, med-itation, and prayer are emphasized. Near the end, patients agree to an after-care plan, which usually includes Twelve-Step meetings and finding a sponsor.

Addiction "treatment" during the 1960s remained, largely, a matter for the police and courts. The field matured and expanded rapidly during the 1970s and 1980s, and the Minnesota Model emerged as the dominant approach in both inpatient and outpatient care. Two other well-known forms of rehabilitation, methadone maintenance and therapeutic com-munities, involve fewer than 10 percent of all treatment programs. Even these often encourage clients to attend Twelve-Step meetings.

Most outpatient programs carry on elements of the Minnesota Model. Patients attend classes and therapy one to eight hours a week, more at first and less later on. According to the research, outpatient care shows comparable long-term outcomes to inpatient for far less money.[54] Outpa-tient care, given its limits, often relies even more on their patients' use of outside Twelve-Step meetings and mentors.

Almost all addictions treatments seek to change addicts so that they will no longer drink or take drugs. The person must act differently, usually through some internal change. Joseph V. Bailey simplifies matters in *The Serenity Principle*: addiction involves a search for completion, and its root is the entirely human need to feel good and the cause is insecurity. The solution, brought about by personal change and the exercise of free will, is mental health and serenity.[55] AA found one way to do this. But even the modern scientific approach to addiction recognizes that the addict must change.

"People take drugs for two reasons, to feel good, which we call sensation-seeking, and to feel better, which is self-medication," said Alan I. Leshner, director of the federal National Institute on Drug Abuse, speaking at a conference in 1998.[56] From his bully pulpit, with single-minded verve, Leshner has promulgated the theory, based on extensive research and backed up by brightly colored CAT scan images, that drug addiction is a brain disease. At the conference he explained that drug use spikes dopamine levels in the brain, which makes addicts feel euphoric, and changes the brain by, among other things, reducing its ability to produce dopamine. (A neurotransmitter, dopamine helps regulate movement and emotion levels. Many researchers believe inadequate dopamine levels prompt addiction; others disagree.)

"But addiction is not only a brain disease, it is a brain disease with embedded behavioral and social context aspects," Leshner continued on to say. In this we hear an echo of AA's approach, which relieves the addict of blame but makes her or him responsible for recovery. Steven Hyman, director of the National Institute of Mental Health, also promotes the brain disease theory with room left for personal volition. "Take heart patients," he said in a 1998 interview with Bill Moyers. "We don't blame them for having heart disease, but we ask them to follow a certain diet, to exercise, to comply with medication regimes. So it is with the addicted person—we shouldn't blame them for the disease, but we should treat them as having responsibility for their recovery."[57]

At Joseph Molea's Florida clinic for doctors, his scientifically trained clients are often skeptical. In a dramatic display for new patients, Molea, also an M.D. and recovered addict, will slap down a copy of *Alcoholics Anonymous*, of which the first 164 pages cover the program of recovery, and then the text of the American Society of Addiction Medicine, "which is about the size of the Washington, D.C., phone book." Molea's lesson is simple. "Pick which one you want to read. They both end up saying the same thing: Spiritual solutions to alcoholism have not been replaced by medication or surgery."[58]

Interestingly, most of the expensive private rehabs, such as Hazelden and the Betty Ford Center, have stuck to the Twelve-Step approach. Sometimes these publicize the disease concept as the primary aspect of their philosophy. But their goal for the addict is spiritual transformation. "A large number of our members make that the primary part of treatment," said Ronald J. Hunsicker, president of the National Association of Addictions Treatment Providers.[59]

Faith's Utility for the Addict

Treatment programs use spirituality to help patients remain clean and sober after they quit. "The role of spirituality is not so much for them to get off drugs as to stay off and to enhance the meaning of life," Herbert D. Kleber, a psychiatrist at Columbia University active in treatment and research for 30 years. He estimated that spirituality is critical to recovery for about half of addicts in treatment.[60]

The book *Alcoholics Anonymous*, written when that fellowship had about 100 members, concludes that the nondrinking alcoholic reacts to life much like other people. Once he does drink, "something happens, both in bodily and mental sense, which makes it virtually impossible for him to stop."[61] Then the book makes a critical point: to avoid drinking, the alcoholic has to change.

"These observations would be academic and pointless if our friend never took the first drink, thereby setting the terrible cycle in motion. Therefore, the main problem of the alcoholic centers in his mind rather than in his body." Alcoholics are those who "have lost the power of choice in drink," and are beyond the power of human aid. Mere moral codes, philosophies, self-knowledge and willpower did not work for these alcoholics, so something new was needed. "We had to find a power by which we could live, and it had to be a *Power greater than ourselves.*"[62]

A higher power can defeat the lower power of alcoholic compulsion. This need not be the God of others, it could be the individual's conception: "the Realm of the Spirit is broad, roomy, all inclusive." Just admitting the possibility of a higher power led to a "new sense of power and direction, provided we took other simple steps."[63] This spiritual approach combines complete flexibility with a mandate that it be undertaken.

Working the Twelve Steps cements the change. AA defines these as "a group of principles, spiritual in their nature, which if practiced as a way of life can expel the obsession to drink and enable the sufferer to become happily and usefully whole."[64] The alcoholic opens his mind to new ideas, follows several suggestions, and is transformed.

"The great fact is just this, and nothing less: That we have had deep and effective spiritual experiences which have revolutionized our whole attitude toward life, toward our fellows and toward God's universe."[65] While turning to a higher power is recommended, just turning away from the god of self and addiction seems to change the person. Hamilton Beazley, an author and associate professor of organizational behavior at Butler University, spoke of the utility of prayer in these terms. "It's suggested that AA members pray in the morning, to just say, keep me sober, that is sufficient, it doesn't matter to whom the prayer is directed. And to say thank you for keeping me sober at night. This is for newcomers to orient them to the fact that they are not God."[66]

The remarks have a behaviorist tone. Treatment and support groups seem more directed at checking the ego of addicts by eliminating self-centeredness than at finding God. The two can coincide. Finding a God or god or some higher power has a profound effect on a former addict whose entire life once revolved around finding, using, and recovering from drugs or drink. It has a profound effect on most human beings who are, by nature, prone to self-centeredness. But even without a deity, prayer, meditation, service, and spirituality can move people from the center of their universe such that they live differently.

In more religious language, obtaining salvation may be a matter of dodging hell. William James saw the therapeutic process of religion in a similar light. For the damaged soul seeking respite, James wrote, conversion is "a process of struggling away from sin rather than of striving toward righteousness."[67] What is the end result? One version is described eloquently in the other main AA text, *Twelve Steps and Twelve Traditions.* "When a man or a woman has a spiritual awakening, the most important meaning of it is that he has now become able to do, feel, and believe that which he could not do before on his unaided strength alone. He has been granted a gift which amounts to a new state of consciousness and being. He has been set on a path which tells him he is really going somewhere, that life is not a dead end, not something to be endured or mastered. In a very real sense he has been transformed, because he has laid hold of a source of strength which, in one way or another, he had hitherto denied himself. He finds himself in possession of a degree of honesty, tolerance, unselfishness, peace of mind, and love of which he had thought himself quite incapable. What he has received is a free gift, and yet usually, at least in some small part, he has made himself ready to receive it."[68]

Put simply, recovered alcoholics have changed their minds—about a lot of things. Rowland H. recalled Carl Jung telling him that his type of condition was usually hopeless, with exceptions. Jung continued: "Here and there, once in a while, alcoholics have had what are called vital spiritual experiences. To me these occurrences are phenomena. They appear to be in the nature of huge emotional displacements and rearrangements. Ideas, emotions, and attitudes which were once the guiding forces of the lives of these men are suddenly cast to one side, and a completely new set of conceptions and motives begin to dominate them."[69]

Does Spirituality Make the Difference?

Generally, AA participation seems to improve the chances of recovery. Based on a 50-year study of 660 men, George E. Vaillant, a psychiatrist at Harvard Medical School, concluded that changing an addiction required four elements: a substitute dependency; ritual reminders that one drink could cause relapse; repair of social and medical damage; and self-esteem. Self-help groups such as but not only AA provided all four in the simplest manner.[70] Members of AA and other spiritually based programs would insist their method for recovery involves something much more profound, but Vaillant's summary serves as a practical description.

Of the men who achieved three or more years of sobriety "40 percent did so through Alcoholics Anonymous, their biggest source of help in recovery."[71] Indeed, Vaillant reported in his 1995 book, *The Natural History of Alcoholism Revisited,* that more recovered alcoholics began abstinence at AA than in treatment.[72]

Vaillant cites other researchers who found the same pattern. In one study, treated alcoholics were twice as likely to abstain for six months if they attended AA. Another found in a ten-year follow-up that AA involvement was the only major predictor of abstinence.[73] Vaillant concludes that though direct proof is elusive, the research shows more and more indirect evidence of AA's effectiveness, such as its growth among all groups, regardless of age, sex, income, race, and education.

A 1998 review of studies by William R. Miller of the University of New Mexico found that spiritual or religious involvement reduces the risk of substance abuse and that increased involvement appears correlated with recovery. "One drives out the other," Miller wrote, echoing Jung's formula. Further, Miller found that addicts who practice the Twelve Steps are more likely to remain abstinent than those treated with two other types of nonspiritual therapy.[74]

Two major reviews of the research by blue-ribbon panels support some of the claims made in the area. One, by 20 scientists and directed by Miller in 1996 for the private National Institute for Healthcare Research, found "good evidence" that involvement with AA is associated with better outcomes in out-patient care and that meditation-based interventions are associated with reduced substance abuse and problems, and "reasonable evidence" that AA involvement is associated with better outcomes after in-patient care and that Twelve-Step-style treatment works at least as well as other approaches; Miller's team also reported "some evidence" that motivations for drug abuse and spiritual pursuits overlap, that people in treatment had low levels of religious involvement, that alcoholics often had negative experiences with God, and that the personal sense of meaning increases after treatment.[75]

The other research review, prepared for a 1999 conference sponsored by the National Institute on Alcoholism and Alcohol Abuse (NIAAA) and the Fetzer Institute, involved hundreds of empirical studies on spirituality and substance abuse. It found "strong support" for the protective nature of spirituality and religion (110 studies); of AA involvement (51 studies); and of spiritual/religious interventions (26 studies).[76] The anecdotal evidence of spirituality's role is strong:

Harold P. Brown, a psychologist and clinician, found in his research that sober addicts, compared to the normal population and to addicts new to treatment, gave much greater priority to personal harmony, salvation, forgiveness, love, and service.[77] At the 1999 NIAAA research conference, Lee Kaskutas of the Alcohol Research Group summarized a study, still underway, of 722 subjects assessed upon entering treatment and one and three years later. She found that both secular and religious participants in AA, at follow-up, reported a doubled rate of spiritual awakening.[78]

Critiques of Spiritual or Twelve-Step Methods

Twelve-Step fellowships can be a big target. There are two common features of popular critiques as illustrated by Wendy Kaminer's 1992 book, *I'm Dysfunctional, You're Dysfunctional: The Recovery Movement and Other Self-Help Fashions.* First, these often target caricatures or distortions of the Twelve-Step philosophies rather than the real thing. Critics may acknowledge that AA and NA help addicts, but then charge these groups with making members feel victimized and slavishly dependent on a higher power as an alternative to the hard work of self-realization. Even a casual reading of AA and NA literature, or a talk with several members, or attendance at a meeting, reveals a focus on personal responsibility for past wrongs and present recovery. Further, the message through these fellowships, as well as in treatment programs making use of their ideas, is that dependence on a higher power delivers maturity and independence.

Others complain that using spirituality, or God, to recover simply replaces one addiction with another. This makes little sense, since most nonaddicts believe in God to no apparent detriment. Many newly recovered addicts are often intense, understandably, about their new beliefs, a state responsible for such fears. If spirituality is a new addiction for those in recovery, then at least it is not killing them. Further, accepting the human condition of dependency on others is usually the first step to independence. Edward Sapir, the anthropologist, writes that in all cultures, religion involves accepting one's human powerlessness and, at the same time, irrationally believing that one can gain security by identifying with the unknown.[79]

Often, AA or NA is held accountable for misrepresentations by treatment professionals. These often adapt the Twelve Steps to their own purposes. But then their patients graduate, attend meetings, and repeat these messages as AA truths. Consider two common misrepresentations: the "disease concept" and the issue of whether or not a sober alcoholic ever really recovers. Alcoholism is described as a disease once in the primer *Alcoholics Anonymous*. Instead, the words "illness" or "malady" are used repeatedly, indicating the complex nature of AA's understanding of addiction as a hopeless condition in need of a spiritual solution, or as an illness of the spirit, mind, and body. In 1960, well after AA's founding, E. M. Jellinek's influential book *The Disease Concept of Alcoholism* locked the phrase into the vocabulary of treatment workers, addicts, and, to a lesser extent, the public.

Second, many critics complain that Twelve-Step groups keep members in a state of permanent bondage through the conviction that an addict is always in "recovery" or "recovering," rather than being an ex-addict or a recovered one. In a letter to the *AA Grapevine*, the monthly AA magazine, a writer insisted that the message of AA's founders was one of recovery. The "recovering" camp, he wrote, adheres to "a New Age message which began infiltrating our AA rooms several decades ago and has become accepted by many if not most of our members. Its roots originate in treatment centers and rehabs." The letter also noted that the AA book used the word "recovered" 23 times, and "recover" 28 times, but "recovering" only twice "and then in the context of the newcomer." Interestingly, a dozen or so letters in the same issue dismissed the debate as a matter of unimportant semantics. Many recovered addicts prefer to say that they are recovering, to remind themselves and others of the need for vigilance. Such positions are not central to the embrace of a spiritual approach. What counts is daily effort since AA members remain sober by keeping in "fit spiritual condition."[80]

Of more substance are those charges leveled by Stanton Peele a clinician and author of, among other works, *The Diseasing of America: How We Allowed Recovery Zealots and the Treatment Industry to Convince Us We Are Out of Control*, and Herbert Fingarette, a philosopher and author of *Heavy Drinking: The Myth of Alcoholism as a Disease*. Much of what they fault is outside the realm of Twelve-Step fellowships or spiritual solutions. Groups such as AA and NA are easy targets for the sins of the "recovery industry." As the journalist Joe Sharkey records in his 1994 book, *Bedlam: Greed, Profiteering, and Fraud in a Mental Health System Gone Crazy*, a vast network of rehabs and psychiatric hospitals grew dramatically during the 1980s, before collapsing, by lengthening the list of problems requiring expensive "treatments." These often carried the Twelve-Step label.

Peele and Fingarette oppose seeing alcoholism as a medical disease. AA's literature refers to it as a malady of the body, mind, and spirit and generally avoids the term disease. Along the same lines, Fingarette writes, "alcohol abuse is the outcome of a range of physical, personal, and social characteristics that together predispose a person to drink to excess."[81] Peele, and many others, oppose the medicalization of other social problems and say drunken drinkers and others who abuse drugs should be held accountable for their actions. Personal responsibility is a primary tenet of Twelve-Step groups, their members, and, for the most part, treatment programs that use this approach. Peele states that bad or incorrect beliefs and values can cause alcoholism, and that good ones can prevent or end addiction. Similarly, dozens of recovered addicts have told me that "stinking thinking" caused their problem. The book *Alcoholics Anonymous* states, in one of its few italicized passages, "*After all, our problems were of our own making. Bottles were only a symbol.*"[82] The antidote, repeated many times, is an end to self-centeredness and the start of a life of love and service.

Basically, what both Peele and Fingarette propose as radical alternatives are remarkably similar to the Twelve-Step approach. Fingarette argues that alcoholics are not helpless and must take control of their lives. AA suggests a way to do that. He insists alcoholics must want to change. One hears the same in most treatment programs or from Twelve-Step adherents.

Indeed, the AA approach contradicts the extreme versions of the disease concept. As therapy, this concept is doomed to fail, Jerome D. Frank and Julia Frank write in their classic book, *Persuasion and Healing*, since it implies the person suffers from impersonal forces such as bad genes, absolves the patient of responsibility, and leaves him or her to follow doctor's orders. "More effective treatment, such as the form of psychotherapy embraced by Alcoholics Anonymous, invokes the idea of illness in order to relieve the alcoholic from fruitless feelings of guilt about lack of will power or past behavior. At the same time, the program makes the alcoholic responsible for the consequences of his or her drinking and for following the steps to recovery, which involves moral acts such as making amends to others and helping other alcoholics."[83]

Misunderstandings abound in this field. Even calling Twelve-Step fellowships or other spiritual methods "self-help" is a misnomer. As applied to Twelve-Step-style groups, the term self-help originated with Charles Dederich, who founded the first therapeutic community, Synanon, in 1958 as an alternative to AA for drug addicts, often those with criminal pasts. He called Synanon, with its complete reliance on the group, self-help to distinguish it from AA's reliance on a higher power. The term has since been applied to a galaxy of support groups and it is likely to stick, though more accurate descriptions would be "mutual help" or "mutual aid."

William Miller and Ernest Kurtz, two respected researchers and observers, compiled various outside conceptions of alcoholism mistakenly attributed to Alcoholics Anonymous. AA literature, they write, does not assert that there is only one form of alcoholism or only one way to recover; that alcoholics are not responsible for their condition; that moderate drinking is impossible for every problem drinker; that alcoholics suffer from denial and should be bullied into treatment; or that alcoholism is purely a physical or hereditary disorder.[84] AA's core beliefs do, however, resonate with or resemble those of other fields from which it has often borrowed or which it has influenced.

Fundamentals:
Insights from History, Anthropology, and Sociology

Here's the truth about recovery for many addicts: without a personal transformation, usually spiritual in nature, little happens over the long term. So in an odd way, we have this huge public policy apparatus aimed at effecting an internal change in the alcoholic. As my college theology professor Paul Cioffi sketched it, many philosophies trace a person's life along a radical that continues in a horizontal line, followed by a steep drop to the bottom—shipwreck—and then a new start on a higher plane. Usually this crisis is private. But in addictions treatment, outside forces such as society and state or family, friends, and employers all stand beside the alcoholic and exhort him or her onward. Society intervenes to change the person in a way much like the way medieval European society dealt with sinners. Only repentance and redemption will do. He or she must act differently as an outward sign of inner change.

Medieval rites of repentance bore a striking similarity to those that the alcoholic or addict undergoes. Each follows the trajectory from "sin" to public disapprobation to shame, repentance, penance, and new life within the folds of the community. This community may be social or local, or religious or Twelve Step, or a mix of several. What is most striking is the role of public testimony. While previously this may have served to further punish the penitent, today the recovered addict recites his or her tale as part of their personal recovery to reinforce their commitment to sobriety, as an exhortation to those who have also fallen and are arising to new life, and as a cautionary tale to any outsiders present who have yet to get in trouble with drugs or drink.

Sociology and anthropology offer a useful perspective on spiritual beliefs, practices, and results that they accept as a fact when observed in society. Emile Durkheim, founder of the French school of sociology, based his study of *The Elementary Forms of Religious Life* on the aboriginals of Australia. He understood religion broadly, as that which both expresses and structures society. He describes religion "as a sort of technique that helps man to confront the world more confidently." Similarly, William James wrote that religion makes easy that which is necessary.[85] The historian and theologian Karen Armstrong makes the same point in *A History of God* when she said religion must *work*, or else a people will find another one. From Abraham and Jacob on, and probably before, people picked a conception of God on pragmatic grounds "not because it was scientifically or philosophically sound."[86] God must deliver the goods, or the faithful will shop elsewhere. Thus does each addict find a concept of God that keeps her or him sober.

Durkheim said that religion gives the individual power to live from the group, whose communion and rituals yield a force greater than itself and the individual, a force that sustains a person until the next assembly. "Because he is in moral harmony with his neighbor, he gains new confidence, courage, and boldness in action."[87] Sounds much like an addict who attends a spiritual support group.

The cultural anthropologist, Edward Sapir doubted a person could have a healthy social life or significant personal life without what he called religious sentiments. One he called "a feeling of community with a necessary universe of values." For Sapir, in the religious quest, fear and humility are turned into absolute security, "for once the fear is imaginatively taken to one's heart and humility confessed for good and all, the triumph of human consciousness is assured."[88] This blend of absolute humility and full security is the foundation for an addict's abstinence. It corrects their conduct by reversing self-satisfaction. As the book *Alcoholics Anonymous* puts it, "Above everything, we alcoholics must be rid of this selfishness. We must, or it kills us!"[89]

William James, who distilled the practical function of religion in his *Varieties of Religious Experience*, understood the mystical appeal of inebriation. "Sobriety diminishes, discriminates, and says no; drunkenness expands, unites, and says yes. It is in fact the great exciter of the *Yes* function in man. It brings its votary from the chill periphery of things to the radiant core. It makes him for the moment one with the truth."[90] The sober antidote is that state of mind, known to religious people, when they cease to assert their will and become "nothing in the floods and waterspouts of God. In this state of mind, what we most dreaded has become the habituation of your safety, and the hour of our moral death has turned into our spiritual birthday. The time for tension in our soul is over."[91] This is the same tension described by William Silkworth, the medical adviser to AA's founders, as the alcoholic's state of being "restless, irritable and discontent."[92] It is the same psychic itch described by so many alcoholics and addicts that they tried to scratch with drink and drugs.

For James, the way out lay in the exercise of free will through thought and action. "The whole point of *The Varieties of Religious Experience*," the literary critic Alfred Kazin writes in *God and the American Writer*, "is that the truly religious character begins as 'a sick soul,' is dominated by a sense of lack, of something basically wrong, but through the mysterious accession of faith . . . is given—gives itself—that second chance in life that religion helps to provide."[93] During the late 1800s, religion had lost its certitude in the face of positivism and materialism. Still, James the Harvard scientist had seen the transformative effects of faith as scientific facts. He used the example of a mountain climber whose survival depends on believing that he or she can make an impossible leap to a new ledge. Wisdom and courage involve believing in what is necessary, for such belief saves. For James, beliefs should always and only be tested for philosophical sense and moral use.

A spiritual solution to addiction follows the classic pattern of fall and resurrection, sin and redemption. First comes the sense of unease—common to many, universal among addicts. Then, James writes, "the solution is a sense that we are saved from wrongness by making proper connections with the higher powers."[94]

God/Not God

The starting point of almost any spirituality or religion is the recognition that the believer or practitioner is not the deity. So too in Alcoholics Anonymous, whose text declares: "This is the how and why of it. First of all, we had to quit playing God. It didn't work."[95] When Bill Wilson first talked with Dr. Bob in 1935, as Ernest Kurtz writes, he already was able to present the four aspects of one core idea: "Utterly hopeless, totally deflated, requiring conversion, and needing others, the drinking alcoholic was quite obviously not perfect, not absolute, *not God*."[96] This threshold is so taken for granted that many addicts I interviewed seemed unaware that they had made such a decision. They often spoke of finding a higher power, but rarely of having decided they were not it.

Addicts do not have to profess a deity for a spiritual approach to work. Some rely on principles or guidelines for living, such as "good orderly direction," whose acronym is a handy g. o. d. For those in treatment or new to recovery, the higher power may be their community of sober peers or a Twelve-Step group, a powerful source of hope and direction, just as some anthropologists regard society as the deity behind religion.

The process can occur within the person, without obvious divine intervention. The addict simply has to stop believing in the religion of one, to cease the cult of self. "It is only by ceasing to play God," Ernest Kurtz and Katherine Ketcham write, "by coming to terms with errors and shortcomings, and by accepting the inability to control every aspect of their lives that alcoholics (or any human being) can find the peace and serenity that alcohol (or other drugs, or sex, money, material possessions, power, or privilege) promise but never deliver."[97] By shrinking the ego, the addict makes room for new truths and beliefs, ones that will not kill him.

The first of these is faith, the first teaching of almost every religion. Even here the way is simple: not so much does the addict have to believe in a deity as he has to stop believing in the one which is killing him. In this light, one could say that it is faith, rather than a deity, that provides the power. One certainly sees this in Christianity, where many Protestants preach salvation by faith alone. Jesus, over and over, told people he cured that it was their faith that saved them.

For many, however, only God can displace the god of self-centeredness. "If the definition of spirituality is the power to recognize that there is a power greater than yourself, it's essential," said Ronald J. Hunsicker. "Any treatment has to enable them to acknowledge a power greater than them. Without that, any long-range recovery is compromised."[98] In any of these ways, however, spiritually based addictions treatments offer a practical remedy for the ancient and deadly human malady of hubris.

Profile:
Dennis—Onto and Off the Streets with an Open Spirituality

After a middle-class upbringing in Brooklyn and then a Long Island sub-urb, Dennis began drinking and got into trouble almost immediately. Then came drugs. Eventually, his habits scuttled his college philosophy studies and landed him on the streets of Manhattan for much of six years. To add to his problems, fellow citizens and social workers rarely saw beyond his image as a black, homeless man, just another destitute figure on Manhattan's margins. Today, Dennis has been sober for nine years. A square featured man with a large brow, a ready laugh, and clothes that are fashionably practical and urban—plain leather jacket, heavy-soled shoes, an African cap—Dennis helps run a variety of innovative, hard-headed social programs in Albany and is launching a performance space in a loft above the Hudson River where artists, musicians, and people with mental illness can socialize and perform.[99]

In his career of pain, which lasted from ages 17 to 33, he sees the lesson that keeps him free of drugs and alcohol, leading a happy, productive life. I ask what makes the difference for addicts who recover. "Empathy," he blurts out. "The ability to see others as self. All these questions—where did we come from, where are we going. We don't know the answer to that. What we do know is that we're here, together, in our fear, in our not knowing. That, and that the universe means good for us. There's this force, call it a higher power, whatever, that means good for us."

Something his mother told him while Dennis was being treated at a veterans' hospital in the Hudson Valley turned on the light. "My mother told me on the phone that there was a God, or higher power, who could not want anything less for me than for any other person. I hold on to that.

I always say to myself, 'Me and my higher power.' That's what I do things for. When I was at the Salvation Army, I would work like a dog, filling these bales up with clothes up to 2,000 pounds. Other people were doing maybe 1,500. It was me and my higher power."

Today, Dennis maintains his sobriety by attending Twelve-Step meetings and working professionally with homeless, alcoholic, and mentally ill people. Due to his personal experience, he takes a tough-love approach to individuals who need to change their behavior and insists that his programs measure their results.

"What makes the difference is seeing the higher power through other people. Seeing other people as myself, it broke down the divisions that made me 'other.' AA did that. When I was a counselor (at a treatment center), I would have patients who were millionaires and others who were street people, and I could see that they're the same as me." Dennis prefers the wide-open spirituality he finds in Twelfth-Step groups to other brands. He went through the Salvation Army program, which combines work therapy with Bible lessons, and attended an addicts support group at a black Baptist church. Though he found them helpful, Dennis faults these for being exclusive, for feeding into bothersome images of God, such as a purely white Jesus, and for not providing a lifetime method of support.

The forgiveness he found in recovery transformed him: "Letting something out, unloading the guilt, telling my family when I was in the VA about my use and abuse." Dennis says his insights of sobriety are not new to him, just different. "Yes I knew these things, but I didn't realize the depth of them," he says, punching out the word "depth." As with most alcoholics and addicts who recover, he hit bottom at the threshold to a new life.

"Here I was at a desperate point. I came out of a blackout on 167th Street in front of Columbia Presbyterian, my arm was busted I don't know how, my pants had fallen halfway down and I had my hand out saying, 'Hey, can you give me a quarter?' I was like, 'huh?' Coming out of a blackout like that, 'huh,' where was I?"

Dennis has the extra caution of a man who almost lost it all, twice. He was sober once before, for ten months, and relapsed despite employment, an apartment near Central Park with a girlfriend, and Twelve-Step meetings. "It was anhedonia, the inability to feel happiness. I had a good job and I was still feeling 'blah.' Some of that was just waiting for my brain to come in balance after years of cocaine."

Beyond that, he credits a constructive approach to life. Dennis values his ability to keep promises. "It's 'Word Up,' they say on the street. The idea that your word is bond. The building block of relations with other people is ability to keep a promise. If you say you're going to meet a person or even yourself on the street corner at five o'clock, you feel better. The ability to keep a promise is the ability to create a reality."

CHAPTER II

The Middle Class and Mainstream Treatment

The Obstacles of Pride and Self-Sufficiency

Many middle-class alcoholics reject the notion that they need help, either to stop drinking or to live a good life without the drugs. For that matter, people of all economic and social classes—addicted or not—reject the idea that they need help. An insistent individualism marks U.S. history. Its demands and distortions grip our minds and steer our lives. The ideology of self rules, even after a person's drinking and drug abuse have crushed actual self-reliance. Such a person may not welcome the suggestion that she or he should now reach beyond the self to others or a deity for help and develop a spiritual life. She or he may be a stranger to the idea of faith playing a major role in life.

"There's a big vacuum," says Brad Warner, a counselor and administrator for a private treatment program in upstate New York. "The middle class has been so dependent on the venal, on crass venality. The idea of moving toward a higher power is hard because they didn't get a spiritual background growing up."[1] Beyond that, self-sufficiency underlies the entire lifestyle of the middle-and upper-income classes. For them, independence and hard work earns their place and confirms their status, as much as any general's medals and ribbons. "Who cares to admit complete defeat?" asked AA members in their book *Twelve Steps and Twelve Traditions*, first published in 1953. "Practically no one, of course. Every natural instinct cries out against the idea of personal powerlessness. It is truly awful to admit that, glass in hand, we have warped our minds into such an obsession for destructive drinking that only an act of Providence can remove it from us."[2] William James, the scientist and philosopher who explored the utility of faith at the turn of the century, saw surrender as the key to the conversion that heals the psychically sick or troubled. "There are only two ways in which it is possible to get rid of anger, worry, fear, despair, other undesirable affections," he wrote in *The Varieties of Religious Experience.* "One is that an opposite affection should overpoweringly break over us, and the other is by getting so exhausted with the struggle that we have to stop—so we drop down, give up, and *don't care* any longer." Even a willing person, as opposed to a resistant one, cannot deliver himself to the Promised Land alone. She or he needs to surrender so that the process may be completed. "In the great majority of all cases," Writes James, "when the will had done its uttermost toward bringing one close to the complete unification aspired after, it seems that the very last step must be left to other forces and performed without the help of its activity. In other words, self-surrender becomes then indispensable."[3] Necessary, but not easy.

Most middle-class alcoholics and addicts who get help are pushed toward the Twelve Steps, either in treatment or in self-help groups they attend on their own. The first theme of the Twelve Steps is humility, accepting that one has a problem or is powerless over a drug. Despite all the evidence of personal failure, many resist admission.

Doctor to Doctor

Joe Molea knows about such resistance. An M.D., Molea works with addicted doctors out of a converted brick ranch house hidden on a tropically leafy street in the sprawling, flat reaches of Tampa, Florida. His six-foot-two, 220-pound frame conveys a high, contained energy set off by a shaved head. Molea's voice carries the blunt but drawling punch of his native Buffalo, in upstate New York, where a steelworker and homemaker raised him. He speaks with the authority of two backgrounds: his scientific training and his personal recovery from addiction.[4]

"I had a history of alcoholic grandparents, on my mother's side. My parents didn't drink. There's this theory of alcoholism being skip-generational, that the children of alcoholics are so traumatized that they avoid drinking altogether. But for the grandchildren, my generation, it's a different story. There was no alcohol in my house. My parents translated that energy into workaholism and taking care of the family, a righteous compulsion."

Being what he called the family's "hero child," Molea became the first to attend college, then moved on to medical school and a surgical residency. He was also drinking to satisfy certain inner appetites, to fill some hole in his being.

"I was achieving the real symptoms of alcoholism, what the [AA] Big Book calls restlessness, irritability, and discontent. I was played out, and the only way I could feel better was one of two ways: achieving more than my contemporaries, or thinking that if I work hard, I deserve to play hard. But working 36-hour days, 100-hour weeks, there was no time to drink, so I began abusing pharmaceuticals in order to maintain my serenity. There was always someone willing to prescribe for me." His inner anxiety grew with his abuse, especially in the pressure cooker of a surgical unit where residents were at the bottom of the professional pecking order. By 1992, his addiction was clear to colleagues who forced him into professional treatment.

Afterward, Molea worked for Florida Medical Association's Physicians Recovery Network and is now executive director of HealthCare Connections. At both, he found what works in treating addicted M.D.'s.

"In Florida, we've found that if you complete treatment, go into monitoring—urine testing, professional recovery meetings once a week along with regular AA attendance—you will have a 90 percent chance of being sober five years later." Many of his clients are motivated by fear of losing their licenses to practice medicine. On the other hand, almost all have spent years curing others—a habit that instills no small measure of self-confidence and even arrogance. Asking others for help is hard; turning to a higher power may be impossible. Molea endorses the Twelve-Step approach to recovery. He refits those concepts with language that will appeal to medical professionals. As he speaks, Molea unpacks a white McDonald's bag and devours a large hamburger, French fries, and 20-ounce soda. Done, he warms even more to his subject.

"Spirituality is the most important element in recovery," Molea says. "So I went back to the Big Book and tried to find modern scientific correlates to what it says in there. In the preface, 'The Doctor's Opinion,' Dr. [William D.] Silkworth said alcoholism is a disease whose symptoms are 'restlessness, irritability, and discontent.'

"Alcoholics uniformly will be able to tell you the time they took the first drink or drug," he continues. "They felt normal for the first time. It's a spiritual experience." The solution must be of a related, though divergent, nature. Abstinence comes first. "It will be 90 days before [the addict] can even know what's happening," says Molea. "Then, the person has to figure out another way to deal with being restless, irritable, and discontent."We continue this conversation, over the telephone, a year and a half after my visit to Tampa. As he reviews a few points, Molea switches into a clinical mode. By now, he has further refined his thinking on the topic and often lectures to doctors and medical students on "neurochemistry and spirituality."

He sketches a picture of the brain's three main parts from the bottom up: the brain stem, which controls vegetative functions such as blood pressure, body temperature, and respiration; the midbrain, seat of the limbic system and thus emotions and instincts; and the cerebral cortex, the thinking section. Molea concentrates on the midbrain, or "lizard brain," which evolved earliest and is present in the simplest of animals. "The normal function is to get the message to the cortex that you need to eat, drink. It's like the idiot light on your dashboard that says, 'Stop driving and fix this.'"

But it is in the midbrain where the alcoholic experiences his sense of being restless, irritable, and discontent even when his basic needs are already met. And here in the midbrain, which includes the pleasure center, mood-altering substances work their magic by relieving those unquiet emotions. In Molea's schema, when the alcoholic feels uneasy, the midbrain sends a message to the cortex, which then produces the thought: "Drink! Snort cocaine!"

The active alcoholic or addict is one who has found the cure for her or his symptoms. "They discover that substance abuse takes them from being 'restless, irritable, and discontent' to being 'happy, joyous, and free,' " Molea says, using another AA phrase, this time for a person's state under divine care. The trick is to make changes in the mid-brain without drugs. Thought alone won't make it so. Emotion and instinct shape thought, not the other way around. "If there are 10,000 more pathways or connections leading out of the midbrain into the cortex, than the other way around, the brain system is obviously designed to send messages to the cortex and not the other way." He offers examples. "I can control my need for water for a length of time to be polite with you on the phone, but eventually I will have to drink. I can explain to a person with Parkinson's disease how it operates on their basal ganglia and then say, 'Now stop your arm from shaking.' They won't be able to. With an alcoholic, I can explain that they can't drink safely, and ask if they understand. They'll say 'okay,' and the first thing they do is go out and drink."

In our first conversation, Molea explains more fully. "It doesn't matter how smart you are, you can't think your way out of it. So it's not just a lifestyle change that's necessary. You have a person with abnormal emotions." Molea looks away, out a window and back at me. "Now, this is where it begins to sound like voodoo. There is only one neurologic avenue left and that's through the spirit. But since the seventeeth century, in the West, we don't believe in that, we believe in ourselves and our ability to control life with technology. It's American rugged individualism taken to the nth degree."

But aspects of life contradict materialism, or at least suggest there is more to this world than can be observed and tested. "We all have experiences that are what we call spiritual—dreams, intuition, inspiration—all things we have a hard time categorizing. Alcoholics and addicts can't think their way out of their problem and they can't manipulate their surroundings to get out. So the avenue has to be in the spiritual, and that's why the most important element in recovery is the spiritual experience."

Think of a stroke victim who, having lost the power of speech, learns to do so by utilizing a different, undamaged part of the brain. One of Molea's colleagues at HealthCare Connections, David Meyers, once said that substance abuse treatment was the only field in medicine that treats the soul. Adds Molea, "The Twelve Steps are designed to engineer a spiritual experience in modern man."

Denial or Hubris: Which Is the Problem?

An article of faith in recovery circles holds that alcoholics prevent their recovery by denying their problem. A much-quoted line has it that " 'denial' is not just the name of a river in Egypt." But research, and my interviews, suggest that most active alcoholics or addicts know they are in trouble even when they do not want to admit it publicly or in a prescribed manner such as "My name is Pete and I am a hopeless alcoholic." The issue becomes a stumbling block, especially for people whose outside success makes them unwilling to declare failure.

Reid K. Hester and William R. Miller of the University of New Mexico reviewed 600 studies of treatment outcomes and selected 211 as scientifically reliable for their *Handbook of Alcoholism Treatment Approaches*. "Current research points to no particular personality of defensive character structure that is unique or universal to alcoholics," Miller writes in one chapter. "The resistant behavior that is labeled 'denial' does not just walk through the door with the client, but is strongly influenced by the way in which the therapist approaches the client. Said provocatively, denial is not a client problem. It is a therapist problem."[5]

So strongly and so often is the mantra of denial repeated, at least among those I interviewed, that many if not most recovered addicts attribute it to themselves. But they do so retrospectively. Instead, alcoholics entering treatment appear to be as variable as nonalcoholics in personality, Miller writes, and are guilty of denial no more or less than nonalcoholics. Decades of psychological and longitudinal studies "have failed to reveal a consistent 'alcoholic personality.' "[6]

Nevertheless, counselors and recovered peers assume most alcoholics are madly denying that they are in serious trouble with drugs or alcohol. The first order of treatment then becomes getting the client to "admit the problem," in rehab vernacular, and accept the label of alcoholic or addict. For people with jobs, families, homes, hobbies, this may be unreasonable. They may wonder why, if they are already seeking help—even if under duress from a boss or spouse or judge—they have to adopt a stigmatizing label.

The more likely problem is pride. The addict seeking help usually knows he's in trouble. Admitting it may be hard, not in and of itself, but mostly because admission means accepting help. Instead, the process shortcircuits over the issue of denial and labels. Miller reports that many a counselor insists the client accept the label of "alcoholic," retarding if not halting progress. "Unfortunately, research suggests no strong relationship between self-labeling and outcomes," Miller writes. He proposes that the therapists change their style to minimize patients' resistance.

To this outsider's eyes, then, eliminating the insistence that alcoholics admit in a prescribed manner that they need help would enable treatments to concentrate on persuading clients to actually accept the help, thus circumventing the problem of pride.

Profile: John—A Political Journalist Finds the Poet Within

The desk is large, ornate, carved wood, topped by heavy lamps and paperweights. It resembles one seen in the restored mansions of nineteenth-century authors or captains of industry. A credenza to the rear holds a computer; there is a fax machine and printer. Books fill shelves up to the ceiling. Windows on three sides admit a hazy light from their northern exposure. The Mohawk River, just a five-minute stroll south with Schenectady on the far side, reflects a glow into the atmosphere above the 300-year old hamlet of Alplaus N.Y. Ensconced in this room on the upper floor of a wood-frame Victorian, John puffs on his pipe and contemplates the course that set him here far from the national politics he covers still for various publications.

"I was born in western Maryland. My family was well-to-do." One grandfather was a factory executive, the other a mayor and banker. "I was raised as a prince until I was five, when my father came back from World War II and my secure little world vanished. We moved from a cozy mountain town to the big, strange city. I was what the shrinks call the 'lost child' until I was 12, when I discovered the 'wonders of alcohol,' drinking beer in the schoolyard. I had my first blackout when I was 15, from vodka. I woke up, crawling in a ditch. I heard some guy crying, 'Help, help, help,' and then I realized that it was me."[7] Like so many alcoholics and addicts, John recalls his first intoxication in detail but also in the mythological terms of its transformative power.

"I remember the feeling, the elevation," he says, trailing off into a reverie. "I saw that was there, and afterwards I sought it. After three or four drinks, there were moments that related to serenity, peace, oneness." John remembers his life as consisting of two tracks, one elevated and one in the other direction: "At 15, I was writing poems in the woods, and then I was one of these little hoodlums, pillaging cars in the neighborhood for the bottle of booze under the front seat."

His spiritual appetite was blunted by his ancestors' stern faith, a rigid

Presbyterianism from Scotland. "I remember my grandparents sitting up at night, telling me about hellfire and damnation. I'll be damned if I know what it was all about, it just was terrifying." John soon left that behind.

A last fling with organized religion was a short bout of Unitarianism as a young adult. Yet he still had an appetite for God, for the power he thought was available via a supreme being. John read Carlos Castaneda and looked for the divine power in Mexico, with the help of mushrooms "and all kinds of psychedelics," and in the swamps and bayous of south Arkansas. He drank on a mad dash toward serenity, or was it ecstasy? "I was seeking oblivion. I drank to black out, as often as I could." Twice he stopped briefly, once with self-control for three months, the other in his late 20s inspired by a spiritual vision of himself "standing in the awesome presence of God. It was not a conscious decision to stop drinking. It was just, all of a sudden, all right to be me." Both times he resumed.

John worked most of his adult life as a journalist covering politics from Washington. The social life there provided plenty of free booze and a convenient schedule. He would drink during the night, then write from 2:00 A.M. until 9:00 A.M., then crash, sleep, and rise in the afternoon to start over again. The death of a close friend in mysterious conditions, either murder or suicide, framed and crystallized John's crisis. "My odyssey started, looking up and down the East Coast for a place to live. I was on the run from, from, from feeling mortal, from my spiritual and moral state." John and his wife settled on Alplaus. John's personal hell resumed. One day he sought to end it.

"I was going to kill myself, by walking a couple of blocks to the river. I was going to put a plastic bag on my head and jump in. I was talking with my wife and all of a sudden I said, 'I think I need treatment for alcoholism.' We looked in the telephone book and there was Conifer Park, just down the road." The treatment center, based on a wooded campus in a former county sanatorium, is less than a mile from John's house. The program and counselors there, says John, "reintroduced or welcomed me back to humanity. I thought my life was over, I really did. My biggest awakening was the induction, in May 1997." The counselor's empathy and understanding made the difference, and it connected with John's most basic instinct. "Here was someone who understood the hell of alcoholism. I would have done anything to stay alive. That's what they did, they gave me hope and showed me possibilities, and I began to believe I could survive this."

Every day for months, John attended outpatient sessions—educational classes, men's group, individual counseling. He learned about "cognitive distortions" that could warp his thinking, ruin his mood and lead him back to drinking. Counselors introduced clients to the Twelve-Step philosophy and encouraged them to attend AA or NA meetings. "People brought up this matter of the higher power, which spooked me . . . I thought it was some damn cult. When I saw that I was at liberty to choose my own course," he says, he grew open to the idea. John says he and others get uneasy when anyone gets too specific about their idea of God. "As long as it's this libertarian, 'we believe that there's this higher power whom we salute,' that's fine." Set free to define his own "great spirit," John explored the possibilities.

"At first, I went back to my fundamentalist roots. I bought the Bible and a book of readings and meditations." Later, he read Native American lore and texts on shamanism. "I realized that there is, to this world, a spiritual dimension, that you can enter through prayer. I don't have to wait for the hereafter. Turning my will and my life over to God, rather than just praying to God, that was the turning point."

Doing God's will, says John, is often a matter of letting go. "Sometimes I just sit with problems, instead of trying to solve them. It's realizing that I don't have all the answers and that I don't have control. That good enough things come my way without being greedy, manipulative, scheming, as I always used to think." What he can control, at least partially, is his state of mind, which in turn shapes his behavior. "Now, I'm working on acceptance and gratitude. It lifts me up, somehow." His regimen: AA meetings, almost daily, prayer, morning and night, and contact with other alcoholics. Of mutual aid among peers, he says, "There's some magic in it."

T. S. Eliot wrote that at the end of all our wandering we would arrive at the place where we began and know it for the first time. John's life has orbited into an almost complete circle. An urge recently moved him to wield his pen, and keyboard, on fiction, the first time in years. "I really felt something telling me, 'Move, get going.' As soon as I gave up, it started to flow." Which is where he started.

"This creative writing is the best writing I've done, period. I became a hack because of the booze. Now, I'm back to who I'm meant to be, back to that 16-year-old kid who wrote the poetry."

Coercion: Forcing the Unforceable

While anyone can stumble over pride in recovery, professionals accustomed to respect and success may find it a large obstacle. For instance, how does a relative or counselor get a doctor to accept treatment when to do so suggests failure, the lack of self-control and self-mastery, and the need for help from some kind of outside power?

"They're coerced, frankly," says Molea. "Unless they accept this, they will lose the ability to practice. With doctors, he must overcome their egos, their tendency to believe, that, as Molea puts it, "Nobody can tell me anything." In an aside, he tells me that, "Lawyers are the hardest because their whole professional identity is tied up maintaining personal freedoms." Molea insists to his patients—doctors whose preference is for science and medicine—that a spiritual program of recovery pioneered by AA remains their best bet for sobriety despite decades of additional research. "The long hard road is with the skeptic who has to go back and reprove everything," says Molea.

HealthCare Connections puts its clients in several residences or "therapeutic communities" that have room for 20-40 people. They stay an average of four months. The staff tries to impart two difficult lessons: "You're not any different from anyone else and you can't trust your instincts." Molea seeks to open a crack in the wall of ego and resistance. "We tell them, 'You've screwed up so badly that you've given other people power over you, and that will continue until you surrender and let someone help you.' And then the spiritual experience creeps up." Patients confront the difficulty of living without old coping mechanisms.

"We do anything we can to create restlessness, irritability, and discontent (in the addict) in a safe environment where they can't get drugs, so that they'll be left with, 'I can be restless, irritable, and discontent, or I can try this stuff over here.' " Most doctors, accustomed to difficult regimens from their days as interns and residents, can fulfill the outer requirements of treatment for at least a month. At that point, they may rebel and break a rule, or the staff provokes such a rebellion, so that they can revoke privileges and lead the patient to "want" to change. Contriving hurdles is a common technique in various metaphysical disciplines. Consider, for instance, the mind-breaking *koans* or riddles that Zen Buddhist teachers devise for their students. The answer is usually irrelevant while the struggle for a solution pushes a pupil beyond rationality toward enlightenment.

Even those who are complying with treatment are targeted. "We'll find one thing, if necessary, to cause a crisis. We told one guy, 'You're doing everything too perfectly, you need to screw up,' " Molea recalls with relish. "Since you can't get out of it intellectually, the solution is prayer, meditation, reading Twelve-Step literature, going to meetings, working with a sponsor." I ask if this whole process is manipulative.

"It's not like manipulation, it is manipulation," Molea admits cheerfully. "In the sense that all therapy is manipulative. In reality, you let the client out-manipulate him-or herself." Molea is at peace with the process. "Causing pain is a necessary evil to get to the goal."

With other groups, the threat of losing one's job or profession also opens minds to spiritual solutions. At Hazelden in Center City, Minnesota, John MacDougall reports similar success given the combination of personal motivation and outside pressure. "Our best results are with pilots," he says, and ticks off the responsible ingredients on his fingers.

"They have an incredible job they want to keep. They're caught between the union—who assigns them a buddy to attend meetings with—the [airline] company and the Federal Aviation Administration." And given that most have a military background, "They're used to following orders."[8]

A Visit to Hazelden

For many addicts from the prosperous classes, pride collides with survival on a 488-acre campus in the flat reaches of eastern Minnesota. Hazelden was founded in 1949, first as a home for alcoholic clergy and later converted to general use. Its location just outside Center City is an hour's drive north of Minneapolis and St. Paul. The low-slung brick buildings and discreet parking lots tuck into the gentle swells of the earth. Walking paths meander along the perimeters and into some woods but not too far, as if even the patients' wanderings require a controlled freedom. For addicts in primary treatment, there are 128 beds in six units, each named for one of the early supporters of Alcoholics Anonymous.

Its method is commonly known as the Twelve-Step or Minnesota model. As described in a paper by Patricia Owen, Hazelden's director of research, and Randy Stinchfield, a colleague from the University of Minnesota, key elements include: using the Twelve Steps as "a foundation for therapeutic change;" the belief that patients can change and that addiction is a disease; recovering alcoholics serving as counselors and role models alongside professionals; use of peers as "models of change;" a goal of abstinence, and assuming that patients, if treated with dignity and respect, can "grasp the tools needed to become sober."[9]

Though separate from AA, which is not affiliated with any outside program and does not run treatment centers, Hazelden is often considered—if wrongly—"the closest thing to the institutional voice of the AA-based treatment community," according to a 1998 profile in the New Yorker. That year Hazelden, a nonprofit foundation, had 40,000 alumni, a $25 million endowment supported by corporate donors, and $20 million in revenues from its publishing division, the article reported.[10] A month of treatment here can cost about $15,000. The party paying such a sum— patient, employer, insurer—wants results. At Hazelden, with all its counselors and psychiatrists and medical staff and nice touches, the main effort is at inducing a metaphysical transformation.

"Our principal job is to provoke interest in spirituality and the spiritual side of treatment," declares John MacDougall, supervisor of spiritual care. The reason, says MacDougall, an intense man of medium height and rounded edges, is simple: "We want people to get well." He calls chemical dependency "the most complete disease, one that affects you spiritually and emotionally, mentally and physically."

In their paper assessing Hazelden's outcomes, Owen and Stinchfield use more clinical language. When a person applies the Twelve-Step philosophy, they write, "The ultimate goal is personality change, or change in basic thinking, feeling and acting in the world . . . the main agent of change is group affiliation, and practicing behaviors consistent with the Twelve Steps of AA."[11] At all stages, Hazelden reinforces to patients their need for help. Other rules teach patients to know and depend on their group and counselors in a kind of temporary egalitarianism. While visitors may find the atmosphere claustrophobic, many graduates of mainstream rehabs remember their units as hothouses of intimacy, honesty, and mutual aid.

Staffers bluntly describe the predicament of alcoholics as that of "King Baby," and distribute a pamphlet describing the malady. The phrase dates to Sigmund Freud's description of an inborn attitude of self-centered entitlement as "His Majesty, the Baby." When patients sit down for a meeting at Hazelden, someone reads aloud a section from the book *Alcoholics Anonymous* that includes the stipulations, "That probably no human power could have relieved our alcoholism. That God could and would if He were sought." The message, MacDougall says, frustrates or threatens both patients and the social authorities that deal with addicts. "This is very annoying to judges, priests, police officers, newspaper editorialists, and the treatment community because we would like to make them well to solve the problem and to stop alcoholism." MacDougall smiles grimly. "I don't have any delusion that I can make someone well," he tells me during the course of a 90-minute interview in his cramped office. Kim Lundholm-Eades, a chaplain, joins us. Patients are taken through the first five of the Twelve Steps.

"It's really AA or NA involvement over the long run that will keep someone clean and sober," MacDougall adds. If there is power, Lundholm-Eades sees it in the process of a person naming, first, the major problem—the addiction—and then inventorying good and bad personal qualities through the self-examination and confession of the Twelve Steps, notably the fifth that requires "a searching and fearless moral inventory of ourselves." The book *Alcoholics Anonymous* compares the process to a business taking stock: "One object is to disclose damaged or unsaleable goods, to get rid of them promptly and without regret."[12] This self-examination, usually written out, helps patients "name what has worked and what has not worked for them," says Lundholm-Eades. "There's power in naming," she adds, and mentions the German fairy tale figure of Rumpelstiltskin, the dwarf who splits apart when his victim finally guesses his name.

MacDougall thinks, as did the founders of AA and as do many counselors, "if you don't do a Fifth Step you will likely get drunk." Finding the real person, dumping the baggage, and developing the good are at the core of most treatment schemes. At Hazelden, this involves working with three entities—peers, a higher power, and the AA program—in order to change. Thus, spirituality involves how well one relates "to a higher power, with yourself, and with other people," says MacDougall. Physical and mental recovery occurs first—"after 18-20 days, the brain wakes up. Emotional comes later, and spiritual recovery comes a lot later."

MacDougall orders the stages of recovery the same way as do many other treatment professionals. Indeed, it stands to reason that the desperately ill addict has to regain her health first. Most treatment schemes stabilize a new patient medically and nutritionally before proceeding to other therapies. But the reverse order is found in the book *Alcoholics Anonymous*. There, the founding members of that fellowship wrote that, ". . . we have been not only mentally and physically ill, we have been spiritually sick. When the spiritual malady is overcome, we straighten out mentally and physically."[13] Still, today rehabilitation centers often concentrate on stabilizing the health of their patients while, at least initially, soft-pedaling the talk of a higher power, moral inventories, or prayer and meditation. Later, spiritual development becomes the priority and, as an alleged guarantee of sobriety, the foundation of mental and physical health. Resistance and rejection are routine among new patients.

"In groups you may hear, 'I don't want to hear that God crap,' " said MacDougall. "So I say, 'Tell the group about the success you've had handling your addiction alone.' " The counselors also confront suspicions grounded in religion. "A lot of pastors get real edgy with Twelve-Step programs because there's more spirituality in the basement [at meetings] than in the church," says MacDougall, a former Methodist cleric. On the other hand, "some religions see AA as some sort of New Age thing," says Lundholm-Eades, who was raised a Swedish Baptist. AA spirituality does not make a claim on the truth, however, does not require certain beliefs of members and has no written doctrine. What members have in common, said MacDougall, is no personal defense against a drink.

Many in recovery extend this notion to powerlessness over "people, places, and things," in a popular phrase. But being impotent is not the answer either, said Lundholm-Eades. "I focus on what they do have power over, that they do have choices." The idea of powerlessness troubles many, especially those women who are all too familiar with being victims of the powerful. With these, Lundholm-Eades said, "I work on lessening the power of shame, so they can have a change of perspective." That shift underlies a new power, one based in hope rather than fear. They also need trust. Claire Cassell, a chaplain on the women's unit, draws patients into physical exercises—such as walking in a circle of peers while blindfolded—that encourage them to take the risk to trust others.

All three chaplains agreed that recovery along spiritual lines contains paradoxes: the condition is not the alcoholic's fault, but he or she has to take responsibility for it; to regain power over one's life, one has to admit powerlessness. Hope yields the power to change. Adds Lundholm-Eades, "They realize they can re-author their story, and give it a different ending."

Disease, Chemistry, Spirit, and Outcomes

I visited Hazelden the week that PBS aired a series, "Close to Home: Moyers on Addiction." The TV production, by veteran journalist Bill Moyers and his wife, executive producer Judith Davidson Moyers, was a coup for Hazelden. The couple's son, William Cope Moyers, was treated at Hazelden and later worked as its first director of public policy. While serving on an advisory council for Hazelden, Judith Davidson Moyers heard about new research into the brain chemistry of addictions, which helped spark the PBS show.

Shortly before the series aired, however, a writer had profiled the center in the *New Yorker* magazine with considerable skepticism about spiritual solutions. He also cast a gimlet eye on Hazelden's—and other treatment professionals'—lobbying of Congress to mandate increased coverage of mental health services, from which it could benefit handsomely. At the same time, the writer, David Samuels, typified a common hostility toward spiritual solutions. Near the article's end, he visits a laboratory where anti-addiction pharmaceuticals are tested on monkeys, none of whom, he writes, "take the Fifth Step, or surrender to the will of a higher power." When one crack-addicted simian grunts gutturally, Samuels quips that "maybe he is appealing to his higher power."

If the *New Yorker* showed skepticism toward spirituality, "Moyers on Addiction"—oddly enough—was at the other extreme in its silence on spirituality. The series profiled several addicts and alcoholics. Each of these mentioned prayer, meditation, God, and the Twelve Steps. Otherwise, the series barely explored the topic. However, when it came to causes and solutions, from a public and health policy perspective, the series trumpeted research into neurochemistry and genetics. CAT scan images showed parts of a brain as influenced by cocaine. Scientists spoke of turning chemical switches to block cravings or prevent the effects of drugs. The message seemed to be: "Here are a few addicts who found God and got sober, but what really counts in fighting addiction is finding the right pharmaceutical."

Of course, the promise of a chemical solution threatens the treatment industry. Approaching addiction as purely a physical or brain disease, akin to diabetes or hypertension, challenges the Twelve-Step philosophy at the heart of most rehabs. Why bother with Hazelden, Samuels asked, when a pill could do the trick at a fraction of the cost? But even Samuels, and the researchers he visited, conclude that a magic pill is unlikely given the brain's plasticity and "the constraints inherent in the human condition."

Lampooning Hazelden's philosophy may be easy, but the real question regards its results. In their study, Owen and Stinchfield checked up on a representative sample of 1,083 patients at intervals after treatment, most of whom named a family member or associate who could verify the patient's status. They were able to contact 71 percent of the original group, considered an acceptable if not ideal level for scientific studies.

One year after treatment, 53 percent had not used drugs or alcohol and 35 percent had "significantly reduced" their use of alcohol or other drugs. Further, more than half were attending Twelve-Step meetings, most of them at least weekly, and reported better health and an improved relationship with their spouse or mate.

The researchers admitted that the abstinence rate might be less, since research—and common sense—suggests that former patients who cannot be contacted have slightly poorer results. But the results are in line with numerous studies reporting abstinence rates of between 40 percent and 60 percent one year after treatment. As with other research, Hazelden's outcomes show that the effects of treatment fade somewhat over time. One month after treatment, 77 percent were abstinent, and at six months it was 59 percent, before dropping to the one-year level of 53 percent.

Profile: Angel—Embracing Spiritual Dependency

At the age of ten, Angel sought to change herself. "My first drink was old wine in the cellar of my foster family's house. I knew that I would be altered based on what I had heard from my cousins." Did it work? "The taste, it was disgusting. I crashed on the bathroom floor, but it felt good not to feel. I was living in a highly abusive household. After that, I drank as much as I could without getting caught."

All this seems far away when one talks with this poised and forthright woman who has a cheerful musicality in her voice. She laughs when I ask if she has always been so composed. Today, Angel—a pseudonym she chose to protect her identity—works as an advertising executive for a local cable television firm in the Minneapolis area. She is a single mother of a ten-year-old boy. An African-American, Angel was raised by a white Lutheran foster family. Like many alcoholics who grew up in the middle class, Angel fell out of it during her addiction and climbed back in afterward.

She ran away, for the second time, at age 15 and lived on the streets until a woman took her in on the condition she finish high school, which she eventually did. By·this point, Angel smoked marijuana and took LSD regularly. She left, got her own apartment, found a job, and began snorting, then smoking cocaine. In her early 20s and desperate, she called various rehab centers and settled on Hazelden because "I thought it was the cheapest in Minnesota." She entered in 1987 and stayed 31 days, then moved into a halfway house for three months. Angel relapsed the next year but has abstained since. She completed college and attends Cocaine Anonymous and AA regularly.

"I continue to grow with God. My definition of my Goddess is that it is both male and female. She's not so condemning as my previous God, who was always throwing me into hell for cursing and doing other things. I got that idea from church and Sunday school." Feeling damned came easily, Angel says, "when you're five years old and you're wishing your [foster] mother dead."Today, her "core concept" of God is Trinitarian, including Jesus and the Holy Spirit. "It's still three in one. But I have a different connection with him, her, it."

She was never without faith. "Even on the streets, I believed and I had these powerful experiences. One time I was sleeping in a restaurant on the bathroom floor and I prayed all night for food. In the morning, this waitress laid out this breakfast before me." Another time, a penniless Angel prayed to resist the urge to steal a pair of shoes she needed for a job. At the store, a salesman gave them to her for free. Though she felt a "powerful connection" to God, it lessened over time as the drugs continued. There was another quality to her prayer life: "I prayed not to stop but to get more." What changed?

"The third step, the 'as you believe part,' " she says, referring to the third of AA's Twelve Steps, namely, "Made a decision to turn our will and our lives over the to care of *God as we understood Him*." AA literature italicizes the phrase, suggesting its importance. "You can come in as a Buddhist, a Hindu, Protestant, in some Native American religion—it doesn't matter, so long as it's something greater than yourself."

"Before, all decisions started and ended with me. 'How will this benefit me?' With a power greater than myself, I do have some inclinations to decide how my actions could benefit others. I'll ask, 'God, what is your will for me? How can I help the other person?' I had a hard time with that the first six years, because I had a hard life and I felt I was owed." In the first few years after Hazelden, Angel became a single mother and attended college. "Life was unbearable and my program [of recovery] was unmanageable because everything was me-focused." The night she was to mark her AA anniversary, by receiving a medallion, or "chip," at her group meeting, she could not think of any close friend in the room she had frequented for six years. "There was no one I knew well enough to give me my chip. I broke down. I was crying hysterically." Someone came to the rescue, but the night was a turning point. About the same time,

Angel graduated from college and got off welfare. She found an AA sponsor—a combined mentor and confidante—and began helping AA protégés, or "sponsees," of her own. Shifting the focus to other people made a difference in her life, spiritually and economically.

Angel encountered life on a spiritual basis in treatment. "My counselor held back on the Twelve Steps, but in the first week he did ask me, 'Where are you at with God?' "The question—especially in a clinical setting—threw Angel off. She did not attend many AA meetings while at Hazelden, but she did work through some of the Twelve Steps. "We did Step One in the first week, with this pamphlet, listing our symptoms and the consequences. I came to One before treatment. Now Two ['Came to believe in a power greater than ourselves.'] was a little tougher." The Third Step—deciding to turn her life and will over to God—happened to her after a crisis.

"I had a 'regular' from my work visiting me. One time I knew he had drugs on him and I became enraged because he wouldn't give me any. We went outside for a walk and I, I basically tried to beat him up. He didn't give me any. He told me I was a mess and this place wasn't doing anything for me." Later in her room, Angel kneeled in despair. "I was saying the Third Step over and over. 'I'm making that decision, I'm making that decision.' I didn't know what that meant, but it was my first spiritual awakening. Something came over me at that moment. I became more accepting."

She followed that up with the personal inventory suggested in the next two of the Twelve Steps. Hazelden included classes in meditation, health, and nutrition, a psychological inventory, and counseling, family therapy, and regular exercise. Angel endorsed all of those. But the main benefit of her 31 days there?

"Hope, I got hope." She pinpoints a moment.

"A woman in a red dress who came and told us her story. Something about it, I just identified with her, and that gave me hope that I could recover. That woman actually gave me hope that I could not smoke crack cocaine."

Now, she adds, "I hope to do God's will. I hope to see my son graduate high school. I hope for many things, because I know that without hope nothing is possible."

Hubris and Its Discontents

Two elements of Twelve-Step-style treatment particularly offend well-educated, middle-income people: the twin notions of admitting powerlessness over addiction and relying on a higher power. Marianne Gilliam's 1999 book, *How Alcoholics Anonymous Failed Me* (New York: Eagle

Brook/Morrow), embodied this critique. "In the fear and helplessness of our addictive natures, we created these authoritative, rigid systems such as AA and religions in order to be absolved of the responsibility for our own lives."[14] These are common complaints. But it is safe to say that for most believers, religion amplifies, and enables them to fulfill, duties to self, society, and God. Ideally, religion grounds responsibility in the relationship to God. Faith helps the believer to live faithfully. God cannot be observed but results of faith are visible. Religion long has been invoked as remedy for addiction, sometimes to good effect, sometimes not. In interviews, dozens of members reported that AA allowed them to disentangle spiritual solutions from organized religion. At the same time, Twelve-Step fellowships draw some of their most powerful ideas from religion.

Most religions define grievous sin as a rejection of God and an elevation of the human person to a paramount position. For the ancient Greeks, the great sin was hubris, the presumption rejection of limits on human freedom. In Judaism, there is the sin of "averah," a rejection of the will of God. Similarly in Christianity, pride tops the list of the Seven Deadly Sins, and involves rejecting God's will. This is the nature of Original Sin as depicted in the tale (Genesis 3:5) of Adam and Eve, who ate of the tree in the middle of Eden on the serpent's promise that "your eyes will be opened and you will be like gods who know what is good and what is bad."

Pride is first invoked in the addict's life during the active days, when the drug distorts clear thought and often makes the person feel ecstatic, invulnerable, godlike. Then, in the final throes of an addiction, counselors and addicts report, life condenses to a self-centered round of getting, using, and recuperating before starting all over.

In recovery, pride can trip up the client, who would prefer to do it on his own or without some maudlin reliance on God through practices associated with childhood. AA literature, and reports from addicts themselves, indicate that reliance on a higher power, however defined, liberates. The Twelve Steps, and other spiritual paths to recovery such as native American religions or even the secular Women for Sobriety, all lead addicts to assume responsibility for their problems and their lives. "Our problems were of our own making," the book *Alcoholics Anonymous* declares. "Bottles were only a symptom."[15] The other common and related criticism aimed at Twelve-Step spirituality charges that it promotes victimhood among addicts. Not so, says MacDougall at Hazelden, who notes that addiction itself shackles people. "Alcohol has traditionally been a tool of oppression. You know the old saying, 'Candy is dandy but liquor is quicker.' It helps exploit people. On plantations they used to give free liquor to slaves on holidays so that they wouldn't run away. In the 1980s I visited Soweto in South Africa, and the only place in the township with electricity was the government-owned liquor store."

For MacDougall and others, recovery liberates victims. "We don't teach powerlessness. We do teach powerlessness over just one thing, alcoholism or addiction. If you admit that, you gain power over the rest of your life."

Cognitive Behavioral Therapy and Spirituality: Two Routes to One End

The otherwise successful addict who stubbornly rejects a new perspective on his or her life reminds me of a fiction workshop I took at the University at Albany with Doug Glover, a Canadian novelist who lives near Saratoga Springs. Writers, especially of fiction, have a hard time with criticism. During the first session with Glover, three or four students almost rebuked his opinion of their craft, and even his right to have an opinion. At the start of the second class, with many of my peers still fuming, he sat down, looked over us in silence and diagnosed the situation. "Resistance," he said plainly, almost glaring at the fact of it floating in the air. "Resistance." Glover explained that resistance to criticism is normal and even a good sign that a writer has invested herself in her work. But resistance does not eliminate the need for correction and change.

Years later, I see further into the writers' rebellion. Each of their short stories said something fundamental of who they were. They were balking, in part, because they did not like being told to look at their lives differently. So too with an alcoholic, especially one armed with family, job, hobbies, house, cars, and vacations. She sees her life in one way, in a way that has worked for her so far. To overcome an addiction, she is told to see it differently. And she resists.

The religiously inclined see addiction as a failure of the individual self or even the individual spirit, who must find relief in a transcendent power. Not so differently, the psychologically inclined see the problem as one of bad—dysfunctional, if you please—habits of mind. Cognitive behavioral therapy, increasingly popular in the addictions field, seeks to change how a person thinks and acts. In the patient's "internal dialogue" lie the problem and the solution. "Cognitive restructuring helps a client control emotions, and, ultimately, behaviors, by convincing the client that certain ideas are irrational and by teaching more rational, less defeating ideas."[16] In a Vermont state prison, a "cognitive self-change" treatment group tries to correct the "cognitive distortions" that incite criminals to violence.[17]

One hears similar talk from AA members. Once abstinent, many routinely say that they now "have a thinking problem, not a drinking problem." A man recalled for me complaining, early in his recovery, that the AA program amounted to brainwashing. His leathery sponsor shot back,

"If anything needs washing, it's your brain." New thinking is paramount. As the book *Alcoholics Anonymous* declares, "Some of us have tried to hold on to our old ideas and the result was nil until we let go absolutely."[18]

Twelve-Step and similar programs aim to change the way members think and act, often with little overt reference to God, though a spiritual life underpins the transformation. Through various slogans these groups express the effort to change one's daily life. These include: "Live and Let Live," "Think, Think, Think," "One Day at a Time," "First Things First," and "Easy Does It."

"The slogans and steps should be put into behavioral cognitive terms so that [medical and mental health] practitioners can see we're not about burning incense and waving crosses," says Patricia Owen, the research director at Hazelden. "We may be talking about the same thing but in different language." Much, maybe 75 percent, of Hazelden's treatment could be described as behavioral cognitive therapy, she says. Putting the idea of a higher power in an addict's mind may enable that person to think and act differently—the whole point of cognitive behavioral therapy—in order to abstain and recover. As George Vaillant points out, the messages of AA already resemble a cognitive approach: don't take the first drink; avoid getting tired or lonely; find new friends; get help; enjoy living free of drugs; take responsibility; think positive.[19] These slogans and advice express the pragmatism that radiates through most American efforts at self-improvement, religious and otherwise. But there are differences between spiritual and cognitive approaches.

Many addicts and professionals regard addiction as, primarily, a problem of thought and attitude. Cognitive counseling, as developed by psychologist Aaron Beck, regards errors of thought as the cause of upsets and improper actions. Thinking shapes feelings in this scheme, which reverses the order given in the book *Alcoholics Anonymous* and described by Joe Molea. Through cognitive restructuring, the client learns that certain ideas are irrational, or harmful, and replaces these with useful ones. Clients learn to talk to themselves differently, to see themselves and life differently, and thereby to think and act differently.

Fran Steigerwald and David Stone, researchers at the Department of Counseling and Higher Education of Ohio University, looked more systematically at the cognitive behavioral aspects of mainstream recovery. "AA meetings provide an atmosphere in which cognitive restructuring can take place," they wrote. "The 12-Step group encourages and supports alcoholics to explore and own selfish, self-seeking, and self-centered thinking, which brought them to AA in the first place." The aforementioned slogans, Steigerwald and Stone write, "reflect some of the issues, like control, power, and distorted thinking, which alcoholics have struggled with while drinking."

The first three steps "provide the basis for a cognitive restructuring that allows for the distorted alcoholic cognitions, emotions, and behaviors to change. Step 1 challenges the cognitive distortions of grandiosity, defiance, and isolation by admitting powerlessness together with other alcoholics, 'We admitted we were powerless . . .' Step 2 restructures this powerlessness into reliance and hope through belief in a higher power. Step 3 is the action step that cuts out self-will and begins dependence upon this higher power."[20] What seems complex and mysterious is actually simple, at least in its main element: the addict must be willing to try to change. In his 1990 textbook, *Counseling the Chemically Dependent: Theory and Practice*, R. L. George writes, "Effort simply means to be willing to think new thoughts, to try new behaviors, to make an effort to do those things which are necessary to 'working the program.' "[21] To a degree, this "effort" may involve the work of the midbrain as described by Molea, in a process where instinct and emotion—influenced by spirituality—shape thought.

Spirituality goes a step further. The idea of a higher power starts a process in which a person has complete freedom. Believing may be hard, but most anyone can act as if there is a higher power helping him abstain. Says Owens, "We find that the best way to start is with a personal, unique concept of a higher power, and that will lead to a universal concept." Changes in thought and behavior that follow can cement belief, which further transforms the person.

In early recovery, change washes over an addict because he or she, at some level, decided in favor of abstinence, recovery, and change. Saying yes, then, may be all it requires. There are many levels of yes. What counts is helping patients say yes to beliefs and thoughts that will help them, according to Brad Warner, the counselor in upstate New York. He speaks in rapid bursts, punching out sentences in a raspy voice of conviction and enthusiasm.

"The first thing I do is look at the client's beliefs. We go through an exercise called, 'I believe.' We go through all the different beliefs they have about the world, about God, about whatever. Then we look at which beliefs are helping them in recovery or not." At Hazelden, both Owen and the chaplains spoke of AA's moral inventory in the same utilitarian terms. Warner, who alternates between AA talk and clinical language, regards developing a new set of beliefs as a spiritual endeavor. But he distinguishes this from religion, a loaded topic for many of his patients, by referring to the Latin roots of each word. Religion derives from *religio*, meaning conscientiousness or piety, and *religare*, which means to tie or bind. Spirituality derives from the Latin word, *inspiritus*, which means a breathing. Perhaps doomed by its roots, religion still carries that air of coercion for many who prefer the sense of freedom and inspiration conveyed by spirituality. With some justification critics call popular spirituality, "religion without the rules." Next, Warner reminds his clients that, if or when they have the sort of spiritual awakening that is the aim of the Twelve-Step program of recovery, it will be of the slow, gradual educational variety, as described in the book, *Alcoholics Anonymous*. Strong winds and bright lights are unlikely for most people as they plod through a wholesale alteration of thinking and living. This seems more acceptable to well-educated patients who prefer reason, proof, and order.

"We teach that by changing beliefs, you will change your reactions to the world, which will be necessary," says Warner. "Looking at it from a cognitive point of view, you can make a lot of changes in a short period of time. That's what AA does. People come in thinking they have to drink, they talk [and listen] for an hour at a meeting, they don't drink, and the effect is revolutionary."

Conclusion: Out of the Thicket

Professionals, addicts, and much of the public agree that addiction is not a moral issue. But if the solution is spiritual in nature, it necessarily invokes morality. At Hazelden, the three chaplains respond to the association in quick, tag-team fashion. "I don't see that paradox as a problem," says Kim Lundholm-Eades. "I don't see it as a problem either," adds Claire Cassell, the women's chaplain. "You have to take responsibility for your actions." Lundholm-Eades quickly continues. "The medical model has never absolved anyone of responsibility." MacDougall chimes in with a critique of purely medical or scientific approaches to addiction. The trio of chaplains worry that the trend toward medical treatment relies too heavily on patient's changing by mere virtue of insight and ignores the critical if intangible role of spiritual aspiration. Says Cassell; "Hope leads to change." Whence comes hope when treatment consists of purely scientific solutions—a prescription, a pill—remains unknown.

Even expressed in the language of cognitive behavioral therapy, there is no mistaking what is essentially a conversion experience. "The change in beliefs is at the core of the spiritual experience," says Warner. "We see it as primary to recovery."He continues, paraphrasing a definition from the book *Alcoholics Anonymous* and also referring to the famous, if outdated, chart of addiction's decline and recovery's rise created by Elvin M. Jellinek, the physiologist who wrote *The Disease Concept of Alcoholism* (1960). "Unless the patients have made the spiritual change, defined as a vast change in feelings and outlook, then they're not getting better physically or emotionally," says Warner. "They're just on hold, waiting for the next drink. If you look at the Jellinek chart, on the upswing, most of the changes are not changes in symptoms but changes in attitude and outlook. A person can wipe out all the symptoms but without a change in outlook, they are way down the chart. I see this all the time in people who relapse."

"People come in and you know they're going to relapse because they are only looking at external symptoms and not at the internal changes they need to make. It's a matter of the internal locus of control versus an external one. But that's what we do, we try to change the patients thought processes." Warner quotes from the AA Big Book.

"With few exceptions our members find that they have tapped an inner resource which they presently identify with their own conception of a Power greater than themselves. . . . Most of us think this awareness of a Power greater than ourselves is the essence of spiritual experience."[22] But most of his middle-class patients may be just as happy to credit new beliefs for their recovery. It sounds more reasonable than "spiritual awakening," even if one phenomenon passes for the other.

CHAPTER III

Women's Treatment, Women's Spirituality

For decades, alcoholic and addicted women were treated alongside men. This often meant that they were not treated at all. Those who had children could not usually enter treatment, especially residential programs. When women did enter treatment, they often walked into a heightened version of the man's world that had exacerbated their drinking in the first place. Most of the clients were male. Counselors and senior clients preached and practiced a confrontational approach to recovery. The alcoholic was seen as a wild creature, criminal and shrewd and perverse, who needed to be lassoed, corralled, and branded with the consciousness of their addicted state and their utter need for help from others, often including a higher power. Clients talked tough, even about their feelings, and picked up the habit of referring to their "alcoholic personality" as a separate entity they had to wrestle to the ground. Graduates of the typical treatment center practiced a form of hero worship—something most men develop a knack for as little boys—in their exaggerated gratitude to counselors "who kicked my butt" into accepting and recovering from their addiction. Schedules and regimens were often military in nature, especially at the publicly funded centers.

Into this milieu would walk a woman alcoholic. Nothing was tailored to her needs, personality, or hopes. Though many did well and recovered, many dropped out. Others, especially mothers with small children or other dependents, were unable to enter at all. "It used to be, essentially, a system that served men—with a few women in there," Nick Gantes, who directs the Illinois Office of Alcoholism and Substance Abuse, told me during an interview in his office, buried deep in the cubicled warrens of a curved sky-scraper in downtown Chicago.[1] Over the last decade or two, government agencies and private groups have created or expanded programs for women. By 1996, women constituted 30 percent of the 1.5 million people admitted to treatment programs.[2] In Illinois, Gantes reported, women make up 40 percent.

By another measure—people who help in support groups—women are now represented in proportions closer to the actual occurrence of abuse or addictions. According to the 1996 membership survey of Alcoholics Anonymous, 33 percent were women, an increase from earlier years when this fellowship was largely male. The proportion is likely to grow since, among younger AA members—those under 30 years of age— a full 40 percent were females. In some other countries, the percentages are even higher: 44 percent in Austria and up to 50 percent in Switzerland. In all countries for which there is data, women are over-represented in AA compared to their presence in treatment, which an international research team found to be evidence of AA's flexibility and its appeal to women's values and attitudes.[3]

Women Conceiving God

A women's spirituality, created to save lives and crafted from old and new elements, emerged in rough outline during a morning's conversation with seven residents at The Next Step Inc. The recovery home for chemically dependent women is housed in a former convent in the racially mixed West Hill neighborhood of Albany. The women—black, white, alcoholic, some ex-cocaine addicts, most from upstate New York cities and villages—are in their 30s and early 40s and have been sober for periods ranging from 1-15 months. One December morning, they talk about the origins, nature, and role of their spiritual lives as they lounge on the overstuffed furniture of the living room.[4]

"I believed in God, when I was out there, but I always asked 'If he's such a good guy, why is he not doing anything for me?'" says Tina. "In recovery, I was baptized in the water and I felt clean and whole and, like, 'whew.' I started reading the Bible and going to church." How has she answered her old question?

"I began hearing the word, that he's not a mean God, that he's a forgiving God." She heard that as a child in a Pentecostal church, but was not listening. Tina points to a crude oil painting of snow-draped pine trees flanking an icy stream. "When I think of God, I think of that picture, of something beautiful. I don't think of a person.

"When I was younger, I would think of God as man, a king who ruled everybody. When I think of him as a person, I think of people who can change their minds. But when I think of God as that sort of picture, I think nobody can take it away or change it."

For some of the women, the faith they knew in childhood remained valuable but blocked by drugs. "Before treatment I felt unworthy of the people I loved," says Maureen. "This led me to faith in a higher power I call Jesus Christ. It gave me the courage to look at myself. Spirituality comes from within. The deepest, goriest feelings I can get out, because of God, and not be fearful of rejection from other people."

Yes, Maureen believed in a God before. "I knew he was there but that he didn't care because I was out there, drinking on the streets.

"I did it to myself, following my will." Under this new light, her past appears differently. "I see that all these experiences were for a purpose. I'm starting to feel that God was there, after all."

It's surprising how few have a single, clear picture of God. "I think of God more in nature, as a spirit, not as a man" says Robin. "I don't need to go to a church, I just sit next to the woods." Most describe a deity in terms of their apprehension of love, peace, communion, and acceptance. "For me it's a feeling of softness and warmth," says Maureen. Robin prays "to a spiritual being that's watching over us." This unclear if effective image contrasts with her childhood notion of God "as a man holding everybody in his hands."

Others employ varying schemes. "My higher power, God, I call 'good orderly direction,' " Beatrice announces. "It's doing the right thing at the right time." During a previous treatment regimen, she got stuck on the spiritual content "for the reason that God didn't keep me from drinking or drugging. But he loved me, or I would be dead."

Beatrice keeps her religion apart. "I had clean time before, but it wasn't from going to church but from going to [Twelve-Step] meetings." Her image of God is "dark-skinned, almost black. Sometime my God is a woman." She laughs, then offers some explanation. "I had a lot of surgery, mostly for woman's problems, with woman doctors. They were more understanding."

Further, she formed some ideas while attending Catholic schools. "I'm not Catholic, but there it was always, 'Hail *Mary*, " Beatrice says, emphasizing the name of the woman who bore Jesus. "Without Mary there would be no God, so God would have to be a woman. Then you look at the saints—a lot of women there. And so many things in the Bible happen to women." The increased role for woman in society confirms the fact for her. "God doesn't necessarily have to be a man," Beatrice concludes.

Without blaming themselves for their addiction, the women tended to trace their decline and recovery in terms of losing and then regaining faith.

"I believe we have a spirit, a soul, and sometimes it gets out," Robins says. "It was lost and now I have to get it back."

For Susan, "I never thought God left me, but I stopped asking him for help. I took my life back in my own hands." At night, she gives thanks and asks for rest; in the morning Susan asks for patience, love, tolerance.

I ask whether God would stop helping once she stopped asking. "No. I just wouldn't be aware of it. And he may watch over me, but I'll do a lot more struggling."

Turetha was raised in a church-going family. "I knew the way, but I chose not to follow it, not to listen to my mother." Almost dying from drug abuse "gave me more will power to serve God." Now she feels God's presence while singing hymns, reading the Bible, praying. "I know there's a place for me. So long as I surrender he'll show me."

The Next Step encourages spiritual development with daily meditation sessions and at least five Twelve-Step meetings weekly. "We try to saturate them with that because it's going to be their ongoing lifeline," says Sally Peters, the program's wiry, blunt clinical director who has worked here for 23 years. "Spirituality is a big part of the recovery process. A lot of people have a blank spot there."

In a change from ten years ago, Next Step's residents tend to become heavily involved in a church during their recovery. Peters suggests the women are seeking any refuge from "all the chaos in the world." Audrey Kibrick, the director for the past four years, says today's client—here and elsewhere—tends to be more impaired than in the past and thus open to more types of help. Many of the women attend black Baptist or Pentecostal churches that offer their own recovery groups, usually centered on Bible study and discussion. For Kibrick, the presence of help outweighs its form. "We're happy because when they leave here they're going to need a lot of support," she says.

Women, Addiction, and Treatment

Fewer women than men report abusing or depending on alcohol or other drugs at any point in their lives, though the rate is still high: 18 percent in 1991, compared to 35 percent among men.[5] When people over 12 years of age were asked about the past month in the 1993 National Household Survey of Drug Abuse, 4.1 percent of women reported using illicit drugs, compared to 7.4 percent for men. And 1.5 percent of women reported heavy drinking compared to 5.3 percent for men.[6] This ratio, with two to three times as many men abusing drugs or being addicted held true in most age categories. Interestingly, abuse in both sexes peaks in the years between 18 and 25, then declines steadily—supporting the thesis of a vocal minority that addiction is not simply a medical disease, since so many people taper off and usually without much help. Finally, surveys indicate that women are catching up, so to speak, in rates of abuse. Young women, for instance, are doing more of the binge and abusive drinking once considered exclusive to men.

Treatment programs have amended a once-common conviction that there is one path to recovery. Programs for mothers and other women have led the way with tailored approaches. In the single most striking accommodation, many allow a woman to bring her small children into treatment. Others allow pregnant women. Therapy often differs. Counselors confront their clients on important subjects—"You are an alcoholic"—but less aggressively. They do not get in the addict's face. More experienced residents may show newer women "tough love," but the emphasis is usually on the latter.

Consistent with traditional treatment, women's programs address their clients' spiritual needs and development. Many or most do well with the standard approaches, such as the Twelve Steps, conventional religion, or generic styles of prayer and meditation. For those who need "women's treatment," does the spiritual part of their recovery differ from men?

The simple answer: women often understand God differently than do men, or emphasize different roles of the divinity. More strikingly, they tend to see recovery in terms of empowerment, rather than embracing powerlessness—one of the core beliefs in the Twelve-Step model. That difference often originates in the damage done to women during or before their drug abuse and addiction.

"Ninety percent of our women report being victimized—in relationships, by incest, physical abuse, etcetera," Florence Wright, clinical director of The Women's Treatment Center in Chicago, a professional who combines warmth and directness, told me during a tour of the facility.[7] I ask if this abuse coincides with their predispositions to addiction or if it contributes to it. The issue is a sticky one, often pitting the findings or predilections of scientists—who tack toward genetic and neurochemical explanations for mental illness—and patients and advocates, who often see the root of their problems in traumatic or violent pasts.

For Wright, the connection is direct. The history of victimization, she says, "contributes, particularly if it occurs at a young age and damages the spirit. Adding alcohol and drugs further damages one's spirit. A lot of their recovery involves undoing that damage. I don't necessarily think there is a spirituality that's unique to women. But it is a matter of empowerment and helping them to heal. And the healing part can be very difficult, because they have to deal with other things, along the way, that have damaged their spirit."

Research collected by the National Institute on Drug Abuse indicates that up to 70 percent of drug-abusing women report histories of physical and sexual abuse. In 1998, the first large-scale study of sex abuse and drinking found that women who were abused as children are at much higher than normal risk for life-disrupting alcohol dependence as adults. Study leader Sharon Wilsnack, a psychologist at the University of North Dakota, Grand Forks told USA Today in 1998 that while not a cause, "the relationship is powerful. Abuse is the single strongest predictor of alcohol dependency, even stronger than a family history of drinking." Her team interviewed 1,099 women. Other researchers at the time said that a strong link between abuse and alcoholism was obvious in treatment for years. Of the estimated four million female alcoholics, Wilsnack estimated that half of these may have been sexually abused in childhood and that many drink to alleviate their psychic turmoil.[8]

NIDA also reports that among addicts or abusers, women are far more likely than men to have had alcoholic or addicted parents.[9] Women also seem to become addicted more readily to certain drugs, such as crack cocaine.[10] During the late 1980s, the great scare of a generation of "crack babies" growing up with numerous defects let flow the funds for women's treatment. The spread of AIDS among women, and especially those of childbearing age, added urgency to the need for treatment solutions.

Yet by choice or necessity, women avoid treatment for many reasons. They often feel twice stigmatized: by the addiction and by the loose morals or irresponsible motherhood associated with it. They also tend to see their addiction as one piece of a larger problem. According to a pair of Swedish researchers, Lena Dahlgren and Anders Willander, who followed up on 200 women two years after treatment, "They usually regard the alcohol abuse as only part of a life-crisis and want more comprehensive assistance."[11] This finding dovetails that of Dr. Margaret L. Griffin at McLean Hospital in Massachusetts, who studied 95 men and 34 women hospitalized for cocaine abuse. She and colleagues found that women were more likely to cite specific reasons—depression, health, family or work pressure—for their drug use compared to men, for whom cocaine was part of a larger pattern of antisocial behavior.[12]

Being a woman also restricts choice of treatment. Most programs do not accept pregnant women and they drop clients who become pregnant. In many locations, addicts have to wait to enter crowded facilities. Since there is no delaying a pregnancy already underway, postponed treatment can damage two people—mother and infant. Only a fraction of agencies will take a mother with her children. In New York State, long a pioneer in rehabilitation, only 14 out of 1,000 or so treatment centers in 1996 took in addicted mothers with children, according to the Office of Alcoholism and Substance Abuse Services.[13]

Consequently, mothers often refuse to go for help since they have, or trust, no one to watch their offspring. They often fear that child protective workers will take away their children. Even while in treatment, many women told me that this fear haunts their days and nights. Among a group of four women I followed through treatment in Rochester for a year, the only one who left before finishing treatment was a mother of eight. Though she had one child with her, the others were scattered among relatives—a lot to worry about. When she dropped out, the impact was all the greater since it was spread among her kids. Women, especially those who have received welfare or committed crimes, often avoid treatment for fear they will be sent to jail and denied public assistance.

Profile: Lisa—Recovering through Women for Sobriety

In 1995, Lisa's counselor told her it seemed she had a drinking problem.

"I thought he was full of crap. To me, a person with an addiction or alcoholism was one of these old bums I saw downtown." But Lisa, a working mother of two in Cincinnati, Ohio, did attend a few meetings of Alcoholics Anonymous, enough to be turned off by an emphasis on the disease and the ostensible need for a spiritual solution.[14]

"I always felt worse when I left. I felt uncomfortable that every time I wanted to say something, I had to say, 'I'm Lisa and I'm an alcoholic.' We heard the same stories over and over, but I didn't want to talk about my drinking all the time. I would come out of the meetings and try to prove that I'm not alcoholic. That didn't work. I would do one or two drinks that night, and more the next night, and keep going.

"The drinking affected my family, my relationship with my husband. I was depressed and I always blamed him. I had no major health problems. I thank God I was very lucky with how little it affected me." But the habit was long-standing. Lisa remembers drinking as a teen, even bringing alcohol to school each morning as a teenager.

One thing that turned her off about AA was the suggestion—to Lisa it seemed to be more of a mandate—that she find some higher power to help her. "They kept cramming this higher power down your throat. You could call it whatever you wanted: nature, God. That was how you were going to stop drinking. No, it wasn't, I had to make the choice to stop. Once I stopped, spirituality could help me, as soon as I admitted that it was my choice to stop, not my higher power's choice." Lisa remarks that she is not anti-religious, and that she is a practicing Catholic with a well-developed spiritual life.

But seeking alternatives, she also attended a meeting of Self Management And Recovery Training, or SMART, held at a local hospital. Though SMART is primarily for those seeking abstinence, it also offers help to people who want to drink responsibly. While first impressions, especially as reported by still-active alcoholics, can be incorrect, Lisa did not like the message "that you don't have to be abstinent to get better. I said to myself, 'Oh no, I am not one of the lucky few.' " Her local council on alcoholism referred Lisa to a local session of Women for Sobriety. Groups exist around the country. A meeting lasts 60 to 90 minutes and is led by a certified moderator. Members are asked for a small donation. People begin by reading from WFS literature, including the 13-part New Life program.

At Lisa's first meeting, she liked the philosophy of the ten women she found there. "They introduced themselves and not one said the word alcoholic or addict. Each said, 'I am a capable woman,' or 'I am a competent woman.' " That night, Lisa committed herself to try Women for Sobriety for six weeks. "We go around the room, each takes a turn—'I'm Lisa and I'm a competent, capable woman,'—and you say something positive that happened to you that day or since the last meeting, or something negative."

"We do 'crosstalk,' unlike AA," Lisa says, using a common term for responding directly to another person's comments. "You allow them to get it out, then you might say, 'I had something like that, and here's what I did.' "

Lisa did not stop drinking immediately, nor was there any rapid, profound change of mind. Meanwhile, she attended WFS meetings twice a week and followed its daily regimen of readings and contemplation. "It took another year, and then my denial was gone." Lisa realized she had changed when she was preparing to celebrate, even though she is not Irish, St. Patrick's Day. "On March 17 1997, it just hit me over the head. It just hit me that I could not go to bars and celebrate. I said that to some friends who were *not* part of my WFS group." The admission outside of her group was significant "because I always felt very shameful, and to say it to my husband and best friend and not feel shame was important. 'I'm alcoholic,' like yeah, 'I have diabetes.' Now, if I have a craving I can talk about it and not feel the guilt."

Lisa still attends the same WFS group. There are four long-term members—"lifers," she calls herself and the other three—and a rotating cast of other women. "A lot come, become competent, capable women and then go on with their lives, maybe checking in once in a while. You can do it on your own—read the 13 statements in the morning to start your day right, reflect on doing one for the day, like Number Three, 'Happiness is a habit I will develop.' At night you review the day."

As for discussing God at the meetings, "You can, but we don't a whole lot." The emphasis is on a positivist philosophy that many women find empowering and suited to their needs. Lisa develops her spiritual side in other realms, such as a retreat she recently attended. "Now it plays a big part in my life. I have a problem with the old religion, before Vatican II," she says, referring to the pivotal sessions of Catholic Church leaders in the early 1960s that led to a procession of progressive reforms. Lisa now attends a large suburban church—Good Shepherd—in Montgomery, Ohio that she considers welcoming and modern.

"Once I understood what spirituality was, that it was not what it says in the Bible or church, it helped me gain control over my addiction. Spirituality? It's an inner calmness. If I feel stressed, I can meditate on the inner spirit. I say 'Help me, Inner Spirit,' over and over, and this flooding sensation comes over me of peace, of calmness."

Relationships and Powerlessness

The idea that women define themselves in terms of relationships and that men define themselves in terms of accomplishment has spread through our society. Though one may quibble with its fine points, the assumption resonates with some research and many people's experience. The idea is also relevant in addictions treatment and recovery. Stephanie Brown, an author, researcher, and clinician who directs the Addictions Institute in Menlo Park, California, has found that most men and women understand their addiction differently and in a way broadly determined by gender. "The meaning of alcoholism may differ. Men may see it as a failure in their sense of masculinity and competitiveness. Women have a number of different meanings, but usually as a failure in relationship to men, or as a failure in being a wife and mother."[15] Addicts in treatment are typically advised to avoid romantic relationships for a year. Often in support groups, both the informal ones formed among clients and the traditional ones in the community, newcomers are encouraged to withdraw from their old social networks in order to concentrate on recovery. Combined with the emphasis on powerlessness, this can harmfully isolate women who often tend to define themselves more in terms of their relationships. To generalize: compared to men, women are more often and more deeply embedded in a variety of family, romantic, friendly, and other networks. "Relational therapists have noted that women often enter drug treatment to maintain or enhance their relationships and that this desire to change their personal lives should be built on as a strength, rather than interpreted as resistance," Margaret Kearney, a nursing professor at Boston College, wrote in her 1997 paper, "Drug Treatment for Women: Traditional Models and New Directions." When a woman arrives at the threshold of treatment or recovery, she usually understands the critical notions of powerlessness and humility based on past relationships. "Many women have been socialized to accept abuse, shame and powerlessness, which perpetuate emotional pain conducive to drug use," Kearney commented.[16]

The syndrome not only keeps them out of treatment, but also can make traditional methods such as confrontation backfire. Traditionally, counselors and veteran clients drum into newcomers the notion that they were in denial about the true nature of their addiction and their self-destructive personality. New clients were told that they had to accept their powerlessness over drugs and also over the "people, places, and things" that could prompt a relapse. This is not always a comforting, or useful, message to a woman who has been abused by others and beaten down by their own addiction. Further, if a woman can arrange for a break from her responsibility for children, home, and work in order to attend treatment, she may still be hampered by shame for her temporary "neglect" of these roles. Thus, women's treatment must address many practical and emotional elements not usually considered in traditional centers such as low self-regard, the shame and pain over past abuse, child care, maternal training and support, and advice on relationships.

Women's Spirituality

The spiritual element of recovery seems especially important for many women. While some critics say the entire notion of a higher power is patriarchal and demeaning to women, many on the ground level of recovery see it as a means to self-sufficiency and dignity. An addict with a God of her own conception is more fully armed to return to her family and neighborhood, and less likely to submit to other authorities.

Among the women Florence Wright sees at The Women's Treatment Center in Chicago, "powerlessness" does not mean "weak," she insisted. "We're all powerless over something," Wright said. "We talk about regaining a sense of power and control over their lives. If we can redefine it for them, that helps."

Research by Roy J. Mathew and colleagues from Duke University Medical Center and Kerala University in India is that women differ from men in their experience of spirituality before and after recovery. Using two different scales on a sample of recovered addicts in AA and NA and a control group of non-AA members, the researchers measured, among other things, belief in a god or higher power, in religious faith and practice, in mystical experiences, and in personal values such as morality. Before recovery, the women tended to score lower than men on belief in religion, a god, and mysticism. After recovery, they scored higher. Females also reported more significant changes in beliefs measured on the character subscale.[17] The same researchers previously reported that their study and similar research, in India, found that women generally reported higher spirituality scores.

While it is hard to say what explains the higher scores after treatment, there may be one explanation for the lower scores beforehand: many women postpone seeking help more than men do. At Clean & Sober Streets, a long-term residential center in Washington D.C. for hard-core, homeless addicts, men usually stay a year. But women, on average, stay 18 months before they are ready to return to the community. "Usually it's because they've just gone down a lot further," said cofounder and director Julia Lightfoot.[18] Unquestioned is that spirituality matters for so many. Wrote Kearney, drawing on the work of others, "As women discover their own internal strengths and increased self-knowledge, many find that their spirituality is a source of centering and affirmation."[19]

Spirituality in Treatment

While addiction treatments have long emphasized spiritual development, mainstream healthcare has begun to pay more attention to the role of spiritual beliefs and practices both for maintaining good health and for healing from accidents and disease. Spirituality also helps people with terminal illness. While AIDS may erode the human form and dignity, "those with the disease search for meaning in life as they seek ways to prolong survival," a team of researchers at the Morehouse School of Medicine found in a study of the meaning and use of spirituality in 45 women infected with HIV/AIDS.[20] Six major themes emerged in their interviews: relationship with a supreme being, prayer and meditation, healing, peace, love, and religiosity. "The acceptance of spirituality as a component of health and quality of life," they concluded, "requires a shift in perspective that may allow for the development of new treatment and care strategies that are meaningful to those whose conditions are presently incurable."

Eating disorders, which afflict far more women than men, are another example. While professionals have clinicalized these, legions of women have found respite through spiritual development, often in Overeaters Anonymous. In a compelling article, C. J. Garrett, a nursing professor at the University of West Sydney in Australia, argued for seeing recovery from anorexia nervosa as a ritual of personal transformation, rather than just a medical or clinical disorder. Using an understanding of asceticism promulgated by French sociologist Emile Durkheim, Garrett studied 32 people in various stages of recovery.[21]

"Participants in this study referred to anorexia as a spiritual quest and for them recovery involved a re-discovery (or creation) of a threefold connection: inner, with others and with 'nature.' These connections are, for them, the defining features of spirituality. The negative phase of the ritualistic quest (anorexia) involves a confrontation with the inevitability of death as a condition of the positive phase (recovery) in which people actively choose life." While fasting or even starving oneself was a common route to a certain power among medieval saints, such asceticism has less currency today. As such, Garrett concludes, recovery through self-transformation constitutes "the active and metaphorical 'rebellion' against forces of social control." Other clinicians have developed models for addressing spirituality in treating depression among older women.

Some female patients, and even more professionals it seems, find the AA concepts of a higher power and the encouragement for the alcoholic to admit powerlessness demeaning to women. Some feminist theorists trot out arguments against the Twelve-step approach, or almost any spiritually based method. Stephanie Brown, of the Addictions Institute in California, told me she feels these critics are seeing something that is not there. "They're big on politicizing the field. They bring a hierarchical structure that emphasizes power, gender, sex to AA. They're imposing an outlook that does not match the structure of change." This process of recovery through the Twelve-step philosophy is the same for men and women, Brown says, and is rooted in the basic experience of addiction and alcoholism. The drugs or alcohol take away the person's "structure of power." At the same time, Brown added, "All humans have a fundamental sense of powerlessness, of frailty. This is not the same as the politicized view of power, where someone is in power and someone is not." In treatment and recovery, both men and women realize the limits to their power over alcoholism, and turn for help in that area to a higher power, "something greater than the self." Usually, this is a nonhuman entity that each person defines for herself. "Actually, there is a great deal of autonomy," Brown says. As with all members of such groups, women can choose their own concept of a higher power.

If a woman sees her addiction as a failure of power—relational for most—she may then find a higher power that redresses this imbalance. Her spiritual source of power may enable her to repair these relationships, or it may help her to abandon destructive relationships, or it may help her see the same relationships differently and in such a way that they are no longer problems.

Spirituality in Recovery

The necessities of treatment suggest the basic elements of a spirituality that would enable women to abstain from drugs, change their lives, and be fulfilled. For Kearney, nurses who work with female addicts in a "woman-centered approach" should follow some broad principles: mutuality, respecting the woman's perspective as valid, and not exerting authority; supportiveness, especially of an addict's readiness to change; avoidance of confrontation, while presenting consequences of drug use in "a warmly concerned, factual manner;" and harm reduction, or help for addicts who are not ready or able to stop.[22]

The thicket becomes thorny because much of contemporary spirituality, in and out of recovery circles, originated in mainstream religions. That these modern notions also rebelled against tradition does not alter the chronology or causality. Consider the case of lesbians. "Much of the homophobia we experience in this society has some connection to Judeo-Christian roots, or is ascribed to religious views," wrote Eleanor Nealy of the Lesbian and Gay Community Services Center of New York City.[23] Treatment programs fail to address "the problems lesbians may have in working 12-step programs, the fact that many lesbians feel alienated from traditional religion and their difficulty finding a definition of a 'higher power' that works for them." For Nealy, reconciling sexuality and spirituality is critical in the recovery of an addicted lesbian. It is worth noting that thousands of gays and lesbians have found Twelve-Step spirituality flexible enough to overcome problems with organized religion.

The Twelve Steps and support groups are good, but not enough, said Florence Wright, whose program relies heavily on "women-focused groups" and the interaction between female counselors and female addicts. A network of mutual-aid groups for women stressing positive thinking and behavior modification has spread widely since its founding in 1975. Women for Sobriety was begun by Dr. Jean Kirkpatrick, who found that the primary admission in Alcoholics Anonymous "that we were powerless over alcohol" encouraged dangerous dependencies among women. Kirkpatrick reasoned that the Twelve-Step strategy of "ego deflation in depth," articulated by AA's founders in its text, may undermine a woman's need to overcome feelings of helplessness, powerlessness, and dependence. WFS teaches that members are the authors of their own scripts, whereas AA recommends members decide to "turn our will and our lives over to the care of God as we understand him."

Lee A. Kaskutas, of the Alcohol Research Group, in Berkeley, has written extensively on Women for Sobriety. With a sympathetic imagination, Kaskutas has looked deeply into the internal mechanics of change in order to determine its cause. Kaskutas sees a "cognitive behavior modification approach is evident in WFS meetings, aimed at changing one's thinking from negative to positive affect."[24] For members, thoughts shape and create behavior, negative emotions destroy serenity and threaten sobriety, and a person controls how much she allows negative thoughts or problems to bother her. AA members make a similar suggestion when they allow that while the alcoholic may occasionally think of a drink, he or she can decide not to dwell on the thought. In another similarity, WFS members seek abstinence, self-esteem, and spiritual and emotional growth. The difference arises in the source of help. For the Twelve-Step adherent, help ultimately comes from a higher power, often through very human agents such as sponsors and other members of the group or fellowship. For WFS members, changing how one thinks, feels, and acts—with the temporary or long-term help of other WFS members—makes the difference.

In a later analysis of the group's 1991 membership survey, Kaskutas found that a fifth said their life had gotten out of control, and these were the ones to achieve sobriety most quickly.[25] This bears out common sense, to a degree: those who need help the most are most likely to benefit from it. Kaskutas also found that many members saw little conflict with the tenets of AA, and used both groups according to their individual needs, with about a third also attending AA. Among them, 54 percent attended WFS for support and nurturance, 26 percent for a safe environment, 42 percent for sharing about women's issues, 39 percent because of its positive emphasis and focus on self-esteem. Of those who also attend AA, 28 percent do so primarily as insurance against relapse; 25 percent for its wide availability; 31 percent for sharing; and 27 percent for support. Of members who do not attend AA, 20 percent said they never fit in, 18 percent found it too negative and 15 percent felt AA was geared to men's needs.[26]

Finally, Kaskutas's analysis of the national WFS membership revealed that women who belong to both WFS and AA tend to endorse both AA's teaching that sobriety comes from God and WFS's view that sobriety is something an individual can control through her state of mind. Contrary to impressions that WFS is relentlessly secular, the eighth principle in its New Life Acceptance Program states, "The fundamental object of life is emotional and spiritual growth."

For women, writes Kearny, spirituality "may take the form of participation in traditional religious rituals, exploration of woman-focused religious movements, or development of personal spiritual rituals and practices." For many the combination typifies modern spirituality, where humility in seeking a deity coincides with an emphasis on personal responsibility.

Crafting a Spirituality for Recovery: Liberty Manor

Traveling west across upstate New York, somewhere past Syracuse the terrain flattens out and ushers one into the great American heartland. Rochester is its first outpost. The atmosphere bespeaks a self-sufficient city removed from the orbit of larger metropolises. Its plaques and parks and historic sites paint a tableau of the city in the mid-1800s crisscrossed by abolitionists, philanthropists, and factory workers all seeking their identities and freedoms. To wander about town, its parks and downtown, to talk with residents and authorities is to be impressed by a strong identity, civic pride, and the can-do habits free of Old World hang-ups. In the fall and winter of 1997, I spent time there at Liberty Manor, a residential treatment program with room for 15 women and five preschool children.

On one visit, I walk from the railroad station up Joseph Avenue. Downtown falls behind as I pass into a busy, slightly worn area of housing projects, wooden houses encased in clapboard or asphalt shingles, and small shops. Most of all, there are houses of worship, one after the other. First Antioch Baptist Church, new and angular, of brick; one block up Mount Vernon Baptist, an old red brick church with a timbered entrance; farther on I pass the Full Gospel Tabernacle Church, the Peace Missionary Baptist Church, the Warwick Full Gospel Church, the Deliverance Assembly Church. Several of the churches are in storefronts. Two actually share one tiny space, Holy Redeemer and Full Deliverance Church.

The boulevard also provides a short lesson in the misdeeds of urban renewal. In the projects, the buildings are set far apart, and one complex even has a gated entrance. Farther up, there is a denser settlement of houses, two and three story apartment buildings, stores with indeterminate business hours, bait shops, record shops, and several old German and Jewish meat markets. These features are eclipsed by the houses of worship, of which there are 15 along one mile of Joseph Avenue. The boulevard would provide a good testing ground for John DiIulio, the Princeton criminologist who has complained that there is more research on the impact of used-car lots and liquor stores than of churches in our inner cities. The people of this area are seeking salvation in this life. But in the realm where religious beliefs and architecture come together, a free-market principle often prevails. Buildings that outlive their usefulness for one belief system are converted to use by adherents of another, perhaps more effective, set of principles.

At the end of my walk, I come upon Our Lady of Perpetual Help, a massive building in simplified Italianate design made of rough-faced, tan bricks. The nuns who once staffed the parish and its school are gone. Their expansive convent now serves women who are seeking to regain their selves by following a new set of principles. Most stay for six months, some come with children and others arrive pregnant and deliver while in treatment. At first, they attend full days of counseling and other sessions. Later, job training and school start. Liberty Manor is one part of Restart Substance Abuse Services, an agency of Catholic Charities in the Rochester Diocese. In 1997, Restart had a staff of 100 and a $4.25 million budget.

The director, Carl Hatch, says that clients are usually "very dysfunctional, poor, and with multiple previous treatments." Hatch sees some benefit to his clientele, so many of whom are sent by the courts. "Some literature suggests you can have more success with mandated clients than nonmandated. The best indicator of success is retention and with mandated clients you can retain them longer."[27]

Though clients are encouraged to attend AA or NA meetings in the community, Restart does not follow, strictly speaking, a Twelve-Step model. Hatch does, however, believe that Restart's clients should be exposed to spirituality. I ask him how one can mandate an addict develop spiritually, or, for that matter, get better? "You can't," Hatch admits quickly. "If they are led to water, you can't make them drink, but if you're any good, you can make them thirsty more often than not."

On the first of three visits to Liberty Manor one autumn, I chat with a group of eight women. Most used cocaine, usually crack, and drank.[28] Most have children. Most are poor and have been arrested more than once. Yet the atmosphere of female support, maternal wisdom, and infant disorder resembles that of any suburban mothers' playgroup. Some balance their infants on their laps or help with another's child. Others wander in and out, lending a casual air to a discussion of topics violent and serene, of sin and redemption, of addiction and recovery.

Almost immediately, LaQuinta announces, "I'm learning to deal with a lot of attitudes at one time. If I see someone with a bad attitude, I don't deal with them." Kathy, the only white woman in the room, sounds the tones that underlie the addiction of so many female addicts. Her past as a prostitute hangs over her. "For me having a baby in early recovery, it's hard to find a balance. There's a lot of guilt and there is a lot of shame about how [the baby] got here. Fortunately I was mandated here by the courts. This is my fifth rehabilitation. I'm learning to live life on life's terms." I ask what precipitated this rebound into recovery.

"I had an emotional relapse with all the guilt," Kathy replies. "I was feeling incompetent. I just got to the point where my head just couldn't take it anymore. It was a higher power working in my life. Left to my own devices I would have kept drugging and died." But she sees addiction as evidence of a larger problem. "Drinking and drugging were just symptoms of the disease that we just couldn't cope with life. The difference today is I have a willingness and desire to stay clean, which is what counts."

Shirley, 39, is on her third treatment, the one she says counts. "My self-esteem is higher than ever. I grew up in an abusive family and was in an abusive relationship." She left both to deal with her addiction, she says, and is learning to control her anger and share the secrets she says can keep her sick.

"It's about talking to people in productive ways, not the street ways," Kathy interjects. Some of the women had sober periods before thanks to religious involvement.

"I went to Teen Challenge at Antioch Bible Church, that was my church, and I was clean for a year," Wanda says. "We read out of the Bible and talked about that a lot, that God forgives us for our sins and that just because we do drugs we're not bad people. I needed to get a relationship with God. He's the only one who'll really help me." After being treated twice in a private clinic, Wanda says she feared living in her old neighborhood. "I needed more help so I came here when I was seven months pregnant in July and the baby was born in August. I feel stronger. I have a newborn and I feel stronger."

Karen, 37, had a second problem, which first accelerated her drug use and then helped her to seek help. "I have HIV, and when I learned it it? hit home real hard. To deal with that, I started using more and more." This recovery is for her, she says. Previously, "Anytime I went to treatment, I went for everybody else."

Hearing these phrases and explanations repeated in such a rote but emphatic way raises troubling questions. How original are their thoughts? How much was grafted onto them by the rehab community, whose assumptions about the nature and path of addiction, treatment recovery have accreted into a crystalline form? Their feelings appear genuine. What is likely is that they often express these in the formulas handed them, because they lack the vocabulary or the experience in discussing their inmost thoughts and reactions.

"I feel that time is running out," Karen says, with a broad giggle that dissolves her dignified, even haughty composure, "and I want to do some successful things." She thanks God, and her medication, for being healthy. "I believe in God, haven't been to church in a while. I always ask the Lord and he gives me, not what I wanted, but he always gives what I needed." In a blend of Christianity and free-form spirituality, she reads the Bible and attends AA or NA groups, and works on the Twelve Steps. "I know that without Christ in my life I can't do it by myself."

At 26, Jurina has eight children and is pregnant with another, happily patting her rounded belly. She has a soft, almost giggly exterior over a character still hardening, like a cast sculpture of drying concrete, and acquiring dimension and resilience. She's experienced violence, abuse, alcoholic drinking, and years of injecting free-base cocaine.

"I had seven other kids and I didn't use while I was pregnant with the others. This one I did use and I was scared of Downs syndrome. I came in June and I just stayed." Jurina praised a discussion group, which meets at the house for helping her face some truths. "A group meets three times a week there's a lot of confronting. I learned about controlling my anger." (Interestingly, this contradicts the practice of many women's programs that avoid combative techniques for fear of alienating clients.) Several of the women mention anger as the most difficult emotion. In an interview a month later, Jurina cites her progress. "I'm learning about not going there, to the flying off. I am learning to stop, think about it and don't yell."

Rebecca is one of the senior residents and is on the verge of graduating. While here, she gave birth to a daughter, Arianna, "which means 'holy one.' " Rebecca grew up in a semi-rural, white working class area outside Rochester and was raised after age 11 by her grandmother. When this kindly woman died, Rebecca began taking drugs in a fierce rebellion against heaven and earth. "I was angry at my grandmother for dying, I was angry at God for letting her die. It was a way for me to get back at her, it was a way to get back at God. I wanted to hurt myself, because I wanted to die." Against her basic shyness and modesty, she worked as a stripper and, later, as a prostitute to support her needs and drug use. At the end, she had sold her 1988 Firebird for $75 and was left pushing her belongings down the street in a shopping cart. Fearful of using crack again, she turned herself in for a previous warrant and was sent by the Rochester drug court to Liberty.

"I had a five-and-half-year-old son, and I was five months pregnant when I came here." She appreciates the six months she has had at Liberty compared to the shorter treatment she had before. "At 30 days, your head is just starting to clear." She attends AA meetings, preferring these to local NA sessions, which she called "chaotic" and tainted by the presence of drug dealers.

Karen has been trained to work, to parent, and to manage her own life. All those matter, but she speaks of a deeper aid to her sobriety. "I pray. I don't read the Bible, it's contradictory and hard to understand." Since her family left the choice of a religion up to her, Karen is now looking for one "I feel comfortable with. I need a religion to fit in." She looks up and tells us, "I feel saved by God for something."

On a later visit, in December, I talk with Eloise Copper, who has run Liberty Manor since it opened in the late 1980s. During that time, she has overseen treatment for maybe 500 women. She estimates that about 45 percent finish a six-month stint in the house and that, of those, 50 percent remain clean for at least one year afterward.

I ask about starting a program for addicted mothers with troubled pasts. Her answer reveals a fundamentally spiritual outlook. "At first a lot of the staff couldn't deal with it. They would read [the women's] records and think they're going to be a violent."

I ask what she thought.

"I saw a human being."

The goals remain practical—saving lives. "The advantage of it is that the women have healthy children if we can get them early. A lot of times a woman can go in treatment but they don't have anything for the kids." And Restart concentrates on preparing the women for real life afterwards. Those without high-school degrees study toward their GED or graduate equivalency degree. They attend career counseling, have their skills and interests assessed and are trained for various jobs. Many start working part-time. The Journey Cafe at the main Restart office in Rochester employs many and is also a place where residents can, in a less regulated setting, dine with their families or meet their attorney or social worker.

Liberty Manor does not spend a lot of time guiding residents through the AA or NA principles, which many programs do in what is called Twelve-Step facilitation. There is one staffer who introduces residents to the first three steps, which encourage the addict to admit the problem and to hope and trust in "a power greater than ourselves."

Carl Hatch notes that, by contrast, many residential programs operate on the Minnesota model under which patients are pushed to complete, formally, the first five steps of the AA/NA program. Steps four and five involve compiling "a searching and fearless moral inventory" and admitting that to "ourselves, to God and to another human being."

The patients who object are usually the religious, rather than the secular, men and women. "We run into resistance from clients over the religious element [of the Twelve Steps]," says Hatch. "Rather than the agnostics and atheists, it is generally African-American and Hispanic Evangelicals who don't buy the concept." These are encouraged to continue with their own religious observance.

At Liberty Manor, there are morning meditation sessions, run by the residents. But the entire Restart program avoids excessive reference to spirituality or religion. "At Catholic Charities, we put less of an emphasis on the spiritual than the secular because we're so defensive about the church-state issue," Hatch told me on another occasion. Copper reiterates the point.

"Because of the state, we don't mention religion to [the women]. They have to mention it first, and there are a few churches that will pick them up." But Copper insists addicts need a beneficial and transcendent source of help. Most have lived at the mercy of a "lower power" such as drugs or an abusive spouse.

"For me, those that are going to make it have that spiritual element, a higher power. Those that make it have that higher power, because a lot of them have a mother, father, a boyfriend who's been their higher power before they got here." Without an alternative, says Copper, many women will simply revert to the destructive power. The distinction between this free-form spirituality—find a god, any god, so long as it works for you— and religion was made clear during a housecleaning that took place during the conversion from nunnery to rehab center.

"The convent was filled with crucifixes and statues when we started, and the state made us take them all out," recalls Anna Nick, a volunteer and long-time parishioner at the church next door whose authority and vigor belied her many years. Though Restart encourages residents to attend religious services of their choosing, Copper fears that religion can sidetrack a woman during the first weeks of recovery. "Many of the women see other women who go to church and decide they want to do that. Evangelical Christians think they can bring these women to church and heal them there, like it was some magic stuff," Copper says, shaking her head.

Then there are those who cannot fathom a source of unconditional love and trip over traditional notions, Copper says. "They think they can't, they think that God will not accept them where they're at—drinking, smoking, doing drugs—and they think they have to do this whole turnaround before God will accept them." For mothers, being a poor caretaker of babies that may have health problems due to their addiction easily compounds feelings of insufficiency.

Even when there are a variety of venues, finding spiritual solace can be hard. "Some of the women came back from a Narcotics Anonymous meeting that they said was too spiritually oriented," Copper recalls. "Sometimes they go to church and cry and people accept them so that they feel better, but it's not about that, it's about developing a closer relationship with God."

For Hatch, there are many routes to an effective spiritual life. A tall, slender middle-aged man with a comfortingly hoarse voice, he steers ably between the rocks of these turbulent waters where faith can save lives, but also cause a ruckus. He was raised Quaker but is not personally religious. An employee of Catholic Charities since he graduated from college, he understands the importance of delivering publicly funded social services without a denominational flavor.

"We encourage people to get involved in self-help groups. We don't care if it's AA, NA, or what. But we do know that successful recovery has to have a spiritual component. The research and anecdotal evidence shows that people who establish or reestablish their spiritual connection have a much better chance at staying sober."

At Liberty Manor and a men's residence I visited, Freedom House, senior AA and NA members often picked up patients for meetings. Hatch recruited liaisons from local churches who will help interested residents attend services, Bible study, men's or women's groups, and other events. The brand of help "is not an issue for us," says Hatch. "They need to have a structure and a support system."

Jurina grew up among alcoholism and abuse but only started drugs when she was 23. "My baby's father said, 'Try it,' and I liked it. Later, I started losing things slowly, then they all left—kids, the house, furniture, my clothing."

Jurina seems surprised when I ask if she ever tried to stop before. "No, I had no reason to stop." She talks of learning the rules of life, for the first time. "I'm learning to stay clean and sober, to stay out of the old neighborhood. I'm learning to speak, to let my feelings out and to cry. Never really got into the Twelve Steps yet. I pray, it makes a big difference. My children are coming back home. They're with my mother right now."

Jurina was scheduled to leave Liberty Manor a few months later for a transitional residence. Her dreams are to work and move away from her old neighborhood, perhaps in the countryside, "somewhere way out there."

I wonder about her chances, with the kids and jobs and sobriety, that she'll survive as she envisions. It is the problem mentioned by everyone who works with poorer clients, namely what will happen to them when they return to their old neighborhoods. Perhaps they see the wrong problem. Maybe the old haunts are not the problem. After all, there are plenty of churches and support groups in the cities. Or maybe the challenge is to form recovering communities, as suggested for decades by Father Peter Young, an Albany, New York based pioneer in providing housing and jobs along with treatment. After all, we can't move every recovered addict—and ex-con and ex-juvenile offender and every other person who needs a new start—to a new home in a different community. Young envisions recovery cadres transforming existing neighborhoods.

For Jurina, something spiritual has clicked. Basically, she sees her life from a different perspective. "Because God was with me, because I could have been dead, with some of the things that happened to me. When I was using, I'd believed in Him but now, I thank him for the things I've got such as a healthy baby and because he put it in my mind to come here. I wasn't mandated."

"I pray with my eyes closed, sometimes on my knees. I pray that my family remains strong and healthy and I thank Him for the things He has done for me. If I forget to pray last night I make sure do it tonight. I am still the same person—I just pray."

Adapting Treatment, Checking Research

As noted, women often enter treatment in worse condition than their male counterparts. Two reasons come to mind, though there are more. First, some become addicted more quickly and end up losing jobs, family, health, mind, and spirit sooner. Second, the barriers to treatment keep them beyond help for a longer period of time. A mother may compound the situation by concentrating on her family and ignoring her own condition. A good treatment program for women would, to an even greater degree than one for men, answer such basic needs as food, housing, transportation, legal help, parental training, childcare, and assertiveness training. Traditional treatment programs provide few, if any, of these services. Females in recovery often need a more long-term, consistent relationship with a treatment provider and, moreover, help in rejoining the community afterwards.

There are many aspects to specialized treatment for women. The absence of men is the most significant. While some professionals propose this environment for most or all female addicts, it does matter especially "for those who have suffered sexual molestation or trauma in direct relationship to men," says Brown. "It provides a greater feeling of safety, physical and emotional, which is part of dealing with past trauma, especially as related to men."

This single-sex atmosphere has an additional benefit: women often come to treatment earlier in their drinking or drug-abusing careers because they are more comfortable seeking refuge with other women. The Swedish team, Dahlgren and Willander, found greater success two years after for women treated in single-sex units compared to those in mixed programs. The most important reason, they concluded, was that specialized programs tended to attract women sooner in their drinking careers.[29] Throughout the treatment field, abstinence cannot be the only question. Other improvements—or failures—take place, in the addict's family, work, criminal activity. "If we ask whether these women are forever free of drugs, employed, and useful citizens, then we wouldn't have a great success rate," Loretta Finnegan of the federal Center for Substance Abuse Treatment told the Brown University *Digest of Addiction Theory and Application*. "But, if we look at taking a woman from the streets of any city from nearly death's door and making her healthy during a pregnancy so she carries to term, has a healthy child, [continues taking] a recovery drug and receiving services and becomes a functional human being who may now and then slip back . . . then many programs are very successful."[30]

Other studies have shown that treatment pays off for the women and the children, most dramatically in drastically reduced need for neonatal intensive care.[31] Specialized training—in vocational, social, and other skills—for pregnant and mother teenagers, when added to comprehensive drug addiction treatment, leads to less depression, better relations with peers, more employment, and less drug abuse, two federally sponsored projects reported in 1994.[32]

Current studies do not seem to show a significant difference in rates of recovery or relapse between the sexes. But while males and females share some patterns in treatment and recovery, women often drink or relapse for different reasons or under different conditions. These characteristics should inform the spirituality many construct to help their recovery. In a study of 77 men and 65 women alcoholics during and after treatment, a team led by Gerard J. Connors of the Research Institute on Addictions in Buffalo found that the average age and education were close in the two groups: about 34 years old and college graduates, respectively. In both groups, nearly the same proportion, about 90 percent, had previously attended AA or other Twelve-Step groups. The men, on average, had more years of alcohol problems, 12.3 compared to 9.8. (This seems to belie the contention of several program administrators who reported that women tended to come to treatment later, and with more problems, than did men. However, each addict's story differs in length and severity and the programs that reported this pattern tended to deal with less-educated and poorer clients who were, generally, worse off.) More women did, however, report mental health problems, notably major depression—25 percent compared to 8 percent of men—and post-traumatic stress disorder—28 percent compared to 10 percent.[33]

Though most treatment may be designed more for men rather than women, several studies "have provided no evidence of sex differences in treatment outcomes," a researchers at the Addiction Research Foundation of Ontario in Toronto found. What they did find, however, was that more women (48 percent) than men (32 percent) drank again due to negative emotions. For men, the more common cause of relapse was being with other drinkers.[34] This suggests that the spirituality women develop as an aid to recovery will need a greater emotional content.

Women and men did differ in how and why they relapsed. A Brown University team interviewed 300 subjects from six different treatment centers and found that the women reported drinking less, and less often, than men, though they did drink to intoxication more often than men did.[35] Men relapsed alone more often than did women. Men report relapsing frequently while with male friends; women tend to relapse alongside their romantic partners. As have other researchers, the Brown team found men reported more positive moods during relapse than did women, who report more depression overall.

Women often relapse for different reasons than men. Connors and his team found that male alcoholics who drank most often cited a desire to drink and feeling good as the reasons. Women, on the other hand, blamed a desire to drink, feeling down, pressure from a spouse or partner, and dropping their guard.[36] Many women say that it was their boyfriend or other man who first handed them a crack pipe, or bottle, or other drug. Further, once they come out of treatment, if their partner is still using drugs, abstinence is that much harder. Interviews with hundreds of addicts impress me that, generally, wives or girlfriends support the sober lifestyles of their mates more often than do men in the same situation. When we consider how women stay sober, some differences have emerged. Connors' team found that such factors as treatment, self-help groups, increased leisure activities, talking with people outside the family, and religion had a slightly greater influence on abstinence among women than among men. Other strategies—recalling the pain of drinking and the benefits of sobriety, expressing feelings, talking with family—played a nearly equal role for men and women.

Emerging Issues and a New Spiritual Synthesis

Whether by design or accident, the treatment and recovery of female addicts has nurtured a distinctive women's spirituality. Most of all, it is practical and effective. Women have crafted this spirituality to save their lives. Like drowning ship passengers who grab onto only those items that float, these addicts latch onto spiritual beliefs and practices that work.

Caution is necessary. The women's alcoholism movement had lobbied for tailored treatment since the mid-1970s. But only when the public grew alarmed that thousands of infants were being born addicted to crack cocaine did the funds really start to flow. Money set aside for services to mothers and pregnant women grew by 500 percent between 1988 and 1990, from $24.4 million to $119.3 million, while Congress released millions more through Medicaid and other programs.[37] Auditors for the General Accounting Office regarded these developments wistfully: "Tragically, it is only when a woman's ability to bear healthy children is threatened by the consequences of alcoholism and drug addiction that we, as a society, are willing to take notice. We take notice not because we care about women, but, because we allege to care about children."[38]

Many or most of the addicts who benefit from this largesse will, no doubt, be grateful and not bite the hand that feeds their children while addressing their own addiction. But subliminally, the paradigm could reinforce traditional ideals of a woman's truest role and value: mother, caretaker, nurturer. It reinforces the message that a woman counts only in her relationships; that a mother matters because she is a mother and has children, not because of her essential humanity and individuality. It is a short step from these images to traditional forms of sexism.

Women's treatment could counter such trends and advance equality in two ways. Physically, an agency that treats female addicts is, de facto, a kind of ideological power base, a gathering place for determined women—both helpers and the helped—and a wellspring for further action. The Women's Treatment Center in Chicago is housed in a solid brick building that was built as a hospital, founded in 1928 by female physician Mary Thompson, who faced discrimination elsewhere and who wanted to offer women and children special attention. With its female professionals striding in and out and women chatting quietly as they wait for appointments, the center stands as a powerful advertisement in its inner-city neighborhood of the strength and potential of low-income, minority women. Florence Wright, the clinical director, estimated that 97 percent of the 1,000 women treated there in 1997 are single mothers who were never married. These women represent a cadre who can help change their communities. More elementally, women who have discovered a spiritual solution to their addiction are well armed to deal with many other challenges. This purpose and power could stimulate political action. In Illinois, Nick Gantes spoke as if therapy for abused women runs in a straight line toward social equality. "Many women need counseling tied to having been abused mentally, physically, and sexually. They need empowerment and therapy tied to raising their consciousness and independence and their ability to live on their own. All women's substance abuse treatment should be adapted to the dynamics of treating women, which includes cultural sensitivity and the political perspective."

Being treated by and among women, apparently, grants the female addict the understanding and acceptance of self that is tied to spirituality, which in turn underlies the initiative of women in recovery. "Women's treatment is at the forefront of recognizing that spirituality is at the forefront of treatment," Gantes said. "They are more successful than other programs at treating women and helping them stay sober. Clients are more accepting of women counselors and administrators. They've shared, they've shared many more experiences."

For women who choose this route to recovery, spiritual development can lead to change in many realms—family, romance, work, education, community. As Laura Schmidt and Constance Weisner declare in an astute 1995 summary of the field's history, "it appears that the ideology of the women's alcoholism movement has been institutionalized in treatment programs of the women-only sector. These programs, for instance, tend to combine intensive alcoholism treatment with vocational, childcare, legal, and housing assistance that can support women in achieving independence and in making career life transitions."[39]

Whether the elements of women's treatment and recovery amount to a philosophy is, as yet, unclear. But in its ground-level emergence and practical focus, it could infuse grit and fire into the theories of Rosemary Radford Ruether, Sally McFague, and other feminist theologians.

Ruether, in her book, *Gaia & God: An Ecofeminist Theology of Earth Healing*, characterizes Classical Western culture and the monotheistic religions, as having "justified and sacralized these relationships of domination" that are seen as the divinely ordained natural order. She advocates "a social reordering to bring about just and loving interrelationships between men and women."[40] Domination of women and the earth go hand in hand, with the tendency to link women with earth, matter, and nature while to men belong the realm of sky, intellect and "transcendent spirit," Ruether writes. Even the spirituality of recovery, at once so freeform and liberating, can come in male clothing of generations of men, most recently Carl Jung, the founders, and current members of AA, or most counselors in the treatment field. Some feminists advocate worship of *Gaia*, the earthly divinity more immanent than transcendent, a being personified. But wisely, Ruether questions the value of simply replacing a "male transcendent deity with an immanent female one," and says we need both of these "holy voices."

Sally McFague, in her seminal book, *Models of God: Theology for an Ecological Nuclear Age*, says that very image we have for the deity determines our relationship with it. "We live our lives according to our construction of the world; as Erich Heller said, 'Be careful how you interpret the world; it *is* like that.' "[41] Theology is, basically, the elaboration of key metaphors and models, she argues. Amid all the deconstruction of traditional theology, what has been missing is some construction. McFague proposes to fill the gap by remythologizing the relationship between God and the world. To the outmoded image of God as father she would add those of "mother, lover and friend."

We could use another perspective on God, considering the ill effects of one so long dominated by the male ethos. Many long-standing theologies or belief systems imagine Creation coming to an end in a vast conflagration, a nuclear Armageddon. As McFague points out, the alternative vision embraced from the other extreme—that God the father will take care of our problems—is equally destructive in its escapism in that it absolves us of responsibility to solve our problems. (A popular, modern version of this thinking was the bumper sticker that proclaimed that the solution to certain conflicts should be to "kill them all and let God sort out the guilty and the innocent.")If our beliefs point to a Creator who decides that the most fitting end for Creation is to destroy it, we should wonder about the fruits of any male-dominated religion.

For feminist critics, there is another worrisome legacy of the major monotheistic religions, what some call "dominionism." In Genesis, God instructs Adam and Eve, "Be fertile and multiply; fill the earth and subdue it. Have dominion over the first of the sea, the birds of the air, and all the living things." This directive, these critics argue, has encouraged humanity to exploit and pollute the earth and men in power to rationalize their exploitation of women. For McFague and others, the Judeo-Christian tradition's triumphal, imperialist imagery opposes life. (Some Muslim and outside critics may also blame Islam's imagery for excesses of patriarchy or violence.) "What the father-God gives is redemption from sins; what the mother-God gives is life itself."[42]

This imagery should reassure those who worry that the medical models of addiction absolves personal responsibility. McFague echoes others in her claim that our traditional image of God, as father, shifts responsibility for the earth and life from us to the divine. Inside Twelve-Step groups, members continually emphasize their responsibility for past deeds and—with a higher power's help—their current lives. Some men may find it ironic that the women they once considered the "weaker sex" are formulating a more balanced view of God that will empower humanity with a greater role in creation. As McFague writes, "It is not the power of control through either domination or benevolence but the power of response and responsibility—the power of love in its various forms (agape, eros, and philia) that operates by persuasion, care, attention, passion, and mutuality."[43]

If a combination of male and female is needed, then the higher power as understood by so many women offers one vision of a source of help that is both outside and within, that is greater than a woman's addiction and is also eternally, and often internally, accessible to that woman. The Twelve-Step approach encourages alcoholics to pick their own image of a higher power, one that works. The voice of *Gaia*, long silenced by the thunderous masculine voice of power and law, Ruether writes, "today is finding her own voice again." This voice translates not into "laws and intellectual knowledge, but beckons us into communion."[44]

I have heard these very same sentiments expressed by dozens of women—middle-class, poor, in treatment or in support groups from AA to Women for Sobriety. These theologians could connect their theory with the spirituality crafted by many female addicts to save their lives. The academics perorate against patriarchal religion and society and detail all the modern depredations—militarism, pollution, sexism, agribusiness—and possible redemptions. But they rarely touch the topic of addiction in women, freighted with dimensions of oppression and abuse, and the theology many develop in recovery. When Ruether calls for "healing therapies and spiritualities of inner growth," I want to direct her to a morning meditation at Liberty Manor or a session of Women for Sobriety. "Making healing and inner growth available to us all means unhooking them from professional 'help,' which comes with credentials and high price tags," she writes, quite sensibly. Ruether suggests "base communities," or "local face-to-face groups with which one lives, works, and prays." A fine model for these already exists in the thousands of small groups of women who meet regularly to maintain their abstinence—from drugs, alcohol, and overeating—via spiritual development. That *metanoia,* or change of consciousness, "begins with us," as Ruether writes, has been the keystone of recovery for millions of women.[45]

Kathy, a mother of three whom I interviewed several times at Liberty House in Rochester, exemplifies this potent blend of recovery and spirituality in shaping a new life. Here was a 37-year-old woman who had grown up in an abusive family whose father walked out when she, the oldest of six, was eight. One brother died in an alcohol-related car crash and she herself drank and took drugs from her early teens. Later, Kathy prostituted herself. In a painful instance of female deferral, at her boyfriend's behest, she did not go to the hospital after someone split her head open with the butt of a sawed-off shotgun, for fear the authorities would call the police. She was in and out of treatment since 1987. Two programs kicked her out and by the end, she lost everything—and when these women say "everything," they mean it—and faced several felony charges. By the end, only a long-term stay could help. She entered Liberty House in June. By October, her relationship with a divinity was redirecting her life.

"Before I had an angry God, now I have a forgiving God. I'm not sure about a loving God. But I came to my knees to such emotional pain because I couldn't lash out."

"I have a biracial daughter. I love her, and I always will, but she is a reminder of what I was," she says, referring to her days as a prostitute. "Child Protective took her, but now I have full custody of her. And that changed my ideas about God." Two months later, her infant, Moriah, is six months old and healthy. Kathy has full custody and is five months sober. "I am feeling overwhelmed and grateful." She was about to move to an apartment at the YWCA and plans to be a journalist. Her determination and self-awareness suggest it is possible.

"I changed a lot. I have greater hopes and my hopes are broader. I feel like I belong, that I fit in, that I fit in for the first time. I feel proud, and reliable." Every morning, Kathy attends the morning meditation session. "Each of us says 'I am a worthwhile woman,' or some other affirmation. We do a reading from the meditation book, 'Day By Day,' and give a positive statement about ourselves."

"I am still struggling with a relationship with God." Kathy pauses, as if to wonder at this new person she has become, perhaps the person she buried in years of stripping, prostitution, and drugs. "It's hard understanding all I've been through. I wonder why I'm an addict. But I've had one gift after another if I look at life in its simplest form. My behavior, my acceptance level, my patience, and tolerance are all better. When things are not working out, I know it's for a reason and God wants me to learn."

CHAPTER IV

Native American Treatment
and Indian Spirituality

An Ancient Answer to a Current Problem

Leland Leonard, a Navajo, cheerfully describes himself as an ex-Da Agne'ï, using his people's all-purpose term for drinker. Navajo, which became a written language only in recent decades, makes no distinction among people who drink alcohol based on the degree or regularity, he says. As an alcoholic with many role models, Leonard knew no other kind.

"Growing up, I saw the drinking style: 'Hurry up and drink as much as possible before the policeman arrived.' "[1] Much of the alcoholism he attributes to two causes: the "prohibition effect," which occurred on many reservations thanks to historical bans on alcohol sales and involves making the prohibited substance attractive to people who may not have otherwise been drawn to it; and centuries of living under the thumb of one or another conqueror.

"You grew up watching your father or your uncle go behind the building and drink, and you wonder about that. It's a learned behavior," he adds, then catches himself when his clinical side catches up with the personal. "Yes, it's a disorder, but alcoholism is also a behavior." Conditions encouraged the activity, says Leonard: "Because it was forbidden, that increased the drinking." Leonard has been sober for 18 years and directs the Phoenix (Arizona) Indian Center, which provides social and cultural services, and is married to a physician.

"In the military, I developed a drinking problem. Then I came back here to the reservation and I was pretty unhappy. Life is slow. I had assimilated to the dominant culture. I knew I had to sober up even when I was drinking, I knew that all along.

"One day I was hitching from Cheyenne to Gallup. And my parents picked me up in their pickup truck. They told me about all the things they had done for me and how they had tried to help me. Then my mother told me I was not welcome at home until I did something to help myself. And then they dropped me off. I went into an alley and drank some wine that I bought, and I wept."

Leonard survived several more years drinking, working, and even attending school across the Southwest from Phoenix to Los Angeles. "When I was close to my bottom I quit school and went back home and I told them I was ready."

"They had a ceremony for me in the Native American church. It was an all-night ceremony to get me back in line with Mother Earth." Leonard declines to describe specifics of the ceremony other than to say that it was repetitive and involved introducing him to his ancestors in the four clans to which he claims membership through his paternal and maternal grandparents. His business card notes his two immediate clans.

Within a few weeks, Leonard checked into a residential rehabilitation treatment program and spent 30 days learning the nuts and bolts of life without alcohol. The pivot in his life remains that all-night healing ceremony back on his reservation, which drew upon his people's ancient spirituality and culture.

The Indian Health Service reported in 1997 that despite improvements, the age-adjusted alcoholism death rate for Indians was 440 percent higher than that for the general U.S. population.[2] In 1986 to 1988, about 17 percent of Indian deaths were alcohol-related, compared to 4.7 percent for the rest of the population, according to an analysis by Philip A. May, professor of sociology and psychiatry at the University of New Mexico. After analyzing those same facts, May criticized the assumption—accepted as gospel among outsiders and many Indians—that Native Americans suffer dramatically higher rates of alcoholism. He listed various reasons for increased Indian deaths from drinking, including: a higher demographic proportion of young people, who tend to drink more and take more risks in all ethnic and racial groups; the isolation of many Indian communities leading to increased time driving, often at higher speeds; the greater distance from medical attention when there are accidents; poverty, which typically worsens drinking and magnifies its effects; the prohibition effect on the many dry reservations; and dangerous cultural attitudes and habits, such as not using seat belts. Nevertheless, May said, when alcohol abuse is considered together with alcoholism, these amount to the leading cause of mortality among Indians.[3] Though drug abuse research is less complete, counselors and tribal leaders say cocaine and inhalants are used widely, particularly by youths.

Using Indian rituals and beliefs to better treat alcoholics and addicts is simply a matter of adapting to the size and preferences of a different group of people the methods that have worked over decades for millions of whites, blacks, Hispanics, and other people around the globe. The central formula remains the same.

"Alcoholism has a standard end, and it's death," said Paul Rock Krech, an Ojibwe Indian who counsels men at a program in Phoenix. "Alcoholism has a standard treatment and it works for everyone: one, don't drink; two, get support; three, *change*; four, maintenance." He leans back against the bookcase that towers over his chair and smiles. "Everything in Indian country comes in four."[4]

Mainstream treatment failed many Native Americans, according to counselors and patients around the country. Phoenix, for instance, had many programs based on the typical combination of medical care, Twelve-Step facilitation, group therapy, and education. "We knew something was missing," says Diane Yazzie, the long-time director of the Indian Rehabilitation Center. "If Indians are sitting in a talking circle, they will probably share something personal. Put them in a Hazelden-model medical program in a hospital, and they won't. I would get calls from the people at Good Samaritan hospital. They said, 'We don't know what to do with Native Americans. We can't get them to share, we can't get them to talk.' " As anyone close to a former addict knows, talk is at the heart of recovery.

In 1995, the federal Indian Health Service established a traditional medicine advocacy initiative to enlist traditional healers and others. At meetings around the county, groups recommended that healing practices should first be integrated into alcohol and substance abuse prevention and treatment, as well as other behavioral problems, before being included as part of other treatment protocols.

"Alcohol and drug abuse is our number one social and health problem, and it's been practically in our families for generations," explains Rita Holy Bull, a Dakota Indian.[5] She and her husband, Gary, a traditional healer and Lakota Indian, advised and helped organize the initiative. She says programs such as one near her home on the Sisseton Wahpeton Dakota Reservation have improved success with traditional Indian beliefs and rituals.

Indian spirituality, or each of its many forms indigenous to each tribe or band, represents a whole complex of beliefs, practices, and ceremonies that infuse society and culture with meaning and direction. This occurs on a daily basis, often with cyclical or seasonal rhythms.

Some features and benefits of Indian spirituality in treating Native American alcoholics were summarized by Wayne Mitchell and Ken Patch, university professors who also administrated Indian health programs. They first note that tribal religions "provided an organization and a code of behavior which contributed to an understanding of the meaning of life." These were tied to the natural world, and to a belief in the supernatural world. Goals include personal and communal balance and harmony. Tribal religions or spiritualities served as the basis for social codes and values, and served to explain matters otherwise unexplainable. Mitchell and Patch propose that involving Native patients in tribal religions will lead to stability and enlightenment, a sense of community and support; a sense of worth and identity; and cultural recovery.[6]

During a stint as a federal official, Leland Leonard worked with 80 tribes in the Southwest to craft treatment methods that will work for their members. Practices included talking circles, in which a spiritual leader guides participants through discussions on personal and traditional topics as they pass around an eagle feather or other sacred object; sweat lodges, of a similar nature to talking circles but within a dome-shaped hut filled with steam from hot rocks and water; the use of medicine wheels and other traditional objects as aids to meditation; and healing ceremonies.

At the end of the twentieth century, people routinely distinguish between religion in the institutional sense and its personal form, namely spirituality. American Indians, especially those involved in treatment and recovery, insist theirs is a form of spirituality rather than a religion, especially in the Western, European sense. They maintain that their beliefs were woven into daily life and reinforced by community and ceremony but in a nonsectarian manner. For example, among the Osage tribe of the upper Midwest and Canada, these habits or rituals govern even so mundane and personal a matter as sleeping positions. Traditionally, each Osage town was divided in two parts, representing the sky and earth, and residents on each side slept facing the other in a custom that reinforced their principles of duality and unity.[7] It is more accurate to describe these customs as spiritual and cultural rather than religious. In treatment and recovery circles, addicts and alcoholics often turn to their tribes' practices despite a previous lack of familiarity. At the same time, the use of spirituality in addiction treatment represents a pan-indian approach that combines various practices on a practical basis of "whatever works."

Profile: Mike—"Living in a Spirit World"

Now that he is off the street and the drugs and the race toward oblivion, Mike, an Ojibwe Indian, does something he never has before: pray. Each morning, with a group of other men at the American Indian Services halfway house, he burns some sage. Someone may read a passage from a book of meditations. The men sit in a talking circle and pass around an eagle feather. Holding the sacred object often enjoins a person to speak truthfully about painful topics and effectively prohibits interruptions. Others listen in silence. Mike also prays at night, before bed. Generally, mornings are for asking and evenings are for thanking.[8]

"I'm living in a spirit world. Even after I die, my spirit goes somewhere. And it had to come from somewhere." Like so many native Americans, Mike, 34, grew up in an urban area removed by geography and generations from his people's traditions. His newfound consciousness of a transcendent power—one that watches, loves, and also judges—bolsters his sober habits and hedges any self-destructive tendency to drink. "I feel I'm being judged for how I spend my life here." Spirituality, he says, "has to be worked on more. When I'm drinking, it's not there at all. That's why they call it 'chemical spirits.' It's delusional." Mike objects to being labeled. "I don't think I'm an 'alcoholic,' I just can't handle it." Alcohol, he says, is not indigenous to native American society and culture, but was foisted upon them by outside powers. "Alcohol and drugs was used as a weapon on a conquered people. It's just a label, 'alcoholic,' given us, like Chippewa." Many members of his tribe prefer their own title, Ojibwe, or even "Anishinaabe," their word for "The People."

Mike grew up in Hibbing, a mining town in northern Minnesota that was also the home of folk singer Bob Dylan. Only a handful of Indian families lived there and Mike learned little of his tribe or culture. He began drinking early and knew, by the age of ten, that it was trouble for him. Twenty-four years later, Mike gave it up in his best, fullest effort. That followed numerous dead ends and meaningless jobs, a failed marriage, and a drunk-driving conviction, eviction and, at the end, ten months living on the streets of Minneapolis. He spoke in March of 1998 while living in a halfway house operated by American Indian Services in a lively, gritty neighborhood just west of the glittering towers of downtown Minneapolis.

"I decided I had enough. It was realizing that at the age of 34, I hadn't accomplished anything." A previous treatment, outpatient and educational in nature, helped out at the time, Mike said, "But it was not spiritually based." He seeks the right term for a mismatch, but nods sheepishly when I ask if the problem was that it was "white based." The real problem, Mike says, "was my own delusions." A black-haired man of medium height and weight, he sits slightly hunched over as if still burdened by his past and a fear that his delusions could overpower him. Gratitude and sullenness compete for expression in his demeanor. There seems no danger that Mike will be carried away by ecstasy over a fresh start on life. Instead, he resembles a man trying on a new suit: ready to enjoy the garment but anxious to be sure it fits before opening his wallet.

Mike's solution is neither new nor prescribed from without. Spirituality, he says, is both an individual matter and something "that's always been important in my morals." Today's version, he says, offers a "new beginning."

How does it work?

"You just don't drink and you go to a lot of [AA] meetings," said Mike. I ask if the Twelve-Step approach to life and recovery is foreign to him, given its roots in an outside culture. "No, it's universal. Just because it was started by a couple of white guys. My life *was* unmanageable. That's universal." What makes the difference for him this time on what could easily be a recovery merry-go-round is, he said, is being among native American counselors and patients. "It's a safe place," said Mike, in a rare use of contemporary therapeutic terminology. And the use of traditional Indian healing and prayer rituals hooks him into his personal identity as well as his broader, historical community. Once a week for three months, he and five or six other residents have learned to drum and chant Ojibwe songs from a tribal elder.

"The drumming gives me a feeling of pride, of being Native American and not being a part of the genocide chain. It's your Manifest Destiny, that almost wiped us out. Even Indians do it to each other." The halfway house also holds sweat lodges periodically. An Indian with experience runs the sweat, which is held in a state forest about 60 miles from the city. It follows the usual routine of opening remarks followed by several rounds during which the men comment on various topics.

"It cleans out the impurities and it is a time for prayer," says Mike, "kind of like a church thing. You pray for the things you're dealing with in your life. It's a time to be thankful and share your point of view with the other guys. You talk with, not at, the other guys. It helps me feel good. Nothing will ever help you keep sober unless you want to. But you have to find a new way to vent yourself."

Mike says he treasures "the ideas, concepts, and the discipline," that he has learned and developed in a recovery aided by Native American traditions. "These are the things that I should have developed as a child."

History and Context

In Indian Country, the past lives on the in present and memories are long. Any outsider who visits a reservation or discusses current events with a Native American typically receives a small history lesson, and is struck by a recall of events hundreds of years old as if these happened yesterday. What the visitor soon learns, often with surprise, is that each federally recognized tribe is a sovereign, self-governing entity—albeit within the U.S. legal system and subordinate to Congress—and deals with the federal government in some ways as would another nation. Many tribes assumed their relationship as sovereign powers signing treaties with the federal government, though some of those treaties were of conquest and most ceded lands to the United States. The hybrid status of tribes was articulated by John Marshall and the Supreme Court in 1832 when they declared the Cherokee Nation and other tribes to be "domestic dependent nations," capable of self-government, subject to Congress but not to the states.[9]

Before the Europeans arrived, North American tribes ranged over wide areas and governed themselves. When Christopher Columbus sailed west in 1492, there were, by some estimates, as many as 10 million native Americans in what is now the United States. By the 1930s, that had dropped to about 300,000. In 1996, there were an estimated 2.3 million. Of the nearly 2 million American Indian and Alaska Natives counted by the 1990 U.S. Census, 54 percent lived on reservations and a significant portion lived nearby. About 500,000 people who listed themselves as Indians lived in cities and other areas, usually far from their native lands.

In terms of land, in 1790 they held about three-quarters of the United States's eventual landmass; today they have 2 percent of the total—56 million acres scattered among 314 reservations. The final, and in some ways most hurtful, reduction was in terms of recognition. During the 1950s, more than 100 tribes lost their federal recognition under the Eisenhower administration's policy of "termination" that exchanged cash for the status. Impoverished tribes were pressed to sell their patrimony and many fell apart.

Relations with the United States moved through long periods of losing land and culture. President Franklin D. Roosevelt restored some tribal control with the 1934 Indian Reorganization Act, though many tribes resented the imposition of a Western form of government on their nations. The current period of self-determination has its roots in the militancy of Iroquois and other Indian nations during the 1950s and the Red Power movement of the 1960s. Richard Nixon, a surprisingly good friend of Native Americans, ended the termination of tribal recognition and signed the 1975 Indian Education and Self-Determination Act. The Indian Health Care and Improvement Act of 1976 gave tribes more freedom in delivering services to their people, who are promised lifetime health benefits under various treaties.

Making Room for Indian Beliefs

The war on Indians was also one on the spirit. Early European missionaries sought to supplant spiritual practices, often with good intent but destructive consequences. More than one tribe lost its bearings as belief systems and rituals were washed away by Christian evangelists. More directly, civil administrators discouraged or banned indigenous religious observance. In the nineteenth Century, the federal courts prosecuted and punished native Americans who practiced their ancestral religions.[10] Sioux Ghost Dancers were a prime target: many were killed at Wounded Knee in 1890 and their leaders arrested two years later. As late as 1923, the commissioner of the Bureau of Indian Affairs spoke harshly on the subject in the following letter "To All Indians:"

"Not long ago I held a meeting of Superintendents, Missionaries, and Indians, at which the feeling of those present was strong against Indian dances, as they are usually given and against so much time as is often spent by the Indians in a display of their old customs at public gatherings . . . . From the views of this meeting and from other information I feel that something must be done to stop the neglect of stocks, crops, gardens, and home interests caused by these dances or by celebrations, powwows, and gatherings of any kind that take the time of the Indians for many days."[11]

The hostility toward religion as an impediment to economic production is not new. In Medieval Europe, civil authorities and landowners discouraged the expansion of religious feast days since these kept peasants away from their fieldwork and supposedly cut into farm production. The larger threat to earthly rulers was, and remains so today, that posed by religious belief as a tool of empowerment.

The repression of Indian religions was one of a piece with the larger history of Indians. And this history has also, many Indians and mental health professionals say, contributed to the problems that are now being addressed by changes in how services are rendered. "There is an attitude toward drinking that carries from generation to generation, and it's more than the prohibition effect of alcohol being banned," says Leonard. "It goes back to the Spanish conquest of our lands, and then having the Mexican government rule this area, and then the United States. It's about being under this foreign domain and power, and then being under another foreign power, and then being under another. It's about anger that's been built up for generations."[12]

This anger mixed with frustration and powerlessness to produce a toxic brew that has bedeviled many Indians, Leonard says. From native Americans and on reservations across the country, one can hear similar testimonies. Though he believes that alcoholics are genetically predisposed to the disease, Leonard accords a large role to cultural and social conditions in making a person drink destructively. Terry Tafoya, a therapist at University of Washington Medical School and a Native American storyteller, and his colleague Kevin M. Roeder also endorsed this theory, writing that Indians, as well as gays and lesbians, "have internalized a great deal of this hostility expressed against them, as reflected in a higher rate of alcohol and other substance abuse than most other ethnic and social groups."[13]

Other problems can be traced to a legacy of oppression and loss. Despite dramatic improvements in maternal death rates, infant mortality and other measures, Indians' health and well-being remain worse than the rest of the country thanks to poverty, isolation, and other problems. A

1995 Indian Health Service report found, among other problems, that aside from higher rates of alcohol-related deaths, 340 percent more Indians die of tuberculosis; 154 percent more Indians die of diabetes; 42 percent more die of suicide and 34 percent more die of homicide than the general population. And they are more dependent on publicly funded health care. In 1987, fewer than one in three had private health insurance, compared with 80 percent of whites, 52 percent of blacks, and 50 percent of Hispanics.[14]

Like other groups of people, the health of Indians is shaped by a web of circumstances, culture, and behavior. As in medicine generally, doctors, bureaucrats, and tribal authorities try to address these less material factors as well. "As modern medicine begins to understand and appreciate the healing power of traditional Native ceremony, ritual faith, and herbal remedies there has developed a growing interest in its preservation and integration into health systems . . . . Lifestyle factors which impact on Native American mortality and morbidity are not always effectively addressed through the clinical approaches of modern medicine, and a vast potential for the improvement of Indian health through the integration of tradition healing, culture and spirituality with the health care system."[15]

Substance abuse professionals began using Native rituals and beliefs in the 1970s. Tribal and private programs report good results by drawing upon the legacy of their clients' culture and religion. Private and public funders are more ready to support a spiritual component to health care and addictions treatment. As tribes assume administration of public health programs, they are more able to fit these to their needs.

By 1995, the Indian Health Service was spending 35 percent of its budget on these tribally run programs through 70 compacts and agreements. By 1997, tribes were operating 9 hospitals, 115 outpatient centers, 56 smaller health stations, and 171 Alaskan village clinics, according to a report commissioned by the Henry J. Kaiser Family Foundation. Of the 6 million out-patient visits to federally funded Indian facilities in 1993, nearly one-third were to those operated by tribes.[16] The Indian Alcohol and Substance Abuse prevention and Treatment Act, passed in 1986 and amended several times since, furthered Indian autonomy via "tribal action plans" and set aside funds for counselors and treatment. In 1992, the Indian Health Service began the Traditional Medicine Program to incorporate traditional beliefs and practices within its facilities. In Phoenix, the federally funded Native American Community Health Center, according to the mission statement I saw in its lobby, has dedicated itself, "to improving the physical, spiritual and cultural well-being of Native American families and other underinsured and uninsured individuals in the greater Phoenix metropolitan area."

Such a sign, seemingly bland and generic, heralds a recognition that to prevent, treat, or cure an ailment can require a change in behavior. Changing behaviors requires changing values and beliefs, the personality and character that form and guide daily living. It is an art, not a science, rooted in the deepest and highest levels of humanity, in the subconscious and in the metaphysical.

Potential Challenges to Native Spirituality in Treatment

Deploying the spiritual, or religious, easily collides with professional habits, general culture, and the rule of law. The integration of indigenous spirituality into substance abuse treatment raises the question of whether the trend will violate the U.S. Constitution. The first sentence of the Bill of Rights reads: "Congress shall make no law respecting an establishment of religion or prohibiting the free exercise thereof." Outside of Indian Country, courts have generally ruled that sentencing convicts to Twelve-Step style treatment or meetings violates this separation of church and state.

Questions of whether the Constitution applied on Indian reservations were settled—at least for general jurisprudence—in 1924 when, during the Wilsonian flush of recognition for colonized peoples around the world and also as a reaction to mismanagement in the Bureau of Indian Affairs, Congress declared Indians to be U.S. citizens. But as of this writing, there does not appear to have been any legal challenges to the public funding of Indian spirituality on the grounds that this would amount to "an establishment of religion."

"There was some concern, early on, when we first started funding Indian programs in the 1980s," recalls Cynthia Turnure, executive director of Minnesota's Chemical Dependency Program Division. "Our attorney general had some questions, but it was not a problem." On the national level, the Indian Health Service has been slow, or cautious, to pay for traditional healing ceremonies or medicine man services. However, it does make room for these. "We encourage the accommodation of Western and traditional medicine," an IHS spokesman, Tony Kendrick, told me. "Practically all of our facilities have healing rooms for services and doctors can refer patients to medicine men." In 1998 Veterans Affairs officials in Phoenix told the Navajo Nation it would reimburse certain services of medicine men.[17] The groundbreaking agreement followed an 18-month trial, which yielded good results in mental health care, and officials predicted it would be expanded to other tribes and services. Under the pact, the VA would reimburse Navajo veterans $50 when they go to a tribal hand trembler, crystal gazer, or stargazer, who diagnose the patient and determine which of about 23 ceremonies or hundreds of Navajo herbs are needed. The government also will reimburse Navajos for expenses involved with certain ceremonies required to restore harmony in a returning warrior.

Were the constitutional question raised, one answer would be that Indian spirituality, as used in health care and addictions treatment, may be sufficiently non-denominational to pass muster as something other than a religion. In Minnesota, Turnure says Indian-operated programs avoided problems by offering their patients alternatives to indigenous spiritual practices.

Many tribes even lack a word for "religion." Leonard, Shelton, and others speak of Native spirituality as a way of life, as what one does during each day's march. Outside observers have reached the same conclusion. "A human being's spiritual life is his/her most important expression of his/her humanity," the authors of a 1992 handbook on Indian spirituality and culture declared.[18] "To respect this is something the elders teach in almost every tribal community in North America. Native American sacred ways were not, classically, incorporated, sectarian, or evangelical. They were just ways of seeking life."

Rather than being strictly tribal or sectarian, the rites and rituals are portable and adaptable, say practitioners. "When I go to a Sioux sweat lodge, they ask me to call on my own Ojibwe ancestors," says Donna Isham, director of American Indian programs at the Minnesota chemical dependency division, during an interview at her office in St. Paul. A colleague, Louise Valandra, a senior planner at the agency, interjects, "We're not talking about God as God, it's more—" Isham completes the sentence: "—a way of life."[19]

On the other hand, the use of traditional rituals and beliefs in treating addicts and alcoholics recalls the overlooked fact that religion has always been at the core of a society and its culture, motivating and steering its course. Few societies are as joined in their religion as are Indians. Faith and life, traditionally, are one. For some in Western society, by contrast, religion has become a hobby or one in a range of choices that make up a "lifestyle." Many in what Indians call the dominant society think that allowing spirituality—or religion—to shape one's person and behavior is suitable only for kooks. But in Indian country, transcendent beliefs and daily life may be so intertwined that a separation between church and state may never have any currency, legal or otherwise.

Indian Rehabilitation Services in Phoenix, Arizona

Indian Rehab, as everyone calls it, is located in several buildings on the quiet streets just north of the spotless brick-paved plazas and glassy skyscrapers in downtown Phoenix. In the low-slung central office, brisk administrators pass through clumps of still-foggy clients. Just blocks away is the men's program, located in a large house with a front porch on a quiet palm-tree-lined street and room for 16 residents. The Guiding Star Lodge for women uses a two-story former motel—its 1960s-spare brick lines give away its origin—on an oddly barren street in the low-rise valley between Phoenix's downtown and midtown office clusters. There is space for 40 women and children. Indian Rehab can offer some graduates transitional housing in a small complex of apartments, one of the first such for Indians, according to staff.

Indian Rehab began in 1972 when several Indian men sobered up and sought to help others, according to Diane Yazzie. They rented a house, then won it from its owner in a card game. She considers this irony with a straight face. "It's interesting that gambling got us into our first addiction facility."[20] Though it is open to all, most clients are Native American, from a variety of tribes. They exhibit two of the changes common to patients at other rehabs: most are addicted to both alcohol and drugs and, primarily as a result of that potent combination, most get into trouble sooner. The average client is now about 28 years old.

As elsewhere, counselors have moved from treating the individual in splendid isolation to treating the entire family, who are usually invited in for an abbreviated program. What distinguishes Indian Rehab is the effort, "to use Western therapeutic models with traditional Indian methods," says Yazzie.

"Someone will mention their dreams and we'll say, 'Let's smudge your broom,' or 'Let's take it to the sweat lodge,' " says Candace Shelton, clinical director at Guiding Star and an Osage from Oklahoma. The first phrase is shorthand for a cleansing ceremony "If a woman has a dream that disturbs them—maybe they saw an ancestor or some spirit bringing negative energy, we may clear out their room by burning a bundle of sage."[21]

Alternatives to standard treatment were needed. "I saw the old DWI programs in which they would just give them didactic information, and they would come drunk to meetings. Education alone was a dismal failure," says Yazzie. "Some thought we could treat addiction as a physical problem, but that's not enough. What pulls them all together is the spiritual component, but that's so individual. It could be having a higher power, or it could be just needing other people.

"In other programs, the atmosphere is very white: everything is very organized, everyone has to be on time, and it hooks into the whole dynamic of Native Americans being told what to do." Indian clients, she adds, "would shut down, withhold, and withdraw. That's the last thing you want to happen."

Women stay at Guiding Star for eight weeks. One of those weeks is devoted to spiritual and cultural awareness. Each woman writes about her own tribe and its rituals, seasons and cycles, and history. In addition to research at the library, many interview their grandparents. With the help of counselors, they also go through the first five of the Twelve Steps, Yazzie says. "It all gets brought back to personal responsibility, and we teach them to do it without getting caught up in shame. They need to do it spiritually, because a lot of Native American women are leading shame-based lives." This sensitivity is not born of any reigning social ideology; it stems from a desire for results. "We are a bottom-line-based program," says Shelton.

Each morning begins with a daily meditation with readings from a book of reflections—there are dozens available for people in recovery, including many just for women—followed by a brief discussion. On Fridays, the women gather for a talking circle. "Usually an eagle feather is passed. Then when you hold the eagle feather, you must tell the truth," says Shelton. "Talking circle can last over five hours. You share all you need to share."

The counselors allow for cultural variations among the women. Tribes approach spirituality, and the fundamental questions of life, in varying ways based on history, culture, and other factors. During one three-month period of 1997, Indian Rehab treated people from 54 different tribes. Some tribes do not allow women to hold the eagle feather, a symbol reserved for men. Images vary: Navajo believe that the owl is a death omen, while among Shelton's fellow Osage Indians, the owl is a positive sign, she says. In most of the treatment rituals, Indians are united in the overall format. "The talking circle is a pan-Indian kind of ritual, one they are all familiar with." Other times, sweet grass is used. After the leader speaks, the object is passed clockwise "because that's the direction in which we journey," Yazzie continues. When a person holds the sacred object, he or she often feels empowered to speak of their private demons, to unburden themselves, and to learn the lessons of previous generations. "It's about wisdom from our elders, in my case my Grandma and my Mom. The purpose, in a group of alcoholics or other people, is 'don't be afraid to look behind that door at your secrets.' You talk, and then the feather is passed to the next person. It allows a positive feedback from the group to the person. Periodically, the leader may refocus the group, if it's getting negative, or prod someone to go deeper. For example, someone may have a [post-traumatic stress disorder] issue we need to key in on."

At Guiding Star, the sweat lodge is held every Tuesday night and is open to women of the community. A dome-shaped structure made of poles stands off to the side in the yard of packed dirt outside the old motel. A small pit, about two feet across and ten inches deep, has been dug in the middle. Cloth and hide coverings are stretched over the frame. In the afternoon, residents from the men's house build a fire in the yard and begin heating up a dozen or so rocks, which range in size from that of a potato to a football. During the sweat, these are carried into the lodge

and placed in the pit where water is poured over them. An outside con-
sultant, usually a spiritual leader from one of the tribes, sprinkle sage and
cedar on the glowing rocks. The steam and aroma purifies participants
physically and spiritually. Songs can be sung or chanted; a drummer may
keep a steady beat. At some point, the leader will introduce a topic, such
as healing, discuss it briefly and then ask someone to take a turn before
proceeding on to the next person in the circle. Usually, there are four
rounds. The session may last several hours, until everyone is all talked
out. At Guiding Star, women are strongly encouraged but not forced to
take part, Yazzie says. "I've seen incredible changes in the woman. The
sweat lodge is a profound experience. Sitting in a dark lodge that's very
hot and you're sweating and turned in on yourself—it's like being in the
womb. It's very introspective."

The use of these methods does not hearken back to ancient times so
much as it represents modern adaptation. Powwows arose among tribes
elsewhere in the country, sweat lodges were imported from the Lakota,
and talking circles are a relatively new thing, says Paul Rock Krech, a
counselor at the men's house. "In the old days they didn't have time to
kibitz." Confrontation, so much a part of most treatment schemes, can
easily backfire with Indians and especially women, Shelton says.

"We work real hard at not doing that. We have to be real sensitive in
about how Native Americans have been treated. Many are carrying gener-
ational shame." Conversely, there is a danger that alcoholics will use a
history of persecution to dodge responsibility and retard their progress.
"You can get into this 'oh, the poor victim, oh, the poor Indian,' " says
Shelton. "We work real hard at getting the women to move out of that."

Culturally specific treatment can, however, appeal to the entirely
human desire to be special. The sweat lodges and medicine wheels—a
prayer aid—and other methods "give them something that sets them
apart from the rest of the world," said Krech. "A lot of addicts are looking
for terminal uniqueness, and this is a positive way of dealing with that."
Krech, a stocky man with a long braid halfway down his back and steady
gaze that can yield to a smile, is a Chippewa or Ojibwe Indian from Minnesota. He embodies tradition and modernity. Krech is a trained grass
dancer and wears a thick clinical skin, thanks to both his own recovery
from alcoholism and his counseling experience.

"There is a moral deficit with many of them," Krech says bluntly. During our conversation, I ask Krech if the use of a spiritual solution means
that addiction involves a spiritual malady. "Yes, definitely, the addiction
affects all of them—body, mind, soul." While Krech pooh-poohs many
generalizations about "Indian culture," he also would like to rewrite the
AA text or Big Book from its 1930s businessman's lingo into a vernacular
that most Indians would better understand. Back at Guiding Star, I ask
Shelton what the best grounds are for an addict's recovery.

"From working in the field and from my own recovery, I would say it has to be spiritual basis, whether you call it the higher power or Buddha. It's a matter of being able to turn one's life over. That's the basis for a sustained recovery. You do what you need to not drink, and then it's a matter of following the Great Spirit, or whatever. Many Native Americans live their sense of spirituality, say by honoring the various cycles in rituals of time in the year. That's what we really work with them to reconnect with."

The spiritual practices are key to Indian Rehab's work, according to Wayne Mitchell, director of social services in the Phoenix Area Indian Health Services. "Their success would be impossible without that religious component," he says.

American Indian Services, Minneapolis, Minnesota

One rainy Tuesday night in April, five American Indians sat around a tractor-tire-sized drum in a spare basement room and pounded the skin in a fierce rhythm. The sound mixed with their voices chanting ancient tribal songs, their pitch gliding eerily from basso profundo to alto. The song echoed madly off the cast concrete walls up into the halfway house above and, presumably, down into the earth. Without assaulting the ear, the rhythm penetrated the internal organs of each listener. In a short time, my heart and lungs seemed to clench and relax according to a primeval biological notation.

The atmosphere is both casual and intense, much like that of certain synagogue or church services where the celebrants are not distracted by the comings and goings of congregants. The men drum for their recovery from addiction; they drum for their lives. Off to the side, a boy rolls billiard balls about a pool table, the spheres smacking into one another noisily, before drifting over to stand at his father's shoulder.

In Ojibwe, they chant the Eagle Song, about a visit from the birds revered as messengers from the Creator. The song is repetitive and consists largely of the line "They're coming to see us," sung over and over in a rising and falling pitch. For 12 weeks, Herbert Sam, an Ojibwe elder and spiritual leader, has been teaching a handful of men how to drum and sing. The men are residents of a 20-bed halfway house run by American Indian Services, the region's oldest and last such facility. They have all volunteered for the instruction; American Indian Services does not require its residents to partake in most of the spiritual exercises offered at the house.

Byron stopped drinking four weeks ago. The somber, fortyish man identifies himself as an Anishinaabe. His face brightens as he discusses the drumming with the air of a boy allowed to stay up late with the grownups. "It is a great honor to sit at the drum," he says. Like so many

Indians, Byron grew up away from his people's homeland and learned of their traditions secondhand.[22]

"You feel the message that you're getting from your Creator and he's speaking to us and telling us that the earth is a gift to us. It's a spiritual communication with the Creator." I ask him how the drumming—so prosaic and simple—helps. "Like they say, 'let go and let God,' " Byron says, using an expression popular among AA members. "The message is to let go and let the Creator have his way with me."

Sam, the leader, prefaces many of the songs with a description of their origin and significance. One tells the story of an Ojibwe princess who hid in a pond during a war and had a vision of a drum divided in quarters—a sacred division among many tribes—that she later distributed. He reminds the men that they have choices now—whether to drink or not, how to live—and suggests they absorb and feel the vibrations of the drum as liberating. Another man hovers his hand over the skin and says, "You can feel the song coming off the drum." Just the fact that they are drumming out ancient songs is significant, Sam reminds them, for the mere fact that "we've survived." Afterward, he summarizes what he considers the therapeutic value of what could easily appear to be just five guys banging on a battered drum in a basement rec room.

"I tell them to trust themselves with the drum, to hit it wrong or mispronounce words. They learn about life from this," Sam says with a tap on the drumhead. "If a man learns to take risks on the drum, he learns to take risks in life."

American Indian Services, founded in 1976, is based in a weary building—a former funeral home—on East Franklin Street east of downtown Minneapolis. The Phillips neighborhood was once full of Native Americans moved here during the federal effort to relocate them from reservations to cities. It is now more diverse, with many blacks and South Americans moving into such Indian enclaves as the Little Earth public housing project.

The worn carpets and stained upholstery seem to match the mood of the new residents, many of whom are still withdrawing from the haze and sullen despair of street life. Yet the determined sobriety of veteran residents and the pluck of counselors infuse joy and purpose into the structure. This mixed atmosphere is common at treatment programs for people who are poor, where an enforced asceticism born of low budgets bolsters a singleness of purpose

In its 22 years, the residence reports having had 1,206 men come through for 1,956 different stays averaging 75 days. Most work; others attend school or job training. The house provides counseling, cultural activities, and chores. "We have the philosophy of AA but change it to work into the Native American perspective," said Linda Vermillion, the assistant director and patient advocate. "We don't force the [Indian] spirituality on them, but about half take part."[23]

Last year, 110 men stayed at the house and 47 percent graduated, meaning they left when they and the administrators agreed they were ready to do so. Vermillion estimated that of the 300 patients she has worked with in 1994 to 1998, about 100 are still sober. "The problem with most alcoholics or addicts who stay sober one year is that many of them feel better and then 'forget' they can't drink," she explains. Such centers can be surprisingly good at tracking former clients, whose lives can be constrained by poverty and pathology. Those who fail usually end up on nearby streets or even drop by, like reverse Raskolnikovs revisiting the scene of their last redemption.

Minnesota has been a leader in requiring agencies to track their results. In 1997 American Indian Services reported that six to twelve months after treatment, 35 percent of former patients were abstinent. That constituted an improvement over previous rates that the staff attributed to increased use of Indian rituals and cultural awareness.

At the Minneapolis house, Philip Archambeault, a counselor, seems well suited for making native American traditions useful and palatable to alcoholics, who are almost by definition resistant. A stocky Lakota Indian whose father directed this same halfway house 20 years earlier, Archambeault wears the buzz cut and upright posture of a former Marine. A tattoo of the Corps' insignia adorns a thick upper arm. Perhaps only such a person could recruit men for classes in sewing traditional outfits as well as in drumming. When I visited, several men were stitching up dresses worn during the grass dance performed by warriors to clear a prairie site for an encampment. That provides a practical connection to Indian heritage. He also introduced the drum instruction, which serves a more metaphysical purpose.

"The drumming does a lot for the ego and the individual," Archambeault says. He recalls the emotional and spiritual vacuum left by the forced relocation of families to cities and children to government-run boarding schools, and by the introduction of alcohol sales on many reservations during the 1950s. "The drumming represents the heartbeat of the earth. The drum sound expands into the earth and the heavens. The drum ceremony expands the connection of the guys into the earth and the heavens."[24] Similarly, men may request a pipe ceremony, which involves prayers and lessons and ceremonial tobacco smoking. Archambeault says that in ancient times tribes from all over sent their young men to quarry pipe heads from the red rocks of Pipestone, Minnesota. A stem of wood is usually affixed to the red stone, which is carved in some animal or other shape. Showing the pipe to hostile tribes would guarantee safe passage, he says, which has particular significance for an addict seeking a new life.

While divided on the exact cause of the high rates of alcoholism and addiction among Native Americans, many treatment workers agree that the loss of heritage aggravated the problem by hollowing out countless souls.

"When it was outlawed in the mid-1800s to practice our spirituality, that did a lot to the core of all our people," says Archambeault. High dropout rates among Indian high school and college students, even at the culturally friendly University of Minnesota, may indicate social or personal insecurity. But for many of these youths, withdrawing is simply the means "to hold on to what little dignity they have," he says. Reconnecting alcoholic Indians with their heritage signifies recovery more than it would with European Americans, for whom church and religion often is only "one piece of the pie," Archambeault says. "Spirituality is just a matter of implementing, 'What does it mean to be Native American?'"

Mash-Ka-Wisen Treatment Center in Northeast Minnesota

Mash-Ka-Wisen Treatment Center is on the Fond Du Lac Reservation of the Ojibwe tribe, in the flat woodlands southwest of Duluth. The Ojibwe title means "Be Strong Enough To Accept Our Help," and doubles as a motto.

American Indians from around the country come here, including many Seminoles. The largest group is Ojibwe, a tribe of about 200,000 concentrated in Canada and the upper Midwest, and their cousins among the Ottawas and Potawatomis. The one-story brick building hugs the flat earth of northern Minnesota next to one of the region's countless lakes, which presents a gray-blue reflection of the overcast sky one early March day when winter's gusts and sleet shoulder out spring. To another side lie a timber teaching lodge and a powwow field circled by several ten-bench grandstands. Inside the common room, illuminated by the bright haze from a skylight, about 30 Native American teens, young adults, and a handful of weathered older men pull chairs and wood-sided sofas into a circle. They slump silently or lean into whispered conversations punctuated by laughs or a fall back into the cushions. Then the silence quickens as one man strikes a match and lights a crumpled ball of sage in a large white shell. He fans some of the smoke onto his face and torso with an eagle feather in a traditional cleansing ceremony, then passes it on. Each person does the same, some pausing to spread the smoke over him or herself more thoroughly. The fragrant, grassy smoke awakens one's nostrils gently. A deeper seriousness drops on the group, whose members agreed to let me sit in on the session. They slowly relax to my presence and are soon absorbed with the business at hand. Some know this ritual from childhood; for others it is relatively new. Two women motion for the shell of smoking sage and feather to be passed around them. "They're under the moon," a man whispers to me in explanation, referring to their menstrual cycle.[25]

The feather is important to the Ojibwe, and to many North American tribes, who consider eagles to be divine emissaries. The shell also resonates for many Ojibwes since one—the *megis*—was believed to have guided their ancestors on a great migration from the lower St. Lawrence River. It is set on a sidetable and the feather is handed to a young man of about 19. He begins nervously, a grin hedging some panic in his eyes.

"What's new with me is that, well, the program isn't really working for me yet," he says. "I'm not getting the spiritual part of the program. I don't know. I do like the cultural stuff here. I feel comfortable." As he talks, resolve enters his quavering voice. All others listen respectfully. Considering its dozen itchy teenagers, the group's silence is striking. No counselor is present, in contrast to the group discussions that are a mainstay of many treatment programs. While holding the feather, a person seems drawn to a higher degree of honesty while given the chance to talk without interruption. They may, however, invite reactions from their peers.

This is precisely what happens later when a young man publicly regrets, and then defends, his infraction of house rules. Residents begin interrupting one another with differing reactions as group discipline breaks down before an older patient restores order. By turns, men and women recount their crumbled pasts and short recoveries, their fading or growing desires to drink or drug, their fragile or strong hopes for abstinent lives. Most refer to families that, no matter the degree of dysfunction, sound to be the anchors of their storm-tossed lives. Near the end, one man offers a coda to all the shared experiences and hopes. "I want to feel better about myself. I just want to feel better about myself."

Since its founding in 1978, Mash-Ka-Wisen has treated about 6,500 alcoholics and addicts. There is room for 30 residential patients, usually three-fourths men and the rest women. The agency also provides treatment on an outpatient basis and runs a 21-bed halfway house in Duluth, about 25 miles to the northwest. Counselors say their clients respond well to the cultural adaptations they offer. Upon admission, 83 percent report no previous exposure to Indian spirituality. Though convinced of the value of spirituality, "we don't promote one spiritual or religious belief over another," director Elwin Benton insists. "No one has a monopoly on goodness."[26]

Gauthier jokingly calls that the "party line." But he reiterates the point even as noting that the Ojibwes are "very ritualistic." The tribe's way of life has generally included the rituals of the Midewiwin, a physical and spiritual healing society that once had eight degrees of training for membership. The society's philosophy, which has spread to other tribes, stresses personal balance, respect for other forms of life, and social harmony.[27]

Most clients—Benton estimates 90 percent—take part in some rituals, which can infuse daily and communal life. A bowl of tobacco sits on the front counter for people to use in making offerings outside. "People believe that every day the Noon Spirit takes that up to the Creator," says Gauthier. Periodic sweat lodges are offered. "The belief is that it returns them to the womb of Mother Earth, back to their original state," he continues. "I tell you, the whole atmosphere around here is different for a few days after a sweat. It's a lot calmer."

The center brings in tribal elders for instruction, holds morning meditation sessions, and weekly talking circles and, each August since 1978, hosts the Celebration of Sobriety Powwow, which draws more than 2,000 people. There is a convenient intersection between treatment centers incorporating Indian spirituality and, in the wider world, what Benton calls "a renewed interest in people wanting to learn about the ceremonies, our languages." He says that only a tiny fraction of the 5,000 local Ojibwe speak their language, but that many children now are learning some of it in school.

But what may be a cultural rediscovery outside is a deadly serious business in Indian treatment circles.

"I believe if you don't have a spiritual recovery you won't have a recovery," says Gauthier. "I know you can get into a whole can of worms with that, but for me spirituality is whatever makes you feel a purpose in life." There is a simple formula according to Mike Munell, an out-patient counselor at Mash-Ka-Wisen who is also a recovered alcoholic: "When we were using alcohol and drugs, that became our higher power, and then it turned on us. That leaves a void when you stop, so we have to replace it with a higher power that won't turn on us."

He says he spends a lot of time explaining to clients that spirituality or Alcoholics Anonymous, which they are encouraged to attend and join, are not religious. "A lot of them have had conflict and bad experience with religion," Munell says. "When I was in Catholic school, I got a very mixed message. They would tell you about the Ten Commandments with one hand," with this he snaps back an arm in well-remembered gesture, "and with the other they would crack you with the ruler."

As a result, Mash-Ka-Wisen tries—Benton admits the place is run by humans—to offer patients the widest possible choice in assembling a spiritual life. For instance, the center—as do many—tries to make sure patients complete the first five steps of the Twelve-Step program. Numbers four and five involve making a "searching and fearless moral inventory of ourselves" and then admitting "to God, to ourselves and to another human being the exact nature of our wrongs." Some research, and considerable anecdotal evidence, have convinced counselors that addicts and alcoholics who complete these greatly improve their chances of recovery.

At Mash-Ka-Wisen, patients who need someone to hear their inventory can choose from a list of Indian spiritual leaders—so designated by community consensus—or Catholic or Protestant clergy. One of the former type is Frank Goodwin, a large Ojibwe man with a ready smile who earns his living as a cook in a nearby Head Start program and is not comfortable with being held up as a spiritual leader, which he calls an honor. "I am connected to our spiritual values, what I've been taught by my father. People come here looking for something, and we offer our traditions and, in a way, address their body, mind, and soul." When he meets with patients to hear their inventories, he talks to them about getting a better sense of self and puts the "confession" in a context of travel. "On their journey forward, I tell them to leave that fifth step here." Goodwin concludes the event with a prayer and pipe smoking, which he said had cultural significance as well. "At the end, we smoke the pipe to let it all go to the Creator. A Lakota elder once told me, the pipe is not a peace pipe, but a telephone to God."

Of equal importance to the spiritual component is the atmosphere of a facility staffed and populated by their own kind. "Indian people are clannish and we feel comfortable with each other," says Benton. "They've all suffered prejudice and discriminatory actions, so here they can identify with each other's point of view." He personified this tendency by being guarded and nearly monosyllabic with me when we first spoke, on the telephone and also upon my arrival. Aware their clients generally abhor too direct a social manner, Mash-Ka-Wisen—akin to many other Indian programs-uses a less confrontational approach than that found at other rehab centers.

"Indian people are really uncomfortable with confrontation," says Benton. "They have been put down all their life, so why reinforce that here? Their self-esteem is so low we try to lift that up."

Tensions in Applying Indian Spirituality

Within Indian treatment circles, there are some tensions regarding the proper role of traditional healing and spirituality, paying for such services, and the potential for misuse. The Indian Health Service was established in 1954 and remains the largest single source of health care for Native Americans. As discussed, its mission includes raising the spiritual health of Indians in culturally acceptable ways.

"We really believe in living with nature, which includes the spiritual and healing ceremonies," says Roslyn Curtis, director of health services for the Navajo Nation, which runs its own federally funded programs. While discussing another topic—care of the elderly—Curtis noted a broad sentiment among health care providers to make good use of traditional beliefs in medicine. "One of the things we're teaching is to go back to families and the old ways," she says.[28]

Actual practices vary. Visits to two Indian programs reveal some of the tensions. The federally funded Phoenix Indian Health Center embodies both old and new in Native American medical coverage. The facilities are a bit worn, budgets are tight and militants periodically march outside to protest research projects—that have involved having Indian subjects with obesity or other illnesses living at the hospital for extended periods—as paternalistic or worse. Administrators endorse the move to incorporate traditional spirituality, though the backing is more verbal than financial. For instance, three medicine men conduct sweat lodges, hold healing ceremonies for interested patients, and, each month, bless the nurses in the obstetrics/gynecology division. But they are not on staff as such.

"One works as a janitor, another's on the pharmacy staff," explains John Malina, a doctor and Yaqui Indian who previously worked at the center, during a tour for a group of journalists. "We're working to get them paid under a National Institutes of Health initiative."[29]

While that seems an odd gap in services, there are precedents. Few Native Americans have full-time day jobs fulfilling traditional roles. A long-time prime minister, or "Thadada:ho," of the venerable Iroquois Confederacy, Leon Shenandoah, worked for years on the maintenance staff of Syracuse University. Still, imagine the outcry at a mainstream hospital if a Catholic priest or Jewish rabbi had to mop floors in order to be on hand to minister to patients as a chaplain. "The problem is medicine men, traditionally, don't want to get paid for what they do," says Malina. Such arrangements hearken back to traditional Indian life before the cash economy.

Nor does everyone in Indian country rush to enshrine traditional spirituality in health care. The Hu Hu Kam Memorial Hospital, on the Gila River (Pima) Indian Community south of Phoenix, represents the bright hope of tribal programs, with its modern facilities, gleaming hallways, and patient-friendly atmosphere. Native Americans hold most seats on the board of directors and many of the jobs, from doctor to clerk. But when I ask administrators whether there are medicine men on staff, they seem startled by the notion. Vi Johnson, a Pima Indian and the chief executive officer, says patients can arrange visits, on their own, from several traditional healers who live nearby. She and Joel Brill, the chief medical officer and a non-Indian, speak in virtually the same distancing tones on the topic. At the time I was with a group of visiting journalists, and several of us sensed they were eager to show that an Indian-run hospital could be as modern and clinically competent and removed from ancient, nonmedical beliefs as any facility in the outside world.[30]

Even many professionals who endorse the use of native American spirituality do not insist on its necessity. Theda Starr, a Pawnee woman with two master's degrees and the blunt, no-frills manner of a social services veteran, runs Desert Visions. The 24 bed treatment center, also on the Gila River reservation, treats chemically dependent Indian youths from

41 tribes in four states. A spiritual experience, while nice, is not essential for recovery, she says. "They do need to admit they are powerless. What's hardest for these kids is to trust. Their first feelings to come out are anger and rage, so it may be difficult for them to believe in a higher power." Nevertheless, during the program's eight weeks the youths attend sweat lodges. Starr says many have spiritual experiences, but she emphasizes the physical effects. "It detoxes the kids like that," she says with a crisp snap of her fingers, "and gets all the poisons out." Each youth researches his or her own tribe, attends weekly talking circles, goes on a camping trip to a sacred site in the nearby mountains of the Tohono O'odham Nation. At first, some families resist having their children attend the explicitly spiritual rituals, but usually agree later on, especially given the flexible approach taken at the federally funded Desert Vision. "We don't foist any one particular culture on them," Starr says.[31]

The wise are cautious in prescribing solutions for complex and deadly problems such as addiction or alcoholism. Attitudes toward indigenous spirituality have veered from rejection to warm embrace. In 1924, Commissioner of Indian Affairs Charles H. Burke dismissed Native religion "as a crutch preventing the useful assimilation of the Indian into white society," and ordered his underlings to have the Pueblo people rid themselves of their religion "within a year."[32] Now, far from Indian Country, many well-educated outsiders borrow willy-nilly from tribal practices, with non-Indian youth groups holding "vision quests" and retreat houses sponsoring sweat lodges. Yet some of these same people dismiss religion in their own circles, and discuss fundamentalist Christians, Orthodox Jews, or conservative Muslims in the same language that Commissioner Burke called Indian customs an impediment to progress. The contradictions will have to be worked out.

Some Native Americans worry that their spiritual practices will be distorted even among their own people due to ignorance. Many Indians live far from their homelands and often know little about their culture or traditions. Counselors at Indian treatment programs report a significant percentage of clients arrive nearly ignorant of their tribe's spirituality. "Indian people aren't all into tradition the way most professional people think they are," said Paul Rock Krech, the counselor in Phoenix. "Most are ghetto people." Sometimes they can recall from childhood only a fragment of ritual or belief passed on by a grandparent or tribal elder, Krech said. To help patients bridge the gap with mainstream AA-style treatment, Krech and other Native counselors use a version of the Twelve Steps rewritten with reference to a Great Spirit rather than God or a higher power. Purification is added to the need for prayer and meditation, and several references to family and brothers and sisters are included.

As Krech and others caution, Indian spirituality can mean many things, is easily corrupted or made superficial, and does not "cure" anyone. While Archambeault "bombards" his clients with lessons on their role as Native American men in their tribes, families, and the world, Krech merely suggests spiritual practices. He considers sweat lodges, for instance, as more of a health measure than a metaphysical experience.

"My grandfather, who died at one hundred and eleven, didn't do sweat lodges as something spiritual. Sure, you can go in there and say, 'Let's go to the east, let's go to the west, let's do this thing with the sticks and let's dig this pit,'" Krech says in a sing-song voice with a rapid pantomime of ritualistic motions. He leans back and smiles broadly at the image.

The danger exists that certain practices can be elevated into something other than their original form and function, and that bastardized rituals can be cast like magic powder at people who have a deadly ailment. On the other hand, adaptations may be welcome. In some locales women now take an èqual role in some sacred rituals. "Until just recently, the women used to sing behind the men, who were drumming," says Donna Isham, of Minnesota's Department of Human Services. "Now they sit right at the drum."

Rituals and rites designed to aid proper living can still congeal into a lifeless dogma or creed. "My grandfather said that our spirituality will come back," Archambeault says, "but it will be different, that it could come back as a religion, so we should be careful." Indian religious traditions can be so integrated into communal and daily life that individual use—such as when an alcoholic in a treatment program burns sweetgrass and meditates alone—would deprive practices of meaning and dimension. The individualist ethos of Western society pervades recovery circles and could distort the communal spirit of Indian practices. Another threat arises in the appropriation of one tribe's ceremonies by a treatment program in a distant location. According to George Tinker, an Osage who teaches at the Iliff School of Theology in Denver, "Perhaps the most distinctive aspect of American Indian religious traditions is the extent to which they are wholly community-based and have no real meaning outside of the specific community in which the acts are regularly performed, stories told, songs sung, and ceremonies conducted."[33] Indian spirituality tends to involve places and settings, generally where power resides. Will practicing ceremonies outside their original context or locale lead to misuse and even mutation? Will they lose their power, or have quite different effects? These questions await answers not so much in scientific study as in the experience of addicts eager for what works in their quest for life.

Profile: Jan—"It's My Spirit That's Getting Better"

Jan's early life could stand in for a mythological retelling of the great break in Indian life from homeland, tradition, and society. When she was two-and-a-half years old and living with her family, who were members of the Potawatomi tribe, on the Hannahville Indian Community in Michigan, her mother died.

"I remember my Mom lying in the casket, and telling my father I wanted to sleep with her because she would get cold out there all alone," Jan says. A second loss followed when her Finnish father transplanted the family 14 miles to Escanaba, Michigan. "I remember my father and my grandfather moving us out, because the roads were so bad they had to use a horse and wagon," Jan, now 51, recalls, speaking from her home in Minneapolis. The loss reverberates in her voice: "That's where my roots were." Escanaba, at that time, she says, was not friendly to Indians. She yearned for home and, especially once she was in high school, frequently visited her grandparents. They spoke Potawatomi, did not drink—common among traditional Indians—and, though they attended Christian services, also observed tribal rituals. "They always made sure there was tobacco on the table and they would sprinkle some in the stove as an offering. When there was a feast, they would feed the spirits with a plate of food they put in the fire so it would go up to the sky."

In Escanaba, her family lived on the proverbial wrong side of the tracks as her father struggled in a variety of jobs, made worse by periodic drinking episodes. Soon came her turn, at the age of five. Like so many alcoholics, Jan remembers that first taste.

"My father and my aunt were at my grandparents, who were away, and they were drinking wine but they kept the bottle in a hiding place. I was getting it for them. Each time I would take a drink, and I liked it, the taste and the effect it was giving me. I couldn't navigate my feet and the kids were laughing. I remember the taste of the wine. It was muscatel."

She continued to drink "when I was seven, eight, nine years old. I heard about alcoholics, but that was not me I thought. Not until I was 40, when I caused a three-car accident and was arrested for DWI." Before that, she had wrecked a car "at least once a year," but without involving the police. She also had three children, moved about the country, got married and separated, and worked in factories and wood mills. After her arrest, Jan attended the first of five treatment programs, a 28-day residential program in Marquette, Wisconsin with a Twelve-Step philosophy and a largely white clientele.

"I loved the feeling I got from it, but the spiritual part, I didn't quite understand. I didn't know it was a way of life. I grew up Catholic. I knew what was right and wrong, but that was religion. I knew that if I went to church and I went to confession, you'd be all right. When I left that program, I was still looking for that answer: 'What is spirituality?' " Jan drank again and later went through—twice, thanks to another relapse—a native American based program near Baraga, Michigan.

"I learned who I was there," she says. Jan credits the experience for helping her to overcome some of the shame she experienced as a child growing up in a prejudiced environment. For three years, she abstained from alcohol and drugs and immersed herself in Indian culture—pow-wows, sweat lodges, education, and even separatism. "When I was first learning to walk the Indian way, I was very prejudiced. I didn't think whites belonged in our meetings, with us."

Eventually, Jan drifted from her practices and from AA meetings, and drank. She spent 21 days at the Mash-Ka-Wisen center on the Fond Du Lac Reservation in Minnesota. "I wanted to have what they have. I got back in touch with my culture there. I just opened the door and let it in." Jan appreciated the Native American elements of Mash-Ka-Wisen, such as the talking circles. "When I'm holding the feather, I feel closer to nature, to mother earth, in the circle because that's what we are, a circle. Life has lots of cycles. I have a few eagle feathers in my keeping so I have to take care of myself."

Jan lives with her boyfriend, who is also "in recovery," as the saying goes. They have an apartment near East Franklin, once a strong Native American neighborhood, now more integrated, that she calls the "war zone." Jan commutes two hours daily to a casino north of Minneapolis. The work is not ideal, but she is glad to have it and is proud of her relia-bility. Sobriety involves a blend of AA and Indian culture, and her recov-ery offers hope for what Jan considers a particular scourge of her people.

"I like going to the meetings at the American Indian Center, on Franklin, where it's mostly Native Americans. It's really sad to walk down the streets around here and see so many Native Americans who are lost." Alcoholism among her people, she said, "started way back when Indians took that first drink. People don't have that spirituality because our par-ents were too drunk to tell us about it."

Jan attends sweats, but "you can't do too many; you have to keep things in balance." She still remembers the power of her first, back in 1991. "There were seven women in it, and I felt like, like I wasn't even on this earth. We left and went to a powwow. I didn't sleep all night because I felt so good. Later we met a security guard in the parking lot and we just sat with him and we talked AA all night, about the Spirit and living the spirit way. I was reborn again."

She and a friend who is a recognized pipe-carrier periodically perform the pipe ceremony, with its ritualized praying and tobacco smoking. Jan prays most mornings to remain sober. "You put down your tobacco, and talk to your Creator, and ask to do his will and to not be judgmental of other people. I even put the tobacco on cement if I have to, but I prefer to do it by trees, because they're our grandfathers and without them we would not have fresh air."

None of these rituals solve her alcoholism or other problems.

"Life is a process. We all have our own journey," Jan says, her voice brimming with joyful confidence. She seems tickled to be alive, but sure of what is keeping her that way. "Spirituality is a way of life. You can't be perfect. But if I have conscious contact with the Creator, I will have peace inside, and no one can give you that but you and the Creator."

One of her joys is the fact that her children have made her a grand-mother. "I feel like I'm 20, but my body lets me know I'm not." Jan laughs, a deep, bubbling sound. "It's my spirit that's getting better."

Outside Pressures on Native American Treatment

As are most rehabilitation centers, and health care generally, Indian-run programs face several concurrent challenges: limited or reduced funds, managed care, and a need to show results or at least report the outcomes of treatment. "We are moving to a world where everything is measured by rates and numbers," said Keith Longie of Indian Health Service. "You've got to prove what you do." Welfare reform is another challenge. As gov-ernment bodies administering social programs, tribes are required under federal laws adopted in 1996 to move many recipients off cash assistance and into jobs. Combined with cuts in other federal Indian programs, trib-al and health care officials predict that more Indians will be poor and chronically ill.

One lack that is not new, nor unique to Indian programs, is the shortage of help for addicts after they complete treatment. That is usu-ally considered the toughest time to remain abstinent, and is exacerbat-ed for the many Native Americans who live in small communities deep in the desert, woodlands, or High Plains. From Indian Rehab in Phoenix, many return to homes that are 60 or more miles from any form of aftercare or support group. To extend a helping hand, or ear, the program has set up a toll-free telephone line for graduates to talk with counselors or a peer. Mash-Ka-Wisen runs a halfway house in Duluth for graduates of its treatment programs, a service more pro-grams are establishing.

Administrators say they are eager to show good results, though in most locales the business of developing and applying detailed and uni-form measurements is just underway. Researchers are trying to pinpoint the elements of success. A survey of 63 Minnesota Indian women who had been sober for at least one year found that the most commonly cited aid to sobriety—by 73 percent of the group—was traditional religious and spiritual ceremonies and powwows. Overall, 95 percent attended such ceremonies, compared to one in ten who went to formal aftercare and 56 percent who attended AA meetings. The study also found a correlation between overall mental health and traditional lifestyles: while 22 percent of the individuals who grew up in homes where their native language was spoken attempted suicide at some point, 56 percent of the women from households without that practice did so.[34]

"There are higher completion rates when treatment is culturally appropriate," says Turnure, who has sat on several panels convened by the National Academy of Sciences to establish outcome measurements for mental health and substance abuse services.[35]

At Mash-Ka-Wisen, Gauthier reports that follow-up surveys were able to contact one in three former clients and found that 40 percent are abstinent a year later, better than many programs. (There is a loss of what researchers call the "treatment effect," meaning it wears off. At three months, 78 percent were abstinent; at six months, 68 percent.) Anecdotally, Benton estimates that of the 6500 people who have gone through Mash-Ka-Wisen since its 1978 founding, about 25-30 percent are now abstinent. "Twenty percent do it right away, and that goes up after several attempts."

An Historical Precedent in the Good Message of Handsome Lake

The mainstream incorporation of Indian spirituality and healing methods into health care can be seen as part of a broader assertion of sovereignty in recent decades. Just as the Red Power movement of the 1970s was fading, many tribes secured a new battlement to fortify their sovereignty. In 1988 Congress legalized gambling on reservations, provided states agreed and signed a federally approved compact with the tribes. By 1997, one-third of the tribes had some type of gaming enterprise generating total revenues of $6 billion.[36]

The casinos have given many tribes the lawyers, money, and courage to assert their will and sovereignty. Even those without gambling feel emboldened. Sometimes with money and sometimes with only the resourcefulness of a tenacious people, many tribes have breathed new life into old languages and customs. Their muscles flex in the form of lobbyists patrolling the polished corridors of the U.S. Senate to a band of two dozen self-designated Mohicans convincing a mayor and village council in upstate New York to back their bid for recognition. Outsiders easily overlook the degree to which a political resurgence can have a religious and cultural foundation.

Confronting addictions with traditional beliefs is not a modern phenomenon among native Americans. After the American Revolution, the six tribes that comprise the Iroquois Confederacy lost much of their land to whites. Their once-heralded social and political organization deteriorated. Depression, alcoholism, suspicion of witchcraft, and even suicide spread among men—many of whom had lost traditional roles—and even women, according to the dean of Iroquois studies, William N. Fenton.[37]

During this time, Handsome Lake (1735-1815), a Seneca Indian living in western New York, descended into alcoholism. In 1799, he awoke from an apparent catatonic state and began teaching both moral and ceremonial precepts he received in a vision he had while unconscious. First among these, he taught that alcohol was once useful for celebrations and certain rituals but had become the greatest of evils. It was to be renounced, as was gambling and witchcraft. Other Indian leaders, such as Crazy Horse decades later, also denounced "the white man's poison." Handsome Lake's code eventually endorsed unity, domestic morality, preserving land holdings, a degree of acculturation to white society and economy, and the continued use of certain ceremonies, songs, and dances.[38]

His clarion call of hope and self-sufficiency, fittingly called the "Good Message." (*Gaiwi:yo:h*) galvanized many Iroquois, coming as it did in a time of social despair, Fenton writes in his book, *The Great Law and The Longhouse*. In later years, Handsome Lake's dictatorial manner and paranoia alienated many followers. But his teachings had a renaissance in the mid-1800s and the Good Message became a force for traditionalism in modern times. Among other changes, abstinence became common in certain tribes. In the 1830s, the Iroquois established the first temperance league in the United States, according to historian Laurence M. Hauptman.[39]

Handsome Lake and his code have implications for treatment of alcoholics and addicts in Indian Country. First, the Good Message may be useful in and of itself. Many of Handsome Lake's teachings resound in rehabilitation programs and recovery circles, where personal responsibility, service to others, adaptability to circumstances, and respect for a deity or higher power are emphasized. Handsome Lake even called for a rite of confession of personal sins, akin to the moral inventory suggested in the Twelve-Step programs.

Second, it is worth considering the role of religion in reviving political power. "The political consequences of the Good Message were revolutionary," wrote Fenton.[40] Handsome Lake's teachings spread to other reservations in Canada, where many Iroquois had moved in the eighteenth and nineteenth centuries, and in upstate New York. In both regions, what is still called the Longhouse religion became the center of the new traditionalism. A decentralized people regained their unity and identity. Though the parallel is not exact, treatment centers have spread, and adapted traditional Indian spirituality in its many forms to modern times. Alcoholics who find in these a support for their recovery are likely to be dedicated practitioners. It will be interesting to see whether these scattered bands of people can invigorate Native identity and political power.

Since at least 1970, Indian alcohol programs have incorporated the Indian Medicine Wheel to emphasize the balance among the physical, mental, spiritual, and emotional realms. One method, the Red Road to

Recovery, is used in dozens of states and Canada. One panel of health and Indian experts prescribed an even broader use of spirituality in promoting the well-being of native Americans. "Clearly, the lifestyle related health problems which plague Indian populations today are those most likely to be addressed by the spiritual revival, cultural survival and reintegration of traditional Indian teachings and belief systems."[41]

Addicts, alcoholics, and counselors are not interested in wasting their time on rituals without effect. Neither do they worry much about what more secular non-Indians would consider encroachments by church on society or the state. Most Indian tribes are adept at adaptation and survival.

"The Ojibwes have a long history of dealing with their own and foreign religions," said Gauthier, the program director at Mash-Ka-Wisen. Jesuit missionaries arrived in the 1600s, leaving a forlorn, graying, timbered church just south of the reservation, but never succeeded in replacing indigenous religions. Here, as elsewhere, Indians took what they liked of foreign practices and left the rest.

"Indian people are real adaptable," Gauthier says. "If it makes sense, they do it."

On the other side of the country and during a similar conversation in his air-conditioned office in midtown Phoenix, the Navajo Leland Leonard grabs a three-by-five-inch yellow stick-up note and fixes it to the top of a copy of the Twelve-Steps as rewritten for Indian culture. He draws a circle, quarters it with two lines and labels three of the four points: physical, mental, and social. He adds the fourth, "spiritual," circles the word and jabs his pen to draw seven arrows pointing at it. "That's where it all comes together."

CHAPTER V

Measuring Results, Measuring the Soul: Science and the Spirit

Magic Pills, Hopeless Cures, and Public Understanding

Addiction is a moral failing. No, it's a malady. No, it's a disease with bio-medical and psychosocial aspects. Better yet, it's a brain disease. This progression of terminology over the century leads us to the point where many people think the answer lies in a pharmaceutical agent that will curb cravings, restore well-being, and ward off the effects of drinking or illegal drugs. Indeed, the public discussion of addictions treatment lurches from declaring that the problem is rooted in genes or biology or neurochemistry to the promise of yet another magic pill in the offing. While science should reveal its findings, the public could be forgiven for wondering how the "answer" of one moment gets swept aside in the next.

Consider the hoopla over dopamine, once thought to be the key to addiction. Working on the theory that drug addiction develops, in part, due to neurophysiologic reinforcement, scientists in 1995 announced that at least one "reward pathway" has been identified in the brain that involves neurons that originate in the ventral tegmental area and project into the forebrain or cortex. Drug use stimulates the release of dopamine from these neurons into receptors in the cortex, producing positive reinforcement.[1] As a team from Yale University explained, the action of dopamine on these neurons strengthened basic human drives such as motivation and volition even to seek and use drugs—"whatever it takes to get a person moving in a goal-oriented, directed way."[2] Then, within a few years other researchers were suggesting that dopamine was not the key player in drug addiction, as previously thought, that it was only a messenger and one of several factors involved in the pleasure process. By that point, however, scientists had spent decades seeking a medication that would cure addiction by blocking dopamine.[3] They have company. In mid-2000, more than 100 drugs were in the works for the treatment of mental illness, including cocaine dependence and opiate addiction.[4] Researchers were also busy on the pill for alcoholism. The outside enthusiasm for this Quixotic search bespeaks the conviction that a human being really is, or should be, a machine or a computer or a vat of chemicals and tissue, one that could be made perfect through scientific interventions.

Consider this exchange between Pete Wilson, then governor of California, and winemaker Ernest Gallo as reported in *The Wall Street Journal*. Wilson said that Gallo became "terribly excited," about research aimed at finding a pharmacological way to prevent alcoholism.

" 'Are you saying they think they can create a block to this addiction?' the governor asked Mr. Gallo.

'Yes,' he replied.

'My God!' the governor exclaimed. 'That's incredible.' "[5]

Wilson went on to propose an unprecedented $143 million in state funding over five years to accelerate the project, whose director said it could find in only five years what could have taken 15 to 20: identifying four to six agents that can combat alcoholism and addiction. Later would come the multimillion dollar contracts with pharmaceutical companies for testing and sales. Yet the findings of research have been modest. The federal Agency for Health Care Policy and Research assessed various studies and trials on pharmacotherapies for alcohol dependence. It found, for disulfiram, mixed evidence as to its value but also that "compliance is a strong predictor of outcome;" for naltrexone, good evidence for reduced relapse and drinking; for acamprosate, good evidence that it enhances abstinence and reduces drinking for alcohol-dependent subjects but minimal evidence on its effect on craving and the rate of severe relapse; for serotonergic agents, minimal evidence on its efficacy for treatment of alcohol dependence; and for lithium, evidence that it is not helpful for treating alcohol dependence. The potential role for these would still be, the report noted, in tandem with Twelve-Step or other psychosocial approaches.[6]

To recover, addicts must decide to not abuse drugs. If found, a magic pill will only work so long as a person takes it, which means she or he must be engaged at the level of will, responsibility, values, and the spiritual life supporting these. Recovering addicts must ultimately be true to their real selves, not the addicted selves, and thereby become the persons they really are, or are meant to be, as they so determine. But a pill, one that truly delivers a "cure," forecloses that opportunity since it would no longer be necessary to grow as a person. Instead we would have groups of people akin to methadone users, on it forever, with symptoms eased sufficiently to avoid the need for personal transformation. Joe Molea speculated that there will one day be a pill for alcoholism and addictions, one that will normalize defective reward pathways in the brain and speed up treatment. Addicts would still need to clean house and make amends, unlearn bad habits and acquire good ones, and grow spiritually. "That's true even if you could snap your fingers and solve the neurological problems," Molea says.[7]

Even scientists call for caution and admit ignorance. "The question of putative mechanisms of action continues to haunt psychopharmacology. Put simply, we know these drugs work, but we have very little idea how. We make guesses based on the neurochemical effects of these compounds. We have very little proof, and sometimes very little data, about whether the neurochemical effects that we find have anything to do with the therapeutic effect of the medication."[8]

A Disease of the Brain or the Person?

Seeing addiction as a disease serves many purposes. The theory reassures scientists, politicians, and others that we will someday have a final cure. It reassures nonaddicts who envision a sharp divide between their own habits and those of addicts, so they can think, "Well, I don't have it." It reassures addicts, usefully, by freeing them of moral blame so they can concentrate on taking responsibility for the solution. And the concept suits society's temperament. Disease concepts are a touchstone of public thought, as Fingarette writes, and "moral and social ills were now perceived as pathologies of either the individual or the body politic."[9]

Interestingly, AA cofounder Bill Wilson was reluctant to term alcoholism a "disease," because, he explained, "technically speaking, it is not a disease entity."[10] Wilson preferred the terms "malady," albeit a potentially fatal one, or, more commonly, "illness." By my count using a digital version of AA's main text, "disease" is used once in *Alcoholics Anonymous*, while "malady" appears six times and "illness" 12 times. Wilson said that AA avoided the term disease so as to not "get in wrong" with the medical profession for sloppy terminology. In his magisterial survey, *Not God: A History of Alcoholics Anonymous*, Ernest Kurtz sheds light on this seminal struggle to define terms. Wilson was deeply influenced by his friend and mentor Dr. William Silkworth, whose experience treating 50,000 alcoholics led him to conclude: "alcoholism is not just a vice or a habit. This is a compulsion, this is pathological craving, this is *disease*."[11] This thinking appears in *Alcoholics Anonymous*, notably the definition of alcoholism as "an obsession of the mind that condemns one to drink and an allergy of the body that condemns one to die." The National Council on Alcoholism, an influential group founded in 1943, borrowed from AA the term "alcoholism" and the idea of the alcoholic as one who has lost control in order to promote it as a medical disease.[12]

Despite the emphasis on alcoholism as primarily a spiritual malady in need of a spiritual solution, the "disease concept" was widely propagated by AA members and is considered one of the group's signal contributions to public understanding. However, this reductionism highjacks a single idea out of context and applies it monolithically to a complex problem. Most critics, incorrectly, blame AA alone for the popularity of the disease concept. Yet the phrase never appears in *Alcoholics Anonymous*; moreover the word "concept" indicates a continuing uncertainty. A study of the field's history and interviews with more than a hundred addicts, AA and NA members, and dozens of professionals have convinced me that the medical and treatment communities are most responsible for spreading this questionable notion. Since the public appears unconvinced, officials have gone further to insist that addiction is not just a disease, but a brain disease. Over and over around the country, government officials and program staff told me, as if they were reading from talking points distributed by Washington, "Well, it is a brain disease, you know."

On the public policy level, the "chronic brain disease" initiative purports to reduce stigma and increase support for treatment. The idea was borrowed from the mental health field, which had more of a basis for such claims and used the theory to reduce prejudice. In addictions, proponents point to genetics and neurochemistry and those vivid images of brains under the influence. The evidence is incomplete, constantly being revised, and contains contradictions and ambiguities.

Several can be seen in a 1998 article by its most prominent defender, Alan I. Leshner, director of the National Institute on Drug Abuse. In the article, versions of which Leshner has published and delivered elsewhere, he disparages the old notion of addicts as weak or immoral and "unable to control their behavior and gratifications." Instead, addiction is "a chronic, relapsing illness characterized by compulsive drug seeking and use." So, he tells us, "It is time to replace ideology with science."[13] But then in the next paragraph he tells of research showing that addicts can modify their behavior, which suggests their compulsion is less than compelling and that they can act differently. Later we read that most drugs of abuse act on the mesolimbic reward system. Prolonged abuse seems to throw a "metaphorical switch," moving the person into the addicted state with a brain different from the nonaddict's. Isn't that liberating? All the stigma gone? Leshner concludes: "If the brain is the core of the problem, attending to it needs to be part of the solution."[14] He acknowledges other components, but the entire thrust of this initiative seems to be diagnosing and treating brains apart from people.

The brain disease theory so dominates the upper levels of treatment and research, and focuses so much attention on medical interventions, that other approaches and factors are ignored or given short shrift. "More than two decades of research clearly shows that drug addiction is a chronic relapsing illness that comes about because of the effects of long-term drug use on the brain. State-of-the-art approaches to treating drug addiction will be the focus of the National Conference on Drug Addiction Treatment." So trumpeted the announcement of this April 1998 conference in Washington, D.C. It lived up to the promise. Many of those in attendance, counselors, and program administrators, wandered about the halls dazed and pummeled by the reams of data on modalities, pharmacologies, genetics. "What about spirituality?" someone finally asked nervously in an open session. "That's how most people we work with recover." Oh yes, came the response, addiction has a psychosocial and behavioral component. But spirituality? Hard to study, difficult to set up the appropriate randomized clinical trials, maybe we should look at that.

The message was clear, and in line with society's preference to reduce problems to biological, chemical, even molecular levels. Breathlessly the media announces each new finding of the chemical root of addictions and the magic pill that is just about in hand. When the National Institute on Alcohol Abuse and Alcoholism issued its "10th Special Report to the U.S. Congress on Alcohol and Health," Health and Human Services Secretary Donna Shalala, announced in the foreword that "Alcohol problems can yield to scientific investigation and medical intervention in the same way as other health conditions."[15] In the midst of chapters on genetics and chromosomes, neurology and medications, the volume acknowledges that participation in AA or Twelve-Step-style programs are the dominant approach in treatment and that their effectiveness has been confirmed by research.[16] But this is said in one page out of 492 pages, as if to indicate that, well, a spiritual approach is interesting, but let's get back to neurochemistry. Similarly, NIDA's booklet, "Principles of Drug Addiction Treatment: A Research-based Guide," devotes a brief paragraph to Twelve-Step programs as an adjunct to treatment.

Well, yes, scientific proof may be lacking in some regards—repeatability, control groups, random assignment—but the affiliation or experience of recovered addicts should count for at least an acknowledgement and explanation of spiritual methods. This mindset permeates the scientific community and its publications. NIAAA and NIDA fund the vast majority of research into alcoholism and addiction, and their funding continues to increase given the public or political demand for a solution, if not a cure. In academic and scientific journals, terminology further divorces the person from the brain. Some publications direct contributors to avoid such allegedly stigmatizing terms as "addict" or "alcoholic" and insist on such awkward phrases as "person with substance abuse disorder." The rejoinder comes in the practice of actual recovering people who almost universally refer to themselves as alcoholics or addicts, or recovering, or recovered, addicts.

Nevertheless, science moves on. Determining the neurochemical basis of addiction may not suffice. In December of 2000, researchers at the University of Texas at Austin announced findings to the effect that chronic alcohol abuse disrupts the brain's molecular programming, specifically the neuro-circuitry of the frontal cortex, seat of judgement and decision-making. These findings are useful, but are predictably presented in such a way as to further position addiction as a process occurring independent of its human carrier.[17] Far from having a personal basis, addiction must be a matter of bad genes, miswired neurons, or even defective molecules.

Other findings have challenged the dominant aspects of the disease theory. One invariably hears from disease proponents that children of alcoholics are three times more likely to become addicted themselves. They point to research showing that about 18 percent of sons of alcoholics became alcoholics compared to the 5 percent of sons of nonalcoholics. But as Fingarette, and others, point out, that also means that four out of five sons of alcoholics avoided the habit. He concludes that "Any genetic factor must be but one possible factor among others and that this genetic factor makes a difference in only a minority of cases."[18] The English science writer Alexandra Wyke, in her 1997 book, *21st Century Miracle Medicine*, reported that, "Recent studies with twins, though, have suggested only a tenuous genetic link between people and alcoholic tendency." She dismissed the reduction of a person to his or her DNA as "genetic essentialism."[19]

As for neurochemistry, G. Alan Marlatt and colleagues found that alcoholics will drink to excess when they think they are consuming alcohol, even if the (heavily flavored) beverages contained none. Further, these subjects would drink little when they thought the beverage was alcohol-free, even if it was not.[20] In Fingarette's review of the research, he concludes that rather than "an uncontrollable abnormal, chemical-physiological reaction" to alcohol, it is the drinker's mindset, beliefs, and attitudes about alcohol that determine her or his consumption.[21] "Instead of looking at heavy drinkers as victims of some wayward gene or physical abnormality, we can now see them in a truer light: as a diverse group of people who for diverse reasons are caught up in a particularly destructive way of life."[22] A regular part of brain disease presentations is the vivid CAT scan images of addicts' brains lighting up under the influence of cocaine or other drugs. But as Sally L. Satel says, "You can examine brains all day, but you'd never call anyone an addict unless he acted like one."[23] No drink, no drug, no problem.

If alcoholism and addiction are diseases, strictly understood, then why are other conditions so routinely associated with these maladies? Female addicts report, at disproportionate levels, having been sexually or physically abused, even before drug habits rendered them vulnerable. Questions about the organic origins of mental illness were raised by findings that so many women hospitalized for such disorders had been abused earlier in life, which cracked the prevalent contention that schizophrenia and other problems were almost entirely a matter of genetics and neuro-chemistry. Long-term studies among youths found that "a history of childhood maltreatment is associated with increased risk of at least 25 percent" for such problems in adolescence as drug use and mental ill-ness.[24] Ditto for alcoholism or addiction. At Clean & Sober Streets in Washington, D.C., a well-regarded program that works with bottom-case addicts, psychotherapist Marsh Ward told me that almost every resident has had a horrific childhood of one kind or another. Sara Kershnar of the Harm Reduction Training Institute states flatly: "I have yet to meet a per-son with chaotic drug use who was without some form of trauma in their past."[25]

Addiction begins with a person choosing to drink or take a drug, and recovery involves the decision to abstain. Many recovered alcoholics regard their problem as a disease, but paradoxically, they find their solu-tion in a spiritual program, the Twelve Steps or AA-style treatment, which is replete with moral content and overtones. The challenge of recovery is "change or die," an essentially moral formula that is not so far from the biblical declaration that "the wages of sin are death."

If addiction is understood as a problem with a large role for personal change and responsibility, it would not be alone. In 1998, A. Thomas McClellan disputed common opinion that drug abuse is a "voluntary activity" while diseases like asthma and diabetes are not. Instead, these other diseases are also contracted through voluntary choices. "Many, if not most of the people who end up being treated—medication-depend-ent—for their conditions would not have to have been medication-dependent had they complied with initial recommendations," McClellan said.[26] Rather than addiction being a disease like other chronic condi-tions, perhaps those are more like addiction, with plenty of room for per-sonal choice in the development of and recovery from the problem.

Patricia Owen, research director at Hazelden, offers one explanation for the preference of those who dispense research funding. One official told her that, "Alcoholism will not be accepted as a disease until they have a pill for it." But even neurology suggests a pill will not solve the answer. "I personally don't think the medications are going to work on their own," Marilyn Carroll, who directs an addiction research lab at the University of Minnesota, told the *New Yorker*. "The brain has ways of being unbeliev-ably plastic, of getting around whatever roadblocks you try to put up."[27] At the end of the research, there would still be a person.

Owen continues: "Even with other diseases, just taking the pill alone doesn't cure. The patient has to comply with treatment and many don't." As with many diseases, and especially addiction, she adds, "there's a per-sonal transformation involved in making the decision to take a pill."[28] Even NIDA's Alan I. Leshner usually expands his description to include room for personal choice and responsibility. "Today's version," he told the *New York Times*, is that addiction is "a brain disease expressed as compulsive behavior; both its development and the recovery from it depend on the individual's behavior." Well.

Hostility of Science

The behavior behind addiction and recovery consists of choices. Choices are based on values, values on morality and beliefs and these on the core, or soul, of a person. Any lasting solution needs to touch the person there. But scientists and health care workers, and a public full of modern sensitivities react strongly to this line of thought. Not much has changed in the hundred years since William James analyzed the issue in his report, "What Psychical Research Has Accomplished."

"No part of the unclassified residuum [of human experience] has usually been treated with a more contemptuous scientific disregard than the mass of phenomena generally called mystical." Medicine dismisses these or regards them as products of the imagination. "All the while, however, the phenomena are there, lying broadcast over the surface of history." James compared this disregard to that of a religious believer who refuses to acknowledge scientific considerations that weigh against his or her cause: "Certain of our positivists keep chiming to us that, amid the wreck of every other god and idol, one divinity still stands upright,—that his name is Scientific Truth, and that he has but one commandment, but that one supreme, saying, Thou shalt not be a theist." James wanted a more radical empiricism; a science freed of preconceptions, for which the issue of religious belief had not been foreclosed ahead of the evidence.[29]

Yet, we yearn to be done with messy humanity. "Science must replace ideology as the foundation for drug abuse, addiction, prevention, treatment, and policy strategies," said an audience member at the 1998 American Society of Addiction Medicine.[30] Good luck. Beliefs and values will always drive treatment since they are at the core of an addict's habit and recovery. As recovered addicts, relatives, and others often say, no one stops until they want to stop. Writing earlier this century, the anthropologist Edward Sapir pinpointed one source of the scientific distrust of the transcendent. Psychiatry, frustrated with its inability to solve all mental disorders and envious of hard science, reverts to seeking cause and solution in biology, chemistry, or genetics. In his essay on "Psychiatry and Anthropology," Sapir wrote: "The conventional companionship of psychiatry and neurology seems to be little more than a declaration of faith by the medical profession that all human ills are, at last analysis, of organic origin and that they are, or should be, localizable in some segment, however complexly defined, of the physiological machine." Scientists distrust psychiatry, and psychiatrists themselves, wrote Sapir, "worried by a largely useless medical training and secretly exasperated by their inability to apply the strictly biological part of their training to their peculiar problems, tend to magnify the importance of the biological approach in order that they may not feel that they have strayed away from the companionship of their more illustrious brethren."

Despite periodic headlines about science finding religion, the portion of scientists professing disbelief or doubt about God remained nearly constant between 1914 and 1996 at about 60 percent.[31] The uneasiness may explain a divide even among scientists. Dan Blazer, a psychiatrist at Duke University who has studied the intersection of religion and health, told me that surveys indicate, generally, that physicists, chemists, and others in the "hard" sciences are more likely to be religious or at least open to spiritual issues, while those in the "soft" sciences are more likely to be atheistic, agnostic, or even hostile.

"If researchers write about spirituality they're afraid they wouldn't get tenure and it's quite true. The social sciences are very concerned about being a science and not being about religion," said William Sonnenstuhl, an associate professor of organizational behavior at Cornell University and associate director of the Smithers Institute in New York.[32] Given their insecurities, social scientists strain for empirical respectability. They arrive at academic gatherings armed with surveys they "unpack" and data they "mine." This vernacular reveals preference rather than reality.

The hostility or discomfort with the spiritual or human element of addiction and recovery manifests itself in a lack of research. Studies on every other aspect of addiction—neurochemistry, biology, pharmacology, and so on—cram the scientific and medical journals. A reader would hardly know that it is a person who picks up or declines a drink or drug. This neglect, at least until recently, is remarkable given the long history of spiritual solutions, from religion to Twelve Step to meditation. "Serious scientific research on the spiritual side of addictions is rare indeed," William R. Miller, a prominent scientist and clinician, declared in 1990. "Traditional spiritual concepts have been relabeled to remove their transcendent dimensions, and addiction researchers have acted as though spirituality plays no role in the lives of those they study."[33] The problem runs through the broader field of psychology and mental health. "In major psychiatric journals, measures of religion are reported only rarely, and, when assessed, over 80 percent of studies examined only one variable, usually affiliation."[34] Spirituality is certainly scanted compared to the volumes of studies done in the search for a magic pill. Money may be why. "You have all these huge pharmaceutical companies looking for a solution and there is not a lot of money to be made on spirituality," said Russell Greenfield, a doctor and fellow at the University of Arizona Program in Integrative Medicine.[35]

Professionals who will one day work with addicts can pass through their education hearing little on the topic. Doctors and medical students routinely report little exposure to the spiritual basis of many addicts' recovery while in medical school, other than attendance at a Twelve-Step group meeting or a short lecture. Charles J. Shaw, a doctor at the St. Luke's Hospital treatment program in Phoenix, Arizona, polled several of his interns for me on the extent of their coursework on addictions in general: "none," "zero," "three hours," "maybe two weeks in the psychology track," came the answers. "It's just not taught, for a lot of reasons I don't know," said Shaw. Addictions and spirituality, he continued, "makes them uncomfortable because they just don't understand it."[36] The same is true for those at the microscope. Wrote Miller, "Diversity training of psychological and medical researchers typically includes no serious consideration of spiritual and religious issues, despite the presence of a large volume of studies showing positive relationships between religious involvement and health."[37]

The message filters down to counselors. The index in a major textbook for the substance abuse field lists three citations for "spirituality," one related to AA and two for "drug use as catalysts for."[38] Addicts are also divided from their helpers. A 1985 Gallup Poll found that while 96 percent of Americans professed a belief in God, only 40-45 percent of mental health professionals did so. Not that counselors and doctors have to share the beliefs of patients, but the gap suggests a lack of sympathy or understanding.

Sometimes, it takes quite a lot of digging to discover the spiritual basis of recovery in treatment. Program administrators often describe their regimens as entirely medical and psychological even when a copy of the Twelve Steps hangs on the wall or patients meet daily for morning meditation. When I asked about spirituality, some directors reacted strongly, as if I had focused on the wrong detail. "Are you some sort of preacher?" was one response to my query. Patients, by contrast, rarely mentioned medical interventions but loved to discuss their spiritual lives. Counselors may tell a different story. The Delaware Valley Clinical Trials Network surveyed staff at 50 programs in three states and found that 83 percent agreed with the statement, "Spirituality should be emphasized more."[39] (Yet a portion of this same group, 33-52 percent, also favored increased use of medications such as methadone or naltrexone.) Addicts and clinicians told me that a spiritual life, of almost any kind, was critical to recovery. Daytop Village, an old-line therapeutic community, conducted a spiritual survey of about 700 adult clients and found that 81 percent agreed that "your relationship with God helps you in your treatment" and 89 percent agreed that "having a relationship with God is important to being clean and happy." A slimmer majority of teenaged clients also agreed with those statements.[40]

Despite the lip service, however, treatment can involve precious little spiritual direction or development. "A three-year study of 441 patients called the spiritual the most neglected part of therapy. This was borne out by a 1985 report that 91 percent of patients in treatment centers complained that their spiritual needs were not adequately taken care of. Other research indicates the percentage of success of treatment is in direct proportion to attention to the spiritual aspects of the disease."[41]

Professionals may acknowledge this element merely to suggest it be diminished. A news account timed to AA's sixty-fourth anniversary suggested the group's methods needed scientific supplementation. "Today, alcoholism is largely considered a physical, psychological, and possibly genetic addiction, rather than a moral weakness." (As if morality—or values—could be excised from psychology.) Thus, a symposium of the American Society for Addiction Medicine "concluded that AA continues to be successful, but would be more effective if supplemented by modern interventions, such as inpatient hospital treatment programs and group therapy."[42]

Behind this hostility lies a centuries old and worsening divorce of body and mind or spirit, something that accelerated with the reductionism of René Descartes. Further, as Miller argues, science expands its authority into the spiritual realm by recasting terms in psychological vernacular and stripping away the transcendent element. Meanwhile, science pretends to be unburdened by beliefs or ideology. "Scientists (and therapists) do not and cannot proceed in a vacuum free of values or beliefs," Miller writes. "The perception that one is operating with total objectivity, unbiased by personal beliefs, is a dangerous assumption, both in science and in therapy."

Actually, science has parallels to the spiritual endeavor. When we regard religion, we concentrate on its doctrine, rituals, and rites. But more broadly, as Durkheim defined it, religion consists of "a system of ideas whose object is to express the world." Thus, religion and science both seek to explain the same natural realities. Science too rests on the opinion, or faith, of its believers. "Science can succeed in this task only if it has sufficient authority, and it can gain such authority only from opinion. All the scientific demonstrations in the world would have no influence if a people had no faith in science."[43] Scientific concepts convince us because we can test them; adherents of a religion or faith test those concepts against their experience.[44] People believe in that which helps them. Addicts pursue spirituality insofar as it assists their recovery.

During the 1990s, medicine and science began to study faith and religion due to its observed effects. Given spirituality's central role in treatment and recovery, some addiction researchers are now putting it under the microscope. "A few years ago you would never have heard of the National Institutes of Health being involved with spirituality," said Margaret Mattson in July 1998 while she was organizing a conference on the subject for the NIAAA. In the drive for results and accountability, governments and other funders are tacking spirituality on to the lists of variables and factors measured before, during, and after treatment.

Outcomes: Measuring Results

Years ago, a friend tired of his endless succession of sessions with his psychiatrist. "How are the rest of your patients doing?" he finally asked. "Are any of them getting better?" Good question, and one that is being asked throughout health care, which for a long time relied more on experience than real data for evaluating methods. Similarly, for decades, though there were major national evaluations, individual drug and alcohol treatment programs, and even funders rarely tracked results. New York State, a leader in the field, spent billions of dollars over years on treating alcoholics and addicts with little idea which programs were working and why. After newspaper and legislative investigations, a 1995 law required that programs report objective outcomes of individual programs. Ahead of many other states, New York launched a comprehensive assessment of how many patients complete treatment, how many were sober or clean, and how many remained so afterward and how they changed in terms of criminal activity, employment, and health.

"Most states are moving in that direction," David Mactas, former director of the National Center for Substance Abuse Treatment told me. Granted, national evaluations and other research have demonstrated that rehabilitation has results, that each dollar spent on helping substance abusers recover saves several in police, court, welfare, health, and other costs. Even if they relapse, time in recovery is better than no time at all and prevents what harm would have occurred were the person drinking or drugging and driving a car or committing a crime during that period. Armed with these talking points, counselors, program managers, and government officials love to chant that "Treatment Works!" But given the wide variation in the nation's 11,000 rehabs, the question now is, does *this* treatment program work?

That's what the average potential patient and, more importantly, her or his family wants to know. "It's a very reasonable question: 'Is what you're doing working?' " John Coppola, director of the New York State Association of Alcoholism and Substance Abuse Treatment Providers told me.[45] Not that everyone embraces the idea. While I was writing a series of newspaper articles on the cost and results of treatment, numerous program directors took umbrage when I asked about the fate of their graduates, about the exact payoff for the funding they received. Good intentions and a few anecdotes were, presumably, enough. No longer. Another reason for resistance is the mutual-aid nature of treatment. During the 1960s, the pioneers in the field were largely ex-addicts who set up programs to help others like them in all respects save recovery. Personal validation sufficed as proof. "If you look at the whole treatment field, it all began with a few guys who went through a TC [therapeutic community] in 1964 and then decided they wanted to help people with what worked for them," said Coppola.

Others resist "because the results are going to look so bad," said Deirdre Oakley, an analyst at the Policy Research Institute, which studies a range of social services for difficult groups. Relapse is the most common treatment outcome. Rare is the alcoholic or addict who goes through treatment once and stays clean or sober forever. A. Thomas McClellan, the University of Pennsylvania outcomes researcher, told Bill Moyers for his PBS show that of the more than 100 programs his team has evaluated, "there's a good 20 percent which actually make people worse."[46]

The difficulty of measuring results bedevils all of health care. Even after years of effort, only a few states were able to offer candidates for heart surgery the rates of success at different hospitals. That too is changing as part of the effort to curb health care costs. In addictions treatment, insurers, managed care organizations, the federal, and most state governments have begun to track results in all areas of life from employment to criminality to health to family stability. New York, for instance, implemented a system to look at a representative sample of programs and their clients at different stages before, during, and after treatments. Massachusetts began checking admission, discharge and billing, and also employment status; substance abuse and treatment history; goal achievement; use of state, health, and social services; service utilization; and costs and has, in one report, analyzed the results.[47] After reviewing 3,200 possible measures in the public health, substance abuse, and mental health fields, the National Research Council settled on four basic objectives to assess: health status, social functioning, patient satisfaction, and risk status.[48]

Many follow-up evaluations rely on what patients or graduates say about themselves. Common sense suggests that addicts are unlikely to report honestly on their failings. Not so, according to Patricia Owen at Hazelden. "Self-reporting is generally accurate. We do periodic samples of self-reports compared to what their significant others report, and there is usually an 80 percent accordance." The remainder is split between patients who lie about relapsing and those who overestimate such slips. "It's very consistent with what other researchers find."[49] Other studies with drug addicts have found similar or even higher agreement between self-reporting and testing of urine samples.

Thankfully, abstinence is no longer the single measure of success. The Physician's Leadership Council, quite reasonably, demanded that alcoholism and addiction be judged in the same light as other chronic illnesses with behavioral aspects, such as diabetes and hypertension. With all these illnesses, repeated efforts at change may fail but eventually lead to recovery. To judge one relapse as proof of failure is harsh, unreasonable, and medically useless. Progress, not perfection, should count.

Outcome measurements will evolve in several ways. First, individual programs will be evaluated. Second, though national studies indicate that treatment in general pays off, scientists do not know which form of treatment works best for whom. And third, some want to look at each person more carefully. Deirdre Oakley suggests that the field take a cue from the treatment of people who are dually diagnosed with addiction and a mental disorder, where specialists measure progress by asking people about the pattern of their drug abuse—more, less, or abstinent. By charting the cycle of abuse and relapse, counselors can see what factors contribute to reduction or recovery. Similarly, Patricia Owen advocates a case-management method, in which Hazelden would contact graduates at regular intervals to see how they are faring. Graduates would be asked about abstinence, AA or NA attendance, relationships with family, friends, and even their higher power, and more empirical measures such as legal troubles, employment, and health. "I want to see the entire picture," said Owen.

Outcomes: Measuring Spirituality

Exactly what leads to recovery remains, in large part, unknown. A national study tackled this question and found better results among individuals who completed treatment, received more treatment, and were treated longer (though other studies dispute the value of treatment duration). "However, the study also found these treatment factors and other patient characteristics such as gender, age, legal pressures to enter treatment, and the severity of all problems at admission, explained relatively small proportions of overall variations in outcome, ranging from a low of 5 percent for psychiatric outcomes to a high of 19 percent of variation for medical outcomes."[50] Similarly, Alan Kott, the assistant director of evaluation at the New York State Office of Substance Abuse and Alcoholism Services, told me that about 80 percent of the variation in outcomes was due to unknown factors. In 1997, he speculated that spirituality might explain a portion of that. Four years later and with all due caution, Kott said evaluations of program outcomes suggests spiritual development may explain 10-15 percent of the variation. Much of the rest, he predicted, could be related to differences in programs and staff.[51] Others would put the role of spirituality much higher. Why? Because it serves to change people, and change is the core of recovery. "You show me a chronic medical disorder, any one, and I'll show you the need for behavioral change if the treatment is to work," said McClellan. If patients don't change in addition to taking insulin, or hypertension medicine, or, in the case of addicts, methadone, Antabuse, or naltrexone, "you will see relapse." Citing the support and practice of Twelve-Step and other groups in changing behavior, he added, "Every study that looks at this finds that participation in the self-help groups is quite consistent with maintained change."[52]

The widespread and varying use of the Twelve-Step philosophy by programs confounds research by making it hard to separate its effects from other elements in treatment. Another difficulty is self-selection: do people who attend AA or other groups fare better because of that, or do they attend because they are already in better shape because of family, work, or other stabilizing factors? Researchers often reduce the spiritual element of recovery to a type of social support. In a related field, however, scientists studying the role of religion in the health of older Americans found that even when they separated out social support as a factor, those participants active in a religion lived longer and better, Dan Blazer, a geriatric psychiatrist at Duke University, told me.[53]

Addiction invites scrutiny along spiritual lines. But immediately the discussion touches on moral and even religious issues. Many people still think addicts are to blame for their problems. People in the field disagree, but they have borrowed from AA whose founders shrewdly combined two ideas: alcoholism is a malady but the alcoholic is responsible for recovery. This makes measuring outcomes, and the factors behind those results, trickier. Two types of scrutiny are necessary: personal assessment and scientific measurement of spirituality's utility. It invites a performance-based evaluation. Even the frothy appeals by preachers of the past were based on a belief that God would relieve the drinker of their bottle. Indeed, the primary method of the Twelve Steps was developed during a time when doctors and others sought the causes of alcoholism, as they so continue. AA, by contrast, concentrates on a solution and avoids naming causes other than to suggest alcoholism stems from a spiritual deficit. Personal transformation provides the sense of well-being that the addict would otherwise seek through substance abuse. "If you don't have a spiritual awakening, you won't have a sober lifestyle as I see sober," said Peter Hayden, the no-nonsense director of Turning Point, which serves about 2,000 predominantly black clients in Minneapolis. He criticizes elements of the Twelve-Step philosophy, such as "powerlessness," but is resolute on the need for a conversion experience. "You may be dry or not drinking but without spirituality you will not be living with elements you need," he said, ticking off such virtues as love, dignity, and responsibility. "These are the issues that only spirituality can deal with."[54] Those with addictions agree that this sort of change is central to treatment and recovery.

How to measure it? Ask people.

One checklist, the Alcoholics Anonymous Involvement Scale, asks a patient point-blank if they have had a spiritual awakening. At Hazelden, John A. MacDougall developed a questionnaire people can use to assess their spirituality by grading answers to such questions as "I have experienced awe and wonder," or "I have surrendered to the care of a higher power," or "I try to help others." Some measure spiritual change. Daytop's spiritual survey asks 47 questions grouped into past, present, and future categories. These cover previous beliefs and religious education affiliations; current beliefs such as "does God forgive you" or "do you forgive yourself," and practices such as prayer and meditation, and future inclinations, such as plans to attend Twelve-Step meetings or the desire for nonreligious prayers at mealtimes.

Addictions professionals could also borrow ideas from general medicine, in which interest in tapping faith to help patients is on the rise. Christina M. Puchalski, a doctor and the director of education at the National Institute of Healthcare Research, suggests taking a spiritual history of patients structured around faith and beliefs, their importance and influence, religious community, and the patient's preferred role for these issues in care. The institute reports that more than 60 medical schools have begun to train students in taking a spiritual history. Puchalski said it is simply a matter of finding out what is important to a patient. "Spirituality can be defined as whomever or whatever gives one a transcendent meaning in life."[55]

In studying spiritual transformation, a panel of scientists sponsored by the Templeton Foundation recommended a general approach that considered three broad areas of human existence: beliefs on the nature of reality, transcendence, deities, and individual purpose; motivation, including morals, goals, and higher values; and experience with the transcendent.[56] These all shape behavior. But, the panel cautioned it might be hard to determine in which direction cause and effect flow. For instance, is enhanced spirituality a cause or product of recovery? There are other questions to answer. Which spiritual interventions make the difference? Does a lack of spiritual development predict relapse? The panel even recommended charting the role of spirituality in the controversial "harm-reduction" approach, which skips the traditional insistence on abstinence. The Templeton panel, which was directed by William R. Miller, also suggested that research measure both the quantity and quality of spiritual and related factors in addiction and recovery, and the interplay between the personal and the societal. Thus, this group of scientists opened the door to scientific scrutiny of the most personal and intimate experiences and beliefs.

Along the same lines, scientists have to look deeper than mere affiliation with a spiritual approach such as Twelve Steps or the Christian methods of Teen Challenge, a popular treatment practiced at sites internationally. Consistently, researchers have found that mere attendance at AA meetings, for instance, does not predict the deep-seated change associated with continued abstinence. What makes the difference is involvement in AA: helping newer members, leading meetings, volunteering all contributed to a person's well-being and meaning in life. Looking even deeper, researchers could gauge the shift in values a person experiences, especially since recovery often involves a dramatic turnaround.

AA or NA participants generally pass through three levels of change by practicing the Twelve Steps: surrender, action, and maintenance. These are suitable "domains" for research, according to Scott Tonigan, a colleague of Miller's at the University of New Mexico. Speaking at a 1999 conference sponsored by the NIAAA and Fetzer Institute, Tonigan also encouraged research on the relationship with the higher power, and on common beliefs of these fellowships and the means by which these are passed on.[57]

The simplest method may be to measure change in spirituality. Richard L. Gorsuch of Fuller Theological Seminary notes the considerable research showing that the classical religions—Catholic, Protestant, and Jewish—of Western culture have been a major bulwark against alcoholism. So why do so many people raised in these become alcoholic? Gorsuch points out that alcoholics consistently report a judgmental, vindictive God. This varies from mainstream religious teaching, grounded in the Bible, that stress forgiveness and love. "Hence, psychologically and theologically the 'Christianity' of alcoholics is not the Christianity of most other American Christians." That is, alcoholics are generally distinguished by a poor connection to their own, or any, religious tradition. Put bluntly, they were not brought up right. "Theirs is a theologically immature faith, and because it is immature, it is also ineffective." Again, we return to the matter of results. Gorsuch says answers may emerge by measuring the change in a person's spiritual life related to the change in their alcohol abuse or addiction.[58]

Science and Society Must Believe Believers

Traditionally, scientists were uneasy about AA's unscientific approach to a medical problem. Many remain puzzled by this anarchic fellowship that helps members recover from addiction on a spiritual basis. There are hardships in studying Twelve-Step fellowships. These do not take public positions on outside issues such as scientific findings or treatment methods. Members often express personal opinions that can be mistaken for group doctrine. And the anonymity of members, the voluntary nature of their participation, and the autonomy of each group confounds attempts to pin them down for clinical studies.

Support group members resist scrutiny out of suspicion or even hostility toward doctors and scientists. Some recovered addicts think medical professionals failed them in the past, say, by prescribing antidepressants to them while still drinking. Many believe doctors and researchers misunderstand the role of spirituality in addiction and recovery.

"It is hard to get AA, CA, and other groups to cooperate with studies," said Milton Bullock, director of addiction and alternative medicine at Minneapolis General Hospital. Instead of tossing up his hands in frustration, he suggested that rather than waiting for a sufficient number of randomized clinical trials to include AA members, professionals should simply reach some conclusions based on participation. "I believe the Twelve-Step approach is efficacious without research, simply due to the mass of evidence," Bullock said. He suggested a different approach, such as by surveying current members about their drinking or drug careers and recoveries.[59] This type of review could balance the experiments that require a control group of people who are denied treatment, a risky proposition given the dangers of addictions and a difficult one given the personal nature of spiritual development. To ignore the sheer numbers involved in Twelve-Step groups, or religious programs, because these lack the proof of randomized clinical trials is akin to saying that the parental wisdom on child-rearing was not valid until modern psychologists could prove the efficacy of each reprimand and hug.

George E. Vaillant, a Harvard psychiatrist and author of *The Natural History of Alcoholism*, a 50-year study of male alcoholics, has suggested this retrospective approach. He proposed that researchers should examine differences between alcoholics who recover and those who do not, rather than limiting research to the contrasts among professionally run treatments and control groups.[60] This suggests the earth-shattering conclusion that science could just take people at their word. If an alcoholic says, "God saved me," what could be wrong in believing her?

Durkheim based his work on what people said and did in the religious and spiritual realms. He argued, sensibly, that "the unanimous feeling of believers down through the ages cannot be mere illusion."[61] He dismissed the critics of religion, who say it contains nothing but an illusion, declaring it "impossible to understand why humanity should have persisted for centuries in errors that experience would very quickly have exposed as such."[62] People will discard that which does not work, especially something as important, time consuming and life directing as religion or spirituality. We can even set aside the debate over God's existence. Durkheim said believers were not in error when they sensed an external power, since that power is society, the root of all religious sensations. Through religion, individuals envision and structure society. This may make spirituality more palatable for addictions researchers. Take the deity out of the picture, or assume that this higher power is merely society acting upon each believer in hidden ways but with obvious results. By this way, observers can study spirituality as a realm that does not necessarily involve God and chart the results of such faith.

William N. Fenton, the dean of Iroquois studies, distinguished himself early in his career from the archeologists and anthropologists who dominated the field by a readiness to listen to the rituals, stories, and histories passed on orally for generations. "I realized I could learn more from interviewing survivors than digging holes in the ground," he told me.[63] As a young scientist on a dig in Wisconsin, Fenton unearthed long, man-made poles from a previous era. None of his academic colleagues could determine the purpose of these until Fenton asked one of the Indians working on the site. The man told Fenton that tribal members still used the poles as javelins in a traditional wintertime sport that involved sliding them along the ice. Many scientists, peering at pictures of brain slices or defective molecules, sometimes resemble these archeologists digging in the dirt when they could just ask a recovered addict, "Why are you sober?" Such frank investigations into transcendent experience can reveal and magnify concrete truths. For Durkheim, the mythologies and theologies of religion afford a glimpse of reality, a reality that has been "enlarged, transformed, and idealized."[64] The addict who says, "I conceive a loving God who helps me abstain and live to good purpose," shows the fruit of his belief in his daily life.

People may think science and religion cancel out each other. Witness the public debate over the teaching of evolution and Creationism. We say it must be one or the other, rather than allowing both to shed some light on the other despite irreconcilable differences. "But religion exists; it is a system of given facts; in short, it is a reality," wrote Durkheim. "How could science deny a reality?" These supposed opposites actually bear on the same subject, reality, in order to express and master it. "Scientific thought is only a more perfected form of religious thought. Hence it seems natural that religion should lose ground as science becomes better at performing its task." The scientific scrutiny of religion will grow. Nevertheless, religion will remain to help humans think in concepts, as does science, and thereby to participate in "a collective consciousness [which] sees things only in their permanent and fundamental aspect, which it crystallizes in ideas that can be communicated."[65]

Another struggle between psychiatry and science continues. Medicine, despite periodic calls for attention to the patient and not just the disease, continues to become more scientific, at least in its yearnings. Over the past 50 or so years, many doctors have narrowed their focus from the person to the organ to the cell to the molecule. Psychiatry, due to its urge for empirical respectability and also new findings on the material basis of certain disorders, continues along a similar path. Other times, however, psychiatry seeks to gain ground at the expense of medicine by finding psychological causes for various maladies. "There are, indeed, signs, that psychiatry, slowly and painfully delivering itself from the somatic super-stitions of medicine, may take its revenge by attempts to 'mentalize' large sections of medical theory and practice," Sapir predicted back in 1932. Nevertheless, he continued, psychiatry—or its lesser cousins of counsel-ing and therapy—often must apply itself to such immaterial or unscien-tific realms as the spirit. "The locus, then, of psychiatry turns out not to be the human organism at all in any fruitful sense of the word but the more intangible, and yet more intelligible, world of human relationships and ideas that such relationships bring forth."[66] For addicts in recovery, building a relationship with themselves, peers, loved ones, and, perhaps most of all, with some kind of deity or ultimate truth is the basis of their new lives. This deserves scrutiny and understanding.

William James, in *The Varieties of Religious Experience*, distilled what was left of the age of faith after its eclipse by science: "Faith is a personal gift, and if you have it, you are beyond argument." This summary was written by the literary critic Alfred Kazin almost 100 years after James's book appeared, during which time its truth has become only more com-monplace.[67] Daily, in private and public, one hears people assert the per-sonal experience of faith as infallible. At the same time and with no sense of contradiction, these same people will deny religious doctrine and its claims on society. Both positions can confound outside scrutiny. But belief has concrete results; "by their fruits ye shall know them." In an arti-cle updating James's thought, Dimitri Tymoczko summarized research that found emotional health to involve overoptimistic presumptions and an insensitivity to failure, and that optimists tend to be better adjusted and happier than realists are. "Overall, the psychological consensus seems to be that there can be a reasonably widespread conflict between truth and happiness," Tymoczko wrote. "The best beliefs, as James clearly intuited, are by no means the truest ones."[68]

With addicts, the matter may be simpler: either their spirituality works and they abstain, or it falters and they relapse or die. Addiction or death are obvious to outsiders; lesser shortfalls may not be. Addicts after treat-ment generally report accurately on their activities. But complicating mat-ters, and in a curious twist, the advent of the scientific age has allowed personal testimony to prevail over creeds and doctrine. Science has cast aside the broad religious declarations of truth and left only personal reli-gious experience beyond its reach. What a person said about her life of faith could not be doubted. As Kazin saw it, we convert not to God but to a realization of our own possibilities. The objective judgment of science restrains, but does not block, the truths we discover within. Experience verifies truths. If not, we find new ones to live by. In this approach, Tymoczko explains, beliefs can be seen as evolutionary adaptations and are justified only to the extent they help people survive.[69]

The truths reported by addicts could also smooth the rancorous contest between the penal and the medical approaches to addictions. A broader understanding of addiction based on the testimony of recovered addicts, which recognizes the role of spirituality, could accommodate the sentiments of a citizenry that must endorse treatment for it to succeed. The public senses, deeply and intuitively, that addiction inherently has a personal component, be it based on will power, morality, or spirituality. Doctors and policymakers routinely lament the alleged prejudice and ignorance of a public that sees alcoholism and illegal drug use as a moral rather than a public health issue. Could it not be both? Scientists just dig in their heels. When the Physician Leadership on National Drug Policy issued its 1998 findings that put addiction in the same league as other chronic diseases, colleagues spoke as if this was the final rebuke to non-scientific understandings. Chairwoman June Osborn told *USA Today* that though addicts bear responsibility for their plight, the evidence is unequivocal that addiction is a disease. "We were telling people to 'just say no' when addiction is a biological event," Osborn said.[70] A biological event? Where is the room for the person, for choice and responsibility? Scientific fundamentalism contradicts the experience of millions of recovered addicts.

Dangers to Spirituality

Using scientific measures to analyze and quantify a transcendent realm could wreak havoc in a sensitive area. "One of the most spiritually harmful things I have seen therapists and treatment centers do is hand patients a 'spirituality assessment' in which a patient's spirituality is measured by a belief in God, the frequency of prayer and the number of times they think about God during the day, and the amount of services and sacrifice they give," writes Leo Booth. He favors evaluating the damage done by religion, especially in promoting a childlike dependence on God. Treatment needs to concentrate, Booth writes, on "finding the best tools for changing beliefs and behaviors of each patient to promote a healthy spirituality based on choice, responsibility and action."[71]

Another danger lies in the scientific quest for the soul. Scientists, and addicts, know that certain illegal drugs influence the pleasure center in the brain. Roy J. Mathew, director of the Duke (University) Alcoholism and Addictions Program, found that drugs such as marijuana stimulate the pleasure centers in the brain—by increasing blood flow to the anterior cingulate, where emotions become conscious—that are also acted upon by spiritual experiences. Both produce feelings of altered consciousness and dissociation. Mathew cautioned against one-dimensional genetic or neurochemical approaches to treatment, and lauded the ability of AA participation to induce spiritual experiences. But at the same time, Mathew speculated that addicts might be somehow defective. "My hope is that someday, we will understand the pleasure mechanism physiologically," Mathew says. "In other words, is there a fundamental flaw unique to an addict's pleasure sensation, and if so, what can you do to bring about change without taking more chemicals?"[72] While endorsing a treatment that induces pleasure without drugs, this line of reasoning promulgates the picture of addicts as physiologically handicapped. There may be points beyond which science cannot go. By another token, spirituality is inherently subjective. A person's report on these experiences is both irreducibly personal and uncontestable. From a scientific point of view, until we have a CAT scan image and the neurochemistry of the brain going through spiritual changes, we are left with what people say. That may be a good thing.

The real danger may lie in the drive for a purely physical approach to addiction and its treatment. During the early wave of managed care and other cuts in health spending, an addictions counselor in Washington, D.C. told me that patients at his program were being allowed a minimum of out-patient sessions, if that. More often, he said, the new regimen was a prescription for antidepressants and a list of Twelve-Step meetings. The temptation to cost-cutters can be strong. In one three-year study of 201 alcoholics, those who chose initially to attend AA were found to have total treatment costs that were about half of those for people who attended professional out-patient care. Both groups experience significant improvements to the same degree.[73] In general health care, it may only be only a matter of time before those who pay decide that for some problems prayer and faith should suffice and procedures beyond that are unauthorized. A survey of executives of health maintenance organizations found that more than 90 percent believe that personal prayer, meditation, or religious practices can help medical treatment or speed healing, and nearly three-fourths believe spirituality can cut health care costs. As Martin Miller of the *Los Angeles Times* noted, it is "a finding that could have implications for health care coverage."[74]

Granted, some addicts may need only a list of support groups and a prescription. A sizable portion of addicts requires the medical attention, nutrition, stability, and counseling treatment can provide. At the far extreme, treatment with a purely medical approach could also shut off a proven avenue for recovery, one that recognizes the higher faculties of patients.

While in Florida for my research, I looked up Sandy B., a recovered alcoholic and popular speaker at AA conventions and medical gatherings. After talking casually for a couple of hours at his apartment overlooking Tampa Bay and then at dinner, he told several stories of doctors who were eased out of professional treatment circles because they favored a spiritual solution to addictions and had promulgated this in the rehabs they ran.

"It's ego, just pure ego, because it's something they can't control," he said of the scientists and health professionals who focus research and treatment on chemistry and biology and neurology to the detriment of simpler, and road-tested, methods of Twelve-Step facilitation and support groups. The spectacle of wasted effort had Sandy reconsider the value of what had seemed a liberating stroke of insight and efficacy by AA's founders. He paused at his kitchen table, stacked with neat piles of personal financial forms and reports, stamps, stationery, and correspondence. His lively blue eyes, set off by a golf tan, stilled with regret. "Sometimes I'm sorry we ever said it was a disease."

Finally, if we treat addiction as a spiritual problem, at least for some people open to this sort of treatment or solution, we may begin to judge the person harshly. That is, a relapse could become a sign of a defective spiritual life, of sin, of a bad soul. This is the reason the AA founders declared alcoholism an illness or allergy, to remove or ease the moral stain and shame. At the same time, they also made the alcoholic responsible for taking steps into recovery, primarily by being open to a spiritual way of life, one that is largely self-determined but also invariably involves questions of morality. Ideally, society could learn to live with this paradox as well. I would argue that we have a better track record, as a society, of welcoming back the sinner—or behaviorally disordered, if you please—than we do those who have been labeled with brain diseases and disorders.

Free to Change

Those promoting the brain disease concept claim it reduces the stigma of addiction. But how will addicts benefit if other people view them as having a chronic, relapsing disease brought about by defective brains? To say addiction is not the person's fault, in this way, is to say they have a permanent condition—faulty neurochemistry, reprogrammed molecules—over which they have no control. While they may stop drinking or drugging, that deformed brain will still be in there, ready to high jack the addict back into their habit. So it should have come as no surprise when a 1999 Hazelden Foundation survey found that although most Americans believe alcoholism is a disease, many are biased against recovering alcoholics and addicts.[75] "The best way to combat stigma is to expect drug users to take advantage of treatment, harness their will to prevent relapse and become visible symbols of hard work and responsibility," wrote Sally L. Satel, a psychiatrist who has worked in methadone clinic. If you had to make a choice between having either a brain disease or a malady whose cause and solution rested with you, which would it be? By the same token, granting people with mental illness some role or responsibility in their recovery liberates. In that field, one result of the brain disease concept is that many of those in need can obtain medications, but not the more human treatments such as counseling, training, and housing.

Bill Clinton's final *mea culpa* a year after admitting his adultery marked the success of a choice that, though moral and true, also allowed him to sidestep a permanent psychological classification. For while sin is temporary, a mental health diagnosis can be forever. In the eyes of a scientifically inclined society, those so labeled cannot change. When the misdeeds in the Oval Office were first revealed, some labeled Clinton a sex addict. The president short-circuited the public psychoanalysis by saying he had done wrong and would repent. Instead of being labeled a compulsive sex-seeker, the public saw him as an adulterer and, rather quickly, moved on.

We are in danger of denying this choice to normal people whose behavior is habitually harmful and self-destructive—those with addictions and some forms of mental illness. As with any chronic condition, recovery from drug or alcohol addiction requires the person to assume responsibility for getting better. The mandarins of addictions and mental health research and administration are pushing another agenda.

Scientists may think that naming a purely physical basis for addiction liberates the addict. Instead, it reduces the addict to neurochemistry and burdens him or her with a permanent condition. Separately, two recovered alcoholics who have directed various treatment programs expressed the same truth to me: "You mean I have a brain disease? Now I'm really screwed." A survey of benefits personnel in 1998 found that "while most viewed mental illness as a biological problem, many viewed substance abuse as a character flaw."[76] More rigorous polling would, I suspect, find the same confusion among the public. Belief in a purely biological basis for mental illness has not accelerated acceptance of schizophrenics. To the average person, character is far more tractable than biology.

The founders of AA called alcoholism an illness or malady that affected the body, mind, and spirit. This reduced the moral stigma while also giving the addict the primary role in her or his recovery. "Change or die," newcomers are told. Other routes to recovery—whether secular, nonsectarian, or denominational—invariably emphasize personal responsibility and growth. For decades, alcoholics have been coming out of the closet. But once their problem is considered a brain disorder, they may rush back in. Consider the mentally ill person who commits a crime. Lawyers often advise such a defendant to take the rap rather than seek a defense in a psychiatric diagnosis, a permanent label that could lead to endless court-ordered incarcerations.

Several alcoholics, sober for years, told me they no longer inform new doctors of their past condition lest it hurt their health coverage. Brain disease sounds pretty hopeless. Better they say, with Clinton, "I erred," make amends and move on. For some, prescription drugs can help resolve mental illness and addictions. Even so, the person has a role, one that adds effectiveness, freedom, and dignity. The only way people can control their behavior, in whole or part, is if they feel responsible, to some degree, for their thoughts and actions. Calling addiction a brain disease threatens to steal that freedom and eliminate the chance for a new life. Spiritual approaches to addiction and recovery insist on personal accountability for damage done in the past and for present recovery. As the first 100 members of AA wrote in their seminal text, "But it is clear that we made our own misery. God didn't do it."[77]

"It is not really wrong to be alcoholic," says John MacDougall, Hazelden's supervisor of spiritual care, "but to recover the person needs a way of life that is more moral than that of the rest of the population. The [Twelve] Steps are a way to convert shame to guilt, guilt to responsibility, responsibility to amends, and amends to freedom."

A. Thomas McClellan of the University of Pennsylvania is among the hardest of hard-nosed scientists when it comes to measuring results. Despite his preference for data, he gives a big nod to the role of the transcendent in recovery when we spoke during a break at a conference.[78] "Spirituality is a matter of getting in touch with the senses that are blocked to you when you are in search for drugs," McClellan tells me in his hurried, practical tone. He also called it a byproduct of sobriety, but one cited by many recovering addicts as "the antithesis of the selfish quality of the addicted state." For most people who complete treatment, aftercare "functionally" consists of AA, NA, CA, and "the spiritual connection" these provide. "If you had to build a machine to help people with substance abuse you could not find a better one than AA—it's free, it's everywhere, and I am constantly amazed at what it does for people. I can tell you for a fact that people who go and stay in AA or NA get and stay better." Medications said McClellan, "relieve the symptoms but they do not give the person the interpersonal sense of well-being that comes from being in contact with a group." Joe Molea, the Florida doctor who treats other addicted professionals, takes it one step further. "If chemical dependency is a function of neurochemical imbalance, then recovery—prayer and meditation, conscious contact with a higher power, meetings—alters our biochemistry and allows our brain chemistry to heal."[79]

A pharmaceutical agent would not have released Eric from the state of mind underlying his addiction.

"For the first time I am feeling happy about myself," Eric tells me sitting in the spare common room of Freedom House, a publicly funded treatment center in Rochester.[80] It is during the early months of his abstinence, though he already shows a level of acceptance. "My ex-girlfriend called my parole officer, so I could face one to three years in state prison." Raised a Christian, Eric once considered his addiction a punishment for past wrongs. "But in talking to my grandmother, who said God wouldn't do that, I realized I gave myself over to the devil." I ask if God is helping him stay sober. "Yes and to stay focused. All I do is my prayers every night and every morning." He attends Twelve-Step meetings but also the Full Gospel Tabernacle, an evangelical church with many young people who put him at ease. "One day, they were talking about being set free. That really hit home with me."

CHAPTER VI

Our God, No God:
Religious Methods and Secular Approaches

Where does a person get the power to stop an addiction? God? Mind? Chemistry? Those are three common answers. So far, we have considered various routes to spiritual power. Chemistry—pharmaceutical agents that curb craving for drugs or block their affects—would be another book. One alternative to most recovery schemes lies outside the spiritual, in the human mind and person. There is yet another path to recovery, at the other end of the spectrum, which rejects the generic spirituality of mainstream treatment in favor of a specific religious approach to God. This chapter considers these two routes to sobriety. Despite stark differences, they share some fundamentals.

Substance abuse confronts a person with her or his dark side, the capacity for self-destruction or evil. To recover, addicts find a source of strength, some new way of thinking, feeling, or living, one that will enable them to survive with happiness, health, and purpose. Many find a God of some sorts, a higher power, through Twelve-Step treatment or groups. But thousands look elsewhere, either to some secular combination of right thinking and group support, or to a denominational God reached, say, through the Bible or the Qu'ran. Picture the spiritually inclined in the broad middle of a horizontal line. To the left place the "No God" people and to the right picture the "Our God" crowd. Many in both camps reject various elements of the AA philosophy or programs that utilize it. These usually include the notion of powerlessness and the need for a higher power, the importance of fellowship with other addicts and the emphasis on seeming religious exercises such as moral inventories, prayer and meditation. Both secular and religious camps seem equally wary of the so-called disease concept of addiction, universally preached in treatment programs.

In contrast, both religious and secular approaches focus on the person and her habit, not her DNA or neurochemistry. Both refuse to explain addiction in purely materialist or reductionist terms. Both offer a radical accountability, and say the person has to make a choice. Help in some form—God, willpower, rationality, email chat—is then available. The religious call the addiction and its related behaviors sin or, reasonably enough, evil; the secular or rationalist terms it a bad choice, or a problem that comes from heeding what one program, Rational Recovery, calls the "Beast" within.

The religious types may say that God is necessary, but that Jesus is the Way to God, echoing the way the first Christians spoke of their nascent religion. At the other extreme, secular types see no need for a deity in their decision to stop using drugs or drinking. It's a matter for the mind and will. A friend of long standing runs an inner-city drug treatment program and recovered in AA. Over many years he became fed up with its ideas and members and finally found a useful ideology in Rational Recovery. His method of abstinence: "You just don't do it."

In talking before various groups, I have encountered a range of hostile reactions to the generic spirituality of Twelve-Step fellowships and treatments. This was most striking among people who take their own religion seriously but who fault AA as a cult in which addicts "trade one addiction for another." These critics, in effect, say, "Religion or spirituality is good if it inspires you to do good; bad if you need it to stay alive." From another perspective, many well-educated people, both religious and secular, dislike the spectacle of dramatic conversions. These often act as if religion is fine so long as you keep it private and don't take it too seriously. As Thorstein Veblen warned years ago, society will tolerate many things except a breach of decorum. Deep faith, the kind that keeps an addict clean and sober, constitutes such a breach. Finally, Twelve-Step spirituality irritates many religious conservatives who consider it nonbiblical and, in its "whatever works, works" philosophy, nearly pagan.

Utility as a measure of an ideology's value offends many in mainstream religions as well. Catholic and Protestant intellectuals routinely dismiss "self-help" groups and their "feel-good" spirituality, reducing these to caricatures while ignoring their capacity to save lives. But what measure other than the effect on humans should we use to evaluate a belief system? "By their fruits ye shall know them," the Bible has it, not "by their roots."

In his entertaining and often well-reasoned jeremiad, *Diseasing of America*, Stanton Peele concludes that treating addictions is a matter of common sense and human coping. "The best thing people can do to solve or prevent addiction is to learn to control their destinies, to find social and work rewards, and to minimize stress and fear, including their fear of the addiction."[1] Who'd disagree with that? The question remains, what enables the addict to live in this manner?

Our God

All through history, lost souls have retrieved themselves with the help of God and religion. The success of mainstream treatment and the mainstream recovery movement—each propagating a nonsectarian, results-oriented spirituality—eclipses the fact that countless numbers of addicts sober up through denominational channels. Some draw on the traditional elements of their faith—prayer, liturgy, dogma, piety, community, sacraments, meditation. Others use denominational treatment schemes. In most cases, these are run by the more conservative or fringe denominations, such as evangelical and Pentecostal Christians or the Nation of Islam. Mainstream religions—Episcopal, Jewish, Catholic, and the like—tend to support mainstream, nondenominational rehabs, often through a separate agency as Jewish Family Services or Catholic Charities. Usually, these agencies do the work for religious reasons, but their respective religion is not part of the aid given an individual. To some eyes, it appears as if they lack faith in their own religion. For them, the answer lies in clinical treatment and the diffuse spirituality of Twelve-Step groups. Their generally more conservative counterparts unabashedly promote a specific faith as the answer. Denominational approaches to recovery share certain elements: a religious faith with varying degrees of doctrine; reliance on the group; confession, which fits with the testimonial tradition of evangelical churches; conversion and support within the larger church community.

Though a religious regimen will not appeal to all or even most addicts, it has great potential for some. "Religion remains an almost universal attribute of our culture," John Muffler, John G. Langrod and David Larson wrote in an authoritative textbook chapter on religious treatments.[2] In 1922, Max Weber made the same point of all societies in *The Sociology of Religion*. And religion, as Abraham Joshua Heschel argued, offers insights into the ultimate questions, taking us where reason cannot. The religious milieu reverses the tendency of our science-based society to trivialize humanity even as it helps us search for meaning. As Muffler and colleagues write:

"The religious traditions remind us that humanity is quite willing to endure sacrifice, discipline, and moral and spiritual exaltation in pursuit of an ultimate commitment to freedom and dignity. We are also reminded that, in the name of human freedom and dignity, we are accountable for our choices and actions; and, as such, people are capable of forgiving and being forgiven, of starting anew."

Further, religion is a communal product and experience. It transforms and reinforces the group, which in turn preserves and renews religious content and ritual. Religion serves a purpose: it is an aid to living. In and through the group, a person feels the joy, security, peace, and energy that she or he then sees as proof of the religion's power.[3] A person who feels these emotions strongly often senses or declares that she has undergone a conversion—a critical stage in many religions, especially those that favor treating social and personal problems as addiction with their religion in undiluted form.

Teen Challenge: Saving Souls and Regaining Lives with Jesus

Teen Challenge dates back almost as long as other long-standing forms of treatment such as the Twelve-Step-style Minnesota model or therapeutic communities. David Wilkerson, who ministered to street gangs in New York, founded Teen Challenge in 1958 and told the story in his best-selling *The Cross And The Switchblade*. Forty years later, Teen Challenge had grown to more than 120 centers in the United States and 250 centers worldwide. The philosophy states that there is hope for every addict, sin is the root of the problem, and Jesus is the only cure.[4]

For most, the program lasts 12 months. The first three to five months are at a local induction center in a small, "home-like" setting with time for Bible study and character development. Teen Challenge announces in its literature that "this new way of living can only be achieved and maintained for life when built on a personal relationship with Jesus Christ." There is work, group, individual, music, and recreation therapy. Then comes eight to ten months at a training center, the main one in a rural setting in Rehrersburg, Pennsylvania.[5]

Charlie Muller is an ex-boxer and car salesman who founded Victory Christian Church in a one-story former post office on a commercial row in the heart of a busy working-class and commercial Albany neighborhood. With a muted red-and-blue nylon shirt and longish hair—the style of a man bridging youth and age, the streets and the pulpit—he flops down into the embrace of a stuffed chair. Muller manages to be both garrulous and weary at the same time. He's enjoying life, but it's a burden. Off to the side of his office, a receptionist murmurs a prayer on the telephone with a caller. In a recent project, Muller is starting an induction center, Albany Challenge, that will help young addicts, aged 16-22, stabilize and find Jesus before they move on to the Rehrersburg training center.

Once he gets talking about the young addicts he has seen find sobriety through Jesus Christ, Muller leans forward, jumps up to fetch pamphlets from a file and speaks with a mix of faith, joy, and street-savvy qualifiers. "You probably were an English major," he tells me, "and you know about words. There are only so many ways to read the words in the Bible, in Romans 10 that you must believe in Jesus Christ and believe with your heart to be saved."[6]

For Muller, Jesus is the doorway—the only one—to God. And for an addict to get clean via Christian faith, man's role is limited to helping

God, who issues the call. "It's the move of God in a touch upon a person's life that we're looking for. When these kids get indoctrinated with the Word of God, hear lessons, and read the Bible, that's when the Lord can come in to work. It's got the answer for everything in life."

Such a single-minded faith led the church to cancel its food pantry, which once drew long lines, as a distraction from the real answer for those with problems. "Now if a person comes here and says, 'I need help and I'll walk your way, give it a try,' we'll help them." During the induction phase of Teen Challenge, there are Bible study and chapel services daily. It's a matter of laying out the meal and seeing if the person eats. "We want to see if they'll make the trip," says Muller, who is happy to leave the heavy lifting to the deity. "We have prayer time, and God shows up."

At the next stage, the training camp in Rehrersburg, Pennsylvania the youths continue Bible and chapel as they begin learning new work skills in farming, roofing, auto mechanics, and other crafts. Muller knows that not all will accept the challenge. Of the 20 youths who graduated from Albany Challenge's induction phase, only half completed the training camp phase. He tells the parable of the farmer who sowed seed, some upon fruitful soil and most upon infertile or weedy land. All Teen Challenge can do, he says, is offer the addict the choice. "Many are called but few are chosen," Muller says.

Since its early years, Teen Challenge claimed a 70 percent "cure rate" for graduates of its program. A study funded by the National Institute on Drug Abuse tracked all students in the class of 1968 that entered a Teen Challenge program in Brooklyn, New York and checked their status seven years later. Catherine Hess, a doctor and former government health official, directed the study and the National Opinion Research Center of the University of Chicago developed it.[7]

Of all 186 boys who entered, 24 percent reported they never returned to the use of narcotics after their time in Teen Challenge. Many dropped out, as is true of all types of treatment—Hess put the graduation rate at 18 percent. Of the 64 youth who had completed the entire program, including time at the Rehrersburg Training Center, 67 percent were drug-free as indicated by the urinalysis test while 86 percent reported being so; 75 percent were employed; and 88 percent did not require additional drug treatment. Hess found one anomaly, which may indicate nothing more than the tendency of adolescents to reject the way of their parents even in matters of faith. Nearly three-fourths of boys who were not religious upon entry completed the program, while 80 percent of those who had been churchgoers at age 12 dropped out during induction.

Like many treatment schemes, Teen Challenge tries to give addicts what they are missing, but in personal and religious, rather than clinical, nomenclature. "Teen Challenge evaluates the weakness in a person," says

Muller. "You really listen to the person, see where they went wrong. 'Who raised you? What was it like?' Kids come in here, they have no home life, no discipline. Teen Challenge focuses on that and trains them. Some come here, and they were never loved so they can't love themselves." Nevertheless, he sees plenty of room for hard-headed pressure.

Down the street from his church, stands a house long-used as a "wet" shelter for street alcoholics. Abstinence is not required, which Muller says merely enables the sin to continue. "There has to be challenge in a person's life, or a pressure. I know a lot of the guys on the street. They'll go to jail, sober up, get out, and go back drinking. The system will take care of them." He stares at me dolefully and shakes his head. For Muller, AA-style recovery can fall short. "They go to God as a higher power, but the Bible says you can't get to God unless you go through Christ. He's the door."

Profile: Jim—"God touched my mind"

Jim, a self-employed insurance inspector who lives in a semirural area southeast of Troy, New York, stopped his self-destructive drinking and drug abuse 20 years ago through Teen Challenge. The program opened his eyes to an essential lesson: "God is love and he's good and he wants to bring us all to heaven. I found that out from the Bible, and the Teen Challenge Bible study gave me a start." That conviction keeps Jim sober.[8]

He grew up on the New York side of the Berkshire Mountains in a home that had horses, a tennis court, and a pool, but little love and lots of drinking, he says. Jim drank from ages 13 to 21. "If I was awake, I was partying." Then several criminal charges and a bad LSD trip coincided with his parents' conversion to Christianity at a Pentecostal church.

"They told me they would help me if I went to this program, Teen Challenge. To me, I didn't need Jesus, I needed help. I had no hope, no joy, no feelings. But my father had changed, I saw the change. I watched him pour several hundred dollars worth of booze down the drain. Then they started saying grace before meals. I thought, "Maybe there's something to it." After a few days at the Teen Challenge induction center in Harrisburg, Pennsylvania, where he began reading the Bible, Jim came home for the funeral of a brother he had always resented. His life changed.

"When I heard he died, I thought, 'That's what happens.' I didn't feel anything. But at home, I walked into my mother's bedroom and I just started to weep. I thought, 'What's going on here?' I hadn't cried, or felt anything, in years. I ran out of the house and walked down the road and I just started to notice things. The grass was green, the sky was blue." Jim speaks of this moment as if the colors and smells were still before him.

He returned to Teen Challenge and completed the year-long program after moving on to the training camp in Rehrersburg. A drug-induced confusion left him thanks, Jim says, to the prayers of others and his own growing faith. "God touched my mind. I still had problems, but from that point on I was in my right mind. I'm not Mr. Holy Roller, believe me. But I still believe in Christ—I'll never leave him."

In God, Jim found the means to transcend his addiction. This simple but profound change in perspective resembles the shift sought in every form of addictions treatment, from cognitive behavioral to Twelve-Step-based to native American to secular, albeit in different terms. "God gave me something higher to live for, because if you don't have something higher to live for, what's the point? These kids, they don't have that, and they're just, 'Let's just live it up and die.' That's the problem."

Jim says most religion, even most Christian churches and ministers, confuse the issue and preach bad doctrine: "God is not religion, He's life." Jim emphasizes that though Teen Challenge got him going, he does not agree with all its teachings either.

Paraphrasing the popular verse from the Gospel of John, Jim speaks breathlessly as he dismisses the popular Christian notion that God tests humans with periods of suffering and trial. "Jesus died so that we may have life and have it more abundantly. That doesn't mean we're not going to make mistakes, but Jesus paid the price once and for all of us. We don't have to do that over again." I ask about avoiding the near occasion of alcohol or drugs. Jim laughs as if reminded of something he forgot. "I enjoy life now, I don't need it. If God is real and on your side, what's there to worry about?"

Nation of Islam

Muhammad's Mosque, a Nation of Islam outpost, occupies a white and red storefront on the northern end of Lark Street, where Albany's condensed version of Greenwich Village fades away. Mothers and children sit and play on the front stoops of several of the brick and stone townhouses, while other buildings sport signs for software firms. Though surrounded by Arbor Hill, a proud but struggling neighborhood where drug busts and sirens are common, these blocks are calm. An outsider on foot feels safe. No clumps of men with cell phones and leather jackets loiter suspiciously on the corner waiting for motorists to pull up and buy packets of cocaine or heroin.

Even when the Nation's men, in their narrow-lapelled suits and stiff bowties, are not on patrol, selling their newspapers or foodstuffs such as bean pies and frozen fish, one senses their presence. Minister Linwood Muhammad, the long-time Nation leader here, explains why. "When we came here, drugs were being sold like food at Price Chopper," he says, naming a local supermarket. "We put flyers out, that there would be no selling drugs from Washington Avenue to Clinton Avenue on Lark. We cleaned this up."[9]

Tall, poised, his ebony skin shining across the dome of a shaven head, Minister Linwood seems amused by his imposing presence. I'd be afraid to litter on this block. The force that tidied up this neighborhood, leaving a penumbra of fear and awe in the air, also works in the lives of many Nation members who were once hard-core drug addicts. As of 1997, the Albany mosque reports 55 members. At the time, Linwood also led a group of about 60 in Montreal. (Linwood and his two groups later split off from the Nation and in 2000 he died of a heart ailment.)

The Nation considers itself a branch of Islam, the monotheistic faith that has about one billion members worldwide. Islam teaches that God delivered the fundamentals of its faith through the angel Gabriel to Mohammed in the seventh century. Adherents live by the five pillars of the faith, which require them to worship Allah, the one God; pray five times a day; fast during the month-long Ramadan; contribute to the needy; and, if possible, make at least one pilgrimage to Mecca. They view Jesus as a prophet along with Adam, Noah, Abraham, Moses, and Muhammad.

While hard to pin down, estimates of all Muslims in the United States range up to five or six million and the total is growing rapidly.[10] Among these, the Nation of Islam is a tiny but visible slice: 20,000 in 1993. By the late 1990s, Albany had about 100. The Nation of Islam was founded by Elijah Muhammad in Chicago during the 1930s and has been the target of complaints about racial separatism and anti-Semitism. After Elijah's death in 1975, his son Warith Deen Mohammed broke with the Nation of Islam and led followers back to traditional Islam, which has no talk of separating people by race. In turn, the fiery and eloquent Louis Farrakhan revived the Nation with appeals to black responsibility and empowerment. In Albany, civic leaders regarded the group's work with disadvantaged people with wary respect.

One evening at the mosque, Minister Linwood and three of other men—each smartly dressed, short-haired, stiffly erect in posture, and scarily alert—tell me of finding surcease from lives of drugs, alcohol, crime, and chaos. They address each other using the title "Brother" followed by the first name. (And like most recovered addicts, they want to protect their identity.) The Nation teaches that most black family names in America are those of slaveholders, and these are often replaced by "X," as in Malcolm X, until a new name, based on a desirable quality, is assigned.

Brother Harun, 25, recalls how his greatest desire, as a 19-year-old in Brooklyn, "was to live a life of hurting people." His family dispatched

Harun to a brother in Albany. When Harun kept up the drugs and failed to stay in school, the brother kicked him out. "I was walking down the block with a quart of gin in my pocket when someone invited me to the mosque." Though still mentally befogged, Harun liked what he saw and heard. "They were about helping other black people. I knew it was right but I didn't understand it. I came back the next day and made up my mind to join on the doorstep."

While attending a lesson by Minister Linwood, Harun spoke out of turn, violating an informal rule of silence for newcomers. "These men all swarmed around me but Minister Linwood stopped them and said to me, 'Look at these men. They used to drink and drug like you but today they stand proud.' " Harun continues. "I continued to come and I continued to come and I slowly gained the power to leave behind that life and habits and associates."

Today, he works as a construction laborer and has repaired relations with his family. Harun reads the Qu'ran, sells the Nation newspapers on the streets and attends lessons and services at the mosque. Naming the reason for his rehabilitation is difficult, though Harun points to a mix of religion, decision, and example. "It's not hard if you don't think it's hard. You just know what's right and what's wrong. Before I knew but I didn't have the power." He nods toward Linwood. "Here, it's the message and that man."

Brother Edward, 44, knew about the Nation as a boy. His grandmother was involved with an earlier incarnation of the local mosque but his strict father opposed the group. Years later, despite an education and a good job, Edward used and sold drugs. Then, "I found myself in search of God." In 1985, he heard Farrakhan speak in New York and later attended a lecture by Minister Linwood. "He told me to seek refuge in God and said to change the way you've been making decisions. That alone touched me enough to want more, to change."

Brother Edward joined in 1991 and has been clean of drugs during that time. "I'm different because there's God in my life." He lives, works, and even socializes with whites, and sees the Nation's message of racial separation as a means to each group earning the other's respect. Nation members believe that separation—the degrees vary—will lead to self-sufficiency. Then, blacks will be able to live alongside whites.

Minster Linwood grew up in a family of preachers. An early lesson in the value of separatism came when, as a child during the 1960s, he had to leave the comfort of a black school for the pain of being a minority in a white school. "It brings tears to my eyes remembering that," he says with feeling. (Many older African Americans, and sociologists, trace the collapse of black communities and enterprises to integration.)

Linwood married young, and began drinking and taking drugs. To "cure" his heroin habit, he ended up on methadone. He was living in the

South End of Albany, where he was impressed by the Nation of Islam members who evangelized the neighborhood. In 1970, Linwood joined and kicked the methadone, "cold turkey, in one month and two weeks." In the mid-1970s, the Nation split over the departure of Warith Deen Mohammed and the Albany group fell apart. Many members returned to drugs and the street, he says. Linwood became a Baptist preacher and resumed drinking until he was treated at a Veterans' Administration program in 1987 and became a counselor.

One night while driving home from counseling sessions at a prison, he had a vision of Elijah Muhammad sitting in the back seat of the car saying, "That's not your message." Despair over the plight of fellow blacks rose up within him. "I came back to Albany and saw people on the street, on drugs and drinking, and I said, 'Oh God,' and I began to cry. I didn't want to preach anymore." He knew he wanted to help others recover, and to rejoin the Nation, but there was a stumbling block: Elijah Muhammad's teachings, reiterated by Farrakhan, that white people were the enemy.

"White people in recovery had been like a father, uncles, brothers to me, and now I was supposed to cut them off." In 1989, he resolved the issue. "I heard that my higher power speaks through other people. I wondered, 'What about this thing that white people are the devil?' I just prayed and went back and studied the Bible and God gave it to me—it's not a person's color that makes them the devil, it's their mind. It's what's inside you, the content of your character, as Dr. King taught."

Linwood compares his journey to that of Moses and others whom God tested in order to teach. "I was brought up in a good family, I had religion—the Nation of Islam, orthodox Islam, the Baptists—and I still fell. God allowed me to become a homeless alcoholic so I could have a spiritual experience, so my relationship could be based on God and not on Minister Farrakhan or anyone else."

Linwood seeks out African-Americans with drug or drinking habits, which is central to his own recovery as well as his ministerial mission. "Most of our members come from a lifestyle of crime and drugs." Members—most are men—must work, respect and provide for their family, and not drink, smoke, or swear. (The Nation teaches women to stay home and rear the children.)

"We don't sit and wait for sinners to come, we go out and look for them on Clinton Avenue." Linwood predicts the races will meet on spiritual grounds, and notes that many Nation members have a white parent. "A lot of [black] people say, 'Well, white people should do this or that.' I say no. As Elijah Muhammad said, the best thing white people did was set us free. Now be free."

Linwood says he learned a lesson during his own recovery, when a new relationship with God enabled him to stop killing himself with drugs and alcohol. "We need to come up out of the basement and into the spirituality of God. Racism will exist until we realize that we will only heal with God."

As I sit in the sanctum of Muhammad's Mosque, what had been my interview changes into a lesson from Linwood. The group in the room falls into its more familiar roles: Minister Linwood preaching vigorously, the men listening and affirming.

"Yes, sir. Mmm-hmm. Yes," came the intent chorus.

I interrupt to ask a question and violate protocol. The men snap around, ready to throng about the interloper—me!—I realize with alarm. Linwood rears back, then smiles magisterially. He waves the men back into their seats and laughs in that rich, bracing tone of his that is so much like his ministry, at once an embrace and a challenge.

Union Gospel Mission in St. Paul, Minnesota: "Here Jesus Is the Boss"

On the northeast, industrial edge of St. Paul, a 20-minute stroll from downtown's glassy offices perched above the Mississippi, tractor-trailers rumble along a pitted boulevard under an overpass to and from several nearby highway ramps. Off this byway turn old cars and workers' vans into the parking lot of the Union Gospel Mission, one in the venerable, international network of missions that help "the least, the last, and the lost" of society in a nondenominational Christian atmosphere. The missions date back to 1826, when David Naismith founded the first in Glasgow, Scotland.

Drivers steer past the main building, where several grizzled men slouch and the meals are handed out, to the Christ Recovery Center in the back—no slouching here, perhaps the difference between handouts and self-help. A growing crowd crackles with Friday-night energy. About seven in ten are men and eight in ten are white with ages averaging 40. They pour into a modest brick building that could pass for a state college dormitory. A handful linger at the edges, dirty and smelly and shy—the before picture. Most of the others are clean, happy, and well-pressed men who bear fading traces of life on the streets—a wind-burned forehead or cavernous wrinkles. That's the after shot. Some more prosperous types—business people, retirees, housemakers—arrive as well. I surge in with the various groups, everyone calling out names and pumping hands and beaming at the transformed versions of so many former drunken hobos. We array ourselves around cafeteria tables in a tiled room. On a small stage in the front, a band warms up—three rhythm guitarists plugging and tuning, a singer, and a lead guitarist tapping the microphones.

A tall, vigorous guitarist with white hair and bushy mustache—Christ Recovery Center's director, Larry Bonniwell—leads the crowd into "On the Wings of a Dove." The crowd, cajoled and berated by Bonniwell, sings lustily, half in pleasure and half in deadly earnest: "On the wings of a snow-white dove; He sends His pure sweet love; a sign from above, on the wings of a dove." Then it's into "One Day at a Time," which harnesses the popular AA slogan to Christian hope: "One day at a time, sweet Jesus; That's all I'm asking of you."

Posters on the cinder-block walls record a late twentieth-century blend of Bible-thumping evangelism and addiction self-help: Warner Sallman's painting of an long-faced Jesus pleading for his life in the Garden of Gethsemane, the Optimists International Creed, the Twelve Steps of Alcoholics Anonymous. Between songs, Bonniwell congratulates several people on their progress into sobriety. A female singer speaks a few inspiring words. After an hour or so, the group throws itself into the soul-ful "Me and Jesus." The hymn blends our society's cantankerous individualism and what Harold Bloom has characterized as the search of the American Protestant for time alone with Jesus in the garden. "Me and Jesus got our own thing going," they sing. "We don't need anybody to tell us what it's all about." The finale, "I Saw The Light," draws in the last reluctant singers.

Flushed with exertion and adrenaline after leading the sing-along, Larry Bonniwell talks briefly about his use of the Twelve Steps. "Yes, we tell them to find a higher power, but here Jesus is the boss." The next day, sitting in his cramped office adorned with plaques and baseball caps and small stacks of paper, Bonniwell speaks in more measured tones.[11]

Union Gospel Mission in St. Paul dates to 1902. In 1970, two recovering alcoholics—George and Mary Jo Robinson—founded Christ Recovery Center on the basis of AA-style treatment "but with an evangelical-style Christianity added that offered brotherhood and acceptance to lost souls."[12] One graduate, 48-year-old Tommy says the faith-based fellowship is the program's critical ingredient. "You feel like you're a part of the family, and most of these guys have no family."

Along with the mission's smaller Drydock program at rural Snail Lake Camp, the center can handle 66 men, 22 of them in the three to five month primary treatment program and the rest in the transitional phase, which can last up to two years. The center subscribes to the once-traditional notion of addiction, best articulated in the book *Alcoholics Anonymous*, as a three-fold malady of the spirit, mind, and body, with treatment focused on the first element.

Almost all funds come from donations. Residents pay nothing, though they share in chores. "Work therapy" is a key part of the treatment. According to a brochure, the Christ center is dedicated to the "Master Healer." But the highway is broad and the mansion has many rooms. "The three cornerstones here are AA, spirituality, and brotherhood," says Bonniwell. "They will be exposed to Christian values and concepts while here. But it is still 'God as they understand him,' " he adds, using the catch-all phrase from the AA Twelve Steps. "From time to time, we see come through native Americans, Muslim, Jewish men. They roll with the punches."

"Our thrust is spirituality. If we can energize a person's spirituality and that becomes part of them, then the other elements, the physical and mental, will improve and the recovery will be long-lasting."

If properly recognized and developed, Bonniwell says, "Our spirit will never allow us to use. Spirituality varies with each person. It boils down to truth, what is the truth for that individual." The days start early and last into the night. Residents attend morning meetings, usually keyed to a meditation or prayer, Big Book meetings for the study of the AA text, "feelings" meetings, and "attitudes" meetings. There is also a regular "Stepping Through Scripture" meeting, a spiritual study of the Twelve Steps of AA or NA and how these relate to the Bible.

In its use of the AA Twelve Steps, Christ Recovery Center differs from most Union Gospel Mission programs, which generally offer solely a Bible based Christianity. No one can be mandated here by legal authorities given the center's religious character, though Bonniwell reports that some are steered this way quietly through Minnesota's centralized referral system. As a result, the residents—almost all chronic, impoverished street alcoholics—come and stay voluntarily. One impediment is that most are rehab veterans who can put on a show of compliance without changing inside.

"The main body of men have been indoctrinated in this stuff, they've been through treatment four or five times," Bonniwell says. The staff and senior residents try to break through any resistance a newcomer may have. "You can't play games here. If you do, you're out." The center works to energize the residents' souls and, through "repetition and affirmations" to give them the tools—practical hope, coping skills—necessary for a sober life. A foundation of willingness helps, Bonniwell says. "All are here because they want to be here."

The center has tracked 210 persons who went through the Christ Recovery Center. Over the years, about half the entrants regularly complete treatment, Bonniwell reports. Of those, about one-third are sober five years later. He takes no credit. At most, Bonniwell says the center helps the person find in Jesus, and the Twelve Steps, a path to abstinence. "The miracle we see here is to walk down the hall and see a guy looking different and say, 'Holy s——, he got it!' And it's nothing we did here."

No God: Secular Approaches to Recovery

Some in the secular camp see no role for a deity in their recovery, while others insist on using only the most oblique reference to matters transcendent. In their attitude toward spirituality and the monolith of Twelve-Step-style treatment, secular recovery groups run the gamut from being open or tolerant, such as Women for Sobriety, to the outright hostility of Rational Recovery. In the middle, as it were, is the newest but perhaps the fastest growing of the lot, Secular Organizations for Sobriety or SOS. Like AA or NA, these are self-help and not treatment. Only a handful of rehab programs make use of their methods. In the most common scenario, if a client resists the Twelve-Step approach, a counselor may refer that person to a secular support group meeting or hand over some literature. Most members of these groups join directly on their own. All three groups draw on the lessons of cognitive therapies and believe in the power of the person to change their habits and lives.

Secular Organizations for Sobriety

In 1978, James R. Christopher sobered up from alcoholism, which dated to his teen years, with some help from AA. Uncomfortable with the emphasis on a higher power and what he considered a religious atmosphere, he explored secular humanism. Christopher expressed his philosophy in an article, "Sobriety Without Superstition," in *Free Inquiry*, a journal published by the Council for Secular Humanism. Hundreds responded and Christopher moved temporarily to Buffalo to work under the auspices of the council while starting SOS.

The council is based in nearby Amherst, also home to the American Humanist Organization, Prometheus Books—that publishes SOS and other secular humanist volumes—and the Committee for the Scientific Investigations of Claims of the Paranormal. A common thread is the philosopher and State University of New York professor Paul Kurtz, who edited the American Humanist's magazine and founded the other three entities. A colleague jokingly explained the concentration of groups there: "Once you've experience a couple of Buffalo winters you lose all faith in a loving God." The American Humanist Organization also helped start Rational Recovery.

Christopher moved back to Los Angeles to run a branch office of the Council for Secular Humanism, and held the first SOS meeting in 1986 in North Hollywood. By the early 1990s, SOS reported 20,000 members in all states and several foreign lands. In 1999, membership was up to an estimated 100,000. In its literature, much of it listed on a thorough website, SOS describes itself as a support system free of religious or spiritual content and based on self-reliance and free thought.

Christopher laid out the SOS philosophy in several books, initially *How To Stay Sober: Recovery Without Religion*. A more recent volume is the product of a maturing fellowship and aims to introduce members to the basic ideas and help them start meetings. In *Sobriety Handbook: The SOS Way, An Introduction to Secular Organizations for Sobriety*, Christopher notes that while SOS groups vary, all share three features: "they are secular, they are sober, and they are self-help."[13]

SOS draws much of its thinking from cognitive-behaviorist and motivational schools of thought. It draws on the person's "vital inner desire to remain sober,"[14] just as the AA literature refers to the alcoholic's survival instinct and the fact that "nature abhors a vacuum." Also like AA, SOS stumbles in the thicket of mind and matter. Its website section on *Frequently Asked Questions* states that, "We tend to think that alcoholism is fundamentally a health problem and that religion has no more role to play here than it does in the treatment of diabetes, melanoma, schizophrenia, hay fever, or psoriasis, for example." Elsewhere the group welcomes scientific inquiry into addictions and solutions. But then *The Sobriety Handbook* ridicules "the few books by 'scientists' seeking to revolutionize recovery by 'proving' that the process of addiction can be reversed, or cured, or that it doesn't exist to begin with."[15]

Such contradictions are ubiquitous. Throughout the treatment field and recovery movement, people call addiction a disease over which a person has no control, but then prescribe solutions that involve a great deal of personal initiative. People in all types of self-help, spiritual, and secular, talk about their responsibility to work on recovery. At the same time, many objectify their addictive tendency as if it were an outside, demonic entity. Many AA members say such things as "my disease is doing pushups," or "my disease is talking to me." Rational Recovery refers to the self-destructive desire to drink as the beast, and SOS, which sets abstinence as the goal, warns that unbound appetites can drive the addict to relapse. The paradoxical nature of addiction, a malady that affects body, mind, and spirit, is responsible for the confusion, which may never be fully resolved. Safest to say that recovery, also, involves body, mind, and spirit.

Tom Flynn, a senior editor at *Free Inquiry* and a colleague of Christopher at the Council for Secular Humanism, traced the success of SOS to the need for a meaningful alternative to Alcoholics Anonymous, both in self-help and in treatment. "There are differences from meeting to meeting, but overall the AA experience is pretty intensely religious," Flynn says. "Primarily, there is an insistence that the person surrender to a higher power. If a person doesn't do that, he will probably have a hard time fitting in." AA and related groups concede room for the agnostic and atheist and members emphasize that each defines her or his higher power and pursues their own spirituality. But AA's defining characteristic, says Flynn, "is that the person has to rely on an outside power for recovery. In SOS, the person draws on their own resources and takes the credit for their sobriety and achievement. AA is other-empowerment, SOS is self-empowerment."[16]

Indeed, SOS—much like Rational Recovery—defines itself largely as the uncola of self-help. On one level, this seems sensible—any new recovery scheme has to set itself apart from the mainstream. Oedipal animosity tinges all breakaway movements. A 1997 guidebook, *The Sobriety Handbook: The SOS Way*, makes many such references as to AA's "pronounced religious orientation," or the group's "compulsory religiosity." SOS makes clear "we are not a cult," and that it does not require or suggest that members undergo "a religious or spiritual 'awakening' or conversion experience."[17]

Many a visitor to Twelve-Step meetings has been impressed by what appear to be religious trappings: moments of silence, recitation of the Lord's Prayer, mentions of God and higher power, and an emphasis on spiritual awakenings. These do drive away, or at least discourage, many people, especially those mandated to meetings by a judge or spouse and looking for a reason to reject any recovery scheme. As the testimonies of SOS members in their book attest, seemingly religious practices such as recital of the Lord's Prayer can drive away those uncomfortable with that ritual. However, many who stay report that these Twelve-Step fellowships prescribe little in the way of a spiritual life other than an addict develop one to her or his own liking, one that aids recovery. When utility is the test, dogma rarely survives.

In the early 1990s, the Buffalo based Research Institute on Addictions surveyed 158 SOS members. Gerard Connors, the primary researcher, said SOS deserves study since it was being presented as an alternative to AA and due to its rapid growth. The survey found that a majority of SOS members surveyed were white, well-educated, employed men over the age of 40. A quarter were women. Though 70 percent reported no religious affiliation, only 37 percent were atheist, 33 percent were agnostic, and 22 percent fell into the "spiritual/nonchurchgoer" category. Most— 70 percent—reported being abstinent from alcohol, on average 6.3 years. As for drug use, 68 percent had used drugs at least once and 88 percent were drug-free for an average of 7.7 years. While many chose SOS for its secular character, antireligiosity was not a defining characteristic for members. In the RIA survey, only 43 percent said that what they liked most about SOS was "no religion," while 48 percent cited "people, interpersonal factors." Among the elements of SOS that were not helpful, 15 percent checked off "AA- or religion-bashing."[18]

While secular self-help groups have usually been founded in a rejection of AA, SOS professes a benign attitude toward the Twelve-Step fellowships. Many members make use of both, which is also true among Women for Sobriety members. Connors and his colleague, Kurt H. Dermen, found that almost all SOS members surveyed had attended at least one AA meeting, with half having gone to more than 100. And 29 percent planned to continue with AA, in addition to SOS, over the long term. Connors and Dermen speculated that many find the two organizations complementary, given AA's stability and ubiquity and SOS's freedom from dogma and religion.

An SOS member from Ohio wrote to the group's newsletter that Christopher's writings "did seem able to take the best of AA—the one day at a time, the daily commitment to sobriety, keeping it your first priority (all the practical stuff I never had a problem with)—without the worst." Interestingly, this woman objected to AA precisely because she was religious, a Catholic convert active in her church. "Yet every time I go to AA I lose God," she wrote. "The God of AA is harsher than the one I had. The God of AA is one who demands submission and sees intellect as the enemy."[19]

SOS, like other secular approaches, has grown in numbers and in its use by rehabilitation programs as an alternative to the Twelve-Step approach. Many SOS members, without a local group to attend, stay in touch with others—often around the world—via the organizations' email list. Officials at prisons and jails, alert to the court rulings against exclusive use of the spiritually oriented Twelve-Step methods, are expanding their offerings. SOS reports that it is now the leading alternative to AA-style treatment in Texas state prisons.

In letters reprinted by SOS, prison officials there told Christopher that "SOS is flourishing inside the prison settings" and that it helped addicted convicts who "had serious personal misgivings whenever the issue of God is raised, even 'the God of your understanding.' " They welcomed a secular approach for the "growing segment of our population" that rejects spiritual concepts.[20]

Women for Sobriety

Women for Sobriety, founded in 1976 by Dr. Jean Kirkpatrick, helps women achieve abstinence through positive reinforcement, cognitive strategies such as positive thinking, and "letting the body help" via relaxation techniques, meditation, diet, and physical exercise. The basic philosophy: "Forget the past, plan for tomorrow and live for today." While encouraging spiritual growth, WFS does not preach it as the solution nor does its literature refer to God or a higher power or other explicitly religious concepts. "I tried to straddle the fence on that one," Kirkpatrick says during an interview, speaking in a kind, husky voice—a product of the sensible compassion evident in her writings and her assorted respiratory ailments. "There are so many women who have a problem with a higher power. It certainly helps to have a spiritual awakening, but it is not necessary. Authority is an issue with women, and AA adds more dependencies: upon a higher power, upon a sponsor, and upon meetings, which they are supposed to attend for the rest of their life."[21]

Kirkpatrick even recommends members avoid excessive or long-term reliance on the WFS. That suggestion guarantees an unsteady membership as women come in, recover, and move on, Kirkpatrick tells me. "Two, three years is about it. We don't grow because people come in and they move on. It's a negative organizationally, but a positive for the women."

When we spoke in 1999, the group reported 5,000 members; many participating through literature, email and telephone calls. There were 200-300 WFS groups with an average of five to seven members each. WFS differs from AA or NA, where the idea of graduating to self-sufficiency draws laughter and is considered the prelude to relapse. Hence WFS membership is neither stable nor an indication of all those who have recovered through its methods. Based on mailing lists and meeting rosters, Kirkpatrick estimates that at least 36,000 women have gone through the WFS program.

The 13 affirmations of her "New Life Acceptance Program" lead the member to take charge of the problem and of life; cultivate optimism, happiness, love, and self-regard; to grow emotionally and spiritually; and to realize that "I am in charge of my mind, my thoughts, and my life."[22] WFS recommends members spend a quarter hour reflecting on these in the morning and an equal period at night reviewing one's progress.

WFS aims to help female alcoholics with problems such as guilt, shame, powerlessness, and depression; dependencies; lack of self-identity; histories of abuse; being a victim, and "being Daddy's good little girl." The association is based on a "philosophy of thinking," Kirkpatrick told Sober Times. "She must come around to believing that our thoughts are the strongest thing that controls us. Changing our thoughts automatically dictates what actions will follow."[23]

Kirkpatrick readily admits that not all women will accept the primacy of thought. This radical rationalism coincides with an insistence that a woman be responsible for herself. This strong independence, so very American, embodies the transcendentalist philosophy of Thoreau and Emerson, especially the latter's essay "Self-Reliance," which was also a favorite of Charles Dederich, founder of Synanon and the modern therapeutic community. While getting sober herself, Kirkpatrick drew strength from Emerson's conviction that, in her words, "God is in all of us and that we are a portion of God." In a final departure from mainstream treatment and recovery, WFS does not dwell on the alcoholism or addiction itself. RR and SOS take the same tack. As Kirkpatrick told Sober Times, "Once you've stopped drinking, you've treated your alcoholism. So then you begin with your mind."

Profile: Lisa—A More Human Intervention

This is what Lisa remembers about her drinking at its worst: "No matter how excruciating your pain is, it erases it. If you drink a bottle of vodka, you can be out of your pain in 15 minutes."[24] She recites this as if it were an article of faith. Her abstinence from alcohol rests on an equal faith in herself, which Lisa has developed with the support and suggestions of various secular approaches to recovery. Most of all, she thinks differently. "Before it was stress, boom, drink. Now, I never go with the thought. I cut if off." Not for her the reliance on spirituality or God.

"It struck me as scary to say you're not in charge of your sobriety. There's precious little I can control in life, but whether or not I drink is one. If it's up to a higher power, then it can be taken away from me at any moment."

Lisa works as a legal secretary in Washington, D.C. She is a forceful person of fluent and vivid speech. She is thankful for her recovery and the support of peers, and convinced of her responsibility for its continuation.

Born in 1958, she grew up in Annapolis, Maryland and had "a very 50s childhood," one that included church until she was 12 years old. She drank "maybe once" as a teenager and only socially in college. Lisa studied business at the University of Maryland and, after graduating, managed restaurants before taking a job at an international bank. During the financial chaos of the late 1980s, the bank closed and the loan on her property was foreclosed. Lisa's fall from bank vice-president was precipitous and she began drinking heavily.

"I did it for my nerves. I honestly thought that if I stopped I would spontaneously combust." Asking for help was out of the question. "I thought I had to take care of myself." Even after she regained her professional footing, she had a drinking routine: abstain during the workweek, binge on weekends, and sober up Sunday afternoon with the help of sleeping pills. She lost days in blackouts, tried killing herself, and finally sought help with support from the partners at her law firm. Though at first referred to part-time counseling, Lisa says, "I fought my way into daytime treatment, 9:00 A.M. to 5:00 P.M." She also insisted on being prescribed Antabuse, a drug that makes a person extremely sick if they drink. (Research indicates that Antabuse, or disulfiram, works best with alcoholics who are well-educated and motivated.)

"Antabuse cancels the urge to drink. I'm not physically predisposed—alcoholism doesn't run in my family. Maybe mentally I am." She took Antabuse during her first six weeks and considers it a handy tool she may use again during a stressful period. The month-long treatment revolved around the AA program of recovery. "The Twelve Steps were hanging on the wall. They would work on the steps in class. They basically beat you over the head with it."

"One counselor was adamantly religious, saying that unless I found God I couldn't stay sober." She found such ideas diminishing to her person. "They told me to make a 'God box' and to put all my troubles in it. That struck me as so unrealistic and bizarre. It takes more human intervention than that." Lisa recalls disdainfully a fellow client who wrote her wish for a new car on a piece of paper and put that in her God box instead of saving her money.

"It was all voodoo stuff. The responsibility for not drinking every day is up to me. I knew that I would have to learn new techniques for living and I pursued that with a vengeance." A counselor steered her to Women for Sobriety, which Lisa found too similar to AA and too focused on female passivity. "The training there is geared to women standing up and having a voice—that's not an issue for me." She then found Secular Organizations for Sobriety. Most of all, Lisa appreciates the group support of fellow SOS members, with whom she communicates daily via email. (Lisa and others are trying to settle on a location for an SOS meeting in or near Washington. SOS is more established on the West Coast.)

"For the first time I have really felt this sense of belonging. If I have a problem that's really bothering me, I can go on the list or just address one person." Just before we spoke, Lisa sent off a message to a new SOS member in Sweden she has been helping along. Support from peers helps. "There's a group of six of us from treatment that are still sober— most of them are in AA. It's been crucial that we all kept in touch or on the phone with each other."

Thinking differently—what therapists call "cognitive restructuring"— also matters. In Albert Ellis's "rational emotive behavioral therapy," Lisa says she found "techniques for looking at things in a rational manner." For example, she is considering a job offer. Instead of thinking she has to make the perfect decision that will shape the rest of her life, Lisa realizes, "I'm just deciding between two good jobs."

She also learned more about shifting her mental focus away from drinking in the literature of Rational Recovery, though she did not like that organization's disparagement of support groups. For instance, she associates the 7-11 convenience stores that dot the Washington region with drinking. Now when in or near a 7-11, Lisa sings her own version of a pop song with humorous, nonalcoholic lyrics, "to change my focus."

RR also helped Lisa understand herself differently. "When the thought of drinking pops into my head I think of myself as a nondrinker. Why would I think of drinking? I don't drink. The word 'alcoholic' has a certain connotation. The word 'nondrinker' has a certain connotation. What am I supposed to say? 'Oh, I'm alcoholic, I've got to struggle, struggle, struggle.' Why would you?"

Lisa seems engaged in a great mental renovation project, each day throwing up a new scaffold or excavating a faulty foundation or, with the help of like-minded SOS members, looking at the same walls from a different vantage point. Recently, a legal decision involving a financial obligation hovered over her.

"On the email list, I said that I was waiting for this date for my fate to be decided. Someone came back and said, 'You will decide your fate. They will only decide the circumstances.' That really helped me."

Rational Recovery

Rational Recovery was founded in 1986 by Jack and Lois Trimpey, of northern California, in response to what they considered to be the lack of choice in the field of addictions, then and now dominated by the Twelve-Step approach. RR grew quickly. Organized as the Rational Recovery Self-Help Network, it had a reported 600 groups with 10,000 clients in 1996, peaking out at 1000 groups before being disbanded, the Trimpeys told me during sequential interviews from their office in Placerville, California.[25]

Basically, RR became popular as a cognitive alternative to AA. Instead of prayer and moral inventories, thought would stop the addiction. Meetings were often convened and moderated by a therapist. RR derived some of its earlier methods from the work of Albert Ellis, a psychologist whose cognitive approach culminated in Rational Emotive Behavioral Therapy. Through rational self-examination, a person can understand and surmount the irrational beliefs—rather than spiritual deficits-that cause difficulties. Ellis has criticized AA-style treatment for, allegedly, contending that alcoholics have no control over their alcoholism.[26]

In 1999, citing problems with the basic premise of the entire recovery movement, the Trimpeys canceled their groups. "Any recovery group is just a way to continue an addiction," Lois Trimpey says. "It's an individual responsibility. If you want to quit, you just want to know how." She notes that many smokers quit on their own, "and they don't have to attend these groups every week where they hug each other." Jack explains that recovery group members bind themselves to each other with the glue of their problems. "Any group of unhealthy individuals has to survive and nobody can get better because the group would cease to be active."

The Trimpeys replaced the network of groups with the Rational Recovery Society Network, which they call a grass-roots agency of social change. (Dissident members of the RR board who valued self-help groups spun off an alternative, the SMART network.) The group also severed connections with the health profession, Jack says, "because of its intransigent adherence to the medical and psychological disease models of addiction."[27] And along the way, RR dumped the Rational Emotive Behavioral approach, which Jack dismissed as unnecessary nonsense. The core of RR remains what the Trimpeys call the "Addictive Voice Recognition Technique." It speaks of the beast, the animal side of a person rooted in their midbrain that seeks pleasure. People drink or drug themselves toward self-destruction for one reason: "It feels good," Trimpey says. In AVRT, a person learns "to partition off the 'voice' from the authentic self," he continues. "We end the inner debate by saying, 'I will never drink again.' When that is said with conviction, there is relief from addiction." Trimpey describes AVRT as a "simple thinking skill which objectifies thoughts and feelings which support continued use of alcohol or drugs." He characterized AVRT as "the lore of self-recovery in a brief, educational format." AVRT is also taught during eight 90-minute sessions to small groups of alcohol and drug dependent individuals, who can commit themselves to permanent abstinence. "There is no discussion of medical, psychological, or spiritual matters, except for a simple presentation of addiction as a normal function of the healthy human body," Trimpey writes. "Given that human beings generally do exactly what they want to do, it should not be surprising that so many follow the instructions of AVRT and become securely and permanently abstinent."[28]

While acknowledging that AA may help some people, the Trimpeys excoriate AA as "an ersatz religion" based on "a discredited cult, the Oxford Group."[29] Trimpey believes AA fosters the dependency at the root of the addict's problem. Some counselors agree. "In AA, it is constantly pounded into the alcoholic's head that you cannot stop drinking by yourself, that you are powerless, that without AA you will die, end up in the gutter," Norma Campbell, a cognitive therapist in Towson, Maryland told the *Washington Post*. "RR does exactly the opposite."[30]

Many mental health professionals readily admit that AA is not for everyone, though they may not always offer alternatives. "I'm embarrassed to say it never entered my mind that AA was the problem," Joseph Gerstein, a Boston internist said in an interview with the *New York Times*. "It has so infiltrated every aspect of the mental health system that it is accepted as revealed truth." Gerstein cited his discomfort with seeing people mandated to AA's "religious environment." In the same article, Ceane Wilis, a psychologist, said, "I'm a strong supporter of AA, but we see a lot of people who aren't able to relate to it."[31]

During a visit to St. Luke's Behavioral Health Center in Phoenix, Arizona, Charles J. Shaw, a doctor, tells me that he sometimes, and reluctantly, will refer a patient who resists AA to Rational Recovery. As for the likelihood of success in RR, Shaw's face darkens and he shakes his head.[32] I met the same reaction elsewhere, lending credence to Trimpey's charge that RR is frozen out of mainstream treatment. Nevertheless, publicly funded referral offices often supply callers with the telephone numbers for RR, Women for Sobriety, and other alternatives to AA and NA.

Research has indicated RR's promise, at least during its earlier phase

when group meetings were being held. In 1993, Marc Galanter and colleagues at the New York University School of Medicine published results
of their study of 433 substance-abusing people who were attending 63
established RR groups.[33] Most were college-educated, employed men
who had previously attended AA with drinking problems dating back an
average of 24 years. Membership was brief—on average, five months
with 2.3 meetings in the prior month. Overall, 77 percent had not drunk
for at least one month and 58 percent were sober at least six months.
Cocaine abusers reported similar rates of success. RR's success was, however, helped along by two outside sources. Galanter and company concluded that previous attendance at AA helped many RR members get
started on their abstinence and taught these the value of group cohesion.
They also noted that a significant minority of RR members were also seeing therapists and taking medication.[34]

RR appealed to people who were not religious. The Galanter team
found that only 53 percent of the RR members believed in a deity and just
13 percent said religion was "very important" in their lives. That was
much less than the comparable figures for Americans overall—94 percent and 55 percent respectively.[35]

For Trimpey, God is not the issue. "RR was not designed for atheists or
agnostics," he writes on the RR website. "It was designed for addicted
human beings of all persuasions who want to quit drinking or using
drugs. Our method, AVRT, dovetails with any religion except Alcoholics
Anonymous, and does not alter one's religious or spiritual beliefs. The
Big Plan of AVRT is not unlike a pledge to God to remain abstinent, a
common expectation in many religions. People who quit addictions face
the same problems as others, and may draw upon religious faith as a precious resource in solving life's problems and in their spiritual growth."

Human Power

Many in the secular camp reject religion and its trappings, the dogma and
the ritual and the "shalt nots." The more positive basis for the secular and
rationalist methods lies in the effectiveness of cognitive therapies that
help addicts to see their problems and lives differently and arms them
with "tools" that enable them to curb or stop the drugs.

William R. Miller, the researcher and clinician who developed motivational enhancement therapy, points out that there are many ways "to help
people move toward such recognition and change."[36] Generally, his
approach helps the addict see the problem and alternatives, accept
responsibility, and tap her inner resources to change thinking and behavior. As treatment, brief motivational interventions have shown consistently good results in studies conducted in 14 nations.[37] Many cogni-

tive/behavioral therapies that boost confidence and competence or, in clinical terms, "self-efficacy," have proven effective in research. Other behavioral methods that emphasize coping and social skills, or that promote self-control through goals, self-awareness, and coping skills, have also proven successful in helping alcoholics.[38] Thus, many addicts learn to use their brains and will to curb or stop drug abuse. Regardless of the cause or course of the addiction, the addict becomes the person who can do something about it. Confidence and hope ensue and build on one another. Through these rational, nonreligious treatments, addicts become their own therapist or higher power, at least for the purposes of abstention.

Sacred and Secular

Both the sacred and the profane, the spiritual and the secular, seek a change in the heart and mind of the addict. For the heroin-addicted gang members he wanted to help, the founder of Teen Challenge "sensed that a reality more powerful, attractive, and rewarding than the needle was needed."[39] The secular and the religious approaches share certain elements in their routes to this new reality. Confession or admission—of the addiction and, perhaps, all the troubles or sins it caused—is usually the addict's ticket into the treatment scheme or recovery group. An addict can convert to a religion or to a new and entirely secular way of thinking and living, either suddenly or over time. For most addicts, conversions come gradually. So too for the secular recovery schemes, with one exception. Rational Recovery, with its emphasis on making a radical decision to never drink again, seems to favor the sudden conversion—also favored by the Evangelical rehabs. Indeed, many Christians urge newcomers to "make a decision for Christ."

Both the "No God" and the "Our God" camps insist that the addict or alcoholic assume moral accountability. Only when the person—assisted by right thinking, new maxims, the group, Jesus, whatever—becomes responsible for the decision to not drink, will she or he not drink. Both insist the person change bad or immoral habits and live properly, whether for the practical reasons espoused by secular groups—such as avoiding the inner conflicts that can cause relapse—or for religious reasons—to avoid offending God—or both. Similarly, AA, and NA call for a moral inventory, amends of past wrongs, continued self-searching, and right living. Despite rivalries and bickering, different roads to recovery cover much of the same terrain.

CHAPTER VII

Harm Reduction: Challenging Tradition on the Street with Transcendence

Saving Lives, Losing Lives, and the Spirit

As many friends and relatives or treatment professionals say, helping alcoholics and addicts recover involves loving the sinner, not the sin. Treatment begins with the sinner stopping the sin in order to get help (though most people avoid this moralizing language). But what about addicts and alcoholics who are still out there, who cannot or will not stop? Can they be helped, even brought toward a better life? To continue the religious paradigm, can society love the sinner in the midst of his or her sin? Advocates of harm-reduction strategies say yes. To help the still-active addict without demanding they abstain or enter treatment invokes a deep level of spirituality in order to reduce the harm caused by substance abuse and bring the person closer to recovery.

The philosophy is to "meet people where they are," and work from there. This practical spirituality is the type of faith that can change behavior. For instance, treating skid row alcoholics with dignity and respect by offering shelter—without demanding reform—can awaken their humanity, their transcendent connection with others. Without reference to a higher power or the other marks of recovery spirituality, harm-reduction advocates deal with addicts as spiritual creatures who are more than their drug addiction. This recognition opens a window for the addict to transcend the problem.

Touched by this electrical pulse, such men and women are often newly able to tap their inner resources and virtues to power and redirect their lives. At the least, they may be kept alive until, one day perhaps, they do sober up. In the meanwhile, they are prevented from dying on the streets. Yet many people see this as "enabling" the person to keep drinking by shielding her or him from the effects of their addiction.

In Albany, New York, a debate played out that was repeated around the country. Various parties—from social workers to anti-poverty advocates to the mayor and church leaders—were eager to do something about a group of 30-50 chronic alcoholics who inhabited storefronts and alleys on the fringes of the state capital's downtown. The Homeless Action Committee, an irreverent group of dedicated volunteers, operated a "shelter-of-last-resort" with a low-demand or harm reduction philosophy. Abstinence or treatment was not mandated. Then they received a federal grant to build a single-room-occupancy facility for chronic alcoholics, a "damp shelter," which operates under similar guidelines. It houses people who would otherwise drink and maybe die on the street, especially in winter. If abstinence or treatment were required, these people would most likely choose the street. There, they would typically experience a series of medical crises that often end with pricey ambulance rides to hospital emergency rooms where the costs of care end up being paid by the public. Despite both pragmatic and humane reasons for damp shelters, the mere ideas that they can drink and still have a place to live yanked at many people's sense of propriety.

"In the public's mind you're encouraging abuse," said Edward DeBerry of the National Resource Center on Homelessness and Mental Illness, located in a suburb of Albany.[1] The harm-reduction model evolved because, he added, "many people came to the conclusion that the heavy-handed approach has not worked." Harm-reduction advocates say stubborn cases will simply deteriorate. "Now, unless you stop the drugs, you get pushed further and further from services," says Sara Kershnar of the Harm Reduction Training Institute in Manhattan.[2]

The philosophy poses a major challenge to the addictions rehabilitation field, where its tenets are already changing assumptions and procedures. The idea that we should risk or countenance evil in order to avoid some harm constitutes a major shift in dealing with problems where the traditional approach has begun with "No. Don't. Stop."

Take the idea of giving clean needles to addicts who shoot drugs into their veins. The idea is to prevent them from sharing needles and spreading the AIDS virus. Usually in these needle-exchange programs, which exist in dozens of cities around the globe, the addict hands in a used needle for each clean one. Research indicates that fears of encouraging additional drug abuse have gone unrealized, says Jeff Stryker of the Center for AIDS Prevention Study at the University of California, while risky behavior, such as sharing dirty needles, have declined.[3] An exchange also provides a time and place for health workers to help needle users with other problems. Some addicts ask how they can get into drug treatment, especially if they are pregnant, a common time for women to get clean.

The aspects of harm reduction most excoriated have been needle exchange and the provision, in some European countries, of "heroin maintenance" to drug addicts. Critics maintain that research has been shoddy, that these measures encourage abuse, and, most of all, that harm reduction shields addicts from the effects of their habits, thus removing the incentive to quit, recover, and rejoin society. "In fact, most needle exchange studies have been full of design errors; the more rigorous ones have actually shown an *increase* in HIV infection," Sally Satel, a psychiatrist, wrote in the *Wall Street Journal*.[4] Legitimizing heroin addiction, albeit through public health measures, *does* seem a risky way to reduce self-destructive habits. It could be, as Satel argues, "the public policy manifestation of the addict's dearest wish: to use free drugs without consequence."

Leaving aside needle exchange, harm-reduction advocates provide services without conditions in an effort to gain trust over time while reducing the most immediate source of danger. This spiritually based effort may reach the most isolated and marginal groups. With pink and blue tattoo-covered forearms, a bright red crewcut, and a silver bone through his nose, Kyle Ranson of the San Francisco AIDS Foundation seems a natural for his work with runaway, homeless youths in San Francisco. He may spend months, even years, getting to know some of these teens and young adults before suggesting they go home or stop selling sex or using drugs. "You have to meet the kids where they're at," Ranson told me during a briefing in San Francisco. "Some are ready to stop. With others we try to keep them alive long enough so they reach the point where they will stop." His group runs writing and art workshops and other activities such as regular barbecues in Golden Gate Park, which tap the runaways' creativity and boost their self-esteem. The low-key approach helps many to feel their lives are worth saving.

Proponents do worry about condoning self-destructive actions. "Oftentimes, I just feel like I'm encouraging these kids to continue using drugs," said Sara Parks Urban of the long-established Larkin Street Youth Center in the Haight-Ashbury section, which even runs a hustlers support group for young male prostitutes. But the work can renew in hustlers or addicts a spiritual connection. "If they know someone's concerned about them, who knows, maybe in five years they'll get off the street," said Roger Hernandez of the Larkin center.

In other cases, an emphasis on behavior, rather than cures, characterizes what harm-reduction advocates consider their realistic approach. One reason for the new approach is frustration over trying to help a core group, perhaps 5 percent of all alcoholics, who go through numerous treatments without much success. A 1993 Minnesota study found that the average chronic, recidivist alcoholic cost taxpayers $23,000 annually, largely in terms of detoxifications and treatments, more than twice the cost of providing shelter.[5] Among Albany's core group of homeless chronic alcoholics, most have been through at least five treatment programs, according to my own interviews and those by Deirdre Oakley of Policy Research Associates.

As most people in the field say, little happens with an alcoholic or addict until he or she decides they want to get better. Much of addiction treatment consists of getting people to that point. Advocates of wet shelters say that's their aim as well with chronic alcoholics. "A lot of people can't grasp the concept that you can accept where they're at and still encourage them to go into treatment," said Donna DeMaria, executive director of the Homeless Action Committee. "We'll spend hours with people when they're at a turning point, in a crisis, thinking that this might be the time. The person has to want it, yet the guy on the street can't get any more uncomfortable, and still they continue to drink." DeMaria sees a spiritual process at work with these people. "When you start giving people some compassion, a support system, and have them feel a part of community, start feeling good about themselves, that might start them thinking about making a change," she said.[6]

Understandably, the public suspects the measures and implications of harm reduction. No one wants to encourage deadly habits. We may need to accept, as Ethan Nadelman, director of the Lindesmith Center, wrote in *Foreign Affairs*, "that drugs are here to stay, and that we have no choice but to learn how to live with them so that they cause the least possible harm."[7] More hopefully, we may need to engage addicts and alcoholics, at least those not ready for abstinence, and in ways that will lead them to curb and even taper off their habits. And in this small opening, we may reach for their spirit, for that part of them that is most human and most amenable to help.

Philosophy and Spirituality of Harm Reduction

One chord runs through traditional treatment and harm reduction—a spiritual approach. Though it takes many forms, the presence of spiritual motivations and methods in each field reinforces the notion that addictions touch and warp a person so deeply that something is often required in addition to medicine, psychology, or chemistry. For the stubborn addict, those still happy or fully hooked on drugs, harm-reduction workers go into shooting galleries with instructions on how to inject more safely, where to get clean needles, and, when the time comes, where to get help stopping. In a blend of Jesus and media theorist Marshall McLuhan, their presence is the message. To addicts they say, "Despite your drugs and anti-social behavior and your refusal or inability to stop, you are worth our effort to reduce the damage you do yourselves and others."

Take Edith Springer, who quit social work in 1988 in frustration over the widespread refusal to deal with AIDS forthrightly through needle exchanges and other methods. She spent two years studying harm-reduction methods in England, Holland, and Sweden. Springer now teaches this philosophy and its methods to social workers and counselors for the Harm Reduction Training Institute in New York City. Springer talks more like Leo Buscaglia than a clinician. "Most drug users have a very low sense of self-esteem, of self-efficacy," she tells me. "We give them unconditional love."[8]

I ask Springer how she can love people who appear hard to love. She laughingly denies the categorization, and explains her values. "It's based in a belief system that we are all spirit. Ram Das [an author, speaker, and expert on Eastern religions] spoke at our conference and he said, 'Don't be fooled by the bio-social-psychological symptoms of the addict. Look in the person's eyes and see the spirit.' It's very Christian, though we're not religious in that way. Jesus was the first outreach worker. He was not judgmental." Making conditions for receiving help contradicts that approach.

"The whole abstinence thing can destroy the spiritual connection with the people," says Oakley, the Albany based researcher. "People will talk about how this is the first time in so long that they've been treated with respect and dignity, that it's the first time in so long that someone has given them hope. It gives them some meaning, some purpose."[9]

Sara Kershnar, who trains thousands of health workers in these techniques for the Harm Reduction Training Institute in New York City puts it simply: "Harm reduction is trying to move us from a spiritless place where the pain is their own fault because A, it's a moral failing, B, it's one that's punishable, and C, it's something we don't treat the same as what we call a disease, to a more spiritual place where we're saying, 'Okay, no one says, When I grow up I want to be a chaotic drug user.'" The assumption, she says, is that every person has the capacity for love and healing. "We try to let people know that they are capable of changing and offer models for that a clean needle is the first time they've got the message, 'You're worth saving." But the aim is also eminently practical. "We would not be concerned if people using drugs were not causing harm," Kershnar adds. "But there is an epidemic of harmful drug use."

Profile: Tommy-"I've got to Do Something"

With most people who end up living on the streets because of their drinking, going through an expensive detoxification and then a rehabilitation program is just part of the routine. Like Tommy. "I was using detox as a place to wash my clothes," he says. "I must have gone through there 40 times." While that may seem like the exaggeration of a tough guy, it is the sort of figure that comes up often in interviews with chronic street alcoholics. They are a particularly hard sort to help. Tommy is one of a tiny but growing number in the nation who were helped toward recovery by a wet/dry shelter, an innovative type of shelter for homeless, chronic alcoholics where neither abstinence nor treatment is mandated. Typically, drinking or misbehaving on the premises, however, is grounds for dismissal. These programs can keep alcoholics alive until they are ready to sober up. For Tommy, 18 months at one such program, the St. Anthony Residence in St. Paul, Minnesota, floated him that much closer to the sober life he now leads.

He grew up in Montana and alcoholism soon defined his life. "I had my first blackout when I was 16. I got into drugs when I was 19, but that was too expensive so I didn't keep with it. I drifted all over the United States, from Florida to California, up to the border and into Canada." He was homeless and lived on the street from 1985 on. Tommy came to St. Paul in 1986, when he was near the bottom of his career as a hard-core alcoholic. There were yet more rough moments. During one drinking bout on Harriet Island in St. Paul, he saw a friend fall into the Mississippi River and get swept away to his death. Then there was the time during one of St. Paul's brutal winters that the police rescued a sleeping Tommy from a snow bank in a hidden spot next to the city morgue. It was a locale favored by homeless people, especially in more clement weather. "It was out of sight, and the police let you sit there," he explains. In another episode, Tommy got out of jail after one of innumerable incarcerations and began drinking. Within hours he was drunk. And airborne.

"I fell off the Wabasha Street Bridge about 70 feet onto the rip-rap," he says with a bemused, detached smile as if he were an anthropologist recounting the behavior of an exotic species. "I landed there and I was laughing, looking at the view, saying, 'Wow, what happened?' I broke some ribs, I busted seven vertebrae, I collapsed my left lung."

Aside from his routine detours to the detox unit, Tommy also went through treatment once in Montana and 12 times at the Minnesota State hospital in Moose Lake, north of St. Paul. "I would get committed to Moose Lake, brought up there, then I would escape and race the cops back to St. Paul." He was not ready to stop. "I understood I was going to sober up one day. But I kept on because I wasn't going to let them force me to do anything," Tommy says.

During such periods, especially for homeless alcoholics, being kept alive can be a form of treatment, at least under the rubric of harm reduction. In 1986, the courts sent Tommy to the St. Anthony Residence. "I was still drinking—rubbing alcohol, Lysol, mouthwash, vodka. I was drinking as hard as possible, whenever I could." For six months he abstained, mostly in order to hold on to a job as a janitor at the shelter.

I tell Tommy that many outsiders would wonder, "Why give this drunk guy Tommy a place to live if he's not ready to stop drinking? What's the point?" For most of our talk, he had been leaning back in steel-framed, cushioned chair covered in burgundy vinyl. Now Tommy snapped forward and talked about himself in the third person. "I'd say, 'Because he survived for a year and a half.' There's a point when you finally say, 'I've got to do something.' " Something added up for him during three separate stays at the Christ Recovery Center, a nondenominational, Christian oriented residential program run by the St. Paul Union Gospel Mission. "The last time I got out of Moose Lake, I called a friend and said it was time to do something." At the Christ Recovery Center, "I had to abstain, it's required. And I did for a year and a half there and worked as a residence manager.

"I always believed in God, I just never gave him any of the weight on my shoulders to carry." Even his stay at the Christ Recovery Center served one purpose above others: "It was a place to live, go to meetings, and to abstain. For me, it was enough time to be able to think again." But in the mysterious alchemy of treating alcoholics and addicts, the point at which an alcoholic says, 'I've got to do something,' is famously elusive. It is the point when a person realizes he or she is worth saving. Counselors, relatives, and friends all find that realization cannot be forced entirely from without. Tommy knows that as well from his work as clinical director of the St. Anthony Residence. But he can't resist giving a selective push or shove to some of the men he thinks are near to ready.

"The guys here, they don't think that, that they've got to do something. I have three or four guys here now I pound on and say, 'When are you going to do something about yourself?'" In his own case, Tommy remembers that one moment began a life.

"It was time." Maybe the change can be put simply. Before, Tommy believed in some sort of God. Today, he uses his belief. "I know there's a higher power. Sometimes when things get too heavy to carry it around, I give it to him."

Challenging Tradition, Grabbing the Torch

Dan McGill, a spokesman for the New York State Office of Alcoholism and Substance Abuse Services, is an old hand in addictions treatment. He began working for a previous state agency, the Narcotics Addiction Control Commission, in 1970. One week in 1997, he had contrasting visions of two camps; both equally concerned about addiction.[10]

"I attended a conference of treatment agencies in Hudson Valley. It was the same faces I had seen for years. The meeting was well attended but it was not overwhelming. The very next day I went to a Harm Reduction Coalition conference at John Jay College in the city. It was packed, standing room only. I didn't recognize any the people but they clearly dealt with a lot of the same issues." An assumption distinguished the younger activists from the older group.

"One speaker said that sobriety was not necessary for everyone. That's very controversial. Other speakers were saying that the traditional recovery/abstinence/sobriety-or-nothing attitude may need revising. Compared to the treatment agencies meeting I had been to just the day before, there was this whole other pulse to the harm-reduction conference. It was much more controversial and had much more momentum. In a sense, it was a passing of the torch that I was seeing." McGill saw a parallel with the activists who, 25 years ago, pushed treatment into new fields such as drug addiction. Now, the harm-reduction advocates are on the street level. They are spreading the message to receptive health and substance abuse treatment workers. In the 1995 to 1998 period, the Harm Reduction Training Institute taught its beliefs and techniques to 7,000 workers at 1,000 programs, Kershnar reported.

But harm reduction—with its emphasis on "engaging" the abuser "where he or she is," instead of mandating abstinence and treatment—is a far cry from the harsh methods deployed in treatment during the late 1960s and early 1970s. Then, confronted with the heroin epidemic, New York's Narcotic Addiction Control Commission established more than a dozen enormous rehabilitation centers surrounded by barbed wire and staffed by guards and social workers. "Patients" were either convicts or regular citizens sent there after being civilly certified as drug dependent. In the 1970s, high recidivism rates at these centers, a growing suspicion of large institutions, and a shift toward community-based treatment led to their demise despite having benefited many people.

The closings were part of a general easing of punitive measures and other changes that added up to a dramatic shift in treatment toward the spiritually based Twelve-Step approach. Harm reduction still represents a giant shift once again from prevailing treatment philosophies. "We are the future," is the cheerful, confident assessment of Edith Springer. We shall see. But the new philosophy riles many who work in the treatment field. At a men's residence run by the American Indian Services on East Franklin Avenue in Minneapolis, Philip Archambeault, a beefy ex-Marine and native American, works hard to coax mostly hard-core alcoholics to stay sober. He is disgusted that some of these same men could live down East Franklin at a wet residence, the Anishinaabe Wakiagun House, and continue to drink.

"It's a joke, it's our opposite," says Archambeault. "I haven't seen that work yet." For him, this aspect of the harm-reduction philosophy merely confirms the alcoholic in their habit. "It's all part of the lifestyle—you get up, get high, stagger around, get jump-rolled, you know, when they knock you down and take your money."[11]

Anishinaabe Wakiagun, the name means "people's house" in Ojibwe, opened in 1993 and offers long-term residence to 40 men and women—late-stage, chronic inebriates with little chance of recovery. The main purpose is to provide shelter to people who might otherwise die on the streets. Most controversially, residents are allowed to drink in their rooms, making it a wet shelter, unlike damp shelters, which only allow residents to drink off-site. "When we were developing the program we got opposition from people in the treatment field," says Kelby Grovender, the director. Often, the charge was that Wakiagun would enable drunks to keep on drinking. "Enabling means that you're shielding people from the consequences of drinking. These people have already felt all the consequences—they've lost jobs, homes, and families. Some do drink less because they're more comfortable. If you're sleeping under the freeway bridge in the winter, you have to drink a lot to feel comfortable," says Grovender. A small fraction "move in the direction," of abstinence and a handful have remained sober for several months at a time, he adds. "As Americans, we hate to admit that there is something we can't change. But some people are going to use chemicals no matter what, so to deny them services is not right. You cannot punish people into staying sober."[12] Even this idea can be expressed in religious terms: humans are sinful and redemption possible but not automatic.

Still, just the idea bugs people who have so long labored to help addicts give up that which is killing them. "The traditional approach to treatment other than methadone maintenance has been total abstinence, and people get quite upset over the suggestion that something other than that will work," Jean Somers Miller, the New York State Commissioner of Alcoholism and Substance Abuse Services, told me one day. "I was at a treatment conference where a speaker mentioned that maybe abstinence can't be the goal for everyone. There was quite a reaction."[13] In a chapter they contributed to a book on homelessness, Deirdre Oakley and Deborah L. Dennis, two researchers who have studied harm reduction in practice, call fears of enabling the biggest barrier to making low-demand services available. "Research indicates that people are actually more likely to accept treatment once their basic needs have been met," they wrote.[14] The reason for these considerations is that abstinence-based programs do not work for everyone, just those who want to stop. "Harm reduction is particularly effective for people who aren't looking to change," explains Springer.

New Problems, New Answers

Harm reduction is not entirely new; its tenets have infused treatment all along. Few people who have tackled the addictions problem, from the founders of Alcoholics Anonymous in the 1930s to researchers at the National Institutes of Health, profess to have the answers for each case. And even when something works, there are no pat cures. Those who relapse are encouraged to try again, and their time abstinent certainly counts as an improvement over the alternative. Just as in treating diabetes, asthma, and hypertension—wherein patients are also asked to change their behavior—a reoccurrence is better seen as a setback, even a normal event on the road to recovery, rather than absolute failure that disqualifies the person from future help. Most definitions of addiction include a proviso that it is an illness characterized by relapse. The stories told by hundreds of addicts, to other authors, and me include repeated attempts before abstinence endured over the long term. In some cases we have, as a society, decided that since some addicts cannot or will not stop, we would be better off controlling their drug use.

Methadone maintenance does precisely that. The drug, doled out to patients in regulated doses, can relieve acute withdrawal symptoms and ease craving, and has shown good results in cutting heroin use, crime, and death, and in increasing employment and social stability.[15] Still, who likes handing out drugs to addicts? Methadone treatment has expanded only marginally since 1980. Despite their radical reputation among treatment professionals, harm-reduction advocates say they are doing the same thing.

If existing methods worked for all people, harm reduction would not have been invented. Certain new groups—such as the masses of people without homes who have appeared on the streets in recent decades—need new forms of help. From the late 1970s through the 1980s, more than one million single-room apartments were eliminated thanks, usually, to urban gentrification. During the same time, state and federal mental hospitals continued to discharge residents while government did little to provide community services. These forces helped create modern homelessness. By the mid-1990s, according to various estimates, 600,000 Americans are homeless on any given night; during the course of a year, the count rises up to one million people. Of those, about 25 percent are seriously mentally ill, about 40 percent are alcoholic or drug-addicted, and perhaps 10 percent are both, that is, are dually diagnosed.[16]

Some older groups also need new answers. Psychotropic medications have stabilized many homeless people with schizophrenia and other disorders, even removing them from street life. But many have not been helped. "A significant portion of mentally ill people are not helped by any medication," according to Deborah Dennis of Policy Research Associates, New York, who oversees the National Resource Center on Homelessness and Mental Illness. It is a position that many therapists find difficult to accept. "Mental health professionals are pretty eager, and educated, to *treat* mental illness," Dennis explained. They often resist the idea of making fewer demands on clients, or lowering their expectations.[17]

"Harm reduction has become more and more popular in terms of serving and encouraging homeless people with co-occurring disorders, mental health, and substance abuse disorders, because the abstinence model is not working," said Deirdre Oakley, who oversees eight sites for a federal homelessness program. After 10-15 years of concentrated government efforts to combat the problem, she adds, "we can reach some conclusions about what works and doesn't." One of the latest endeavors, born of this experience, is the Safe Havens program, which originated in the findings of a federal commission and its report, "Outcasts on Main Street." Since 1993, about 70 of these low-demand shelters for the mentally ill homeless have been established around the nation. In 1998, another 40 were being developed, Oakley says. Many of these make few demands—such as abstinence—of their residents, people who invariably were not helped by high-demand programs.

Pressure for change came from other quarters. By the mid-1980s, civic leaders realized homelessness—though heart wrenching in itself—was bad for business. And they wanted more than shelters and soup lines. "Business leaders and politicians want the homeless off the streets, they want results," said Dennis. "We were finally given the money, so we had to develop an ethos." Consider the vans that bring food, advice, and other help to people on the street. Commonplace as it seems today, it was a radical idea—"What, home delivery for the homeless?"—that caught on. Now almost every city worth its salt has at least one outreach van patrolling the urban demimonde. Two other groups advancing harm reduction were the accountants who watch the bottom line and the advocates or former clients with experience on the ground.

"It's more expensive to provide emergency services to these people in the street," says Grovender. "Allowing them to drink in their rooms is primarily for the safety of the residents. Minnesota has very cold winters, so if they're outside they could freeze to death, as some do every year, or fall off a bridge, or get beat up and killed." Harm reduction coincides with the urge to get a big bang out of each buck. Consider this scenario: a case worker concludes a client is not about to stop drinking, so she works with the person to cut back, under the rubric of what some call "abuse management." This practical, nonmoralizing approach resembles what is happening elsewhere in health care as plan administrators tackle medical issues with a pragmatic eye on the bottom line, starting with the simpler measures as prevention before proceeding to the high tech and costly. To this way of thinking, asking an addict to quit in order to qualify for help would be like asking the sick to get better before being admitted to the hospital.

Consider people with AIDS or with HIV, the virus that causes the syndrome. At Gay Men's Health Crisis in New York City, one of the largest groups serving people with AIDS, people who drink or drug are no longer disqualified from receiving help, according to staff member Laurent Feltman.[18] "It's much more a behaviorally based policy." Clients feel freer discussing their actual drug use, since they are not in danger of losing services. Social workers can then address actual behavior and coax clients to amend their actions to reduce the harm posed to themselves and others. "Before this, to get treatment you would have to acknowledge that you're an addict and give up all your drugs totally," said Feltman, which is a daunting prospect for an addict whose life is already being crushed by AIDS.

Many of the loudest voices for effective and cost-saving innovations such as harm reduction have been the homegrown advocates, former homeless addicts and alcoholics. At a 1994 federally convened meeting in Seattle on the topic there were about 75 homeless persons, at least one from each state. "It really opened the eyes of providers to hear how they were demeaning toward their clients," said Dennis, who helped organize the session as project director of the federally funded National Resource Center on Homelessness and Mental Illness. Since then, about one quarter of participants at the center's conferences are people who are or have been homeless and mentally ill. "They really are the experts," says Dennis. Similarly, the Harm Reduction Coalition, while not minimizing or ignoring the harm done by drug abuse, tries to ensure that current and former drug abusers help shape programs and policies designed to serve them, another level of asserting their human dignity.

Giving a voice to those society seeks to help, or reform, received its biggest impetus from the civil rights movement. It flourished in the mental health field beginning in the early 1970s, when parents, patients, and other activists led the way to deinstitutionalization. When community programs were established, patients, or "consumers" as many now prefer to be known, demanded a voice in setting policy and operations. This was even truer in the modern addictions treatment field, which has been peopled by ex- or recovered addicts from its very inception in the 1950s and 1960s. Taking things a step further, it only makes sense that harm reduction—so radical and grass-roots in nature—gives a big role to the addict in reducing the harm he or she causes.

Harm Reduction in Substance Abuse Treatment

Abstinence-oriented programs work for many addicts. For the others, a harm-reduction approach can—at the least—reduce self-destructive habits. "The harm-reduction model says meet the patient where they are and work toward abstinence," according to Amos James, a substance abuse specialist in the AIDS/HIV program at Albany Medical Center Hospital. "The patient may be able to get off cocaine but they may want to keep smoking marijuana." That may count as progress, especially with AIDS patients. Faced with an abstinence requirement, a heroin addict with the syndrome may simply walk away and continue sharing needles—thereby increasing the risk to himself and others. "I want to enlist the patient to be a partner with me, especially when I have a patient that's acting like an adversary," said James.[19]

To harm-reduction advocates, it makes little sense to ask an addict to give up a symptom—drugs or alcohol—before the causes—homelessness, mental illness, hopelessness—are addressed. "We rip that away, and it does a lot of damage," contends Edith Springer. Better to lure the person toward a new life, bit by bit, than to drive them away with strict demands at the doorsill. "We go to them," says Springer. "It's low-threshold work. We have to get them to buy what we're selling."

Though the hope is that addicts who recover will remain abstinent, Springer advocates being realistic about the high rate of relapse among rehab graduates. "So we better admit that, and prepare people to use moderately if they are going to."[20]

This touches on one of the delicate flashpoints of the entire treatment field: is abstinence ultimately necessary for all those who get in trouble with drugs or alcohol? Or does an insistence on abstinence backfire, and actually worsen both the rate and severity of relapse? Those who say yes to the latter offer two points. First, abstinence for many merely increases the luster of the forbidden fruit. And second, when certain alcoholics and addicts relapse even slightly, their remorse can be so severe—thanks to the lessons about "one drink will get you drunk"—that they go on a tear to blot out the shame, saying basically, "Oh no, I had one beer, my recovery is shot, I might as well drink a case." Marlatt and other researchers call this self-fulfilling phenomenon the "abstinence violation effect."

Harm-reduction programs do not, however, offer addicts or alcoholics a free ride. "We hold people responsible for their behavior, whether they are using or not," adds Springer. "We're very strict about a person following the rules." Learning to live with the consequences of one's acts creates and fosters self-control and confidence. Parents know this. And it is one belief routinely voiced by counselors in both camps, abstinence-based treatment and the harm reduction. Both know that confidence based on experience builds hope, which in turn enables an addict to change his or her life. Psychologists call this quality "self-efficacy." Even though it hurts to see one's child suffer from the consequences of their acts, sometimes it is best for mom or dad to hang back and let life's little blows fall on the provocateur. Ditto for adults helping other adults, albeit addicted ones, find their way.

Once they have the attention of the addicts, harm-reduction workers deploy a variety of alternative healing methods—Reiki, medication, massage. Though some are explicitly spiritual in nature or origin, "we don't require them to believe in anything," says Springer. Her colleague at the Harm Reduction Training Institute, Sara Kershnar, finds in such moments a time to ask about destructive habits. She speaks in the coalition's well-used, high-ceilinged offices on West twenty-seventh Street in Manhattan's Chelsea neighborhood. Kershnar does bodywork—massage and related physical therapy—with many youthful addicts who use needles. Direct appeals to stop can drive these people away. "It's not a great entrée to say, 'Have you thought about getting off drugs?' Instead, I may say, 'Your arms are not looking good, have you thought about rotating sites?'" She recognizes how awful this sounds: "I say to myself, 'I'm talking to a 17-year-old about rotating sites!' But over time [injecting drugs] becomes absurd to them too and they ask themselves, 'What am I doing here?'"[21]

For Sam Tsemberis, a harm-reduction approach filled in a gap he saw during years working with homeless, mentally ill addicts. Though he could personally engage the people, he could not get them to swear off drugs totally in order to qualify for housing. "I couldn't get them to the next step," he recalls with frustration.[22]

Traditionally, to enter a treatment or housing program for the homeless, a person had to be sober, or at least appear so. (Shelters, especially of the huge warehouse variety seen in New York City during the 1980s, were more relaxed since their goal was emergency short-term housing.) Drinking, on or off premises, was grounds for dismissal. A primary concern was preserving the safety of other residents. But for this reason, many refused to approach a shelter. Among those who did, a contingent never seemed able to stay sober. Shelter workers would kick them out, and they would return to the streets and, typically, a cycle of panhandling, drinking, and nuisance making. When they made trouble, the police would come. When they had seizures or got seriously ill, it was an ambulance ride to the hospital. Both are expensive and time consuming.

After a decade of studying and designing services for this group, Oakley and Dennis declared it clear that they "are willing to use mental health services that are easy to enter and that meet their needs as they perceive them."[23] In 1994, Congress approved the creation of "Safe Havens" for such people. The legislation, under the Supportive Housing Program, specified that an eligible person be hard-to-reach homeless, seriously mentally ill and "currently unwilling or unable to participate in mental health or substance abuse treatment programs." Whether or not they intended it so, the language endorses harm reduction and acknowledges that it is possible to help chronic homeless alcoholics who are unwilling to help themselves.

Of the 70 Safe Haven shelters established around the country since 1994, most are damp, according to Oakley, meaning residents are not kicked out if they drink or take drugs off site, as are a minority of other homeless programs. These usually ban violence and, on the premises, drugs or drinking. In some areas, as Minnesota, these called wet/dry residences. The bottom line, as one New England shelter director put it bluntly to a shocked audience in the mid-1980s: "no guns, no bottles." Those who drink elsewhere are allowed back in so long as they behave properly.

The emphasis on actions coincides, for better or worse, with the wholesale move toward behaviorism in mental health and substance abuse treatment. This change in language dovetails with the demand for results, for the change in behavior needed to halt or curb addiction. Often those wariest of wet or damp policies are the residents, whose caution is often inspired by their own experience getting sober and a fear of peers under the influence. At a Safe Haven in Randolph, Vermont, the mental health consumers in charge decided to ban drugs and alcohol, as well as people under the influence, altogether.

St. Anthony Residence: A Second Chance for Drinking Drunks

Following directions to the St. Anthony Residence, a damp shelter for chronic alcoholics, I leave the six-lane east-west highway that joins the Twin Cities and drive past two dozen blocks of warehouses, small factories, and drafting shops in the east end of St. Paul. On an oddly quiet street, with a dozen trees, sits a small building that resembles a Motel 8 done in Southwest mission style. It seems appropriate, given the Franciscan title and its management, since 1986, by Catholic Charities. The industrial location is not entirely accidental. Siting a home for 60 or so inebriates—95 percent of whom continue to drink daily—can be hard, though in one direction just two blocks away is a housing project. Just a little farther is an area of winding streets and stately homes. At the end of the visit, I stand outside and chat with Dennis Borgen, the supervisor, and his boss, Jerry Turner, who oversees this and a larger, similar facility. A resident on his way in staggers up to us, extends a hand to me, and holds on. Bobby, 48, exhibits that combination of sporadic concentration and barely muffled anger so often seen in a man who has spent decades drunk on society's margins. He tells me about having flown sorties in Vietnam on a C-130, his quick claim for respect. He closes in, uncannily realizing that I have smelled his breath and perceived his condition. "So yeah, I'm an alcoholic. Call me the walking wounded. But these guys have given me some time," Bobby says, waving his free hand at two St. Anthony's staffers, "These guys have given me a second chance. My country didn't give me a second chance."[24]

A second chance—or a third or fourth or one thousandth—is what St. Anthony's embodies. With cheerful irreverence, Borgen defines the facility as a "wet/dry house, meaning that a number of residents are saturated and a number are sober."Tolerating drinking by drunks was a tough notion for Turner and Borgen to accept. Both men are recovered alcoholics for whom abstinence is the foundation of life.

"I said I would never have sobered up if I had a place like this to come to," says Turner, a rangy man whose aura of easy authority camouflages the rough past one sees in his weathered face. His concern was that the residence allowed the men to go on drinking while shielding them from the consequences of their actions, anathema to the recovery community and the quicksand into which fall many a spouse or relative who is "merely trying to help" an alcoholic. But with this hard-core group, new solutions were needed and quickly proved their worth.

"The almighty buck saves everything. If you can show you're saving dollars, fine," says Turner. "We're saving thousands of dollars. One resident, he had been to 450 detoxes, which cost $400-600 for a two, three night stay. He was living in detox."

A 1985 study by the Minnesota Institute of Public Health found that in Hennepin County, dominated by Minneapolis, 425 homeless inebriates were costing $9.7 million a year in health care, police, emergency aid, and so on.[25]

The staff keeps up good relations with neighbors by having residents shovel sidewalks in winter for the elderly and, periodically, pick up litter and refuse. Since it was saving money and lives so well in its first ten years, health officials persuaded the agency to open a second, larger facility, The Glenwood, in Minneapolis with room for 80 men. Though many counselors were initially hostile, they grew to value this form of harm reduction for two reasons: by removing the most persistent patients, it made more room in detoxification units for other alcoholics; and it removed intransigent alcoholics from treatment programs where they were disrupting progress for others.

Turner's colleagues in rehab programs "realize that not everybody is going to sober up, that there's a time when you need to make the call. A guy's been through 20 treatments and maybe enough's enough and you can't keep pouring money into them."[26]

Though the priority is saving lives, some residents do sober up. About 5 percent is Turner's estimate. What makes that figure significant is the nature of the risk pool: "We are dealing with the worst of the worst," says Turner. The example of the staff and recovered graduates inspires some to seek help. "They know it can be done," says Borgen. The men are generally receptive to the spiritual nature of AA and its Twelve Steps, which is often a major hurdle for people contemplating that approach to sobriety. But if one cannot make a regular alcoholic sober, with these men the game is subtler.

"Our clients have been to multiple treatments, detox maybe 75-100 times," says Borgen. "We'd be arrogant to say we'll get them sober after all they've been through. They have all the tools, so it's a matter of waiting."

They mention one man who lived at St. Anthony's for 12 years before sobering up. "We try to keep them alive until they can make a choice."

The Inn at Ferry Street: The Last Resort

If the Inn at Ferry Street represents what a damp shelter for chronic alcoholics who are unlikely to stop drinking can be, it is a wonder more communities are not clamoring for one. From the carpeted vestibule to the kitchen to the small, tidy rooms for each resident, the facility has a calm, welcoming air. Its managers seem to have found the balance among realism, regulation, and love. Outside, the dark red structure almost emanates calm. It serves as ballast for a busy street in Troy, a small Hudson River city that has cheerfully endured the suburban exodus and whose grand architecture recalls the local magnates of the Industrial Revolution.

The Inn is operated by Joseph's House & Shelter, a homeless shelter founded in 1983 by two nuns, Sister Rita Shawn and Sister Maria Cokely, who have moved on to create other services for homeless and ill people. In 1995, the program moved into a two-story squared-off brick building whose previous tenant was, ironically, a rowdy bar. That switch in use, plus the program's religious pedigree and its vast network of local volunteers, led neighbors and Troy leaders to support an often-controversial type of program.

Upstairs in the building is Joseph's House, a 28-person emergency shelter. People stay an average of eight days and must abide by 20 pages of rules. They cannot be intoxicated. Downstairs, the Inn has a different approach for a different clientele, people who are chronically homeless, persistently mentally ill, and alcoholic or drug-addicted. There are nine single rooms, designated as permanent housing. Residents' ages range from 40 to 60. They pay for rent and food out of their disability benefits, usually federal Supplemental Security Income. Beyond bans on violence and alcohol or drugs on the premises, there are no rules.

"This is absolutely the last resort for people whose drug addiction or mental illness was a barrier to other services either because of their inability or unwillingness to comply with requirements such as abstinence," explains Tracy Neitzel, the director of Joseph's House & Shelter. "A lot of these people could not 'maintain' in the main shelter because they could not come in sober."[27]

Neitzel and her colleague, Kevin O'Connor, think sobriety and recovery are likely for only a few of those they help. For most, "there is something permanently damaged, organically, from years of abuse," says O'Connor. "Most of them, they're not going to get better. If there were an expectation that they move up the ladder, they would fail. We would all applaud if it did happen." Neitzel and O'Connor admit that some residents of the Inn at Ferry Street sneak alcohol or drugs into their rooms. But the administrators, both warm and direct in manner, report a large reduction in substance abuse, usually a product of the pride residents feel in having a home and of the culture that is created among a small group of people who don't want to lose what they now have. "All have made significant improvements in their lives," Neitzel states flatly. Some have reunited with families; most get medical care and take prescribed psychotropic medications. Six have been here continuously since the Inn opened in 1995, one sign of stability and a condition better than wandering the alleys of Troy. For O'Connor, the most important success is that "they are all more engaged with people." This engagement, this return to the human family, is at once the most practical and the most deeply spiritual aspect of the Inn's work. It is a homecoming after what Neitzel calls "the journey of loss" that each resident has endured.

"They develop a sense of community, of belonging to others. It's helping them develop a perspective on life," says O'Connor. He compares the change to that of the co-founder of Alcoholics Anonymous, whose description of a dramatic epiphany of God revealed through wind and light and liberation is part of the Twelve-Step movement lore. "They would not describe it in the same terms as Bill Wilson did his spiritual awakening, but something has happened to these people, that they are able to maintain this new life," says O'Connor.

Profile: Corey—"Glimpses of Hope"

Corey, the fourth child in an upper-middle-class family who lived outside of Schenectady, started drinking when she was 12 years old. "I loved it. It totally took me outside myself. It gave me courage and I was able to talk to people better." Sitting in an airy, glass-walled vegetarian café, Corey does not appear a shy person. Of medium height and good posture, she wears her hair in a stylish buzz cut and has three small silver earrings in one ear. Her evenly proportioned face presents a bold but unchallenging aspect, a good backup to her direct speech.

Just a few years earlier, Corey's best option was to live in a damp shelter. In this case, it was a house rented by the Homeless Action Committee on a lively, tattered street in Albany, New York. "The rules were no fighting, no drinking in the house, no smoking, don't hang out on Quail Street," Corey says. During her time there, she continued drinking—but less than before—and shoplifting. But something touched her.

"I knew there was a better way, I had seen it. I had felt it." If that was the first time that a sober life hooked her, it was not for want of opportunities. Corey spent time at a half-dozen treatment facilities with little success. But the very nature of these—rules and directions and abstinence—turned her off. In 1986, Corey was kicked out of a Catholic high school for drinking, put into a 49-day residential treatment program and kicked out of there. "I wasn't into being there," she recalls. Her parents brought her to another in Vermont "where you get up at 3:00 A.M. and milk cows as therapy. I wasn't into it." Corey stayed home and attended a school for troubled girls "where I was learning how to be a worse child, how to be a better con." Eventually her parents helped her enter a therapeutic community, a regimented and group-oriented form of treatment.

"I got out when I discovered I had no control over any part of my life," Corey says. "I don't like having no control, especially when it has to do with me." Then there were ten weeks of out-patient counseling to no avail. "The night I left, I got high." She lived in a series of homeless shelters. "I kept getting kicked out because I didn't want to follow the rules." To this point Corey exhibited certain characteristics common to many addicts, but are more pronounced in those that the harm-reduction approach may help: rule-resistant, unwilling, lack of interest in recovery. Many recovered addicts say that when they were using, they still sensed that they were not being who they really were. I ask Corey if she thought along the same lines. "No, it was me," she answers emphatically. "I didn't really care one way or another that my life didn't have direction."

There came a moment of truth when the door cracked open. "I was sitting in downtown Albany. I had nowhere to go. I was scared. I was all by myself and had no friends near me. I just wanted to get high. I was in the bus stop opposite Rite Aid and I decided I was just going to kill myself." She contacted a friend, who called a crisis team, which brought her to a detox unit. Corey later went through a women's program, The Next Step, and sobered up. When she relapsed later, thanks in part to a drug-addicted girlfriend, things were different.

"I was really angry at myself, because I wanted to stay sober. At that point, I realized my life was completely unmanageable." Corey and her companion lived in motels until their money ran out and moved into the damp shelter. "There was no curfew, no chores, just 'live and let live.' It worked for me. I was drinking two '40s' a day," Corey says, using the slang for a 40-ounce bottle of beer, "which was enough but less than my usual dose." Without the shelter, Corey says, "I would have drank more."

Inside, she says, "I was in a tug of war with myself. I never could tell right from wrong. When I was young, they told me I was incorrigible." The tale continues: apartments, motels, crack cocaine and marijuana and beer, theft and an escape to Florida. After her second arrest, Corey was sent to Altamont House, a no-frills, Twelve-Step-style program in the Helderberg hills west of Albany.

"I loved it. I had more glimpses of hope." But she resisted the concept of being powerless over drugs and—as is often taught in these programs—surrendering to "God as we understood him." "I hated the idea of powerlessness. I still have some control. But I changed at Altamont. I gave up some."

Corey's experience led to certain conclusions about recovery. "It doesn't really work unless you want it. I don't believe in treatment, because you have to hit bottom." When we spoke in May 1998, Corey was sober for several weeks following a short relapse. Before that, she had been clean four months. Corey attends Twelve-Step meetings periodically, therapy, and three types of group counseling: relapse prevention, trauma education, and gay and lesbian support. Most days, she reads passages from AA literature.

"Every day I try to take a look at what will be the consequences if I use. I have gained a lot of self-worth." Much of that she relates to the meaning she finds in working at the same shelter on Quail Street, which subsequently closed for want of money. While we are eating, an unkempt and disoriented man approaches and asks if he can come by later to shower and wash some clothes. "Come by at four and you can shower, and we'll see about laundry," she tells him before he wanders off.

"I am beginning to see the big picture. I don't just see the street outside." With a deft flick of her wrist, Corey waves toward the window. "I love working at the shelter. There are some things in life I don't like, and I can play a small role in changing them."

For Corey, finally caring about life helps her stay sober. So does the fear of jail. Her spiritual life matters too, though she prefers the nontheistic variety. "I don't believe in God as the higher power, I can't see it. For me, it's water, nature, a stream. I like to find a place with water, even Washington Park, and sit there. I really can't get into the God thing . . . . I keep people in my life that are positive. I pray. I ask the universe to keep me sober one more day . . . . I know there's something out there. I believe God's an energy."

In large part, Corey traces her recovery to the spiritual values she experienced at Quail Street shelter, even though she was spending her days drinking and shoplifting.

"I found this part of me that I didn't think existed. Just knowing that regardless of who I was or what I was doing, I would be accepted. The acceptance, just the acceptance. That gave me hope. The people there, they gave enough of a crap that no matter how many times I fell, they'd still be there."

Pathways to Housing

Sam Tsemberis, a psychologist with decades of experience, has no illusions about healing souls. Five years ago, he founded Pathways to Housing, which installs people who are homeless and usually mentally ill in apartments around New York City. After being frustrated by programs that make many demands of those they would help, he has few. And his goal is simple.

"We are not saying that giving somebody permanent housing eliminates their alcoholism or their mental illness, we are saying that it answers their homelessness," Tsemberis says. "When you make shelter contingent on abstinence, or absence of [mental illness] symptoms, it doesn't make sense. In order to be housed, you have to be homeless. Treatment comes for us when they ask for it."[28]

The program, where I spent a half-day, makes room for people who just will not fit elsewhere, such as Peter.[29] A dusty, grizzled man of 70, whose tall physique has collapsed slightly in the middle from 18 years of walking the streets, Peter drank since he was a teenager. Treatment and support groups never worked: "I'm a lone-wolf type, I've got to do it by myself." He quit only recently, "because I thought I'd die." Peter now spends his time photographing city architecture, notably those of the Bauhaus style. His work, which Guy Trebay of the *Village Voice* praised for its "austere compositional assurance," [30] hangs in Pathways' offices and was in a recent gallery show. Or Qamar, a 40-year-old convert to Islam who left her suburban home at 17 and spent 15 years using "every drug there was." She saw her children adopted by others, a sister die of an overdose. After she was in a Pathways apartment, the staff told her to attend treatment. Qamar's desire to change was awakened because she finally had something to lose: a home of her own. More significantly, having a home had restored her sense of dignity, which she was also afraid of losing. "I was raised in a beautiful home," Qamar says. "I couldn't see being homeless again." The memory renews her fear and she weeps, fussing with the *kimar* that covers her head. She's been clean since 1993.

Aside from need, Pathways has two requirements: applicants must agree to use a case manager—who visits the apartment twice monthly—and to have their public assistance check, usually federal aid for the disabled, go directly to the agency. Pathways pays the rent and distributes the rest to the tenant for food and other personal expenses. Each person signs a lease with the landlord and is subject to the same conditions as any tenant. Pathways has housed 258 people and has 225 apartments.

Tsemberis seems genuinely amazed, even embarrassed, that the method works so well. Over five years, 85 percent of residents have stayed put in the apartments, which he calls "the best retention rate in the city." About 70 percent of clients have had substance abuse problems at some point; 50 percent are drinking or drugging at the time they enter Pathways. Housing eliminates one reason for their drinking, according to Tsemberis and several clients I interview during a visit. Other excuses fall away as life evens out, help is offered, and residents enjoy the privilege of finding that "people are listening to you," he tells me. The operative philosophy: "A radical acceptance of the person's point of view." That seems to change people, from inside out. Eventually, many ask for help and more than half get treatment for their alcoholism or addiction.

Treatment professionals are often aghast at the notion that an alcoholic can go on drinking once in Pathways. "The reaction? They're puzzled. 'Ha, ha.' [they say.] They're puzzled and disbelieving," says Tsemberis. "They're of two minds: they're amazed that this works so well, or they say, 'You don't have the homeless MICAs [mentally ill chemical abusers] that *we're* dealing with.'" A physical man, with broad, quick gestures and an open Mediterranean face topped by swept-back hair, Tsemberis's philosophy serves him well: he appears energized by years of housing the homeless. Any visitor to similar programs knows well that the more common staff aspect is burnt-out exhaustion. Pathways' office is nine floors above Manhattan's West Twenty-Third Street, reached by an old elevator whose clanking chains announce its slow arrival. The offices are cheerfully chaotic, with current and past clients shouting demands or sweeping floors or admiring their photographs in a group show mounted on the wall. Many staffers were once clients, making them both shrewd and sympathetic with current clients.

"Most addicts don't like using, but it's difficult to ask for help," said Winston Chapman, a bright-faced Jamaican staffer who is a recovered alcoholic and addict. Though abstinent himself, Chapman believes not everyone is ready for that step. "I can encourage them. I tell them, 'You're spending $50 a day on drugs and denying yourself x, y, and z. What about spending $30 a day on drugs and you'll have more for x, y, and z?'" Chapman talks to them about God and spirituality in terms of his own recovery with the awe of a man still unsure of what grace restored his life.[31]

Tsemberis's calm and drive stem from what he calls "a Buddhistic loving compassion, where you love the worst parts of the self. Compassion is our core value." The problem with most homeless housing efforts are the entry requirements. "You have to be a 'worthy' homeless person. You can't be a 'bad' homeless person," he contends. Though various sanctions or other measures are employed when people act up, or when their mental disorders flare up—mandatory money management, being banned from Pathways' office, hospitalization—few clients have been kicked out altogether. "In five years, maybe one," says Tsemberis. "Actually, we're trying to get her landlord to kick her out." Another client has been told not to come to the Pathways office after he threw a cup of coffee in a secretary's face. "It was cold coffee. This guy's been in a lot of institutions, so he has a good sense of what line not to cross." Tsemberis also has an acute sense of when a person's bark will not lead to a bite. During my visit, the coffee tosser appears in the reception area and is escorted out, stamping and cursing, after a great commotion. Minutes later, the phone rings in Tsemberis's office. He answers, his face darkens, and he shouts, "No, you can't say those things to me," and hangs up. Tsemberis resumes our talk before I ask for an explanation. "Oh, it was that guy. He said he was coming back here with a gun. What did I do? I told him he can't do that."

Keeping people housed and connected is what works at Pathways. "The easiest thing in the world would be to kick them out," Tsemberis says. "In a crisis, it would be easy to call the police. But when someone's in a crisis, they need comfort and support."

Moderate Drinking, Decriminalization, and Other Harm Reductions

Harm reduction has other implications for treatment. One is the effort to teach some alcoholics and alcohol abusers to drink moderately. Researchers have long known that only a fraction of treated alcoholics abstain continuously. That's why they measure other changes in life after treatment: these improvements can also spell success, or at least indicate that money spent on treatment bears a return. The authors of a controversial 1976 Rand Report found that "Many non-abstinent alcoholics reduce their consumption substantially, either by controlling drinking levels or by alternating between periods of abstention and drinking."[32] The Rand researchers, Harriet B. Stambul and J. Michael Polich, followed up on 2,900 alcoholics and found that 18 months after treatment a majority were in remission: 24 percent abstinent for six months or more; 22 percent drinking normally; and 21 percent abstinent for periods of one to six months. "Clearly, our data, and those from many other studies conducted over the past 15 years, suggest that not all successfully recovered alcoholics must or do abstain from alcohol," they concluded. In fact, if only continuous abstinence counts as success, then treatment programs would have a hard time justifying the cost. Various long-term studies have found that only a fraction—4 percent to 7 percent—abstained consistently in periods of two to five years after treatment.[33]

Alan Marlatt, psychologist and director of the University of Washington's Addictive Behaviors Research Center, has done studies in which binge and other problem drinkers, often college students, were taught to moderate. The proponents of Moderation Management use his ideas in their support groups. Marlatt prefers to see addiction as a continuum rather than the either-or state of the disease model. "The harm reduction approach includes abstinence as a goal," Marlatt told the *Seattle Weekly* in 1995. "But it asks, if you can't achieve abstinence, what can we do to make things less harmful for you?"[34]

The method, Marlatt colleagues say, works best with those under age 40, who drank abusively for ten years or less, who are not physically addicted or damaged by drinking, and who don't have a blood relative who is alcoholic.[35] According to a number of studies and surveys many less severe cases, such as young binge drinkers, eventually stop their abusive drinking on their own. Some may need help, as in learning to drink less. William Miller, a psychologist who wrote a guidebook on controlled drinking, has compared the approach to dieters who learn to control their eating, since abstinence is not possible. Advocates often point to other developed nations. "In Europe, the biggest form of treatment for alcoholics is moderation management," reports Springer. It is also common in Australia and, to some extent, Canada. The reason may be rooted in culture: other harm reduction efforts—needle exchange and legal use of drugs by addicts-also enjoy greater support in those lands than in the United States.

Does Harm Reduction Work?

Absolute proof that harm-reduction efforts work can be elusive. It is hard to run research trials with transient groups as runaways, addicts with AIDS, or street alcoholics. But other indications, and common sense, suggest it can help. For years in Minnesota, chronic alcoholics who have been treated but have relapsed repeatedly are often sent to wet shelters rather than another round of expensive care. With shelter, meals, and case management, they are in less danger and cause fewer social costs in terms of panhandling, crime, and emergency room visits, reported Cynthia Turnure, director of the state's chemical dependency program.[36] Typically, residents cannot drink on the premises. If they do so elsewhere, they will still be required to act properly in the shelter.

Sometimes not making demands of those in need prompts them to ask for help. At the Marian Residence, a San Francisco shelter for homeless women operated by a religious charity, residents were not required to use the case managers, who were available to coordinate services and advise the women on work, housing, family, and other issues. Instead, the managers gain the trust of the women in more passive, low-key ways. "Within three months, they found that almost every one of the women ask for case management," says Ed DeBerri of the National Resource Center on Homelessness and Mental Illness, who formerly directed the San Francisco Council on Homelessness.[37] The Larkin Street Youth Center, another low-demand program in San Francisco, found through their own survey of the 1,808 youths, most of them homeless runaways, that received comprehensive services during 1995 and 1996 that 71 percent leave the streets, usually for their families, treatment, or a group home.

At the New York AIDS Peer Education Coalition, Edith Springer worked with 60-70 mostly teenaged, crack-smoking prostitutes in lower

Manhattan using a harm reduction model that addressed most of their problems and not just the obvious vices. Over eight years, 25 percent of these gave up both prostitution and cocaine, she reports. Deborah Dennis has studied Pathways to Housing as a federal homelessness prevention demonstration project. "Pathways shows that if you offer housing without requirements for treatment, it will reduce recurring homelessness and make people more interested in treatment," she says.[38] For those who don't stop altogether, assistance can reduce problems they cause themselves and others. Though the appeal is strong to common sense and these scattered examples indicate harm reduction's potential, the process of measuring its impact—especially on the course of addictions—is just starting.

Influence and Possibility

Harm reduction challenges the most basic of substance abuse treatment assumptions: the disease concept. Whether advocates say so or not, their emphasis on resolving conditions—poverty, housing, and other illnesses—first, rather than halting the drug abuse, argues for alcoholism or addiction having some origins outside of the person. Tsemberis and others I interviewed maintain that once deprivations are answered, residents usually taper their drug abuse or drinking. Kershnar discounted the disease model: "There may be a predisposition, but not all people with the predisposition [for addiction] fall into it." She contends there are other causes such as trauma, abuse, and poverty. "Drug use provides a metaphor and a deflection for the deeper pain, such as sexual abuse. We say, 'While you're figuring that out, how can we help you reduce the harm you're causing?' "

Put simply, harm-reduction advocates seem to say, "Change social conditions and it will help the alcoholic." Treatment professionals, on the other hand, say, "Stop drinking and conditions will change." But both engage the person on a transcendent level by saying, "You are more than your addiction."

If harm-reduction reforms the treatment community, the change will likely be gradual. In a measure of their growing presence, harm-reduction advocates staffed booths and walked the corridors at the United Nations in June 1998 when the General Assembly held a three-day special session on drugs. On the other side of the United States, advocates have been involved in shaping San Francisco's innovative plan, announced in 1998, to offer "treatment-on-demand," within 48 hours, to addicts and alcoholics who ask for it. Harm-reduction advocates do not take a position on drug legalization even though many—even most— think prohibition causes more problems than it solves. Those who support drug decriminalization—that usually means legalizing possession of certain drugs in small amounts—now range the political spectrum, from conservative William F. Buckley to Kurt L. Schmoke, Baltimore's three-term Democratic mayor. George Soros, the globe-traveling billionaire financier and philanthropist, has helped finance the drive to change American attitudes on drug policy and for harm-reduction initiatives. "He's paying my salary," Springer tells me.

In June 1998, the nation's top drug policy official, General Barry R. McCaffrey, in testimony before the Senate Foreign Relations Committee, called harm reduction, "a highjacked concept that has become a euphemism for drug legalization." Ethan Nadelman, director of a Soros-funded institute, the Lindesmith Center, replied, "The majority of harm reduction advocates oppose drug legalization, and that includes George Soros."[39] If harm reduction was "hijacked," it was from traditional public health policy. Society, and medicine, throughout history have sought to reduce the harm caused by various cantagions and maladies and emergencies. Poverty may cause many if not most health problems, but doctors usually try to ameliorate sickness rather than redistribute wealth. A more complete solution still eludes our will and heart.

Similarly, when we discuss drug addiction on a public health rather than an individual level, we talk of reducing its incidence. We do not aim at societal abstinence. Our last effort at that was Prohibition, notably unsuccessful. While many in the treatment field reject harm reduction, some are seeing what it has to offer. In New York City, several therapeutic communities have hired the Harm Reduction Training Institute to improve their relapse prevention efforts. In September 1996, the New York State Public Health Council endorsed a harm-reduction approach with the following policy statement: "Providing a continuum of care to chemically dependent persons will lead not only to decreased abuse by individuals, but also to reduced criminal activity, leading to safer communities." Other governments have gone further.

To the north, harm reduction is the basis of Canada's Drug Strategy. Eric Single of the Canadian Centre on Substance Abuse, argues that from a public health viewpoint, it would do more good—saving lives, reducing crime and accidents—to reduce episodes of heavy drinking rather than levels of consumption over time, an aim of controlled-drinking programs.[40] Harm reduction characterizes many of the community-based efforts to cut the aggregate harm caused by drinking. One is the campaign to have people, headed out for a night of barhopping, pick one of their group to remain sober and serve as the designated driver. Instead of wishing no one drink to excess, society accepts some may and suggests, basically, that they just take turns. The controlled-drinking debate has been held before, especially in the wake of the 1976 Rand Report and other research. The abstinence crowd won out, and only in the late 1990s did controlled drinking or moderation management as a solution for some less severe alcoholics or problem drinkers get a sustained public hearing. But as the authors of the controversial 1976 Rand Report, *Alcoholism and Treatment*, reported, "Finally, in light of self-fulfilling prophecies, we must question the wisdom of teaching all alcoholics to believe that even one drink leads inevitably to loss of control—especially when the belief has little basis in fact."[41]

The results of more thorough scientific analysis are eagerly anticipated. One reason is that people are dying: of addiction, of AIDS, of drug-related crimes. Another is that while harm reduction seems sensible, if its underlying assumptions are wrong, then many opportunities and lives could be lost if the approach was applied wholesale. Both approaches—harm reduction and abstinence-based—accept that addiction is more than a series of chemical reactions, that the malady touches on the core of a person and implicates their beliefs, values, and perspectives. Both seek to change the outlook of the addict so that she will no longer take drugs to change the way she feels, so that the addict will be able to live in her skin without self-destructing. To do so, both seek to change the person's spirit.

As Kershnar says, "What most people need is a connection with something bigger than themselves." Sound familiar? It could have been lifted from any abstinence-oriented treatment or recovery method, be it the Twelve Steps, or Hazelden, or a religious program, or even Secular Organizations for Sobriety. In this and other ways, the various camps are not so far apart.

CHAPTER VIII

Treating Hard-Core Addicts: From Secular Practicality to Practical Spirituality in Therapeutic Communities

Hospitality House

On Central Avenue in Albany, New York, a mile west of downtown, the businesses and shops cluster together as if to share hope that scattered signs of urban decay—a few empty stores down the block, an abandoned house around the corner—will not infect the whole body. A spunky charm enlivens the boulevard, dotted with shoppers and blue-collar workers. Ballast comes from several grand churches of stone or brick, each with an adjoining complex of school and rectory.

St. Patrick's Roman Catholic Church is one. Though the parish vibrates on weekends with a lively congregation of older Irish-Americans and younger Hispanic families, gone is the full staff that required the large rectory, a muted Gothic fortress just across a sidestreet from the church. The building, red and gray, now serves another type of salvation seeking. "Hospitality House: A Therapeutic Community," says the gold-lettered sign outside. Two young men walk up the stairs with a combined slouch and bop, another stands on the sidewalk talking up a potential sweetheart.

Inside the steel door, a counselor and one of the residents, most of whom are teenagers or young adults, man the front office. A girl mops the hall outside. Other residents hurry back and forth, with staffers riding herd in a friendly, hectic, and stern way. It's like a family whose members love each other but are always on the verge of shouting. Over a loudspeaker, a crackling voice announces a meeting upstairs, now. The controlled chaos and confrontation characterize, to varying degrees, most therapeutic communities. Here at Hospitality House one can almost see a collective energy flow transforming from criminal delinquency into adolescent high jinks and, ultimately, into abstinence and sobriety.

Therapeutic communities aim for their clients to achieve the values and habits and skills that they call "right living." But what sort of salvation is this? Down the hall stands one youth, and around the corner another. Each wears a sullen, sorry expression, and a two-by-three foot sign. Hand-markered in slanted block letters on yellowing posterboard is the following: "I am no longer a member of this community. I have no privileges because I do not deserve any. I am not allowed on my floor alone because I cannot be trusted. It is time for me to grow by being responsible or go back to where I came from. I am a Phase O."

In a borrowed office, I talk with Mark, a thoughtful young man of slight build with short black hair who breaks out of his diffidence and leans forward when his intellect or sense of duty is engaged. His past includes both heroin addiction and the practice of Hindu disciplines. A few weeks earlier, Mark wore the penitent's sign as punishment after he signed out of the house for an AA meeting and failed to attend. During a long interview, he recalls the shame it provoked.[1]

"It sucked, it really sucked. Hospitality House really put a lot of trust in me." But he seems unsure if wearing that sign for 24 hours aided his recovery. "They say they see me going a certain way, that my head isn't in treatment." Now, Mark says, his peers look at him askance but he doubts that the fault is all his. Such a reception typifies a therapeutic community, or TC in rehab parlance, where solidarity is mandated and newcomers routinely are accused of resistance. "From day one I've been accused of disassociating myself from the community," he claims.

Mark was long a seeker. As a teenager, he read Nietzsche and William Burroughs and took LSD. For two years in his early 20s, Mark meditated regularly but also smoked marijuana. He later studied Hinduism and revered the elephant-headed deity *Ganesha*. He appreciated the religion's emphasis on learning truth and wisdom rather than right and wrong. This deep thirst for enlightenment, however, detoured him to heroin.

"When I started heroin, I sat on a porch for four hours in a thunderstorm. It was like, 'Aha, this is it.' It was exactly like I had dreamed, it was like living inside a dream. I was looking in heroin for the same things as in meditation. I just wanted to get to that higher plane of consciousness." Within two months Mark was addicted, and it lasted a year. At the time of our conversation, he had been clean for nine months. Mark came to Hospitality House after violating his probation on a drug-selling conviction. The TC's mix of rough peer-based therapy and its emphasis on spirituality has helped.

"I'm feeling a little better about myself. I'm finding the balance between my feelings and my mind." While unsure if the efforts to corral him helped, Mark is more certain about the spirituality he learned in this and a previous treatment through exposure to the Twelve-Step philosophy. "The first time I got down on my knees I just prayed to whatever, whomever: 'God, I want you to help me take it away.' Now I pray two times a day, sometimes more. That's been the difference. The first time I did it, it made a difference, and the next time I did it, it made a difference. It's just an incredible feeling."

Hospitality House differs from most TCs in that it has endorsed the Twelve Steps for its clients since it opened in 1971 and embraces spirituality as one element of recovery. By contrast, rejecting the AA way virtually defined the first TC, Synanon, and most of its successors. Deliberately and explicitly, TCs eschewed talk of spirituality in favor of a relentless focus on behavior, and its causes and consequences. But as the years passed, many TCs discovered they could not do without the transcendent element critical in most treatment and recovery, and even to the long-term abstinence of their graduates.

Hospitality House was founded by a Catholic priest, Michael Hogan, who drew on the successful lessons of Synanon, Phoenix House, and Daytop but also utilized the Twelve Steps and outside support group meetings. (Another priest, William B. O'Brien, joined Daytop shortly after its founding, in 1963, and continues as president.) In 1998, Hospitality House had a $1.1 million budget and room for 72 clients. Most are referred by the courts.

"Father Hogan saw Hospitality House as a community within a community," says Linn Becker, the director since 1984. With the group as the central therapeutic tool, TCs aim to change lives, rather than psyches. "We are primarily working with behavior modification," says Becker, who has the manner of a worried, affectionate, and sensible mother. Sometimes that is achieved through confrontation and challenge, even on such mundane items as whether a person made their bed or shaved. It also happens through Hospitality House's explicit use of spiritual tools. For instance, when a client has been clean for four months, they schedule a spiritual assessment with a member of the clergy or other person of their own choosing. "A lot of them report a sense of relief," says Becker. Often, the person feels forgiven or accepted. It's a critical point for an addict with a criminal past. "Deep down inside each person is a lot of rage and shame and this thought: 'How can God forgive me for what I've done, or for what's been done to me.' This is oftentimes the key to resolution of their addiction." She says atheists wrestle with a similar question, namely: "God has abandoned me so why should I believe in him?"

The TC Way

How do you get an alcoholic or addict to admit they have a problem? For therapeutic communities the answer is, "With a big push."

"Everything done in a TC is designed to change the individual," said

George De Leon, director of the Center for Therapeutic Community Research, speaking at a conference in April 1998. The member joins, then participates—to an increasing degree—and finally changes. "The TC is quintessential self-help. The community is the trainer and the work is done through peer interactions, job functions, and community roles."

One of the most established and distinctive forms of addictions treatment, therapeutic communities have successfully treated thousands of tough cases, alcoholics, and addicts with long, hard, and, often, criminal careers, who have few social or educational skills or supports such as families and jobs, and many of whom were ordered into treatment by courts or prisons. TCs see addiction as a symptom and the person as the problem. TCs aim to habilitate the addict, arguing that rehabilitation means little to people who were never fully or properly formed in the first place. The Therapeutic Communities of America details the common ingredients: a highly structured clinical environment; community-imposed penalties and a hierarchy of privileges; change in lifestyle through a community of concerned people; residents are members, not patients, who share in decisions where feasible; and peer pressure that leads to change, especially as the members learn from their failures and successes.

The first TC, Synanon, was founded in 1958. By 1995 there were more than 500 TCs in the United States.[2] Treatment comes through the community of fellow clients acting as a family that enforces rules and rewards and punishes accordingly. Residents do most of the managing, cleaning, and other tasks, making TCs cost effective and self-sustaining while also providing real-life lessons in responsibility, discipline, and leadership. Residents move up a hierarchy as they progress, and leave as they are ready after periods of 6 to 12 or more months.[3]

TCs no longer fit the stereotype of a barebones operation run by former addicts where new residents are broken down by harsh and humiliating methods, and recalcitrant members could end up with shaved heads or wearing dunce caps, diapers, or toilet seats. Most now employ professional staffers, many with several degrees—though most of these, still, are recovered addicts. Various therapies and even medications are used at some. Some TCs offer shorter programs with less confrontation or hierarchy. Daytop Village, in Manhattan, has an out-patient TC program for ex-offenders on parole or probation. At all therapeutic communities, the goal is "right living," a productive life free of substance abuse and antisocial behavior. The method has worked for many.

De Leon, who is also a research professor at NYU, analyzed the results of several long-term studies of 9,000 TC patients and graduates who were followed between 1 and 12 years after treatment. De Leon found that 20-30 percent had neither used drugs nor been arrested, while another 30-40 percent showed significant improvement in their lives.[4] In a subsequent conversation, he called those estimates conservative.

James Inciardi, of the Center for Drug and Alcohol Studies at the University of Delaware, studied a prison-based TC program that included 12 to 18 months of residency, followed by a work-release TC, and then extensive aftercare and found success, though modest. After 42 months, 46 percent of those who completed treatment had not been re-arrested; for those who received no treatment, 32 percent were not re-arrested. During that same period, TC graduates also used drugs less often: 1.2 days on average, compared to 6.8 for the untreated convicts.[5]

TCs, like many other forms of rehabilitation, provide "significant benefits even for those patients who do not complete treatment," according to a 1997 federal overview of research on outcomes.[6] In follow-ups and compared to people not treated, those who remain in TCs for at least one-third to one-half of the planned course of treatment reduced their rate of drug use or crime by one-third to two-thirds, and increased their rates of education or employment by half.

To be sure, TCs, like most other treatments for addictions, may benefit from a more realistic measure of success. For instance, graduates who drink or drug are not necessarily flops. "Eighty-five percent of those who do just had to try it. But now they have the skills to turn that around," says Becker of Hospitality House. When relapse is seen in this way, "It's not a failure, it's a learning curve."

For decades, the TC camp saw itself as the opposite of the Twelve-Step approach. "TC administrators were adverse to even the mention of the word 'spirituality,' " said Bosch, who went through Daytop in its early days. (Most TCs rejected other aspects of mainstream treatment, such as the belief that addiction was an incurable disease, and that the addict would always be "sick" and "in recovery.") Although transcendent concepts undergird TCs, these were never explicit. But since the mid-1980s, more have begun to incorporate prayer, meditation, and elements of the AA and NA philosophy or, at the least, sending people to meetings.

The addicts themselves made the jump with enthusiasm. By 1999 at Daytop, 92 percent of clients were attending, or had, Twelve-Step meetings, according to an in-house survey. If it helps heal the psychic wound of addiction, fine, say many. "The problem is a lack of love—their mother didn't love them, their father didn't love them, the abuse and neglect they do themselves," says Michael Bosch, director of the spiritual dimensions program at Manhattan's Daytop Inc., one of the nation's largest and oldest TCs. "The more love there is, the more change there is, the more retention, the more abstention."[7]

TC partisans would argue that they have been spiritual all along in having hope in hopeless addicts. When many TCs were set up in the early 1960s, "the government determination was that there was no cure, that once a dope fiend, always a dope fiend," recalls Tony Gelormino, director of staff development at Daytop Inc., a well-tailored, square-shouldered man who reveals a disciplined mind and memory. TCs offered a powerful alternative by saying that addicts could stop drugs and become responsible adults. Hope is a tonic for an addict, most of all when conveyed by senior residents and graduates who themselves overcame addiction and crime.

So questions arise: Can a program *make* a resident develop a spiritual life? Even short of force, how well does such a squishy idea play with men and women of few resources and many defenses? Most of all, how can spirituality be fostered in a regimented, confrontational atmosphere?

The experience of TCs is significant for several reasons. Between 1970 and 1995, 1.25 million people were admitted to TCs, or about 50,000 a year. Though only a fraction of the millions who go through all kinds of drug and alcohol treatment annually, the cumulative total is high. Second, TCs have a strong—and growing—institutional presence in prisons and in programs for people on parole or probation. Legal authorities routinely send people to TCs, adding credibility along with a steady source of clients. Third, by nature of their clientele, TCs are one of the best known types of treatment. In public debates over addictions and rehabilitation, speakers tend to focus on criminals and others whose drug abuse causes the most obvious problems—precisely the people who tend to be in TCs. Finally, successful graduates of TCs—given their solidarity and their dedication to helping other addicts—often become counselors and program administrators. They represent a cohesive bloc in the field who share assumptions about what makes treatment work and recovery last. Many help shape local, state, and national policy dealing with addictions.

Since the early 1980s, TCs have been entrepreneurs in adapting their methods to other clients and settings. Modified TCs have been established for women and for people with HIV/AIDS or mental illness or who are homeless—or a combination thereof. Sometimes, these serve those who have been victims of abuse and who may be further damaged by the confrontational styles of standard TCs. De Leon reports that preliminary research shows these altered TCs have results similar to standard varieties.

Some History

Two basic TC experiences—public confession and life in a group whose purpose is to change each member—stretch back for millennia. Religious communities and bands have long retreated from the world to better develop along their own values. Two thousand years ago, the Essenes withdrew from Israelite society to Qumran, in the Judean desert near the Dead Sea, to follow their own conscience and community rule. They left the Dead Sea Scrolls as a record of their struggle and success. Even earlier, about 25 B.C., a Jewish sect known as *Therapeutae*—Greek for "heal-ers"—lived in a community near Alexandria, Egypt and reportedly dedi-cated themselves to serving the sick in mind and body. Frederick B. Glass-er, a Canadian psychiatrist, dates the evolution of TCs to this group and others in the field now point to one or another of these sects as "a type of early TC."[8] The modern substance abuse TC germinated in the genius stroke of a frustrated hospital administrator in England during World War II.[9]

A former tank commander, W. R. Bion threw the burden of care back on his unruly patients. Faced with a ward of neurotic, dirty, and disor-dered soldiers, Bion "told his patients at a daily ward parade that he was fed up with them, and henceforth refused to be responsible for caring about, treating or disciplining delinquent behavior which was theirs and not his," a contemporary observer, Thomas F. Main, reported.[10] Bion would see soldiers who presented themselves properly but did not inter-vene to punish. According to Main, after several weeks of chaos, the ward "became the most efficient in the hospital . . . a bold and innovative exper-iment . . . in the delegation of health and responsibility to patients." Resi-dents developed the habit of individuals bringing their problems to their fellow patients, who would hash it out in what turned out to be an effec-tive and therapeutic manner. Because of the perceived threat to military discipline, his superiors relieved Bion of his duties. Who wants the inmates running the asylum? Nevertheless, his six weeks' tenure inspired others to study and adopt his methods. Main, for instance, seized on the idea of an institution or community that was itself the treatment and coined the term "therapeutic community."

British TCs developed amid other influences, such as the social mobi-lizations of World War II and changing psychiatric practice. When the approach was revised and adopted widely in the United States during the 1960s, Bion's practice of letting the patients help themselves recover appealed to the era's rejection of authority and its elevation of oppressed minorities. Similar thinking in the 1960s ignited the return of mentally handicapped people from large institutions to the community.

Tank commander Bion's short-lived experiment at a military hospital embodied concepts that are, decades later, still at the core of TCs: self-help and mutual aid; individual rights and responsibilities; patients seen as "members;" positive peer pressure, and public confessions. Perhaps most of all, like Bion, TCs set far higher expectations for clients or mem-bers than would a hospital or mental institution. This recognition of an addict's higher self lies at the heart of spirituality in TCs. Still, spirituality seemed a distant notion in the militant methods used by the TCs that first developed in the United States.

In 1958, a recovered alcoholic, Charles Dederich of California, became frustrated with the AA approach as ineffective for members with drug problems and criminal pasts. Basically, he thought they needed rougher treatment—brutal honesty—to forsake their old lifestyles and to learn basic values. According to an account he gave in 1963, Dederich thought addicts would benefit from the lessons of sociology, psychology, philosophy, and other fields.[11] Dederich founded a group home, which grew into the powerful Synanon network of TCs. Treatment was free and without staff or professionals. The group helped members face their problems and learn to live in productive and acceptable manners. He favored direct confrontation, long eschewed in Twelve-Step groups, as the best way to cut through an addict's denial. He discovered in early sessions that meetings took on a different quality "when I maintained a stout and rigid control [as] inquisitor and the leader of the group. I began to demonstrate the mechanisms and methods of ridicule and cross-examination."[12]

This developed into the method of Synanon that, according to the assessment of an international team of sociologists, "exerted an extraordinary influence on thinking about treatment for heroin and other drug addicts in the 1960s and 1970s." In his way, Dederich remained true to the essential value of most utopian communities, personal dignity and responsibility. While admitting it was a paradox, Dederich believed that authority and structure foster inner direction in the addict. TCs developed as patriarchal families or "total institutions," with "meetings that emphasized the therapeutic value of a humiliating stripping down of whoever is in the hot seat."[13]

Synanon grew and gained fame—notably among Hollywood types—before Dederich became unbalanced and lost credibility. But Synanon concepts continue to influence TCs large and small. Most significantly, Synanon made confrontation an element in thousands of mainstream treatment centers. Every alcoholic or addict who is hectored by peers to "get honest" should thank—or curse—Dederich.

Today, the term "therapeutic community" covers many forms of drug-free residential programs. About a quarter are traditional TCs lasting 15-24 months. At modified and short-term TCs, clients stay for briefer periods, anywhere from three to nine months. At these, about 75 percent of clients are male and 50 percent in their mid-twenties, with the remainder split between those 30 and older and those under 21.[14] Many have separate wings for adolescents.

Profile: Kim—"It was Scary, then They Become Your Family"

When they speak to the public, scientists love to show us a picture drawn from magnetic resonance imaging of an addict's brain, the different parts illuminated in red or blue according to the effects of cocaine or another drug. It's popular because it's high-tech, it reduces a complex person to the simplistic level of chemistry, and reassures us that we understand the bewildering effect of drugs on otherwise normal, good people.

We don't have an historical series of MRI shots of the brain of Kim, a sweet-natured, 31-year-old woman who grew up in a small upstate community. But were one available it would probably illustrate what researchers have been presenting as the central definition of drug addiction: "a chronic relapsing illness that comes about because of the effects of long-term drug use on the brain."

What happened to Kim?

"It's a disease of addiction," she tells me in our first conversation. We sit in a cramped, stuffy office at Hospitality House Therapeutic Community. On the edges of earshot is the controlled, militant mayhem of a house full of young adults being corralled, and corralling each other, toward a new life.

"I just look at my family. We always worked, we dressed well, went to Catholic school." Kim's father retired from law enforcement; her mother, now deceased, was a housekeeper. Her siblings and close relatives did not addict themselves to alcohol or drugs. None of this seemed to matter once Kim got hooked.

"I tried marijuana, I drank. I probably drugged for ten years, but I was seriously involved with crack cocaine for three years, '91 to '94." Kim was arrested for prostitution and several felonies, including forgery, and spent six months in state prison. She went through Hospitality House in 1994 to little effect. Kim also had two children, who are now cared for by others. Completing those pregnancies is the bright light from a dark period. "I don't believe in abortion. I'm very proud of that, that I went through with them. It was a mistake I made, but I believe God did it so that they could have a life."

Kim gained little from incarceration. "All prison does is teach you how to do it better next time. I got out on parole, went back to the old neighborhood." After a 28-day rehabilitation stint, Kim picked up the crack pipe and other old habits. But soon came the moment, a profound awakening. It was the late afternoon of an October day. Kim was surrounded by other addicts, nodding or smoking or passed out, each absorbed by dark obsessions. "I was sitting in a crack house, and I started crying. I said, 'I can't do this no more.' I thought of everything, I had had some clean time. I got up and left. I said to myself, 'Do you want to go back to being on the street, to prostitution, to being hungry?' I walked down to the police station and turned myself in."

Her parole officer helped out. After three months in jail for violating parole, she entered Hospitality House. So there was a brain, a person, highjacked by cocaine. But while Kim believes she has a disease, she also believes she was, and is, responsible.

"I don't blame anyone else. I did this to myself."

The strict regime at Hospitality House reconditioned Kim, who now works there as an overnight aide and lives in a tidy apartment in a housing project in North Albany.

She treasures the simple routine of her life today: being punctual, taking soapy baths, meeting a sibling for a birthday dinner, being in touch with her children.

Kim lived at the House for 16 months her second time. Treatment included individual counseling sessions, group therapy, and education and community meetings when people reported to each other on their doings and "pulled up" those who were violating house etiquette. Such activities enhance the community's role as a loving support and strict watchdog of each member's recovery. Confrontation is common and valued; certain punishments, such as wearing signs that announce one's intransigence, are variously reported to be humiliating or helpful. Being surrounded by young addicts who, typically, transfer their intense energy to these roles intimidates many new residents.

"It was scary, then they become your family," says Kim. This is the idea.

"They emphasize that this is your family, your community. They make the announcements: 'Now breakfast for the family is served. Now lunch for the family is ready. Now dinner for the family is ready.' "

Kim quotes from the Hospitality House philosophy, which states in part: "When we plunge into ourselves through the eyes of others we will grow and change." Sometimes fellow residents will listen, comfort, and help; other times they will challenge and confront a malingerer. "I was confronted," Kim says. "Some of the things were painful." Special group counseling for victims of trauma helped her deal with having been raped while she was on the streets. Her thinking evokes the painful, paradoxical blend of responsibility and bad luck that characterizes her ideas about her addiction.

"I learned that even though I put myself in that position, it was not my fault. No one deserves that." She also attended NA and AA meetings in the house or at nearby locations, and counselors helped her start practicing the Twelve Steps.

Seen in retrospect, Kim's recovery bears all the marks of a cognitive shift. It is as if she simply stood up in an art gallery, walked several paces, and then looked at the sculpture of her life from a different angle. But she could not take those steps on her own. Will power did not do it. "I'm glad I said, 'Let me go with the flow and do what someone else says.' " With a laugh, Kim recalls that her father always warned her against being a "one-way street" kind of person. I ask if she would be in danger of doing crack again.

"I would be if I stopped going to [AA and NA] meetings, or if I got an attitude, thinking, 'I *got* this.' " She mentions the two safeguards as if of equal importance. Remaining abstinent involves watching and, when necessary, changing her train of thought in the midst of normal reactions. "All humans have feelings: happy, sad, glad, so on." Treatment reinvigorated and redirected her spiritual life, largely through Twelve-Step facilitation and meetings. Kim also had a "spiritual assessment," which is routine at Hospitality House and is done privately with a client's choice of clergy. Kim had hers with a nun at St. Patrick's Church, who serves this role with many of the program's female clients. Today, Kim prays at night, after the daily shower she loves taking.

"Maybe it's a female thing, but I use all these different soaps and go to bed. I may not say a novena or a Hail Mary but I have a conversation." Kim flips one hand back and forth to illustrate an exchange. Later, over coffee on Albany's bohemian Lark Street, Kim says her prayer life has shifted away from petitions.

"I do more thanking now. I thank God for a warm bed and a home instead of a cold cell. Before I prayed out of desperation; now it's out of gratitude. How do I feel inside? It's pleasant, content, peaceful, happy. Definitely happy. My life? It's normal, normal. I get up, make my bed, go to work on time." The spiritual and cognitive shifts led to a social shift.

"The state doesn't like paying for places like Hospitality House, and that's fine. But look at me, I'm off welfare and I've got a job." Kim gives thanks for her second chance. Yet there is a touch of sadness about her, no bitterness, but a sad wonder over a trip through an earthly hell that seems to have been a pointless, painful detour.

As we sit in a downtown espresso shop, where hair colors range the spectrum and skateboarders indulge in a legal vice, Kim falls into silence. Her eyes lose expression and withdraw into her face, which hardens into a wall of defense before slackening. Kim looks down at our coffee cups, then off into the middle distance, then at me. She drops her elbows onto the wooden surface.

"You know Chris, sometimes I wonder, 'What happened to me?' I was a nice girl growing up. What happened?" She leans back in the chair to consider this in her private conversation. "I don't know. I can't put my finger on that one."

Spiritual Underpinnings

Michael Bosch has the endearing accent—like a rough hug—and quick gestures of his native Hell's Kitchen neighborhood in Manhattan. A heroin user by the age of 11, he eventually became the director of Daytop's "Spiritual Dimensions" program. Bosch embodies the evolution of spirituality in therapeutic communities. "I got a bed when I was 16, at the Daytop TC on Tenth Street and Avenue C. It took me a year, since they used to make you prove you were sincere before they let you in. I graduated in April 1972 after 25 months. It was hard-core, old-fashioned, but to me it was a loving place." This, despite the rough, hectic atmosphere brought on by addicts treating addicts, without their edges smoothed off by any professional training. As treatment or punishment, residents could have their heads shaved, be made to wear diapers and tote baby rattles, or carry signs announcing their misdeeds. More than once in several hours of conversation that began in a Daytop conference room, continued over pizza, and lasted through a walk across a bustling midtown Manhattan on a sunny winter day, Bosch recalls the frenzy fondly. "Back then, you were always on your toes," he says with a smile, his (now voluntarily) shaved head gleaming brightly. In various group sessions, some lasting more than 24 hours, addicts would tell their life stories to their peers.

"They would tell their whole life, good and bad, but mostly about the pain. We were always asking, 'How'd that feel? How'd it feel?' When you came out, the family was there. While you were in, people were sending in notes for you, encouraging you. Just like when you're on a retreat and people pray for you."

Bosch worked for Daytop for several years, then relapsed. After several years of travels and searching, he found himself in his mother's apartment weeping uncontrollably. "Then my whole body was lifted up and I felt this great joy. My head twisted around and I saw a Bible and I opened it and saw this line: 'Search for the truth with a sincere heart and you will find it.' " (Bosch says he's been unable to locate the verse again.) After a spell of evangelizing on the street, he worked as a youth counselor in his parish church, then relapsed with marijuana. In 1986, he recovered again, by attending meetings of Daytop graduates, and resumed his employment there. He apprenticed to the program's chaplain, John Magan, a Jesuit priest. After Magan died, Bosch assumed his current job. He works out of Daytop's Swan Lake complex in the foothills of the Catskills, integrating spirituality into TC methods. In April 1999, Bosch spoke on the topic at a conference of Asian TC staffers in Kunming, China. It's been quite a change for him and the field.

"Spirituality has come into the TCs from the bottom up," says Bosch. Many graduates relapsed due to a lack of an interior life, "because spirituality was the one thing they hadn't developed in the TCs." Those graduates who remained abstinent often had developed an internal life through Twelve-Step groups. Seeing that evidence, by 1999 all Daytop outreach programs and one long-term program began sponsoring Twelve-Step meetings. Bosch offers retreats for Daytop clients and he trains staff members in spiritual methods such as prayer, meditation, and the Twelve Steps.

The change was dramatic. It occurred because the old way was not working. A state prison addictions counselor, who asked to remain unnamed, told me that TCs evolved from their punitive and insular model due to a high relapse rate and the need for the life-long help of spiritually based support groups. "TCs have bought into the Twelve Steps because treatment ends and the person is phased out and is on their own. If you look at what has done the best for the most for the longest, you've got NA and AA and the rest."

Peter Collins, a senior counselor at Daytop's adult outpatient center on Eighth Avenue, got clean himself at Daytop back in 1972. No one mentioned transcendent matters. Addicts spent much of their time recounting—or boasting of—their sins, he says. "It was all, 'I did this and I did that,' and a lot of ego." After Collins graduated from this insular and secure world, he turned to Twelve-Step groups and their philosophy for additional help. Incorporating both approaches was hard, personally and professionally.

Now at Daytop graduation ceremonies, "more and more you hear people thanking their higher power," says Charles Devlin, Daytop's vice president for treatment services. Daytop staffers high and low now speak of spirituality in clear and concrete terms. Derek Whitter, director of Daytop's new out-patient program for parolees or probationers, gave me one of the handiest definitions of spirituality: "A self-awareness that brings about peace and allows people to change."

Whitter says TCs, in the early decades, neglected spirituality because dependence on a God contradicted the emphasis on self-determination and on the healing role of the therapeutic community—including counselors looming larger than life before debilitated addicts. "Before, the staff thought *they* were the ones saving lives. Now, I tell clients to attend Step meetings [AA/NA sessions dedicated to discussing one or more of the Twelve Steps], and that will help them get in touch with a higher power." Now TCs are more explicit but still flexible about spirituality. Says Devlin, "We encourage prayer and meditation and there's a nondenominational chapel. We have a shaman, a priest, a rabbi who will come in if residents want. We want to make people aware [spirituality's] part of living, that's part of what will keep them clean."

The shift from finding salvation almost solely in the TC to finding help from some kind of divinity will continue to reverberate given the cohesiveness and influence of this type of addictions treatment. While TCs long avoided the word "spirituality," these programs actually displayed traditional aspects of spiritual methods since their inception in 1958.

A Community Apart

The spiritual forefathers of TCs include the religious and utopian communities of nineteenth-century America, according to O. Hobart Mowrer and others in the field. Charles Dederich, founder of Synanon, read the transcendentalist tracts of Thoreau and Emerson. Early TC leaders were also influenced by the experience of the nineteenth-century Oneida commune of upstate New York, where members preached an enthusiastic strain of Christianity known as Perfectionism, and the Clarion commune in Utah. Like TCs, these utopian communes, "were created by those individuals whose values and beliefs conflicted with those of the larger society and who sought to create their own utopian self-sufficient communities," wrote Thomas E. Bratter and colleagues in a 1986 article.[15]

"TCs have always seen themselves as families, families that are directed at changing the lifestyle and personal identity of addicts," De Leon said at the 1998 NIDA conference. As in real families, the individual must often submit himself to the larger entity for both the common and his personal good. Gelormino recalls long conversations at Daytop with residents and staffers as they sorted out the alchemy of recovery in a community. "We all agreed that something was happening in the community that was bigger than the individual, and if the individual could subordinate himself to that process for a while, until they see the change inside and not just outside, it would work."

People involved with TCs proudly note their heritage from similar groups over history, which also removed them from society to resolve appetites, or sin, through public confession and group acceptance. Today, the group also counters the scientific view that can reduce an addict, or any person, to their parts or just one part, such as their genes or the passage of chemicals between synapses deep in the brain. Gelormino credits Victor Frankl for persuasively arguing that a person is more than a sum of her or his parts. And this spiritual entity emerges in the group of peers, the essence of the TC. "The community is the healer," says Gelormino. "The community brings all the parts of the person together."

Public Confession

"There are basic elements in all healing communities," said Gelormino. "One is 'exemologiesis,' which is open confession before a group as a healing process. That's the beginning for almost all organized religions, and that's the basis of TCs, and of AA too."

The Oxford Group, a back-to-basics Christian movement of the early twentieth-Century, influenced AA with its principles of self-survey, confession, restitution, and service to others. Bill Wilson and Dr. Bob Smith, AA's founders, both attended Oxford Group meetings as they first got sober in 1935. AA in New York, Wilson's bailiwick, separated itself from the Oxford Group in 1937. In Smith's town of Akron, Ohio, AA groups associated with it until 1939. There, new AA members would kneel and pray in front of the group for help with their problems.[16] Public confessions faded away under the objections of Catholics accustomed to the privacy of the confessional booth. Today, the practice of public confession continues in two forms that pose little trouble for people from most religious traditions: telling of personal stories at meetings, and the moral inventory shared in private with an AA sponsor or other person.

Rejection of the Twelve-Step approach originated with Dederich's dissatisfaction with AA etiquette and methods. Many TC proponents also disliked the emphasis on the disease concept of addiction found in mainstream programs. After a long separation, the two camps have reached a détente on common ground. "The common genealogical roots found in TCs and the 12-step groups are evident to most participants of these, and the similarities in the self-help view of recovery far outweigh the differences in specific orientation," De Leon wrote in 1994.[17] Since the mid-1980s, TCs have integrated Twelve-Step meetings and, less often, education into their programs. More and more TCs recommend their graduates attend meetings. These graduates, and the staff members who attend meetings to maintain their own recovery, often return to TCs with the message of an effective spirituality.

Ideally these two elements, the group and public confession, confirm a person's worth and dignity through the love of others. Gelormino credits Mowrer for influencing TCs by bringing "the concept of human identity into the mental health field." Mowrer (1907-1982), was president of the American Psychological Association and used theological concepts to bring a hard-headed compassion to his field. In an idea that influenced many at Daytop and other TCs, Mowrer suggested considering a patient's guilt to be real, rather than delusional, and suggested that self-disclosure or confession be followed by contrition and atonement to achieve psychic equilibrium.[18]

Richard Dunn, a student of Mowrer's, has spent decades exploring the role of spirituality in recovery and at TCs. He has worked with Daytop and founded one of the first programs in addictions counseling, at Sullivan County Community College in New York's Catskill region. For Dunn, Mowrer simply resurrected the "old religious continuum of sin to guilt to crisis to remorse to confession to forgiveness to Grace." This occurred at a time when modern religion has abandoned hoary notions of guilt and sin. Recovery schemes such as AA and therapeutic communities are, Dunn shrewdly notes, "more in touch with the original notion of the church than is much of the modern church." Ideally, that's what the TC does, welcome the sinner back into the fold. The addict is usually eager to step in. "What Mowrer, AA and TCs recognize is that human beings are designed to live responsibly in society," writes Dunn. Addiction, crime, and irresponsible living alienate a person. Recovery must include "some mechanism for restoration to community." Standing in ashes and sackcloth serves as the crucible of recovery. "Confession sets the stage for amendment of life and restoration of community." The readmission reinforces itself since we enjoy and prosper as members of a group. Dunn calls this group membership "social catnip."[19] The social urge, basic to all humans, can motivate and direct recovery.

But the mix of love and confrontation is potent, both for healing and abuse. One person's idea of hurtful confrontation can be another's passage to wholeness. Even though an addict's exposure to an aggressive group of peers can be traumatic, according to Frank W. Wilson of the Life for the World Trust, a British TC, "the results of group forgiveness can be very powerfully regenerative and usually they are."[20]

Right Living and Values

In practice, TCs refuse to buy into the growing tendency to see addiction as a mere function of neurochemistry and genetics. Mitchell Rosenthal, president of Phoenix House, the nation's largest network of TCs, told me that his program "is about helping people gain self-reliance, maturity, and control over their lives, and that aspect of our work is insufficiently appreciated by researchers who are interested in brain chemistry."[21] In the TC worldview, drug use is merely a symptom of bad habits and values—immaturity and irresponsibility. Addicts never grew up or they regressed into a warped lifestyle. Therapeutic communities deal with these attitudes and behaviors with a combination of " 'tough love' and intense mutual support," writes Dunn. Heroin addicts find "more love, acceptance, and helpful structure in the TCs than ever before in their lives."[22] But it is a love that believes the addict will relapse "until he develops some old-fashioned moral and ethical standards and starts living up to them."[23]

In the first phase of Daytop's treatment, eight to ten clients will meet in "probes" lasting up to eight hours under the supervision of a staff member. Participants explore and discuss—or "confess"—their sexual history, an unexplored minefield for most addicts whose habits often distorted their desires and practices. "It's to get that out, the shame that people come in here with," says Bosch. During the second phase of treatment, clients move on to discuss in similar meetings their family histories and conflicts. Adds Bosch, "We hope that by the end of all these groups, clients have out all their secrets."

Conflicts and Resolutions

Several aspects of TCs readily clash with popular notions of spirituality. One is the confrontation, often carried out in the long-and short-term meetings of clients that form the backbone of TC life. The names of the sessions indicate their nature: "probes," "cop-out sessions," and "marathons." To be sure, people in all kinds of therapy and addictions treatment review and resolve internal pains and conflicts. Critics have long worried that TCs hinder or worsen the process of personal examination through harsh honesty, confrontation, and peer pressure. In response, TCs have evolved. Few are run by residents to the same degree as in the 1960s. At Daytop, professional staff direct and moderate most group meetings. Marathon meetings, which at one time could go on for days, are no longer held. Proponents, naturally, consider the danger to be overstated. William B. O'Brien of Daytop and D. Vincent Biase declared that despite fears and outside protests, "no reported data have indicated evidence of emotional harm as a result of supervised self-help TC encounter groups."[24]

Still, endless sessions of confrontation and confession and other TC methods tend to arouse emotions to extreme degrees. The same happens universally to humans who are changing their lives, whether in therapy or during physical or psychic healing or in a religious conversion. In TCs, an already-alienated newcomer often learns, first, that his or her remove from society is greater than she realizes. The return to a group, the community of peers, is all the more eagerly sought. The desire to belong can be the most powerful tool for a TC to wield in helping an addict. But the pain can be great when, for disciplinary or other reasons, this newcomer is kept out of the group. After all, humans tend to sicken and even die when ostracized. Shunning is used by all societies to enforce discipline. As in other groups, the potential for abuse is great at TCs, and greater at those that are insulated from outside society.

Daytop weathered an early crisis in 1968, when some staffers, supported by Monsignor O'Brien, proposed a "reentry" program to help residents return to the world. "The idea was that you change inside, here, and then you go back to your community and be an agent of change," recalls Charles Devlin. Before that and like most TCs, Daytop clients made the TC their primary allegiance even after treatment. The proposal split the ranks at Daytop, with one group suing the other for control, and was ultimately settled in court in favor of the integrationists. The consensus now prevails that, in Gelormino's words, "We're not a forever community."

A second and related danger arises from the character of TCs. Demoralized, vulnerable addicts enter a tightly structured hierarchy where they learn from veteran clients, graduates, and staff. That is, of course, the idea of the community as therapy. But example and emulation can become authoritarianism and blind obedience.

In a protected environment, TCs create a second childhood during which addicts can learn and mature in a manner they missed during their first childhood or that they distorted during years of monomania and criminality. A good parent who becomes a friend, as the child or addict grows, is part of the experience. At first, this figure is more of a charismatic leader or benevolent dictator. "The American self-help TC believes what depressed, despondent, self-destructive, drug-dependents desperately need are charismatic and caring persons who can function as gurus and/or medicine men," writes Bratter. This shaman, he explains, restores hope, maintains high expectations, and instills faith in the addict.[25] That this person—a TC leader, a counselor, a senior resident—was previously also an addict is the primary lesson for the newcomer. Now they can see, perhaps for the first time, a peer who is no longer consumed by drugs and crime. But a charismatic leader, unless his or her power is checked by a group, can become a dictator. Synanon and other TCs have collapsed after their leaders refused the same accountability demanded of all residents.

"The number of charismatic leaders who directed therapeutic communities to greatness only to become consumed by their abuse of power tragically continues to proliferate," Bratter wrote in 1986.[26] While the seeming opposite of spirituality, such abuses are all the more possible when treatment involves opening addicts up to their inmost beings, to the repositories of morals and values and transcendental longings. Since addicts have failed, they are ready to follow someone who tells them they can win if they follow certain rules. "It's the easiest thing in the world to take 200 heroin addicts to a mountain and set yourself up as their king," says Gelormino. "It really is." Sitting in an upper floor office of the Daytop headquarters in the once-stately, former Overseas Press Club on Fortieth Street in Manhattan, Gelormino still looks warily at the example of "all the quasi-religious organizations, with the power of change, that have imploded, like Jim Jones in Guyana."

Whether in a traditional or a modified TC, confrontation and spirituality may not always coincide nicely. Becker readily ticked off the main criticisms of TCs. "We're confrontational, we use humiliation and we're insulated." The insulation is a feature of most residential treatment centers—that are by nature removed from the world. Humiliation springs from the sordid experience of addiction, and can be confronted, or exacerbated, through confrontation. Confrontation occurs in various degrees and can be put to good use—in the right dosage and with care and love.

"It needs a lot of decompression," Becker said. "If it's done for purposes of humiliating someone or causing shame, then it's wrong." Despite Synanon's sad end, Mitchell Rosenthal of Phoenix House said that Dederich's best legacy remains the use of the group to "break through the denial and defenses of the individual members." But Synanon, he added, "lost sight of the organization's responsibility to residents. The modern TC looks out for the needs of the individual rather than the needs of the group."[27] In response to charges that TCs are "hostile places that lack the milk of human kindness," Richard Dunn holds up the fact that "thou-sands of Therapeutic Community graduates all over the world are cur-rently enjoying the fruits of a drug-free life."

On the ground, blending what works remains the goal. At Hospitality House, Becker tells me, about 45-50 percent of clients complete treat-ment lasting from one year to 18 months depending on the person and his or her progress. The fact that many are here under court order cer-tainly helps retention. In seeking the magic cure, the staff has tried many approaches: acupuncture—whose main benefit seems to be making an addict lie still for an hour and feel the physical touch of the clinician—hypnosis, "thought field" therapy, and cognitive behavioral therapy. When government priorities change, so do available funds. With each, the goal has been finding a way to change the addict's outlook. A common assumption, says Becker, "is that how we think affects how we feel and how we feel affects how we act. But there's no consensus." As for the con-tinuing promises that the next pill will ameliorate the addictive drive, she presumes something pharmacological will work for some. "Others will need that defining moment."

Of course, drink or drugs often debase a person sufficiently to provide all the motivation they will need later on in making a new life. Paul, a clean-cut 25-year old from Utica, arrived at Hospitality House directly from the county jail, where he was serving a sentence for drunk driving. "I came here in handcuffs and shackles. It was pretty humiliating, and then they had me sit in the lounge like that for an hour." The experience lessened his conviction that some bad luck ruined his fun. "It was degrad-ing—I never saw myself like that." The memory of being locked up—"where the drinking brought me," says Paul—goads his abstinence.

Paul interested me because he stood apart from the community life at Hospitality. He came from a more middle-class family and his drinking, while abusive, had not wrecked his life. It may indeed have been a tempo-rary aberration. He was willing to benefit from some of the TC lessons and able to detach from others. "The confrontation, I don't let it get to me. If you take it the wrong way, that's on you." Further, Paul did not approach recovery as a spiritual experience. "I was brought up Catholic but I never dropped to my knees and said, 'God, why me?' I brought this on myself and so I'm responsible for getting myself out of it." The senti-ment accords nicely with TC lessons on responsibility.

While grateful he had a chance to quit drinking, Paul does not consid-er it a blessing from any higher power. "I do pray, not to stop drinking but normal prayers, like for my family." His plans for staying sober after his graduation, four months away as we speak, include AA, changing friends, and acceptance. "I like going to meetings and knowing that it's not just me who screwed up my life. About addiction, I learned that I have it. I never liked that word before."

Back in 1919, William James ventured that alcoholics were frustrated mystics. The founders of AA found a practical means for alcoholics to recover by picking up certain spiritual tools. Dunn sees the same recipe working in TCs. "If drinking and drugging became a way of saying 'no' to life, recovery is a way of saying, 'yes.' That means recovery, at base, is a transformation. Nothing less will endure. It comes down to the capacity to find a spiritual meaning in life, coupled with a doggedly practical collection of relapse prevention techniques."[28]

Profile: John—A Manhattan Kid Finds His Way

John grew up on the West Side of Manhattan, in the Hell's Kitchen neighborhood.

He tried marijuana and alcohol but got hooked on heroin. "The first time, it had an effect. I finally felt comfortable around people. I felt safe." Safe from what? "From fear—fear of people, fear of dealing with myself." In 1970, already "a full-blown junkie" at age 16, John was arrested and sent to a therapeutic community, or TC, as an alternative to jail. Daytop Village operated the program on Staten Island along traditional TC lines. He found some of the punishments—being yelled at simultaneously by five people, spending a night in an open coffin, being made to wear a sign detailing some transgression—excessive. Yet, fear of trouble prompted him to change. And the endless group sessions socialized him. "When I came out [of Daytop], I could talk to people, hold a conversation, go for a job interview."[29]

The so-called marathon groups, which could last for hours or even overnight, were more akin to intimate mentoring sessions with peers. "You'd talk about sexual things, the things you're ashamed of. It was like confession, and you'd cry and cry and cry." He felt forgiven, both directly and by example. "You were told that it was okay. And you see other people who did it, or they see me sharing something, and it's 'Hey, he kicked that out and his head didn't fall off.' " John knew the salve of forgiveness, having attended confession as a Catholic youth, often out of guilt over his heroin habit and stealing.

But during his two years at Daytop, other than the religious overtones of the group confession, John heard no mention of prayer, meditation, or the Twelve Steps. In keeping with TC practice of that time, he was taught that drugs alone were his problem and that outside support groups as NA or AA were not necessary. "When I got out of Daytop they told me I was cured. I was a graduate and almost a superhuman being." During the transitional reentry phase, John had drinking privileges. "I got high with a vengeance." Later came pot and then heroin. He attended a methadone clinic, but abused that drug—"It was my Prozac, I'd do my dose and buy more"—and also Valium and cocaine. John worked steadily, as a chauffeur, and maintained a stable relationship with the woman he later married. Despite trouble-free periods, he wanted help.

"I used to pray, pray in my car to God, to the God of my conditioning from the Catholic faith. I was always in pain. The drugs stopped working and I was left with me." In 1987, he entered a month-long hospital-based detoxification and rehabilitation program. "After 21 days I was clean for the first time in ten years." Also there he heard about the Twelve Steps for the first time. "I said 'I don't have anything else so let me try this. When I got out of the hospital I could hardly walk. I had the AA Big Book and other books, like [AA's] *Living Sober*, and it was a job to walk to the bus."

Though some of the lessons he learned at Daytop years earlier conflicted with AA, "I knew it wasn't a religious cult, that nothing was pushed on you. I was clean and sober for seven years, and slipped in 1994 when I got high for a week. I had stopped going to meetings and felt all-powerful. There were no prayers. I felt no spirit. I was like a machine: going to work, coming home. I felt no substance, no meaning, no interaction with others."

He recovered and has remained clean since, with lessons learned during his early recovery at a therapeutic community and his more recent experience with the Twelve-Step approach. John's spirituality involves a simple discipline and a blended notion of God. "I do things I do not want to do. Like, I get on my knees instead of praying in bed horizontally." Acting contrary to desires liberates him from him. "I get out of myself and I'm not so self-centered. It's very hard for me to do. I'm very selfish and when I don't get off it, it makes my spirit poor." John also found a God of his own understanding.

"It's more of a collective thing, a collective spirit or, from Indian philosophy, the idea of nature. Sometimes I use the God of my childhood." His experience at Daytop prepared him for taking the personal moral inventories suggested by the Twelve Steps. When he shared this roster of sensitive secrets with a mentor, "Daytop made it easier since I thought, 'I've done this before.' I don't want to get high again, so I've got to trust. I walked out of there about two feet off the ground. You know, now, I can talk to you about anything. Relating to other people, communicating—I learned that in Daytop, that everything was okay to talk about."

TCs Today: A Big Presence

Given their success, or at least their disciplined focus, TCs continue to grow and, usually with public funds as authorities, turn to a coherent and successful model for treating new groups of addicts such as single mothers, youths, or people with mental disorders. Six former addicts in a West

Side tenement founded Phoenix House along TC lines in 1967. By 1998, Phoenix grew into the nation's largest private, nonprofit drug treatment organization with 70 programs in eight states, room for 5,000 clients and support from foundations and Hollywood luminaries. At that time, it was preparing to operate a New York public high school for troubled students, and its long-time president, psychiatrist Mitchell Rosenthal, was credited with influencing Mayor Rudolph Guiliani's turn against methadone as treatment. Jane Zimmerman, a doctor and city health official, said TCs like Phoenix House "teach work skills and personal responsibility while holding you accountable. It really addresses the underlying causes of the addiction, rather than substituting one addiction for another."[30] (Ironically, to many outsiders TCs and Twelve-Step-style treatments serve, in another way, to replace "one addiction for another.") Daytop's reach is also great. On any given day in 1995 to 1996, it was treating nearly 5,000 people at 33 sites in New York, New Jersey, Pennsylvania, Florida, Texas, and California.

TCs span the globe. Officials from 80 countries have trained in Daytop's method with many completing months-long internships in U.S. programs. China has set up TCs on the Daytop model and Thailand has adopted the TC philosophy for its treatment of juvenile delinquents. The U.S. Department of State's Bureau of International Narcotics and Law Enforcement Affairs has supported TC development in a number of foreign countries, the *National Institute of Justice Journal* reported in October 1999. Bosch said many Asians like the family concept and that Muslims, especially, appreciate the newfound TC emphasis on spirituality and meditation. The *Justice Journal* reported that TCs in the Philippines and Thailand embodied the decorum and personal dignity that characterize those nations.

But here too lie buried land mines regarding the volatile mix of religion and treatment, especially when it comes to official sanctions. "Most therapy is Anglo-Euro-centric, so one of the essentials to translate is the way we deal with spiritual life," says Gelormino. "You have to be careful since in East Europe and Asia, a lot of religious programs are springing up." In those countries, as well as in the United States denominational programs are pushing for recognition, certification and even public funding. If successful, such a drive could drain funds away from nonsectarian programs. It could also lead to a public reaction against funding any treatment with a spiritual component.

The cruel irony appears to be that just when TCs are willing to discuss spiritual concepts more explicitly, they are in danger of being confused with sectarian religion. This is the narrow ridge most treatment programs have had to walk for decades as they encourage clients to meditate or find a higher power, of any sort, while not appearing to preach a religious dogma. Many TC staffers appear willing to venture out along this path, since they concluded they were missing something all along. "Twenty years ago, Monsignor O'Brien told us we were remiss in that we asked clients to confront their sexual identity, to confront their personal identity, to confront their criminal identity, but we did not ask them to confront their ideas about God and a spiritual life," recalls Gelormino. "If you don't want to go to church, fine, but let's see why."

TC officials see broad new fields opening up as politicians act to treat incarcerated addicts. New York, South Carolina, Ohio, Missouri, Texas, Florida, and California all embrace the TC model for prison treatment. In 1998 and based on the success rate of prison rehabilitation, federal officials told states to develop and implement drug testing and treatment policies or risk losing federal aid, according to the *Bergen Record*. The newspaper reported that according to recent studies, including one by Columbia University's Center on Addiction and Substance Abuse, treated prisoners have a recidivism rate about 25 percent lower than the average.

Since the TC model has become the favored one for prisons, most new programs will be of that kind. In response to the growing interest, the trade groups Therapeutic Communities of America and the Corrections Associations of America have worked to develop accreditation standards for prison-based TCs. One reason was to clear up misconceptions, according to David Kerr, a TCA official, that a TC simply involves "loud confrontation" or "making the addict clean things with a toothbrush."[31]

Herein lies a further danger. As more prisons are operated by private firms, more prison TCs will be as well. In 1998, international security and corrections giant Wackenhut Corp. contracted to run a United Kingdom prison, which included a 200-bed therapeutic community. (By 1998, Wackenhut was already operating 50 prisons in North America, Europe, and Australia—with 34,301 beds—as well as the mental health services in many prisons.[32]) In 1998, Kansas opened a privately run TC in its Winfield state prison that will have room for 63 inmates. After finding success with a prison TC it operated in a Nashville, Tennessee, the Corrections Corporation of America adopted the same methods in 20 other prisons it operates around the country. Given the convergence of two trends—commercial prisons and TC spirituality—someone eventually will be trying to make a profit out of spirituality. God and mammon may yet coexist, but the potential for corruption of one by the other is enormous.

The nature of these new TCs has yet fully to emerge. While Daytop, Hospitality House, and others embrace or continue using spiritual concepts and practices, other TCs prefer the old methods. The Delancey Street Foundation, one of the best-known and most successful TCs, still eschews the Twelve Step approach. During a tour of the program's Spanish villa compound on the San Francisco waterfront, Gerald Miller, a staffer and graduate, tells me that residents do not attend meetings of Alcoholics Anonymous or Narcotics Anonymous. "Once they come into Delancey Street, they don't have a drug or alcohol problem, they have a living problem. You have to deal with the fact that you're nasty, that you're criminal." Nor does he attend AA or NA since the Delancey Street community suffices to keep him on the path of right living. Though some graduates do attend support groups, "it doesn't come up while they're here," Miller says.[33]

More than most, Delancey Street remains an insulated, self-sufficient community despite its commercial interaction with the San Francisco public. Based on what I was told and on materials given me, it does not employ professional counselors and receives no government funds other than for specific contracts at, usually, off-site locations. People work for room and board; there are no salaries. A range of businesses—restaurants, moving, auto detailing, Christmas tree sales—bring in several million dollars a year and provide training and jobs for residents and graduates. Its $30 million complex—of coffee-colored stucco set off by cream-colored trim with geranium-stuffed flower boxes and a tiled courtyard complete with fountains and gardens—cost half that to build since residents did most of the work. Founded in 1970 and long directed by the magnetic Mimi Silbert, Delancey Street reported in 1995 that 11,000 addicts had completed its treatment. About 500 ex-addicts live at the San Francisco complex and an equal number in other facilities in several states. Officials report that about 70 percent come from the courts and 30 percent were homeless. Residents stay at least two years and four on average. Basically, says Miller, "You learn how to get through a bad day without falling apart." He likens it to school.

"People tell you how to walk, how to speak, how to sit down and eat," says Miller, a tall man whose poise, speech, and dress suggest he's come a way from his time as a convicted felon. "The first 90 days are like hell, like boot camp." As if on cue as we speak, a group of grim-faced newcomers wearing khaki pants and white T-shirts dogtrot by in straight columns across the tiled courtyard. A fountain tinkles in the background. At dinner, residents come to the nicely appointed dining room and are seated one by one by a *maitre d'*, an exercise that teaches etiquette and breaks up cliques that may form—important given the number of former gang members.

"Accountability and responsibility are the two big things here," says Miller. There are three cardinal rules: no violence, no threats of violence, no drugs or alcohol. Like all TCs, the group rehabilitates members, either in the confrontational meetings where residents work out their emotional issues or in more vocational settings. "Each one teaches one," says Miller. "If you read at a sixth-grade level, you tutor someone who is at the fourth-grade level." Residents earn their high school equivalency degrees before they graduate, and many attend college. "By the time they leave, they should have three marketable skills." Like other TCs, residents gain privileges with time and progress, and the operation is quintessentially self-help in nature but without reference to higher powers or prayer and meditation.

Increasingly, TCs influence other social and medical services. One reason is the method is already employed with addicts who have other problems: AIDS, prison convictions, mental illness, juvenile status. Such innovations expose more social workers to the TC model and, in turn, TC staffers find out about other practices. De Leon foresees "a general treatment model applicable to a broad range of populations for whom affiliation with a self-help community is the foundation for effecting the process of individual change."[34] TCs may help introduce spirituality as a therapeutic tool to fields that would otherwise abhor its mention. On the other hand, traditional TCs—insular, secular, confrontational—are still influential. Delancey Street, for example, has government contracts to help treat juvenile offenders and other groups.

The goal is a moral being or, in less weighted language, a good citizen. Delancey Street teaches former addicts "the interpersonal, social survival skills, along with the attitudes, values, the sense of responsibility and self-reliance necessary to live in the mainstream of society drug-free, successfully and legitimately."

A Hidden Convergence

Could an emphasis on the transcendent ameliorate the excesses of therapeutic communities? A spiritual dimension can provide a more humane approach to the person by acknowledging her or his essential humanity and, at the same time, capitalizing on the person's primordial survival instinct.

At a 1998 National Institute on Drug Abuse conference, William Miller, a highly regarded researcher, counselor, and author, deplored the harsh view of themselves many addicts acquire or refine in treatment. He criticized a NIDA official's use, in a major talk earlier in the same conference, of an addict's remark that appeared in the *Washington Post*. "That quote, 'I am a crack addict, I don't have a conscience. I learned that in treatment,' represents the old confrontational approach," said Miller. "Twenty years ago, the idea was these weren't human beings, that you need to beat them down." He said the basis for confrontation is the widespread belief that most addicts deny their problem, "that they are surrounded by a pernicious shell of defenses." He added flatly, "There is no evidence for that."[35] In his *Handbook of Alcoholism Treatment Approaches*, coauthored by Reid K. Hester, Miller noted the "particular popularity" of confrontational counseling styles throughout the field. Yet, the authors continue, these "have failed to yield a single positive outcome study."[36] The findings do not indict TCs directly, and research shows respectable outcomes from TCs. Further, it is hard to single out which parts of treatment—at TCs or elsewhere—make what difference in a person's recovery.

The two approaches—therapeutic community and Twelve-Step-oriented—mesh better than one would have predicted 20 years ago. Anthony Bates, a counselor at Daytop's out-patient program, admits that while the Twelve-Step philosophy is not confrontational, its practice involves a rigorous spiritual discipline. Many NA and AA members summarize their approach with the acronym HOW, for honesty, open-mindedness, and willingness. Seen so, "the Twelve Steps are somewhat synonymous with the Daytop philosophy," says Bates. At the NIDA conference, Miller said that treatment should evoke—not crush—the person's inner motivation and resources. "A person has the seeds of change within them."

Daytop—with help from Marc Galanter of the New York University Medical School's Department of Addiction Psychiatry—surveyed 322 residents on the topic, according to an in-house report officials gave me. The majority reported that spirituality plays a key role in their peace and happiness, and that it provides comfort and balance. Interestingly, however, while a majority—54 percent—said Daytop should feature more spirituality, only 25 called for more of the twelve-Step variety, supporting the idea that other approaches to a metaphysical life can help an addict abstain and recover.[37]

Another hurdle is the perennial confusion between spirituality and religion. Derek Whitter says many of his court-mandated clients are loath to go near anything, at least publicly, that smacks of religion. "We're dealing with a population who feel that if they talk about church in group, they will be ostracized." To get around the barrier, Whitter defines spirituality as "an unorganized belief system that enables you to change," while religion is an organized one. Beneath the surface, clients are often more open to spirituality than they are to clinical treatment, according to Whitter and his Daytop colleague Collins. Many had jailhouse conversions to Islam or Christianity, or at least sat through visits and lessons from believers. "As time went on, they became more open to the Word," says Collins. "They don't use those ideas in group counseling, but it comes up in individual counseling."

Certainly many TC graduates have been able to incorporate a more spiritual approach to recovery despite the secular nature of their treatment experience. Tony Gelormino estimates that 60 percent of Daytop's 700-strong alumni association attend AA or NA. "They can easily talk about a higher power. It flows in and out of their conversation." This leaves Daytop staff attempting to blend the transcendent and the earthly. "If you want to increase spirituality in treatment," asks Bosch, "how do you put the higher power idea into something concrete that will help the individual?"

Hospitality House operates knowing that the cause of recovery remains elusive, perhaps on some level of the mind or spirit, or in some spark at the nexus of body, mind, and spirit. This or that provision may or may not make the difference. Many treatment managers say that providing housing for patients after care is essential. "I thought that if we could provide long-term housing to our people," Becker recalls, "they would be nine-tenths of the way home. But no, it was only true for some of them."

"I'm not sure what makes the change," Becker admits with a sigh. "Now, if you stop and ask a kid, 'How did you stay sober today? What did you do?' They'll say, 'I don't know, I had a purpose, I had a goal, I kept busy.' " Becker brings me out into the hall and stops several of the harried-looking clients as they rush past on their way to a chore or meeting or to grab a smoke outside. The variety of their answers, inarticulate and uncertain, makes her point: "With each person it's different."

Jerome F. X. Carroll, a prominent TC researcher, has written that when TC members and graduates are asked what factor most aided their recovery, many say, "my peers." Carroll thinks this response should check the egos of staffers who think they've found the right formula for treatment. Beyond that, however, the answer raises some questions about spirituality. Many recovered addicts, especially in AA or NA, will credit a higher power. But even these often follow this up with their opinion, or experience, that "God works through other people." In any case, both responses draw on the whole range of spiritual values and beliefs one finds in treatment and recovery circles. Yet in a way, seeing others as the messengers of enlightenment reinforces TC notions that the group is the agent of change, the main tool in a treatment. In the best proof that TCs are taking spirituality seriously, it has become one of the qualities subject to measurement and analysis in this data-heavy and outcomes-based era. Daytop has begun to survey clients on their beliefs and attitudes—past, present, and future—toward the Twelve Steps, religion, and God.

Finally, the internationalization of the TC model will likely lead to yet more use of spiritual concepts and methods. As Bosch notes, many professionals and addicts in other countries are more open to talk of God, prayer, sin, meditation than are Americans, who are taught to avoid speaking of faith or religion in polite society. Linda R. Wolf Jones, executive director of Therapeutic Communities of America, spent two weeks visiting TCs in Brazil in 1998 and found similarities and striking differences. "A profound spirituality infused each of the programs I visited in Brazil. I quickly grew accustomed to seeing chapels, Bibles, and crosses everywhere. Morning Mass was part of the daily schedule. Prayers, which might be heard at any time of day, were frequently accompanied by the music of guitar, conga drum, and tambourine."

Wolf continued. "Despite the damaged and sometimes tragic backgrounds of the young residents, I quickly learned that joy—*alegria*—was the daily watchword. Joy in life, joy in work, joy in prayers."[38]

CHAPTER IX

The Recovery Movement:
Recovering God, Recovering Self

Walking and living amidst us are members of a group who share basic assumptions about life and spirituality and self-improvement based on their recovery from alcoholism and addiction. These millions of people attend Twelve-Step fellowships or meditation circles or Women for Sobriety; they may be Native Americans returned to tribal practices or beneficiaries of harm-reduction efforts; they may live in therapeutic communities or halfway houses. If they were not so anonymous and loose-knit, they would count as, well, what? Definitely not a religion or a cult. Members agree on little, maybe nothing, other than the effectiveness of a spiritual way of life.

The recovery movement has some religious aspects—transcendent interest, group identity—but is antireligious in origins and temperament and nonreligious in its nature and structure. From religion, as well as medicine and psychology, it has borrowed "what works" for curbing addiction and left the rest. Its primary tenet is for the addict to admit she or he needs help and, therefore, is not God. Belief in God may or may not come—for many purposes it is almost irrelevant. Eliminating the hubris of addiction ushers the addict into recovery. It is this experience and belief that unifies the larger community of such individuals. As Kurtz and Ketcham write so persuasively, AA spirituality is distinct from religion in that it is aware of its own imperfection. Humility, born in the despair of alcoholism, lies at the heart of the recovery community, which extends from Twelve-Step groups to more secular groups as Women for Sobriety and, on the other extreme, congregation-based or other religious programs. On all other issues, members may differ. So rather than a religion, what we have is a new openness toward spirituality.

The recovery movement and the treatment field pioneered a practical spirituality for the modern age, and broadly influenced mainstream religions from the pews and pulpits. To religions of all kinds, as well as society generally, recovered addicts pose the challenge: Do your beliefs save lives as do ours? Though their practices and beliefs are still evolving, problems and criticisms abound.

The current phase of spiritual experimentation and rediscovery represents a swerve away from institutional religion, a foundation of civil society. Adherents cry out that "I pray, in my own way," or "I'm spiritual but not religious." In either case, they herald an unprecedented privatization of spiritual life. Overall, this cohort of people united on a single point has also influenced society. For instance, the decades-old disease concept has been borrowed and applied to many different or less serious problems, and thus trivialized. But such objections miss the success of the recovery movement in promoting acceptance and humility as a wellspring of new life.

Americans, Religion, and Spirituality

Pragmatism and a tension between solitude and community characterize Americans in their spiritual quest. Neither creeds nor dogmas escape the test of usefulness. Today more than ever, Americans believe not because they are told to but as their experience shows they should. As Alexis de Tocqueville observed, "even in their zeal there generally is something so indescribably tranquil, methodical, and deliberate that it would seem as if the head far more than the heart brought them to the foot of the altar."[1] Tocqueville recalled that medieval clergy spoke only of heaven while American preachers speak only of earth. They must persuade their congregations that religion promotes freedom and security. Americans like faith that works, not doctrine issued from on high. Tocqueville captured the American need and enthusiasm for small groups, that fill the vacuum left by the rejection of Europe's social hierarchy and royalty. They overcome their individualism by gathering into groups. Though these may serve a select purpose, such as paving a road or blocking a garbage dump or sobering up alcoholics, groups inevitably serve a larger social, even spiritual purpose. "Feelings and opinions are recruited, the heart is enlarged, and the human mind is developed only by the reciprocal influence of men upon one another."[2]

The recovery movement grew in ready soil, from its start in the grim days of the Depression when people sought new answers, through the rebellions of the 1960s and into the last decades of the twentieth century when books on angels and channeled messages and chit-chat from God spilled from shelves in stores and homes. One could think that America was passing through another Great Awakening. The previous was in the early 1800s, which gave birth to many enduring religions—from Mormonism to Seventh Day Adventists—as well as many now forgotten, such as the free-loving Oneida Community and the soon-astray Perfectionists. What distinguished the successes was a strong sense of community and mission. The same can barely be said for many contemporary fads, which is not to question their potency or appeal.

What all have in common is the fiercely individualistic soil of America, a nation founded and constantly reformulated in the spirit of rebellion. Harold Bloom found in personal religiosity the power of America's energetic religious imagination, one that has created religion after religion. "Revivalism, in America, tends to be the perpetual shock of the individual discovering yet again what she and he always have known, which is that God loves her and him on an absolutely personal and indeed intimate basis."[3] This contributed to the Gnosticism that is, for Bloom, at the heart of the American religion in the post-Christian era. The hallmarks of this homegrown creed, he writes, include "freedom from mere conscience; the reliance upon experiential perception; a sense of power; the presence of God within," and personal innocence.[4] The independence and self-determination that undergirds this religion continues to grow. A national *New York Times Magazine* poll in 2000 found that most Americans reject moral authority and absolutes, including a strong God. They prefer autonomy, and choose which deity serves their needs.[5]

American individualism and groupism coexist paradoxically. We form groups to sustain the individual. The sovereign individual forms groups to share her or his insights. The diffuse, generic spirituality of recovery fits perfectly. The basic creed: rely on God, however you define God, even if it is without God. Even the religious American dislikes group identity. Many demur from even naming their religion or creed, embarrassed by any strongly declared faith despite it being at their moral core. A person or hospital or college is no longer "Roman Catholic" but of the "Roman Catholic tradition." Sensitivity passes for ecumenism, but it also bespeaks rebelliousness. "I'm this, but not quite, because I reserve the right to pick and choose among my religion's dogmas." The recovery movement is a positive example of picking and choosing, positive because its experimentation has saved lives. At the same time, it suits the modern inclination: I like being in a group, it helps me be me, but I'm keeping it private.

The Spirituality of Recovery

Most people know of AA, NA, or other addiction recovery groups as self-help. To outsiders, self-help seems to eliminate the isolation of the alcoholic, offers a sympathetic group of peers who can listen, advise, console, and support. But to members, it offers all that and much more. Some would call them "God-help" groups; mutual-help may be a better term. Primarily, these groups help members grow toward, achieve, and sustain a spiritual awakening, one that will keep them sober.

In essence, the AA program gives newcomers a mandate that can, paradoxically, be fulfilled with complete flexibility, as their main text makes clear. "If the man be agnostic or atheist, make it emphatic that *he does not have to agree with your conception of God. He can choose any conception he likes, provided it makes sense to him. The main thing is that he be willing to believe in a Power greater than himself and that he live by spiritual principles.*"[6] Put simply: Believe in God, any way you want.

Some of the basic and sequential elements of Twelve-Step spirituality are release, gratitude, humility, forgiveness, love and service, and faith. These echo the stages of growth—renunciation, humility, and sincerity—found in some psychological therapies as well as mystical traditions.[7]

Hope infuses the entire process. To recover, a person must believe they can recover. This is as true in a secular course of therapy as in a religious program of salvation. "A therapeutic program must be convincing to the sufferer—that is, rhetorically persuasive—whether or not it is scientifically or universally true."[8] One recovered alcoholic with years of sobriety, Peter Hayden, told me of his pivotal encounter with a social worker shortly after being arrested for drunk driving and sent to treatment. "I asked him, 'Is this going to work for me?' and he said, 'It will work. You will never ever ever have to drink again.' And I believed him."[9]

At the very least, human assent is required—an almost gentle, invisible decision but one that defines human freedom. As the psychologist and author Victor Frankl realized during his time in the Nazi concentration camps, humans remain free, even in the most restricted circumstances, to choose their attitude toward their situation. Acceptance, not to be confused with approval, is the first step in any personal development. "At bottom, the whole concern of both morality and religion is with the manner of our acceptance of the universe," William James observed.[10]

The spirituality found in treatment and recovery is, above all, adaptable. It is a big tent with room for many. Practices range from the Twelve Steps to yoga or sweat lodges. As for beliefs, many people find additional or deeper fulfillment in religion, while others use alternatives to AA that still encourage spiritual development, such as Women for Sobriety. AA itself has groups in almost every country, and half of its members live outside the United States and Canada. Its message has been adapted to environs ranging from mill towns in East Europe to Alpine farm villages to the slums of Mexico City. The higher power is variously conceived, with 40 percent of members in Iceland, Mexico, Poland, Sweden, and Switzerland understanding it to be something other than either the Christian or non-Christian God.[11] A similar variety is found in the United States.

Almost all religions have converted AA concepts to their own purposes, or members have used it in tandem with denominational beliefs. The psychiatrist and rabbi Abraham J. Twerski has explored the consistency between the Twelve Steps and Jewish tradition. A network of groups called Jewish Alcoholics, Chemically Dependent Persons, and Significant Others has spread and adapted the Twelve-Step method. Christians have done the same through an array of denominational support groups. In his book, *Millati Islami* (The Path of Peace): *Islamic Treatment for Addiction*, Zaid Imani, of a Baltimore based group of the same name, reconciles the Twelve Steps to that religion and the Qu'ran with almost no changes in substance. A Muslim AA member from Pakistan speaks of his faith in familiar terms: "I have always found it rather difficult to let Allah's superior and flawless will prevail in my life and govern *my* will. However, when I make humble efforts, serenely accepting His will for me at some moment in my life, I feel absolutely relieved of the load I have carried on my shoulders."[12] Sufis, such as those affiliated with the Portland (Maine) Sufi Order Recovery Support Group, have also sprung up to help members integrate their religion and their Twelve-Step activity. Conversely, many recovered addicts avail themselves of practices from Buddhism or dozens of other spiritual or religious paths.

Despite these different interpretations and various uses of its concepts, AA consistently helps people abstain during treatment and beyond.[13] Many studies focus on the high dropout rate in Twelve-Step fellowships, up to 90 percent during the first 90 days. Don McIntire took a deeper look at AA membership surveys and eliminated non-alcoholics and those who drop out during an introductory period of 90 days. Reduced to this core of alcoholics who are intent on finding help—AA's target audience—McIntire found that 55 percent will be sober after one year, and 50 percent after five years.[14]

Just attending meetings is not enough. In their analysis of more than 50 studies, Emrick and Tonigan found that AA members stayed sober more successfully with greater AA involvement: having or being a sponsor; helping others; working the Twelve Steps.[15] But just attending meetings can engage the reluctant. As a popular slogan has it, "Bring the body and the mind will follow." This is a common discipline in all spiritual and therapeutic quests for improvement and self-realization.

One does not have to be a churchgoer for the program to help. Lee Kaskutas, in a multi-year study of 722 subjects, found that both secular and religious participants who were still involved with AA at follow-up reported "an approximately doubled rate of spiritual awakening."[16] The essential discipline is not a belief in God but the person's acceptance that she or he is not God. Twerski tells the story of an Israeli AA member he met in Jerusalem. Though a committed atheist, the man told Twerski, "I'm sober six and a half years and I pray every day but I still don't believe in God. I don't believe in God but when I pray that tells me that I'm not God."[17]

A Faith that Works

People believe according to their needs. God has to deliver, or else the faithful will find another object for devotion. Karen Armstrong makes this point in *A History of God: The 4000-Year Quest of Judaism, Christianity and Islam.* "When one religious idea ceases to work for them, it is simply replaced."[18] For our purposes, it is the idea adopted by humans that makes the difference. We cannot measure what a deity does; we can only measure the effects of faith.

As generations pass, humans perceive their God to have drifted away, Armstrong observes. Many primitive societies believe in a sky god—transcendent, distant, and inaccessible.[19] Though once intimate, this deity recedes, so people turn to or invent lesser gods who will hear and help them. In reality, these lesser deities may be aspects of the true divine. Mircea Eliade argued that the sky god was not initially an abstract concept but often was transformed over time into philosophical concepts. This makes sense, since to primitive man, Eliade wrote in *Patterns in Comparative Religion,* "knowledge and understanding were—and still are—epiphanies of 'power' and 'force.' He who sees and knows all, *is* and *can do* all."[20]

Consider the current era. Many people in the United States and other industrialized nations complain that the God they learned of as children was a punishing God, the white-bearded man hurling thunderbolts at the sinful. Recovering addicts often tell of rejecting this harsh God and finding one who loves and accepts them. In this epic transformation, the addict abandons his native land—that of the sterile God or gods—and seeks out the Promised Land, much like Abraham left Ur for Palestine or Muhammad departed Mecca for Medina. Our seeker may be detoured by counterfeit gods of drugs or alcohol or food or gambling. But in the end, they find the God of love, the one who delivers, the one belief in whom enables a life without drugs or alcohol.

Jean-Paul Sartre predicted that our existential dilemma would leave humanity conscious of a hole the size of God. Recovered addicts often recall a void they felt within, one they tried to fill with alcohol or drugs. Echoing Sartre, many say they once suffered from "a God-shaped hole." Many now talk of finding a higher power that loves and helps them. Maybe they replaced the God of their forebears who moved into heaven, or they pulled this same God closer. They now turn to a deity who is near, who will hear, and who will answer their prayers. As the former priest and maverick Mexican educator Ivan Ilyich once said, "God became smaller and smaller so that at last we could see Him."[21]

This was the great gift of Ebby T., a chronic drunk who inspired his friend Bill Wilson with his story of recovering through conversion. Even in his cups, Wilson disliked religion. Ebby offered a way through the logjam: "Why don't you choose your own conception of God?" For Wilson, the statement "melted the icy intellectual mountain in whose shadow I had lived and shivered many years." Granted this flexibility, he writes, "a new world came into view." All that was required was for the alcoholic "to make a beginning."[22] For the object of faith—the group, new habits, a deity—to have an affect, the people must place themselves under its influence. Their faith is confirmed in practice.

The God in Need

The sky god of primitive societies may have been translated into a philosophy and forgotten, but in times of crisis—drought, suffering, epidemics—these peoples invariably turned back to the sky god. This may have required them to sweep aside the lesser deities, or golden calves, they worshiped in the interim. The Bible tells how the Israelites took up with idols until hard times sent them back to Yahweh. Addicts, in their crisis, reject the surrogate of drugs and turn to a deity who will help them recover.

In a way, the Twelve-Step programs' emphasis that the addict find a God "of our own understanding," fulfills a prediction made a century ago. Durkheim found that individualized religions, instituted and celebrated by one person, exist in all societies. Ojibwe Indians often pick and revere their own *manitou*, much as Christians may choose and honor a guardian angel or patron saint. He wondered "whether the day will not come when the only cult will be the one that each person freely practices in his innermost self."[23] Similarly, many modern believers proclaim, "I pray, but in my own way."

In and out of AA, the desire to find a God "of our own understanding" may manifest a childlike urge to create a god after each individual's liking. Or maybe people are just finding the God who was there inside all along.

The search for the God within drives contemporary religious or spiritual life. As Bloom concluded, Americans are always rediscovering that God loves me, me, me. Granted, the addict recovers his or her spirit by recovering the Spirit. But at the same time, the free believer cannot serve as the core of faith. "Still, so much radical individualism is bracing as opposition and innovation, never as belief in itself," Alfred Kazin observed in *God and the American Writer*.

Considered from another angle, God may be found outside of the person but somewhere shy of heaven. Durkheim believed that the god of a religion is really society, and society is the cause of religious sensations. Similarly, many new to AA, still uncomfortable with the idea of God, find in the group or fellowship their higher power. Nevertheless, the religious sensations created in such groups provide addicts with the support, safety, and guidance that allow them to transcend their addictions.

Pain-based Groupism

The idea of addicts, joined in pain, finding release is deeply American. From organizations of victims of disasters or crime to the Million Women March on Washington, DC, modern Americans often turn to each other, rather than officials or experts or institutions, to solve their problems. They come together to meet a need through interest-based, ad-hoc collectives. Pain is a great organizing principle. But it is not so much that people are bound together by their grief as that they find in it a compelling basis to band together with others.

These grounds for assembly are even more compelling today, when centrifugal forces—cars, income disparity, global capitalism—can spin each of us away from others. Seeking refuge, we burrow even more deeply into home. "We have tried to make the fact of being in private, along with ourselves and with family and intimate friends, an end in itself," Richard Sennett concludes in *The Fall of Public Man*. When a chance to join with others, even in pain or grief, comes along, we grab at it. The impulse checks modern individualism. Interestingly, AA literature attacks head-on rampant individualism as a form of soul-sickness, and calls "the philosophy of self-sufficiency . . . a bone-crushing juggernaut whose final achievement is ruin."[24] The answer to this was personal surrender to a higher power, which had the merit of avoiding a dangerous reliance on group leaders, professionals, or any institutions. Further, Twelve-Step fellowships, composed of autonomous groups and lacking a central authority, embody organizational anarchy. Even newcomers are asked to act individualistically, be it in defining their higher power, selecting meetings, or sharing their thoughts on an equal basis with veterans.[25] The impulse to form and use these groups expresses the spiritual hunger for moral guidance and security in a world without absolutes.

Can Utility Be the Measure?

If the ends do not justify the means, what does? William James observed that since we are dependent on the universe, our acceptance of that fact shapes our lives. Without religion, we may accept it as a matter of necessity. With religion, we may do so happily. "Religion thus makes easy and felicitous what in any case is necessary," he concludes.[26] "Change or die," recovering addicts often tell each other. "Grow or go." Yet making faith a tool can pervert it. "The utilitarian view makes something else than God the god in our lives, such as money or longevity or victory over our enemies," theologian and author John Dwyer told me. He advised allowing God to define himself in the believer's life. For people recovering from an addiction, faith allows them to recover this freedom to fashion the self after the designs of a higher power, one they choose.

One must be a believer to understand the power of faith, Alfred North Whitehead wrote. "Religion is the vision of something which stands beyond, behind, and within, the passing flux of immediate things; something which is real, and yet waiting to be realized; something which is a remote possibility, and yet the greatest of present facts; something that gives meaning to all that passes, and yet eludes apprehension; something whose possession is the final good, and yet is beyond all reach; something which is the ultimate ideal, and the hopeless quest."[27] The danger here is circular: faith works for believers, and only believers can see that. Critics ridicule spirituality as religion without rules, but a brutal bottom line exists for evaluating the beliefs of addicts.

If recovered alcoholics drink again, or simply become discontent in their sobriety, they may alter their understanding of, or relationship to, their deity. Many speak of judging actions on whether these bring them closer to, or further away from, a drink. As we develop and refine our idea about God, we will be changed by those ideas. The admission of addiction, tantamount to admitting that one is human and flawed and imperfect, leads to acceptance.

Acceptance leads to faith; faith changes lives. Faith engenders hope; hope activates self-preservation. An alcoholic, faced with ruin, accepts his limits in a scary void, drops the security of the addiction, and opens himself to a new life.

Profile: David—Choosing His Religion

David's drinking got real when he caused the death of a friend while driving drunk. Although he did not stop the drugs or drinking entirely until after a few more years, David, a senior at Villanova, remains abstinent and happy with a broad understanding of a deity. He does so outside of any organized fellowship or religion, and thus embodies the range and freedom of the recovery movement. The only absolute, for him as for many kindred spirits in recovery, is to develop spiritually.

David grew up in Woodstock, New York during the 1980s. He drank his first drink when he was 15 and "definitely" recalls the effect. "I had gone to my best friend's brother's house on a Saturday night. We were with a bunch of older people and I felt involved with them, that I was at the next stage. By the end, I did not feel so well, especially when I had to go to Sunday school the next morning. But it was a good experience for the most part."28

At first he drank every few months, then monthly, then every weekend and on holidays. At age 16, David began smoking marijuana and moved on to hallucinogens, especially "ecstasy" and cocaine.

"Looking back on it, I find it to be ridiculous. I was looking for the feelings of euphoria, the release of inhibition, having fun. I didn't feel I could have fun unless I was inebriated." Sports and other activities tapered off in favor of those centered on drinking. His surroundings provided little check. "In the late 1980s, Woodstock was very friendly. It was not like you were looked down upon if you got drunk or stoned."

After high school, David went off to Villanova. He came home for summer vacation. One night while driving under the influence, he got in an accident. One friend, a female, sitting in the front seat was killed. A friend in the back seat was injured. David was charged with six misdemeanors and three felonies. Eventually, in February 1994, he accepted a plea bargain and received a reduced sentence: 60 days jail, 240 hours of community service, five years probation, and counseling. During his time, the Ulster Country Jail seemed like hell. David promised himself to stay out of trouble.

"But it didn't last. I was at a party, someone offered and I said no. At the next party, I rationalized, 'If I [only] drink alcohol that would be okay.' " Soon he was drinking and taking LSD. The police arrested him while he was under the influence, which violated his probation. Beginning in the summer of 1994, he served 29 months in two state prisons. At the second, he lived in a therapeutic community, with its tight schedules, a hierarchy of members, and rough-and-tumble confrontation.

"It was a crazy experience since I was in complete denial. I figured I was being picked on and used as an example. It took me a long time to accept that I was responsible for being there." Though he took drugs through much of his prison time, David said the TC taught him about himself, his relationships, and family dynamics.

He stopped the drugs in February 1996 when he was about to appear before the parole board. But David had also received help in the form of a quiet conversion. He acknowledged the "whole jailhouse religious thing that goes on" given the trials and suffering of incarceration. His churchgoing mother raised David as a Christian. His father was also religious, albeit in a more freewheeling manner, and an uncle was a Protestant minister.

In jail, nearing release, he struggled for meaning, sought for answers to the fact of his newfound ability to stay clean. One thing was clear: "I decided that this was the last miracle. The first one was when I survived the car crash, hitting the tree at 75-80 miles per hour. The next was walking away with only cuts and scrapes." Sobriety seemed his last chance. He held on; he still holds on.

"I was in a Twelve-step program in prison but not now. I use my family and friends for support. I use faith, some kinds of beliefs but not through the Twelve Steps." David finds the AA philosophy restrictive and controlling. Similarly, he faults religious people who accept too much without questioning. But he does endorse the AA reliance on a higher power, taking personal inventories, and the idea that a person may not have control over an alcohol or drug addiction. He meditates more often than he prays. In picking and choosing that which works, David typifies many recovered addicts. David says his values and ethics all flow from his rediscovery of God. And as with many others, his notions about this Spirit sometimes conflict.

"It's a security blanket that you can turn to. My Spirit is a common bind among people. I have that presence that I can turn to. I'm not sure it's a divinity. I am not sure how much of a presence God has in daily life. He doesn't come down. I feel I am more of a cocreator. I'm more responsible for things that go on."

In his anthropocentrism, "humans are right there cocreating, bringing about the future." When good or bad comes, it is not necessarily from God but from the misuse of free will or by fate or accident, David says.

When I return the conversation to the roots of his recovery, David says that his attitude changed. But he also says that could be a function of age and maturity, and that his drinking was a function of his youth. Today, he does not identify himself as an alcoholic or addict even in his work as a peer counselor in Villanova's substance abuse program. "For me, what's healthier is not to use. I know I don't want to be drunk. What I have now works very well. I recommend to people that they develop a spiritual life. Without spirituality, I am tempted to say, my recovery would be very difficult."

Beliefs and Rites

The basic elements of AA life include acceptance and solidarity coupled with group accountability; honesty; guidance toward personal responsibility; the use of classic texts to perpetuate basic concepts; a system of sponsorship by which older members transmit to new ones the AA way of life.[29] In its pragmatist, democratic way, AA allows and supports a wide variety of spiritualities and concepts, while also checking that which divides or isolates members.[30] Beliefs and practices are many; consider several.

Members of AA, NA, and other spiritually based recovery groups vary widely in their understandings of key concepts, such as the disease theory of alcoholism. Though many insist it is so, they talk of this disease in spiritual rather than physical or biological terms. The Twelve-Step philosophies, as an evolving belief system, have been deeply affected by what many of their members learned in treatment programs, causing a certain conceptual muddiness. In a typical sequence of remarks made to me during interviews, an addict would say, "I learned I have a disease," but then go on to detail their addictive actions as immoral. Or they relish how confrontational therapy in treatment broke through their denial, though this type of behavior is foreign to most support groups and research has shown "denial" to be rare among clients. Most addicts seem to have known quite well their situation; they just lacked faith they could recover.

As AA has influenced treatment, so has treatment influenced, or distorted, AA philosophy and practice. AA veterans increasingly complain about the "psychobabble" or "treatment talk" that has infiltrated meetings. To the many original AA slogans have been added mottoes that seem to have originated in treatment programs, such as working the program "24/7" or avoiding the "people, places, and things" of one's previous life, which contradicts advice found in the book *Alcoholics Anonymous*.

Members also vary in their ideas about "working the program." The Twelve Steps are presented as suggestions and each member chooses whether and how to proceed through them. The only prods are personal pain, from a lack of spiritual growth, and the experience or advice of other members. The concept of God varies widely. Some use the AA group as a higher power, others use their own religious notions of God, others turn to nature or truth. In a survey of AA members, 88 percent in Mexico but only 28 percent in Sweden professed certainty about God's existence. Still, 35 percent in Mexico and 59 percent in Sweden said the "power greater than ourselves" mentioned in the Twelve Steps referred to the AA fellowship or the power of the group.[31] Though specifics vary, it is the act of believing, or acting if one believes, that helps people recover.

Dependence and Freedom

AA's core philosophy involves absolute dependence on a self-defined higher power. Alcoholism is seen not so much as a case of bad morals or values, but as a failure of power to carry out one is values. Power originates in a new concept of God.

Richard L. Gorsuch found that alcoholics consistently report a judging, vindictive God. He called this a departure from the Christianity in which they were raised, where love and forgiveness are the keynotes. Alcoholics, he concluded, have a non-Christian view of God because they were not fully encultured in their religious faith. Alcoholism represents a failure of Christianity to grow in certain people.[32] One may say the same about alcoholics from other religions, an idea supported by the wealth of evidence showing that religious involvement checks drug and alcohol abuse.

In this way, addiction represents spiritual immaturity. AA literature repeats the conviction that alcoholics may have faith in God, but that it is the wrong kind of faith. It did not work. The spirituality of the Twelve Steps produces in practitioners both hope and direction.

Finding a helpful deity helps. Albert Ellis, the psychologist and critic of religion, acknowledged that "a good deal of empirical evidence" shows that "people who viewed God as a warm, caring, and lovable friend and saw their religion as supportive were more likely to have positive outcomes and to stay free from substance abuse than those with a more negative view of God."[33] Spiritual maturation for addicts may consist of moving from the God of their childhood religion to a God of their own understanding. In secular terms, the alcoholic's salvation comes from accepting reality, from admitting that one cannot drink safely and can only stop with outside help. In a 1950 talk to the Kips Bay AA group in Manhattan, Bill Wilson recalled how Ebby T. credited his sobriety to the "religion of common sense," a marvelous phrase that deserves wider use.[34] In *Holy Hunger: A Memoir of Desire*, Margaret Bullitt-Jonas summarizes her recovery from bulimia in Overeaters Anonymous as a matter of "saying yes" to life. Many addicts told me that their spiritual awakening came at the moment when they realized they wanted to live, rather than die. Acceptance is not an acquiescence. "Acceptance is not a passive thing," one meditation veteran said. "The more you accept, the more you energize your whole being."[35]

For the addict, attitude is everything. "The way in which a man accepts his fate and all the suffering it entails, the way in which he takes up his cross, gives him ample opportunity—even under the most difficult circumstances—to add a deeper meaning to his life," Victor Frankl wrote.[36] In acceptance or conversion, a new set of ideas move from the person's periphery to his or her center where it can animate and drive consciousness and life.[37] The addict chooses how to feel each day as a matter of life or death.

Cleaning House: Inventory and Amends, Confession and Penance

A prime feature of Twelve-Step groups is a two-stage process of admitting faults. First the addict admits powerlessness over addiction, initially signified by attendance at meetings, and later she or he shares a moral inventory with the self, God, and another person. The admission and inventory, as well as the more informal revelations made in meetings, ease pain and bring the healing of acceptance. These practices bind individuals, one to the other, as they realize that their darkest secrets are both common and forgivable. As the German philosopher Gustav Landauer wrote, "The deeper we climb down into the tunnels of our individual life, all the more are we in a real community . . . . The deepest part of our individual selves is that which is most universal."[38] As recovered addicts say, "You're as sick as your secrets."

For therapeutic purposes, the admission to God could be left out of the equation. Peter Abelard, the twelfth-century theologian, promoted the usefulness of confession for its effect on the person. Abelard argued that though confession was superfluous because God knew the sinner's failings, the process induced humility in the penitent and drew out that which was secret and shameful. As Susan R. Kramer wrote in an examination of Abelard's theory, "While fault and remission are matters for God alone, shame and its expiation are human matters."[39] Seen this way, liberation may come on a purely human plane as one person admits to another his or her faults and loses the *burden* of guilt. Eliminating actual guilt may be up to God. In recovery, the desire for communion with others and with transcendence or reality motivates personal honesty.

Clean & Sober Streets in Washington, D.C. treats chronic, homeless addicts and alcoholics with success, little money, and spiritual methods. Early on, clients confront their past. Clinical director Marsh Ward, a psychotherapist with a soft-featured face, expressing an implacable kindness, puts each resident through a bare-bones but effective inventory.[40]

One warm spring morning 40 or so members of Group 41 gather in the center's tiled cafeteria. Soft winds nudge the white nylon curtains of open windows. A volunteer sits in front facing a microphone and wearing a wary, hopeful expression. "The garbage you bring in here from your early childhood will send you back out there," Ward tells the room. "I can change the way you deal with it so you're not carrying a big bag of garbage into your recovery." Ward turns to the volunteer, whose tough street face seems to be melting as he remembers the past he is about to recount. "Why the tears?" Ward asks, a bit roughly. With little prodding, the man spills out the essentials of his early pain: a mother disabled by an assault; the father who ran away; a grandmother who reared him but also beat him when he failed to steal the Sunday newspaper; the cousins who mistreated him. Ward listens, nudges once or twice, and then puts an empty chair in front of the storyteller.

"Picture your father there. What would you ask him?" "I'd ask why he left me," the man says softly. "I don't know what to say." Ward gives a few ideas, tells the man to say goodbye and, as he does, spins the vacant chair on one leg. "I have to do this or they stay in the chair," Ward explains. The man weeps. Ward suggests he write a letter filling in all the blanks "with the anger and the sadness and the good stuff, about your life now." Despite observing the man's anguish, a dozen people shoot their hands up when Ward asks for volunteers for tomorrow. They, too, want to reconcile with the past, with themselves and others.

Clients "are absolutely desperate, and that's the first ingredient," Ward explains in a subsequent conversation. "The second ingredient is to take all the chemicals out of their system. In about three weeks you have the return of some of the basic human qualities that go into making them spiritual creatures." These include caring for others, regarding the group as family, and revealing personal truths. "They find out they want this closeness with others, and the price they have to pay is to be honest."

Telling Stories

In this age of mass entertainment and digital revolutions, support groups have revived oral culture. In Twelve-Step groups, generally, there are two types of sessions: discussion meetings, where rotating leaders start things off and open it to the floor, and speaker meetings. Both offer members an opportunity unusual in an age of short attention spans and one-liners: to speak their thoughts for several minutes, or tell their life story for 15-30 minutes, without response or reaction.

The general format for NA or AA speakers is to recount the past, the crisis, and the present recovery, or "what we used to be like, what happened, and what we are like now."[41] The personal stories are typically cast as almost mythological tales of spiritual or existential quests, nearly ending in tragedy but instead coming to deliverance. In a remarkable account in *Harper's Magazine,* an anonymous AA member described orality as a spiritual method and discipline. "The fellowship exists to ground the drunk's ladder on solid earth, on common ground, and whether we extend one end of it back up into the heavens or simply lay it down to bridge the chasms between ourselves, it is still made of words."[42]

Telling one's story is a central and universal activity in AA, according to an international survey of eight countries. By talking about their lives before groups, members build a new identity and compose an autobiography that interprets the past in a coherent and useful manner. In listening, members get to know and trust one another. Newcomers find hope; veterans are reminded of the dangers of drinking. Members work out current problems and share ideas on solutions for life's daily struggles.[43]

Recovery groups combine an openness and nonjudgmental atmosphere with an unspoken observance of certain rules: no interrupting, no commenting on other people's remarks, and time limits. Are stories told in this unchecked atmosphere reliable? At some level, one has to believe what people say about their lives. Their stories are not eyewitness accounts, or even case histories, that can be judged as factually accurate or not. The person says, "These are my truths about my life." As in history, what happened is often less important than what people think happened. Even the lapses and distortions of oral histories convey important truths.[44]

Support group members mythologize their lives. They repeat the important and omit the rest, refining their material to tell a truth beyond the facts. Distortions may result when addicts in treatment fit their stories to the paradigms laid out by counselors, something I sensed was occurring several times during interviews at rehab centers. It is a different matter when, as a free member of an unsupervised support group of peers, a person chooses to see her or his life in a certain way. Don't we all? As Goya observed, art is exaggeration and omission. Humans tell their stories in order to become whole. The truth will out. It alone will do.

Finding and telling the "right" version of one's story is a group process. The speaker receives strength from the group, echoes it back and then receives even more in a expanding circular fashion, in the manner of a tornado gathering strength from smaller winds and other conditions. Of this "demon of oratorical inspiration," Durkheim explains, "It is no longer a mere individual who speaks but a group incarnated and personified."[45] This process occurs in all groups, in the office, the neighborhood, or a congregation. Those whose stories do not fit the group paradigm find their way elsewhere, or they change the group or leave to start another one.

These meetings also revive the ancient habit of oral cultures in regarding spoken words as physical entities. Knowledge can be an epiphany of power. Long after God recedes, God is manifest in philosophical concepts. The Gospel of John tells us that God is in the word. Words generate. In group therapy sessions at treatment centers, I saw participants regard the utterances of others as special, almost sacred. They compliment a speaker for a "good piece," or "a good share," as if the utterance had solidified in mid-air into a talisman. In a way, it has—into a carrier of truth, hope, and redemption.

Despite the informal nature of support groups, their ways can ossify. In the *AA Grapevine*, one reader lamented that rituals were creeping into AA. These included communal greetings to those who spoke—"Hi, Bob!"—readings from the AA books, hand holding during the concluding prayer, and final chants such as "It works if you work it." Rituals occupy more and more of meetings and "may be a long-term threat to the Fellowship," Paul M. wrote. He recalled the Oxford Group and its mission to strip away crusty rituals and return Christianity to its roots, a weighty analogy since the founders of AA attended Oxford Groups before escaping its religious and absolute nature. Paul M. predicted a time when an AA meeting would "consist mainly of ritual responses and ceremony, and the sharing will be afterthought."[46] On the other hand, many members worry that AA has no continuity and that the essentials of recovery were being lost under an avalanche of spontaneous revelations of "feelings." Each danger seems overstated, however, and each could cancel the other out.

The Recovery Movement and Society

The recovery movement has achieved a firm spot in the public mind, largely through television and movie characters who become addicted, are treated, or attend support groups. The one million members AA reports in the United States and Canada amount to less than 1 percent of the adult population. That may be conservative. Based on a nationwide survey by outside researchers, 3.1 percent of the U.S. adult population reported having ever attended an AA meeting for their own drinking problem, and 1.5 percent in the past year—three times AA's own membership estimates. When asked about attending a meeting at any time, for any reason, including curiosity or helping a friend, 9 percent of U.S. adults reported having done so ever, and 3.4 percent in the past year. When other Twelve-Step groups are considered, and eliminating overlaps, 13.3 percent of the population attended at least once in their lives, and 5.3 percent in the past year.[47] Through this direct exposure, and the even wider reach of members and media attention, Twelve-Step groups and their concepts have permeated American society. At the same time, comparing the 9 percent of Americans who have attended an AA meeting with the roughly 20 percent who have ever drunk heavily could indicate that AA is reaching the limits of its potential. Other fellowships, such as NA, are far from that point.[48] Still, many times in the past AA seemed near its limits or ready to shrink and disappear, as did the temperance movements of the 1800s. Instead, it has grown to have a "pervasive influence" in American life and across the world.[49]

Older AA slogans have spread into general use, such as "One Day at a Time," or "Live and Let Live." Newer slogans and mottoes, some of them generated in treatment programs, are also popular, such as being sincere enough to "walk the walk" and not just "talk the talk." (Perhaps, ideally, one should "walk the talk.") These dot daily conversations and public remarks alike and shape both habits and culture.

Remedying or Replacing Religion

Recovering God is not so much a matter of rejecting false gods as it is one of rejecting false notions of God. The problem is universal. "We imagine that the hideous deity we have experienced is the authentic God of Jews, Christians, and Muslims and do not always realize that it is merely an unfortunate aberration," Karen Armstrong writes.[50] Seen so, modern atheism may be a stage in finding a new God after the old one stopped working. Armstrong notes that early Jews, Christians, and Muslim were all called atheists by pagan contemporaries due to their dangerous ideas.

"Is modern atheism a similar denial of a 'God' which is no longer ade-
quate to the problems of our time?"[51]

Support groups now complement the spiritual solace of religion. AA
and other meetings convene in church basements and shrewd pastors
welcome these into the heart of their mission. "Some successful [baby]
boomer churches are shrines to secular movements, particularly the 12-
step programs modeled on Alcoholics Anonymous," *Time* reported. Many
congregations have grown by offering help for all types of personal problems among their members. The Twelve-Step philosophy, grounded in an
acceptance of a potentially fatal flaw, fits neatly with the concept of "the
wounded healer," articulated by Henri J. M. Nouwen. A person's own
faults or wounds become a source of strength, healing, and vision in solidarity with others. Mutual confession deepens hope, and sharing weakness leads to strength.[52]

According to research by Robert Wuthnow, four in ten Americans participate in small groups that meet regularly and provide support. Two-
thirds of these groups—such as Sunday school or Bible study—are connected to a church. The remainder includes reading groups, singles
clubs, and so on, but the most noticeable portion consists of Twelve-Step
groups. Most small group members say their participation has shaped
their spiritual lives. Wuthnow concludes that these are fostering community and revitalizing the sacred on a major, if subterranean, scale.[53]

Given the success of small groups, and the fact that their spirituality is
not specifically Christian or religious, Wuthnow writes, churches must
either incorporate these or risk being replaced by them.[54] The latter is
unlikely, since support groups cannot replicate religion's institutional and
historical presence in people's lives. A more likely scenario: congregations will continue to sponsor these groups and be influenced by what
some of their number learn there.

Does it matter that Twelve-Step adherents routinely distinguish spirituality from religion? The point is widely repeated in a society smitten
with easy individualism and eager to rebel against the moral authority of
organized religion. The distinction is not new and has characterized every
religion or religious reform in its infancy.[55] Jesus, Muhammad, and
Moses all criticized religious practices of their time. The distinction can
be simplistic, since most religions contain a range of spiritualities, and
potentially divisive, since religion itself has kept many people out of trouble with drugs or alcohol.

People in recovery are often accused of the same pick-and-choose mentality that colors modern denominational membership. After all, newcomers to AA or people in treatment are often told, "Take what you need
and leave the rest." The charge of cafeteria-style belief simply points out a
difference between religion and mutual-aid groups such as NA, whose

members must apply an individual test of utility to faith. When members of a religion, on the other hand, justify their creed by its utility—perhaps reducing it to social activism—then it loses its power. But to hold recovery groups responsible for this mindset, or to see them as symptoms of it, is to mistake them for something they are not: religions. They can, however, fill some gaps left by religion.

Many people enter recovery spiritually or religiously illiterate. "One of the problems in the chemical dependency field is that so many kids are not connected with any church, so they don't know what you're talking about with spirituality or a higher power," said Peter Hayden, who runs programs for mostly African-American clients in Minneapolis and St. Paul, Minnesota. I heard the same from directors in other parts of the country. People who have an effective spiritual life are unlikely to abuse drugs and alcohol in the first place. What need of a doctor does a healthy person have?

Dangers and Distortions of the Recovery Movement

What works in faith for one addict may be mushy, utilitarian pantheism to an outsider. There is always the danger that belief will become a mere prop, there to advance our comfort and self-satisfaction. Alfred Kazin laments that efficacy is the only aspect to religion accepted in our scientific age. "Religion even among the faithful, like American literature today, has left cosmology to the physicists. No one argues about God today."[56] Similarly, Wuthnow worries that small groups, despite their strengths, adapt religion to culture rather than preserve religion's role as a critical or prophetic witness. These groups encourage a faith that is subjective and personal, and present a God of love, comfort, and security.[57] God thereby attains our society's highest moral pinnacle, that of non-judgmentalism. "I'm okay, God's okay, and I'm sure I'm okay with Him or Her."

These charges could be leveled at Twelve-Step groups. But AA and its offspring never presumed to replace religion; members are encouraged to return to the faith of their youth or find a new one. Many if not most do so. Further, recovered addicts rarely speak of a deity who condones their past addiction or present shortcomings; most do find one who forgives. The recovery movement is, however, particularly vulnerable to one of Wuthnow's criticisms, namely that small groups may become a stand-in for the divine.[58] Newcomers to AA or NA, especially if agnostic or atheist, are often encouraged to find their higher power in the group of recovering addicts, who have achieved a sobriety that has eluded the newcomer. But unlike members of Wuthnow's other small groups, most Twelve-Step adherents attend various different meetings—most communities have dozens, most cities have hundreds. Members rarely pledge allegiance to only one group, and they find God in many settings and interactions.

Wuthnow also worried that small group members may come to doubt that people can find God on other paths. While I have not heard that thinking in my interviews, I have encountered an us-against-them mentality and a conviction that the Twelve-Step approach, or other method, is the only way to sobriety or recovery. Both attitudes contradict AA literature and general practice.

There is also the danger that people will imagine a God in *their* likeness and image, one at their beck and call. Americans suffer most from this temptation, with their admixture of pragmatic optimism and self-centered delusion. The fierce conviction that an individual is loved by God and yet retains an unlimited freedom is expressed in Herman Melville's *Moby Dick*, when the imperious Ahab roars to his sailors, "Who's over me? Truth hath no confines." Commenting on this persistent strain in American literature, Alfred Kazin writes, "What counts is the positive action of American genius to deny and reject everything that affronts his sublime ego."[59]

The danger of hubris cannot be ignored. For eons, humans have tried to press God into the service of our schemes, often at great loss of life. And the ends may not justify the means, since the means can contain the seeds of a greater evil. What works may not be what is true. Truth may not manifest itself in ways that can be observed or verified. History shows that evil can be very effective. That does not make it good or true. Remember we speak of a spiritually based solution to addiction, not a universal philosophy. The approach must have practical effects. It must help a person abstain. Once sober, the recovered addict can construct or embrace almost any philosophy or theology.

Changing Religion and Society

The recovery movement can offer, by some reckoning, a faith without God. At the outset, it helps people admit that they are not God. Spirituality functions in various ways to help addicts recover shy of having them profess a deity. Though possible for many, I doubt that is enough for most. The entire thrust of the recovery movement is for each member to find a God of her or his own conception, one that works. Others stop short, perhaps thinking there is enough divine in the human to suffice for recovery. The anonymous author of the *Harper's* essay concluded that, "the true spirit of these [AA] rooms is the spirit of human life; a thing godlike, perhaps, but not transcendent; not 'high'; a thing altogether human. In AA we dry moist souls on the *logos*, the Word."[60]

Having borrowed principles from religion, as well as medicine and psychology, the recovery movement has renewed religion. The major monotheisms divided the world into human and divine. By making God something *other*, these freed humans to believe or not. Free will lies at the core of humanity. So, too, AA and NA encourage absolute freedom in finding a God, or something else, that works. Listening to treatment staff and addicts, I was reminded of the fundamental option theory. By this theory, that Catholic theologians developed and derived from French and German existentialists, each person makes a deep and basic choice for or against God. Individual acts do not change the person's basic orientation and only when she changes the "fundamental option" by choosing against God does she fall out of a state of grace. So too in recovery, the alcoholic may measure every choice, thought, and action as either enhancing or hurting the original decision to sober up and live.

Mainline religions could learn other lessons from recovery groups, especially by enlivening basic teachings with real experience. When the AA founders set about finding a practical solution to drinking, they came up with counterparts to many ancient Christian beliefs: *felix culpa* or "happy sin," which sees a flaw as the source of blessing; fundamental option; and ever-available grace, meaning that help is available up to the door of death. Any religion could come up with its own list. Religion could also learn about measuring the results of faith, or at least redoubling efforts for devotion to change and save lives. As addictions researchers refine their measurement of spirituality, others could work toward a broader science of spirituality, one that could reveal or examine the spiritual basis of all humanity. "Progress has given us computers, and global markets, but no feeling, no passion, no flavor of life," Faouzi Skali, director of the multicultural Fez musical festival in Morocco, said in a remark that captured a growing consensus. "Then when we discover the beauty of spirituality and the traditions of the sacred, it's just so strong and so deep that it reminds us of what we have lost."[61]

Religion cannot tell science what to do; it remains an object for science even as it explains and activates a reality that eludes scientific investigation. Instead of disappearing under the weight of science, Durkheim predicted religion would transform its beliefs and rites and survive in new forms. "Faith is above all a spur to action, whereas science, no matter how advanced, always remains at a distance from action. Science is fragmentary and incomplete; it advances but slowly and is never finished; but life—that cannot wait. Theories whose calling is to make people live and make them act, must therefore rush ahead of science and complete it prematurely."[62] Even when religion disappoints, usually in its lesser aspects, humans still value its fundamental role, that of helping them to act.

Nevertheless, people often flinch from public revelation of strongly held faith. As Steven Carter has written, "It is fine to be pious and observant in small things," but "Taking religion seriously is something only those wild-eyed zealots do."[63] But society seems more and more at ease with a functional, nonreligious spirituality. A *New York Daily News* article on Darryl Strawberry's return to Yankee Stadium mentioned the baseball player's attendance at 200 Twelve-Step meetings. The paper even named Strawberry's sponsor and specified which support group they attended (though his is not, of course, a perfect success story.) Strawberry, for his part, focused on the concrete reasons for his abstinence during a boozy team celebration: "It didn't affect me because spiritually inside, I was fit."[64]

The recovery movement, with its lack of doctrine and dogma and its healthy tension between the individual and the group, has enabled many people to acknowledge their ideas about a deity and spirituality. It has also disarmed, to some extent, the general reluctance among other people to discuss such concepts publicly. The methods and anarchy of Twelve-Step fellowships have been applied to other social problems. Dozens if not hundreds of networks have sprung up. Even groups using different philosophies, such as Women for Sobriety or faith-sharing groups, have learned lessons from AA and NA. Americans are now in the habit of forming groups to discuss their problems, an unprecedented phenomenon now so widespread we take it for granted. Given their longevity as fellowships without leaders, AA and NA have emerged as a model of organizational anarchy for self-sustaining mutual-aid efforts meeting on a flexible, non-professional basis.[65]

As anthropologists know, a people that loses its religious practices tends to lose its identity and, often, ceases to exist. The thirst for meaning imparted in ceremony and habit is entirely human. Edmund Wilson, the great American writer and critic, recognized the power of ritual and belief, even as he called for an end to religion. Wilson saw the power inherent in faith and practice.

Near the end of his 1959 *Apologies to the Iroquois*, Wilson describes an all-night ceremony he observed on the Tonawanda Seneca reservation. It was that of the Little Water Company, "the most sacred and the most secret" of Iroquois medicine societies. Though only a handful attended, Wilson saw the observance as one that affected the entire people. "They are making an affirmation of the will of the Iroquois people, of their vitality, their force to persist. These adepts have mastered the principles of life, they can summon it by the ceremony itself . . . Ten men in a darkened kitchen, with an audience of four or five of whom the celebrants are hardly aware, make a core from which radiates conviction, of which the stoutness may sustain their fellows."[66] That which works, works, and works for the many beyond the few.

The recovery movement crystallizes, for society, the basic challenge: will it be man or God? Will we live for ourselves alone or for something beyond? Will we be god or will we let God be God? Humans have always wanted to be God; it could be our defining characteristic. This yearning, and our alternating rejection of it, characterizes all of human history. What the recovery movement offers society is the chance to say that we are, at the least, not God. And that may be all that is necessary.

Profile: Janice—"I'm Bringing Me"

In her eighteenth month away from cocaine addiction, Janice would seem to have little reason for hope. She has HIV and is raising three small children alone. At age 34, she fears she will die before her kids grow up. And in the interest of preserving her own sobriety, she has to avoid her troubled family, whom she loves and who need help. Yet Janice exudes confidence, strength, and direction. It rings in her alto voice and shows in her military bearing. She flashes a smile to celebrate insights. Most of all, Janice believes in a God whom an outside observer might think abandoned her long ago.[67]

"I'm really grateful to him. Everything's getting better and better for me. I had my first son with me, then I had the little baby, and I worked hard and got my daughter back so now I have all three."

"I pray every night, 'I can do this, I can do this.' " Unresolved is whether God, or Janice, is making the difference. Though she did not grow up in a religion, Janice has always believed in God. What has changed is the nature of her relationship to God. "Yeah, I believed in God but it was only, 'I hope he gets me out of this mess,' or 'God, I can't wait till I get home and get something to eat.' "

Janis grew up in Rochester and attended Franklin High School, pretty much avoiding trouble. She entered the army, served three years in active duty and three in reserves. An emphatic woman one would not want to see angry or upset, Janice speaks clearly and forcefully, each word a hard-edged unit. In the army, she was busted down a rank after she was caught using marijuana. After she returned home to her family, she began her cocaine habit.

"They were all using, so I started. I felt like I fit in." By the time she was 30, Janice was a deeply troubled addict. She was treated at Liberty Manor, a residential program for mothers and other women, then relapsed and came back in March of 1997, this time pregnant and with HIV. In April, her third child was born.

Janice opened up about the HIV after several chats. Though two of her children were born with HIV, "they shed the antibodies," in her words, and are now negative. But the four elements—her illness, children, maternity, and addiction—required an approach tailored to her special practical and spiritual needs. She spoke about these during her stay in Liberty Manor and, eight months later, when she was on her own. Janice put her recovery first, tough for many mothers but soothing the shame of having put drugs first.

"Before I was here for my child, not for me," she says, explaining her previous relapse. "Kids don't keep you clean, they just be in the way. If you get clean because you're pregnant or while you're with a new baby, the attention is focused on 'that kid.' " Janice looks down at her gurgling infant. "And she didn't ask to be here, and there's a lot of guilt behind that." In women's groups sponsored by her treatment program and the YWCA, she finally feels able to talk. "They can identify with some of the things that went on in our lives—most of all, ignoring our kids or leaving them with other people, you know, abandonment."

"Before, I couldn't talk even with my family about anything unless I was on drugs. Before I was scared to talk; now, I've got a voice." Janice says she would not feel comfortable with men in the room. "The issues are different for them. Some don't live with their kids or," she adds with a clipped laugh, "they left them with the mother."

"And I have a lot of issues around men, since I'm HIV positive."

She attends Twelve-Step meetings, but rarely speaks, due to, "fear of, I don't know, talking around men." Janice's HIV appears almost dormant thanks to medication, with her T-cell count about normal. She summarizes her current credo: "Making changes in my life and being responsible for myself." I ask why her previous attempt to recover failed. "I didn't know that I had to change things other than the drugs. I didn't want it to sink in; I was just trying to keep my baby. Now I realize the baby won't keep me clean." The omission seems odd, since most programs incessantly tell clients they need to change—completely. But her remark underscores the truism that recovery happens when the addict is ready. For Janice, that involves turning away from her mother, who lives with her drug-using brothers.

"I would love to help her, she needs me, but if anything, I'll go down with her. Here's a woman who helped me all my life, who took the kids when I couldn't, who gave me money to buy diapers and food." She chokes up for a moment.

When Janice lived at Liberty Manor, and had only her infant to care for, she attended weekly a nondenominational church, New Life Fellowship. One of her brothers works there as a minister, nine years after recovering from drug addiction through a conversion experience. "He's been saved," Janis explains. As for her, "Not yet, but I am on the way to some spiritual path."

By September, she had stopped going to church since bringing the children to services was exhausting. Nor does Janice practice the Twelve Steps. Daily group meditations at Liberty Manor she would have preferred to skip: "I could have done that by myself." What does she do? "I pray every night to God. I thank him for the beautiful day, regardless of whether it was bad or good. If it was bad, that makes the next day something to look forward to. I've been praying a lot lately that I'll be there when the kids get older."

Sometimes she sees prayer in the simple manner of a child, as Jesus taught: ask and receive. When broke one day, she prayed for food and help. "Then this old boyfriend called and he came over and bought food and took the kids out for school clothes. I guess God sent him my way because if he hadn't, we would have gone hungry."

But prayer, in and of itself, changes the way Janice thinks and reacts and lives. Still, she credits God. "He's just there for me. He knows what's best for me. If something happens, I can't complain because God wants that to happen." In September, Janice was about to be suspended temporarily from public assistance after admitting that she lied last year about working a part-time job. She's grateful for the ordeal, since it has forced her to come clean.

"Even that shows that I was honest, this time. I used to think, 'Am I being too honest?' Ain't no such thing as being too honest. If you're honest with one thing, everything else will follow through."

For Janice, God acts when humans ask. "I thought that even when I was using, I knew He would help me. I didn't want to." Most of all, Janice appreciates the gift of self. Speaking when two of her children were still living with relatives, she mentioned preparing to visit them. "They ask me, 'Mommy, you coming home this weekend? Bring me something.' I say, 'I am, I'm bringing me.' "

CHAPTER X

Faith-Based Solutions in a Democracy

Alcoholics and addicts have demonstrated with their lives that spirituality changes people. Faith in spiritual principles, in a higher power, in the community of fellow addicts fuel personal recovery. Drug and alcohol treatment and the recovery movement, combined or separately, amount to the ultimate faith-based initiative. Indeed, these are more than a faith-based service, these are a faith-based solution. Alone, the recovery movement, free of the institutional trappings of treatment, represents a faith-based solution in its ideal shape: universal, adaptable, free, self-sustaining, nonreligious, lay-run, and effective.

This record has new relevance given the growing emphasis on religious or faith-based services and solutions to social problems. The "charitable choice" provision of the 1996 welfare reform, signed by President William J. Clinton, allowed these groups to provide certain social services. His successor, President George W. Bush sought to expand that effort through his faith-based initiative.

Little mentioned in this context is mainstream substance abuse treatment, the most widely applied solution based on faith. In one rare instance, a Bush spokesman cited AA as an example of a faith-based program.[1] Otherwise, the faith-based initiatives for addictions getting the attention, such as Teen Challenge, were those operated by religious groups. This focus concerns many. Religious persons worry about government influence over faith, liberals envision theocracy and others fear the creation of an unregulated social service sector with power over vulnerable clients. Addiction treatment and recovery show that a method, and the programs and groups using it, can be spiritual without formal religious affiliation.

Values and Change

People act for a reason. To recover, addicts change their actions. To act differently, they change their thoughts and feelings. To do that, they change their values. Solving addiction and many other social problems requires helping people change their values. So simple, so controversial, so difficult, but so effective.

The entire scheme of treatment and recovery assumes that the addict bears responsibility for their recovery. Even with this week's or next year's scientific breakthrough regarding brain waves and neurochemistry and genetics, responsibility will not, cannot, be eliminated or ignored. "This is one of life's four or five great ironies," Robert Wright writes. "We are all victims of (or beneficiaries of) an extremely complex conspiracy between our genes and our environment, yet all of us must be held accountable for the results; otherwise things fall apart."[2] Treatment can help the addict assume that responsibility. From a humanitarian standpoint, we should help addicts. And for the commonweal, we must. Columnist Dan Lynch neatly resolved the disease-versus-responsibility conflict in terms of public safety. "Three in four prison inmates are druggies and most of them are functional illiterates. OK, that's their fault, not ours. But get them off drugs and give them skills to function in the workforce and this state will be a safer place."[3]

The spiritual approach tells the addict, "It's not your fault you have this problem, but it's your responsibility to do something about it." The first part of this statement, a bit of a fib that many professionals call a useful fiction, releases the person from crippling guilt and helps her or him concentrate on getting better. The contradiction is more acceptable if we remember that the disorder has elements both psychological—abnormal behavior and neurotic coping—and physiological—dependency and organic changes that aggravate the condition, according to Ashley and O'Rourke, two Dominican priests and ethicists.[4] This echoes the standard scientific definition of addiction, which includes the aspect of "compulsive drug-seeking activity." The ethicists distinguish between voluntary acts, which may spring from an inner compulsion, and free acts, which are less and less available to an addicted person given the nature of habituation and physical dependency. In the voluntary realm lies the spring for recovery, which is based on a series of decisions by the addict. These actions—to admit a problem, abstain, seek help, cooperate—open and expand the realm of free acts. The spirit inhabits this intimate and dynamic arena and must be engaged.

Not that we've made some shattering discovery here. "What we're doing today in treatment is no different from what we were doing in 1840," William Sonnenstuhl, of Cornell University and the Smither Institute in New York told me. "Yes, that's 1840 not 1940. In 1840 we had the

Washingtonian Society, which was the precursor to Alcoholics Anonymous, and that was fundamentally spiritual. They considered alcoholism a moral issue and were very frank about discussing it that way. We have not moved much beyond that."[5] Despite Americans' disdain for doing things the old way, the continuity bespeaks an unchanged truth: addiction is bad, recovery is good, going from one to the other requires change based in the values that guide behavior. By some measures, the approach of the mid-to late nineteenth century produced results as good or better than those of today. Inebriate homes and asylums reported "cure rates" of about 30 percent to 60 percent of clients in periods of one to five years after treatment.[6]

The public contiunues to promote spiritual development by funding or encouraging treatment that is dominated by the Twelve-Step or related approaches. Approximately 10,800 treatment facilities existed in the United States in 1997. Most are small, serving 100 clients or fewer, and private. However, public funds paid for nearly two-thirds of all treatment. For instance, though 70 percent of drug users were employed and most had private health insurance, 20 percent of public treatment funds were spent on people with limited private health insurance coverage.[7] Through this financing, we recognize that recovery from addiction requires a change in attitude and values, and that spirituality can effect this change. In recovery parlance, "The same person will drink again." Addictions experts and advocates who seem miles apart often are saying the same thing in different languages.

"Contemporary theories of addiction of all stripes rule out faulty values as a cause of addiction," Stanton Peele writes. "Yet evidence from cross-cultural, ethnic, and social-class research, laboratory study of addictive behavior, and natural history and field investigations of addiction indicate the importance of value orientations in the development and expression of addictive behaviors, including drug and alcohol addiction, smoking, and compulsive eating. Furthermore, the rejection of moral considerations in addition deprives us of our most powerful weapons against addiction and contributes to our current addiction binge."[8] For Peele, addicts must develop values incompatible with addiction and its attendant misbehavior.

Nevertheless, professionals and scientists are loath to discuss the idea, partly out of a reluctance to make class distinctions or to grade systems of values. The alternative is to blame addictions, and almost all other disorders, on biology. By denying the role of values in recovery, we deny ourselves a powerful weapon in checking the spread of addiction and the harms and crime alcoholics and addicts commit. We must start with the person. Addiction only commences as the person takes the drink or drug. No one is highjacked out of a normal existence by an evil spirit wielding a crack pipe or bottle of vodka. Peele argues, sensibly enough, that the values needed to counter drug abuse include moderation, constructive activity, purpose and goals, love and respect for others, personal responsibility.[9] One could prescribe the four cardinal virtues of prudence, justice, fortitude, and temperance. Those preferring a religious or spiritual road to recovery may add the theological virtues of faith, hope, and charity.

Just as values govern the actions that lead into and out of addiction or other bad habits, so too do they hurt or help health and life itself. People who are poor, or of low socioeconomic status, have higher mortality rates. Many attribute this to smoking and other behavior-linked health risks. But researchers who studied the lives of 3,617 men and women found in 1998 that four important behaviors—smoking, body mass index, alcohol consumption, and physical activity—account for only 12-13 percent of the effect of income on mortality.[10] Other factors that raise mortality rates among the poor—stress, hostility, isolation, depression, a sense of mastery or control—also have to be factored in. Of course, these medical scientists avoided blaming the victim and suggested one course of action would be to change social structures. All well and good, but the revolution is not coming. The most liberating course may be to start with the person, even if it amounts to blaming the victim. If it's your fault, at least you can do something about it.

It is time to validate morality in a time of relativism and faltering religious convictions. We think we lack absolutes, but a moral sense exists in all humans and all cultures. On the other hand the *practice* of morality, as Aristotle taught, can be learned and good character derived from many small acts. Recovery from addiction entails many small acts that amount to a kind of individual remoralization. In polite society, the current practice of respecting others by never imposing our values deceives. In reality, we merely ignore the moral substrate of daily life, private and public. Such talk of values good and bad puts off most Americans. So judgmental, so dogmatic. But reduced to its simplest level, it is not. Begin at the basics: life is better than death, moderation or abstinence is better than gluttony or self-destructive addiction. Proceed onward, and you are soon talking about morals and values. At the point of refined applications, we will begin to disagree. On the fundamentals, I don't think so. Those uncomfortable with moral language in discussing addiction may ask themselves if the damage and death caused by alcoholism or drug abuse is anything other than profoundly evil.

In addition to the small acts of character building, recovery also consists of the very big act of the addict finding new food for a psychic hunger. Just as substance abuse satisfied deep yearnings, so must the solution. A spiritual life introduces serenity, which is based on acceptance and an openness to new possibilities beyond the addict's immediate person and circumstances. "Serenity, which is the immunity to all addictions, is characterized by feelings of tranquility, gratitude, contentment, affection for others, and a deep inner peace," Joseph Bailey writes.[11] With serenity, a person feels complete without using drugs or alcohol. "Understanding how to maintain mental health and serenity is the antidote to addictions. Because these principles are simple and are based on the common sense we already have, they are relatively easy to teach and learn." For instance: "Seize any feeling of hope and trust it, for hope is the seed that will germinate a new life."[12] Recovery begins when addicts accept the possibility that they can live happily and usefully, without drugs. Many credit their recovery to the virtues of being honest, open, and willing, for which they use the acronym HOW. "I remained teachable," they say.

Like every human being, an addict must become who he or she really is in order to live to good purpose. Inside and outside must harmonize. Many recovering alcoholics try to shed the habit of, in their words, "comparing my insides to your outsides." In support group meetings members reveal themselves in order to eliminate discontinuities between who they *really* are, who they seem to be, and who they want to be. Some AA members draw on advice from the apocryphal Gospel of Thomas: "If you bring forth what is within you, what you bring forth will save you. If you do not bring forth what is within you, what you do not bring forth will destroy you." The "self" is a tricky concept but simply put, life involves both the discovery and the creation of the self.

Much of the discussion of addiction and treatment overlooks the fact that at the heart of the problem is a person, one who decides to drink and one who at some point may decide to stop. That decision is the key. The Rand Corp. found in its 1976 study of 2,900 treatment clients, *Alcoholism and Treatment*, that among those who had a single contact with a center, and no formal treatment, there was a "substantial" remission rate of 50 percent, only slightly less than among those who were treated, suggesting that treatment may play only an incremental role in recovery. "The crucial factor for success may indeed be the client's decision to contact a treatment center for help in the first place and to remain in treatment, rather than something that occurs during the process of formal treatment itself."[13]

A willingness to discuss values would help all around. To set public policy, we exchange and analyze scientific data when we are really arguing over competing or conflicting values. Data becomes a rhetorical weapon to promote values, which go unmentioned. "When policy differences are grounded in divergent value structures, empirical research rarely helps much until participants allow for those value differences," writes John E. McDonough, a professor and former state legislator.[14] This way, parties can settle on a policy even while disagreeing on more deep-seated values. We can even disagree on the cause or nature of a problem such as addiction and agree on solutions, or at least agree that the range of solutions be broad. Until we can acknowledge this moral dimension, we will hold rather flat discussions of serious social issues. In one of many such examples, William Julius Wilson's well-received book, *When Work Disappears: The World of the New Urban Poor*, makes no mention of religion, church, or spirituality so far as I can tell. We cannot discuss, fruitfully, urban poor people without reference to their deeper aspirations, or to the churches or mosques or synagogues that are the most stable element of inner-city neighborhoods. To deny through silence people's spiritual life, and blame their situation only on outside economic forces, steals what power they have and blocks off the most potent avenue for change.

Encouraging people to develop spiritually does not mean we impose a morality so much as we encourage them to develop their own. If that sounds dangerous, remember that recovering addicts are told to find a God of their own conception. It may be a daffy concept of the divine, but one is better than none given the alternative: drugs and the god of self. If it sounds coercive, consider that we do it already with imprisoned addicts.

Prison Inmates: Sentenced to Recover

Prisons can rehabilitate addicted convicts while also fulfilling their other goals of punishment and deterrence. The addicts can be coerced to comply at least outwardly through restrictions and privileges. Inwardly, the mind and will often follow. Eventually, they may choose to develop spiritually thanks to a process that begin in coercion.

Drug and alcohol abuse and addiction played a part in the crimes committed by 80 percent of the 1.7 million men and women in U.S. prisons and jails, according to a 1998 study by Columbia University's National Center on Addiction and Substance Abuse "Those 1.4 million offenders in state and federal prisons and local jails violated drug or alcohol laws, were high at the time they committed their crimes, stole property to buy drugs, or have a history of drug and alcohol abuse and addiction, or share some combination of these," said Joseph A. Califano Jr., chairman of the Columbia center.[15] The Columbia study also found that alcohol is more closely associated with violent crime than any other drug, including cocaine and heroin; that the top substance abuse crime in America is drunk driving, accounting for 1.4 million arrests in 1995 at a cost of $5.2 billion for arrest and prosecution and that, from 1993 to 1996, the number of inmates needing substance abuse treatment climbed from 688,000 to 840,000, while the number in treatment hovered around 150,000. Califano called for "a second front in the war on crime"—in the form of treatment inside the nation's prisons. The study estimates that spending $6,500 for a year's treatment would, if the convict became a tax-paying, law-abiding citizen, yield an economic benefit of $68,800 through reduced incarceration and health care costs, salary earned, taxes paid, and contributions to the economy.

Persuading states to fund the full need seems unlikely. Prison programs were cut during the long get-tough-on-crime spree of the 1990s. In some places sentiments are turning, especially for offenders who have yet to be jailed. California, New York, and other states have initiated drug courts and other programs to steer nonviolent offenders with drug problems into treatment and not in jail.[16] In New York alone, the plan could more than triple the number of convicts being treated from 4,000 to 14,000.[17]

These drug courts are specialized units with trained judges who can sentence a person to treatment backed by supervision and penalties or rewards. With federal funds, the number of drug courts increased dramatically over several years to about 1,000 in 2001. Across the country, treatment has reduced drug abuse and rearrest rates and saved money.[18] With seed grants ending, their future lies with states and localities.[19]

Drunk drivers constitute a large percentage of Americans who are liable to be sent to treatment or directly to support groups in order, ultimately, to develop a spiritual life. A 1999 U.S. Department of Justice report found that the number of people in jail or on probation for drunken driving in the United States nearly doubled between 1986 and 1997. Of those convicted of driving while intoxicated in 1997, 454,500 were on probation, 41,100 were in local jails, and 17,600 were in state prisons. The report further noted that 46 percent of DWI offenders on probation were in alcohol treatment programs in 1997 and even more—62 percent—had participated in self-help groups. Those on probabtion were more likely to receive help than DWI prisoners, of whom only 4 percent received treatment during their sentence and 17 percent attended self-help meetings.[20]

Profile: LaQuinta—When She Was Ready

LaQuinta occupies a chair, solidly and quietly, in a common room at Liberty Manor, a residential treatment center for women and mothers in Rochester, New York. Her strong repose contrasts with the buzz of eight women, one juggling an infant, who sit and perch and lounge in various sofas and chairs as they discuss their recovery. LaQuinta watches and waits. Only in later interviews, alone, does she talk freely and directly. LaQuinta, 37 and single, is a therapeutic veteran practical in human relationships. "You can't come in and dump your whole guts out on the first day. I came here, sat back for two weeks, and when it was time to speak, I spoke." We met three times in three months in the fall of 1997. (A year later, she was still clean and sober, living in Providence House, a transitional residence run by Catholic Charities, and working in the Rochester Women's Bean Project, which produces gourmet soups and mixes.)

The middle of three children, LaQuinta was born in the nearby town of Lackawanna. Her family moved to Rochester in 1968 and lived in a middle-class area on the West Side, and then closer to Genesee Park. Father worked at Xerox, her mother at a state psychiatric institution. One day drugs stopped LaQuinta's life.

"When I was 16, I smoked a joint. On my way to school I found it and I never got there." Repeating an explanation offered by thousands of addicts, LaQuinta explains, "I was looking to fit in." Later, she was caught shoplifting and was kicked out of school, and then began 18 years of trips to jail. At 26, LaQuinta tried cocaine and was hooked, though she later managed to stay off for a period of two years. In a way, she has always been a ward of the state.

"I've been on the welfare all my [adult] life, except when I was incarcerated." LaQuinta's recovery offers some insight into the role of mandated treatment. Can society make someone change? Near the end of her lawless career, she was sent to Willard Drug Treatment Center, a New York State facility used as an alternative to prison for non-violent drug offenders. One form of therapy was called, "Confrontations."

"They put you in circle and people can throw out whatever's bothering them about you. A lot of it's nit-picking. Some don't give up until they make you cry." LaQuinta acted before she was acted upon, a moment of prudent thinking that fits her character when not on drugs. "I changed my attitude the first week I was there. It was my last chance. At Willard, I never did anything wrong. You had ten minutes to eat. If you don't finish you have to carry it around all day. It's all about time management and self-discipline. There's no looking at men."

There were morning runs of several miles, rain or shine, and inmates police one another. "I pulled up a woman for stuffing food in her mouth. I couldn't stand the way she was eating. She didn't change, so we went to confrontation." Spirituality was introduced, indirectly, through an emphasis on the Twelve Steps of AA and by offering inmates traditional worship. "We did not talk about God; but we had church," says LaQuinta. She was released from Willard in December 1996, clean for 30 days. With money from a job and the lottery, she began using drugs with her boyfriend. Two more treatments followed, in Batavia and at St. Jerome Hospital. Then came more drugs and finally Liberty Manor.

LaQuinta, who insists that alcoholics need to be shaken out of their denial and taught discipline, values most the military-style regimen of mandated treatment. "At Willard, I learned to control my temper and to change my attitude. You change there. You learn how to talk, and if you don't try they keep you there." So what's different now? "I'm applying it.

My boyfriend's going away, to Willard, so he's accounted for. Where he is, he won't be cheating on me."

"I'm more secure with myself now. Before too much was based on him. Here, I've got a sponsor, I'm going to meetings, I'm going to church every Sunday at the New Life Fellowship," a nondenominational church of 200 congregants that meets in a rented hall. "I take it personally when I go and listen, it's like they're talking to me. And I say my prayers three times a day. As long as I make a routine, it gives me the strength to walk away from arguments."

"At church I listen—the preacher, he seems like he's talking to me. I believed in God before but I blamed him for the things that went wrong. Now I say 'Let God's will and not mine be done.' Telling my mother that I was an addict, that helped a lot. I haven't been in jail since I did that."

Counselors and other addicts told her to choose her own deity. "Everyone tells you about getting a higher power. At Batavia, they said it could be a tree." She smirks, then expresses some clear ideas about how it will develop for her. "When you feel you've lost everything that's when you have that spiritual awakening. I don't want God to send it, I feel I have to work for it." I ask why.

"Things are not given to you. When you see bums asking for money on the street, I give because they tell you that when you give, you give to Jesus." She purses her lips. "Sometimes Jesus comes too often."

"I don't know when the spiritual awakening will come, but it will come. I prayed for different persons, I pray for a lot of people, because I think it's right. I want the spiritual awakening, I'm working for it."

Coercion: Nudged Toward the Light

Both in and out of jails and prisons, people are pushed towards recovery. Most commonly, many are sent to treatment or directly to recovery group meetings by a boss or judge under threat of losing their job, driving license, or freedom if they fail to attend or relapse. Many recipients of public relief—one in five heads of household[21]—have substance abuse problems, and these are increasingly required to seek treatment under federal and state welfare reforms. By some counts of federal data, the majority of those who seek professional or AA-type treatment for substance abuse in the United States do so on the orders of judges or employers.[22] The number sent directly to support groups have grown dramatically in recent decades, because of the reputation of AA and NA and also to curtail health insurance, prison, and welfare costs. Though the United States is virtually alone in its widespread practice of mandatory referrals to AA or NA, the practice is likely to spread as other industrialized countries face similar pressures.[23] A bare-bones variation on pushing rehabilitation consists of "coerced abstinence," under a model developed by Mark Kleiman of UCLA and others. Maryland and other states have introduced the method that consists of frequent drug testing backed by swift and increasingly stiff sanctions for violations. Several pilot programs report striking success.[24]

Though coercion and mandates suggest the danger of government paternalism, advocates correctly assert that society can and should promote certain generally accepted standards of conduct. Addiction affects us all through crime, accidents, and health, social and economic costs, so society can require abstinence or moderation of addicts who hurt others. Coerced abstinence could allow addicts to choose their own treatment or method of recovery, or none at all, so long as they stay clean. This approach would reduce the level of government control. It would also preserve, for those who pursue a spiritual program of recovery, the necessary level of free-will acceptance.

So can you mandate spiritual development or even an awakening? Simple answer, yes, at least indirectly. "A preponderance of the research literature confirmed efficacy and cost benefits from coerced addiction treatment or providing addiction treatment in lieu of alternative consequences," one team concluded. Coercion works with most populations—employed, public aid, criminal, child welfare—and the absence of negative evidence "was striking."[25] Nor does the addict's willingness always determine success. One review of the research found that several studies "provide evidence that programs do produce effects independent of client motivation to remain in treatment."[26]

Since most treatment stresses spiritual development, it is not too great a leap to suggest that even this most intimate of changes can be stimulated by outside pressure. "Bring the body and the mind will follow," Twelve-Step veterans assure new members. One danger is that the practice could, and already has for some people, made support groups into an arm of the state for social control. When a group member or officer signs the "court card" affirming the probationer's attendance, he or she acts as an agent, basically, for a judge, parole officer, or employer. The practice began in the late 1960s and is now commonplace. Members still debate the propriety of any Twelve-Step fellowship entangling itself with outside authorities. Many also say mandated attendance contradicts the acceptance and surrender needed for recovery in a spiritual program. Others reply, with some justification, that a coerced person can always make their own decision once they complete their sentence. These also point out that most AA members are, after all, forced into recovery by addiction. In religious terms, it is sin, and not goodness, that pushes the sinner to her or his knees. In plain or secular terms, pain makes someone ask for help. One difference: the pressure of personal anguish is internal and perhaps more conducive to personal change than is coercion by outside forces or authorities. "Coercion diminishes a person's core being," a counselor at a state prison treatment program told me. "The addict is used to punishment. He has inflicted enormous punishment on himself. Is this the 'profound personality change' you're looking for?" But it is hard to separate external reasons—car wreck, job loss, divorce—from internal motivations—despair, depression, anxiety—for an addict to want to change. Both coerce reform by promising a person more of the same if the addiction continues.

Pushing people to change fits with a new mood among citizens. By the late 1990s, with the end to welfare and other changes, commentators such as Paul Starobin saw emerging the "Daddy State," a tough-love approach for curbing unwed parenthood, street crime, drugs, and other social maladies. Instead of providing a safety net, as did the old-line "Nanny State," government now serves to curtail bad behavior and enforce responsibility while preserving, one hopes, the freedom to do the right thing. Take drug addicts, who were once either jailed, or mandated to treatment. Instead, coerced abstinence, through a graduated series of punishments for failed drug or urinalysis tests, prompts addicts to stay clean through a method of their own choosing, "We're saying, you have to help yourself and if you don't, we're going to whack you on the head. It's behavior modification," said Robert Farr, a Connecticut Assemblyman.[27]

Faith as a Solution in Public Policy

For centuries, religious groups have served the poor and the needy. The growth of such services, backed by government funds, accelerated after World War II and during the 1960s. By the 1980s, for instance, church coalitions were rebuilding neighborhoods across New York and other cities, while para-church groups like Catholic Charities or the Salvation Army were helping millions of people.

In 1996, federal welfare reform opened wider the door to funding of church-delivered social services. The "charitable choice" rules prohibit discrimination against religious groups in awarding contracts, and allows these to maintain a religious atmosphere and hire only those who agree with their beliefs. For their part, contractors cannot use public funds for religious purposes and must allow clients who dislike religion to receive services elsewhere. Within several years, advocates reported success. According to a nine-state study by the Center for Public Justice, "religious groups accepting government funding are not having to sell their souls, and clients' civil rights are being respected." But in an indication of the lukewarm reaction to the provision, only 125 new financial and nonfinancial collaborations were established in the nine states during the 1996 to 1999 period.[28]

In January 2000, George W. Bush created the White House Office of Faith-based and Community Initiatives. What he called one of the great goals of his administration—helping these groups "change hearts"—could be accomplished, he promised, without changing their mission or threatening pluralism.[29] Again, the public was wary of mixing tax dollars with religion and the plan began to shrink.

Congregations, however, are busy without taxpayer help. A survey by Independent Sector, a coalition of nonprofit and philanthropic groups, found that less than 1 percent of congregations receive government money.[30] In a separate study, the largest ever of the nation's 325,000 religious congregations, 85 percent were found to have community service programs—most commonly the provision of cash, food, clothing, and shelter to needy families and individuals—making these more common than prayer groups or choir practice. More than a third of the congregations surveyed offer day care, substance abuse counseling or health education. Though the researchers concluded that services provided by the nation's churches "would seem to be excellent candidates" for government support, both the faithful and the public remain unconvinced.[31]

Nevertheless, many Americans and civic leaders believe that only religion can fill the moral void of modern society by imparting traditional values to the wayward. Conservative columnist Cal Thomas celebrated the decline of welfare for pushing many homeless alcoholics into branches of the International Union of Gospel Missions. "While rescue missions cannot force people to change, they can lead them to confront the responsibility they have to deal with their problems and can empower them in ways that secular government cannot," he declared.[32] As for the needy, religious groups were supposedly the best at helping them with food, housing, and work. Based on available research, we do not know if this conclusion is warranted. More likely, the assumption simply fits with an antigovernment, traditional-values ethos.

Supporters of public funding argue there are many ways for religious groups to operate with public funds and not offend the Constitution. Many point out that the Bill of Rights promises freedom of, rather than freedom from, religion. These say social service workers can be religiously motivated and offer spiritual help without demanding religious conversion or observance. After all, almost all houses of worship receive some government benefit—public safety, tax exemptions. Further, the Establishment Clause still allows government aid to private citizens, such as Medicaid reimbursement of alcoholism treatment, even if they use it to receive help at a church-run program. "Where the choice of service is truly private and the government purpose is secular, government help does not endorse religion," wrote David Cole, a Georgetown University law professor.[33] Finally, mainstream religious groups, eager to avoid lawsuits and internal conflict, long ago established separate nonreligious affiliates, such as Catholic Charities, to operate with public funds.

Others have judged these programs a failure precisely for leaving out the religion. In a stinging critique, Brian C. Anderson faulted Catholic Charities, the Association of Jewish Family and Children's Agencies, and the Lutheran Services in America for becoming government-funded arms of the welfare state with little that is religious, or even "values-laden," in the services they provide. He accused Catholic Charities of embracing state solutions to social problems and abandoning the Church's "unambiguous moral inheritance—a time-tested recipe for reducing poverty and other social ills as well as nurturing fulfilled lives."[34]

Unexpectedly for the faith-based advocates, the public sang out a chorus of doubt about these plans. Liberals were eager to maintain a church/state divide. Religious conservatives worried churches would be corrupted by government funding and regulations or that objectionable sects—such as Scientology or the Nation of Islam—would be rewarded. President Bush, meanwhile, assured the *Washington Post* that his plans would resolve fears that "government will force a change in their religion," or that "government will force religion on people."[35] Since the most common community program provided by churches is helping the poor, advocates say fears of federally backed missionaries are overblown. But once food, housing, and shelter are provided, the next logical step is to give people a lasting solution—that involves changes in values and character. If church and other groups back away from that, what good are they? And if they embrace solutions based in their faith—presumably the source of power in their lives—how can the government fund it?

Whether these will receive significant public funds remains in doubt given the deep ambivalence about the proposals. A 2001 survey found that most Americans support public funding of religious social services, broadly speaking, but not the specifics. For instance, they oppose funding non-Judeo-Christian institutions. And six in ten worried that religious groups might proselytize, and opposed funding groups that encourage conversion, a central goal for many religious service providers. Finally, two-thirds worried that federal funding might force religious organizations to dilute their views.[36]

Some concerns are practical and humanitarian. Peter Dobkin Hall, an historian of charities, points to the often dismal record of privately run group homes for mentally retarded people and worries that the faith-based initiative will create a whole realm of well-financed, nonprofit agencies caring for vulnerable and handicapped clients but with little oversight or regulation.[37] Despite our sentimental preferences, there is no compelling proof that religious groups are better than alternatives at helping the poor.

We could recognize the power of faith-based services and leave them alone. Without the dollars from Washington, these would still have their power to change lives. In a way, when staffers at a faith-based group give help—food, housing, counseling—but not their faith, they feed fish to a hungry man or woman instead of giving that person a fishing pole. For believers, it is faith that steers and redeems their lives. Why leave it out? It would be like an AA member who works as a addiction counselor but who never, for fear of seeming to preach, suggests the Twelve Steps or other spiritual approach to a still-suffering addict. A Catholic churchman told me of working in a city neighborhood where the local parish ran a food pantry, soup kitchen, and other services without proselytizing. "We didn't want to practice 'rice-bowl Christianity,' " he explained. One day, a family his group had helped regularly began attending a Protestant church. He asked why, considering their many visits to its social services, they did not try the Catholic church. "You never asked," the mother of the family replied.

The ambivalence reflects our discomfort with taking God seriously, at least out loud. Edward Morgan, president of the Bowery Mission in New York, wrote of well-heeled supporters who are "simultaneously fascinated by the transforming principle of turning your life over to a higher power and vehemently opposed to any acknowledgement of God in public life."[38] Ambivalence is well-founded. Religion has remained powerful by not dominating the political realm, perhaps thanks to the Constitution, and by concentrating on the hearts and minds and souls of believers who can then go out and live publicly on the basis of their beliefs without involving their religion. We should be wary of government pushing religious or faith-based services in a democracy even if religion is the most important method for promoting the values and skills that create civil society, and even if religion creates the basic beliefs about humanity, its existence, and purpose that create public policy.

Church and State

Suppose that more than a million people had recovered from a terminal malady thanks to a set of principles. Now suppose that doctors trying to treat others with that illness were prohibited from using those same principles.

This situation faces authorities across the United States as prisoners and other convicts continue winning courts rulings to the effect that they cannot be mandated to AA or NA meetings or to Twelve-Step-style treatment programs. Naturally enough, when wardens set up programs for drug-abusing prisoners or judges seek a place to send drunk drivers, they turn to methods that have worked elsewhere. They see Twelve Step fellowships meeting all over in autonomous groups that cost nothing and ask little of members beyond what they decide to do. Prison officials see these concepts used by clinical professionals in helping a majority of the three million alcoholics and addicts treated annually in the United States. So judges, wardens, and probation officers pick up these tools and put them to use in courtrooms and prisons, probation, and parole.

Considering the spiritual content of treatment and self-help, is it constitutional to require or push these on prisoners and other convicts? No, the courts have ruled by and large. A number of convicts have convinced state and federal judges that such mandates violate the First Amendment: "Congress shall make no law regarding an establishment of religion, or prohibiting the free exercise thereof."

In a landmark 1996 case, a deeply divided New York State Court of Appeals ruled that prison officials violated the Constitution when they required an atheist inmate, as a condition for family visitation privileges, to attend a treatment program centered on Twelve Steps. As such, the 5-2 decision in *Coughlin v. Griffin* declared the program to be "unequivocally religious." Wrote Judge Howard A. Levine, "There is no firmer or more settled principle of Establishment Clause jurisprudence than that prohibiting the use of the state's power to force one to profess a religious belief or participate in a religious activity." The principles and practice of the Twelve Steps entail religious activity and proselytization since "followers are urged to accept the existence of God" and to seek such a God through "prayer, confessing wrongs and asking for removal of shortcomings." The court noted that under a Supreme Court decision in *Lemon v. Kurtzman*, the Constitution is violated not only when the state compels adherence to a sect, but also when its actions have the primary effect of advancing religion. The dissenters in the ruling objected, saying the prison program "remains overwhelmingly secular in philosophy, objective and operation," notwithstanding elements "that some perceive as somewhat religious."[39] In 2001, a federal judge in New York drew on this ruling as he overturned a double murder conviction that was based on the defendant's admissions to other AA members. Since the the fellowship was a religion, he declared, such confidences are akin to those between a priest and penitent. The decision contradicts AA's literature, philosophy, and practice. It also lengthened the string of precedents that, though sensible on the surface, confuse spirituality with religion and jeopardize the critical element of most drug and alcohol treatment programs.

Elsewhere, federal appeals courts have ruled likewise against sending an inmate to NA meetings or requiring a drunk driver to attend AA meetings as a condition of probation. Oddly enough, these rulings have not been widely applied despite the fact that most treatment programs receive some public funding and almost all suggest, push, or require participation in the Twelve-Step fellowships or philosophy.

Do the Twelve Steps or the related fellowships amount to a religion? To a person, the hundred-plus members of AA and NA around the country I interviewed say no. Emphatically, they distinguish spirituality from religion. Most professionals concur. And addicts who find recovery in other spiritualities—Native American, women's, Eastern, and others—draw the same distinction between their flexible methods and organized religion's content. Is there a difference?

By most definitions, religion has a dogma, a deity, rituals, a moral code, and membership requirements. Courts often have used a checklist of four items: belief in a supreme being, a religious discipline, rituals, and tenets for daily life. (Judges have also tested a group to see if it occupies the same place in the lives of members as more orthodox religions, which seems circular and useful only as a secondary proof.) More exclusively than religion, spirituality seeks something beyond the material—truth, community, meaning—and is both open-ended and personal. Higher courts have, generally, dismissed the distinction between religion and spirituality. They may have a point; just asserting a difference does not make it so.

What should give us pause, however, is the sheer number of people who claim a distinction and live on that basis. Further, these people understand spirituality to be essentially nonreligious. By definition, spirituality lacks doctrine, a moral code, rituals—those elements that define religion. Were the two one, we would have to find another word for the spirituality of recovery. It is a close call and I wish I had a simple verdict. Some of the difficulty arises from the distinction, in an earlier era, between institutional religion and personal religion. The latter is what we call spirituality today. Though judges will still hammer out, or on, this distinction, they should consider that so many people now value this divide.

Self-help fellowships often appear religious to outsiders. But there is no dogma, no moral code, and no prescribed rituals—though like all humans, AA and NA members tend to ritualize certain routines. AA declares that, "the only requirement for membership is a desire to stop drinking," which hardly amounts to a religious code. That leaves the question of a deity, always qualified to mean one of the member's own conception. Among the millions of Twelve-Step group members, there are innumerable definitions of higher power or even spirituality. For many spirituality consists of a search for truth, meaning—the *logos* or redemptive significance of life that Viktor Frankl realized allows each of us to rise above the most wretched of circumstances. That meaning may be what others call God. Many atheists and agnostics find "a power greater than ourselves" in the fellowship or its principles and guidance. Others turn to a "great spirit," or to love or Nature. Many practice an outside religion, but invariably keep that separate from their program of recovery.

Judges have been uneasy with their decisions, since most recognize the success of mainstream treatment schemes. Though most treated addicts do relapse—that's the nature of an addiction—a significant portion eventually recover with the help of support groups and spirituality. Further, AA and NA hold meetings everywhere, send volunteers into prisons and institutions, and charge nothing. Where else is a judge without a budget for treatment likely to send a DWI convict—free mutual-help meetings or 28 days at the Betty Ford Center? H. Wesley Clark, director of the federal Center for Substance Abuse Treatment, recalled for me his years working in hospitals that hosted meetings run by outside AA or NA volunteers. "What's attractive about Twelve-Step programs is they're free and the people showed up and kept showing up. Other people talked a good game, but they never arrived."[40]

The issue is a thorny one. The preamble read at most AA meetings emphasizes its independence from any religion or other organization. Its literature elaborates on the freedom of agnostics and atheists to choose a nonreligious higher power. But the lives of members are entwined in the outside world of legal mandates or informal coercion. According to a AA's 1992 Membership Survey, 63 percent of members previously received treatment or counseling—with most of those saying it helped steer them into meetings—and 8 percent were court-ordered to AA.

In and out of recovery groups, many people dislike seeing convicts mandated to a voluntary fellowship where recovery begins with a person's free-will admission to an addiction. Local judges have answered that rather than mandating attendance, they offer convicts a choice: AA or jail. Another answer is for prisons and courts to offer Twelve-Step-oriented treatment as just one of several options for addicts, which is what the New York appeals court suggested. Or AA tenets could be rewritten in nonreligious language, such that of cognitive behavioral therapy. "Treatment programs are aware of the court decisions, so they offer materials that are derivative of the Twelve Steps," H. Wesley Clark told me. Outside of or after treatment, authorities cannot mandate Twelve-Step meetings, he added, but they can require a person find some form of community support, considered a critical element in long-term recovery. "The Twelve Steps don't work for everybody, so there is Rational Recovery, Secular Organizations for Sobriety, even Moderation Management. As a clinician, I would just say you have to go to a support group. But objections (to AA or NA) crumble when people see there is not much else out there, and you have to wonder why." He laughed softly. I asked why alternatives are scarce. "I don't know." He laughed again. In Twelve-Step groups, Clark added, "You can always find someone to talk to."[41]

Allowing prisoners or probationers to choose the antidote to their poison should satisfy the courts. "The Supreme Court increasingly relies on the principle that indirect benefit to religion because of state action is permissible when the direct choice of religion over non-religion was made by private parties," Jendi B. Reiter observes.[42] These secular programs, with their code of beliefs or suggestions for living, could cause other problems given a range of court decisions guaranteeing individual freedom of conscience.

Maybe Americans just need to stop flinching over matters spiritual. Not every mention of the word "God" or prayer leads to evangelization. By all means, keep government out of religion. But the addicts and alcoholics all around us who have regained their lives through spirituality have a good argument that they are not practicing religion. And addicts in court and prison need all the help they can get. As Reiter said of the *Griffin v. Coughlin* decision, while the strict application of the Establishment Clause was "formally correct, the practical outcome defies common sense."

No solution will satisfy everyone. Some problems require answers that spirituality, religion, and philosophy can provide. We cannot leave them aside. If we think of spirituality as a search for meaning, it becomes less troublesome. If addicts are pushed to resolve their problem by finding such a *logos*, they preserve their freedom and responsibility. Such an approach also fits well with America's renewed interest in personal accountability. Sadly, as a matter of public policy, we apply such tests most often to the poor and disadvantaged. But recognizing any person's freedom and responsibility is a great gift that also preserves their dignity.

Mainstream religions often recognize the spirituality of recovery as something apart and different. "One Church-One Addict" is a program in Washington, D.C. that trains volunteers from congregations to help recovering addicts reenter society. Though run by a Catholic priest and based at churches, it insists on spirituality and eschews religion. "Addiction is a spiritual disease and healing takes place through spiritual curing. One Church-One Addict vehemently promotes spirituality." But proselytizing is forbidden and the religion of all participants is "their own concern."[43]

A more substantial constitutional problem lies in the effort to fund faith-based social programs with public monies. What used to be religious is now called faith-based, to put on a softer, more ecumenical face. Semantics camouflage the problem. Most faith-based services are based in a religion, with the possible exception of Twelve-Step-style treatment. And you cannot have a faith-based service without the faith. Omit the faith and it is something else.

"We haven't taken any government money over the past 109 years we've been in business because we don't want to have to water down or not be able to say that Jesus is important to us," Brad Meuli, president of the Denver Rescue Mission, told the *Associated Press*. "We won't compromise on that." The Denver mission's drug and alcohol rehabilitation program includes mandatory Bible studies and one-on-one spiritual counseling. "You don't have to be a Christian, but we're trying to save lives and this is how we believe that can be done," Meuli said.[44]

Leave in the faith, or religion, and public funding of the service violates the Constitution. "It's absolutely incredible to believe you can have a religiously based program that isn't religious," said Barry Lynn, a minister and executive director of Americans United for Separation of Church and State.[45] Around the country, groups like his have challenged state programs that fund programs such as Faith Works, a Milwaukee program providing drug treatment and job training to troubled fathers or a Texas welfare-to-work program that includes Bible based lectures. "There's no doubt, eventually we will have to go to the Supreme Court," said Stanley Carlson-Thies of the Center for Public Justice, which studies faith-based funding.

Currently, the compromise is for all religious content to be removed from publicly supported, faith-based services. In its government-financed work, Catholic Charities is Catholic in name only. Staffers may be motivated by Catholic principles or duties, but services are provided in a secular atmosphere. At the Rochester convent that was converted into Liberty Manor, the local Catholic Charities that operated the program had to remove all the statues and crucifixes. But that same program, which converted the chapel to a meditation room, encourages clients to follow the Twelve Steps and attend AA or NA meetings.

People who find the idea of God or a spiritual life abhorrent can accept the utility of faith if it bears fruit. But at least since the Enlightenment, Western thinkers have spoken as if science would soon render religion needless. Today, this impulse continues in the perception of religion as a hobby that should not influence public remarks or actions. But no less a student of the Enlightenment than Thomas Jefferson endorsed the utilitarian approach. In a letter to a nephew, Jefferson recommended exploring the issue of God. If the effort ends in a disbelief, the exercise would still inspire virtue. On the other hand, Jefferson continued, "If you find reason to believe there is a God, a consciousness that you are acting under his eye, and that he approves you, will be a vast additional incitement."[46]

Dangers to Spirituality, Dangers of Spirituality

Spiritual solutions to addiction face two related dangers: the institutionalization of spirituality and the deferral by the health care system to Twelve-Step and other outside groups. If institutionalized, spiritual methods can become distorted, stale, or dangerous. Institutional use of spiritual methods creates its own ideology—even as simple as the rallying cry, "Whatever works, works." These belief systems can then infiltrate support groups and, through these, society at large. The recovery movement could also harm religious life by cementing into place the current age's desire for freedom and flexibility despite a hankering after rigor and orthodoxy. The twin desires could yield, in religious life, a subjective mush replete with elaborate but empty rituals. Further, entirely secular, psychological, or trivial elements of health care, treatment, or therapy can be labeled "spiritual" and pushed without sound reason. Even the engine of spiritually based fellowships—peer-run discussion groups—can be used to harm participants in an institutional setting. Kathryn J. Fox studied a "cognitive self-change" treatment group for violent offenders in a Vermont state prison. For her, these methods—despite their benevolent and individually focused image—serve to reinforce the "dominant discourse" of governmental power.[47]

Government intervention in, or use of, Twelve-Step methods threatens all these fellowships. Counselors often pass off nonsense as AA fact to vulnerable clients, who then pass it along as gospel at recovery group meetings to yet more newcomers. A larger, more diffuse danger lies in the use of AA or NA as court-mandated treatment for drunk drivers and other addicts. Such convicts, typically, attend meetings and have cards signed by members to show the judge that they are fulfilling their sentence. "Though AA welcomes them, this is something that's basically against what makes the fellowship work," Marc Galanter, a New York psychiatrist and researcher, has said. "Coming in is supposed to be voluntary—an act of spiritual surrender, not acquiescence to some legal requirement."[48] Though the practice continues with seemingly little harm to either the groups or their philosophy, judges should consider other means to encourage recovery or mandate abstinence. A court could mandate the convict choose or construct a program of recovery subject to the judge's approval and conditions such as subsequent checks and random testing. Or courts could simply mandate abstinence, or the absence of trouble, and leave it to the convict to determine the best course of compliance.

Spirituality can be dismissed or ignored, as it is by many researchers and leaders in the addictions field. Some treatment centers profess the Twelve Steps in name only, and do little to introduce clients to spiritual methods. On the other hand, spiritual solutions can be given too great a burden to carry. Spirituality is free—the perfect treatment in an age of budget cutting. While many addicts profit from joining NA or other groups directly, however, others need the medical care and social stabilization of treatment to ease their transition. To say that spirituality is the complete answer to every case of drug or alcohol addiction would be wrong. As for other social problems, the root of many is poverty. Giving out God instead of cash saves a lot of money. Many politicians profess the power of faith, or faith-based initiatives, to change lives. While no doubt sincere, the stance puts them behind a solution to social problems makes us feel virtuous and costs us little.

Profile: Charlie—Sober with Jesus and Others

Sometimes, generic spirituality and vague higher powers are not enough help for an alcoholic to overcome self-destructive drinking. At the Christ Recovery Center, part of the Union Gospel Mission in St. Paul, Minnesota, a man I'll call Charlie spoke to me about his recovery with Jesus.

His middle-class childhood in Columbus, Ohio featured much social drinking at pool parties and barbecues and cocktail hours. As most alcoholics report, Charlie says his drinking and the drugs, at first, "made me feel all grown up, like a hot s——." His face falls from reverie to glum realization. "After I was grown up, it started to be a big mess." Between his expulsion from high school and landing at the mission at age 28, Charlie drank his way into 11 car accidents, shot himself with a gun, and lost a carpet-cleaning business.

In 1995, he went through a pricey treatment in Columbus of the standard Minnesota model, which combines medical attention with educational lessons and AA meetings. "It was a 30-day cram of 'know this, know that,' and then you're back out on your own and I was drunk two weeks later. I was introduced to the Twelve Steps, to everything. It was nonstop meetings, from six in the morning to nine at night. I had depression, and the psychiatrist slammed me with drugs for depression and anxiety—Zoloft, BuSpar, 'endoral.' "

It wasn't enough. Charlie felt a hole in his life, left by the absence of God and of the company of others who staked their sobriety on Christian faith. At the Columbus rehab, which cost his family $12,000, "they don't set you up with a life," he says. "There was no spirituality, no talk of religion, and they would tell you to practice your religion elsewhere. There was nothing about God. It was all higher power."

"I grew up Catholic but I had stopped believing in God. Unless I needed help, then I would be, 'God, get me out of this.' " He looks around the empty, gleaming cafeteria at the Christ Recovery Center, where we were talking, and thinks back. "I came here not believing in anything." And what happened?

"The fellowship. You're living with these guys for three to five months. Some don't get it, but most do. Now Jesus is my higher power. I'm not a Bible thumper. Jesus is somebody to look up to, someone to be like. I thank Jesus for a lot of things. Before I was like, 'give me this, give me that.' " The thanking reorients him.

"It makes me feel better for thanking someone for what I've got, instead of blaming someone for what I don't." He recounts one moment that counts as the sort of eye-opener that many call a spiritual awakening, a moment that converted his knowledge of the keys to a better life—faith, gratitude—into acceptance and use.

"What happened was when I was in court, hearing all these people blaming the police, the judge, or saying, 'Why did they give me so much time?' It sounded so moronic that I wondered what an ass *I* had been. I knew I was like that."

Despite the Christian flavor, Charlie's talks of his spiritual life in the practical though sometimes confusing terms heard from recovered addicts the world over. "God doesn't have to do with your spirit but as far as just doing better things. I'm doing things I never did before without drinking, such as talking to people. I feel better about myself. Before I hated myself. I feel a lot more at peace with myself. I've never seen beauty in things before and, to tell you the truth, when I was drinking, I had just stopped loving."

Charlie reports esteeming himself, "living positive," and supporting himself with a job at an electronics factory as he approaches the end of his time in Christ Center's transitional housing. "I don't need nobody to bail me out. I'm trying to clean up my wreckage. I always thank God for what I've got. There's always something, even on a bad day. Being happier is just taking a better outlook on life."

The Faith-based Future in Addictions Treatment and Health Care

Fifty years of spiritually based addictions treatment and recovery present several lessons for public policy, health care and social problems. As a society, America has shifted from pure self-reliance of the nineteenth century to a communal responsibility for disadvantaged or suffering individuals of the mid-twentieth to the growing demand for personal accountability. This most recent stage, at its best, joins self-reliance and the commonweal. Responsibility perches on one end of the seesaw, rights on the other, and their shifting weights send each end up and down. Most spiritual approaches to addiction, especially AA and NA, contain the paradoxical balance between the seeming inevitability of addiction in many lives and personal responsibility for recovery. This is the human condition, after all: we are helpless, we need help, and we must get help. Some would add that only in helping others are we helped.

The mutual-help nature of recovery groups updates this powerful strain in American civic society, which has fueled labor unions, community groups, and fraternal organizations. Twelve-Step-style groups now exist to help people deal with hundreds of different problems, from promiscuity to gambling to criminality. All concentrate on changing the person. Group solutions or communal reform—ending poverty, reviving city neighborhoods, promoting peace—need other methods.

In Washington, D.C., the founders of Clean & Sober Streets began their work as volunteers at a huge homeless shelter run by the Community for Creative Non-Violence, an influential group that combined service to society's outcasts with social activism. They quickly broke away in a philosophical split over the proper balance between rights and responsibility, according to Marsh Ward, Clean & Sober's clinical director. "CCNV felt that people are criminals because society made it impossible for them to be anything else. In order to help people not be alcoholic the answer is to change society. (CCNV founder) Mitch Snyder said that people are drunk on the street because it's hard to live on street. For us, it's the opposite. We're saying yes, there's racism and injustice. But there's a hole in the wall that you can get through and get a better life. The philosophy that society has to change before people can change is very destructive."[49]

Addiction treatment and recovery also demonstrate that we can discuss spirituality, with its reference to values and character and transcendence, in neutral language and suggest it as a key to change for people who are sick, criminal, the badly behaved, or otherwise troubled. If addiction really does resemble other diseases or behavioral disorders, then its spiritual treatment offers a good example of suggesting changes that lead to different actions. Many doctors grow frustrated with treating illnesses that are caused by behavior but the reform of which remains inaccessible to them. Some address values and spirituality with patients, though the more likely course is a few pat suggestions about changes in lifestyle. Elsewhere in medicine, some practitioners discuss religion, faith, or prayer with patients, usually if they are dying. But many are eager, though they may lack the time or language, to treat patients as complete human beings with internal resources for healing. Greenfield, at the University of Arizona holistic health center (founded by alternative medicine guru Andrew Weil), distinguishes between medicine and spirituality. The latter he defined as "the view that we're all interconnected in meaning, in purpose. We view spirituality aside from and in tandem with the religious beliefs of our patients." Some patients take to it. Others, usually those with strong religious faith, resist the spiritual component of alternative medicine. But this component is inoffensive and simple, Greenfield said. "We emphasize these four practices: relaxation breathing, progressive muscle relaxation, meditation, and yoga."[50]

Medicine and public policy increasingly ask people to take more responsibility for their health. Just as solutions can include or be based on spirituality, so can solutions and services include moral assumptions. Social Role Valorization, an internationally influential theory developed by Wolf Wolfensberger to guide the care of mentally retarded and other handicapped or devalued people, is based on empirical findings and positive values. Though Wolfensberger directs people to their religion to determine what they should do and why, his theory acknowledges that people express their morality in their actions.[51] Some psychologists recognize the deep personal transformations that are basically conversion experiences. AA presents its spiritual approach as one that can change a personality dramatically and, often, quickly when other methods fail. In a broader population, these "quantum changes" involve shifts in value structure and can be measured and discussed in relatively neutral language.[52]

What role will spiritual support groups play in the future? By their basic nature groups tend to be exclusive. Groups organize around certain ideas, and may hold on to these beyond a useful point and denigrate threatening ideas. The predominant effect of the Twelve-Step approach on treatment has been to exclude other options. Educational and medical organizations founded by early AA members or sympathizers promoted that approach, as well as the disease concept and the goal of abstinence.[53] Despite the tremendous usefulness and flexibility of the Twelve Steps, beliefs held by AA and NA members have often been repeated so many times that they become unchallengeable, self-evident truths. "Data that refute the creed are ignored, condemned, or spurned as nonsense or heresy," Fingarette charges.[54]

One hopes for a softening of the either/or mentality that, to outsiders, characterizes these circles: the insistence that one either is, or is not, an addict forever; or that a person is either doing it the right way or is "white-knuckling it." This thinking distorts treatment. It demonizes outsiders and allow counselors to label people as being "in denial" when they don't adhere to the prescribed agenda.[55] Treatment centers may want to develop goals other than just abstinence in the hopes of reaching more people with drinking problems. Since programs already measure their overall outcomes flexibly, they can do the same on an individual basis with certain clients, especially younger people who abuse alcohol but may resist being labeled alcoholic and whose age and healthy social supports increase their chances for remission without abstinence. Treatment professionals could be less doctrinaire, as some already are, about insisting that "one drink will get you drunk," since, as the Rand Report and others have found, it is not true for everyone with a drinking problem.

If the Twelve Steps offer a spirituality that is uniquely aware of its shortcomings, then the message for the recovery movement and treatment professionals both is that its collective belief can and should change. "We must entertain the possibility that addictions can actually be prevented and cured, not just coped with and accepted," Bailey writes.[56] At the same time, the recovery movement's core values of acceptance, humility, and tolerance could benefit health care and curb society's expectations of medicine. There are limits to what medicine or science can do. Though recognizing limits hurts our pride and nags our guilt, it also opens the door to hope—always a powerful tonic.

With a vocal but largely ignored minority, Fingarette raises the valid question of whether our vast network of professional treatment is necessary, heresy to many AA or NA members who began recovery with such help. "Indeed, it has not been demonstrated that such programs add anything at all to the improvement that could be expected in the natural course of affairs without a drinker's having received any professional help whatsoever."[57] Fingarette is not alone in dismissing the effects of treatment. The authors of an eight-year follow-up with 628 subjects found, as previous research indicated, that treatment did not have a lasting impact on the course of alcoholism. At best, Humphreys, Moos, and Cohen concluded, treatment "has the potential to provide short-term relief and an opportunity for lasting change if additional changes are made in the individual's life for an extended period." Spirituality is one means to this lasting change. The research teams reported that even controlling for personal motivation, "we found consistent and long-lasting positive effects of participation in AA."[58]

Twelve-Step groups, as a primary social and community resource for addicts, provides the long-term help needed to persist in a new life. This is not to argue that society should stop treating addicts. Managed care and other changes may whittle down what's available. For a time, a significant portion of AA or NA members came to the meetings during or after residential treatment. This still provokes mixed reactions. One AA member, writing in that fellowship's monthly magazine, the *AA Grapevine*, called upon members to stop criticizing treatment as somehow less than AA. "This is an apples and oranges proposition; there is a need for both. Love them or not, thousands of people now in AA first managed to get off the treadmill in treatment centers—including this writer." But such a norm is declining, he continued.

"I've heard it said that 'treatment is discovery and AA is recovery.' But in the age of managed care . . . 'discovery' has shifted increasingly to AA. In my hometown, there is no longer any inpatient treatment." With managed care and cuts in mental health services, many patients are referred more directly and groups have reported a surge in such newcomers. Many already in recovery groups resent serving as dumping ground for healthcare providers and legal authorities. In response, the *Grapevine* correspondent recalled AA's slogan, "I am responsible." He wrote, "Welcoming the newcomers, whether they come from the street, the Internet, the court, or the hospital, is where this program begins."[59]

In a way, the situation returns AA to its roots, that of the last resort for many alcoholics. Even in the best scenario, treatment invariably ends. Support groups can be there, down the block, for the long term. There or elsewhere, spirituality can be developed for a lifetime. So it is odd that as our society incorporates spirituality into mainstream health care, researchers and scientists who work on addictions and alcoholism seem ever more focused on finding a chemical solution and ignoring what has worked for millions of recovered addicts.

Some professionals say the recovery movement should become more like advocates for mentally ill people. These activists claim to have reduced stigma by emphasizing biological causes and expanded treatment through shaping policy and administration. The example may not be the right one for the recovery movement. Addiction, even if there are biological factors, is rooted in behavior. The person must drink to become alcoholic. (Of course, a person must act or behave mentally ill to be diagnosed as such, but that behavior does not cause the mental illness in the way that drinking causes alcoholism.) As for boosting the role of recovered addicts in treatment policy and funding, they already fill many jobs, especially at the lower and middle levels, in that field.

Treatment professionals are encouraging recovered addicts to speak up for more funding, reduced discrimination and the like. In one such effort, the federal Substance Abuse and Mental Health Services Administration offered funding to help people in recovery, family, and others enter the public discussion of addiction, treatment, and recovery.[60] Bad idea say many, especially William L. White, an historian of treatment. Such funding could dry up and leave dependent groups stranded and discredited. In the nineteenth century alliances between treatment institutions and abstinence groups caused the collapse of the recovery movement and provoked public skepticism about helping alcoholics. White threw water on the agenda of activist leaders in the recovery movement. "I don't think the centerpiece of the recovery movement should be 'treatment works' or 'alcoholism is a disease.' I think it should be that recovery is a reality, that there are many pathways to recovery, and that recovery is a voluntary movement."[61]

Finally, going public may not help the larger cause of recovery. Twelve-Step fellowships have long functioned quite effectively for their members in large part, they report, due to their anonymity. Why tamper with success? Further, it is far from clear that more treatment programs are needed, aside from a large unmet need in prisons and jails. There are 10 or 11 million alcoholics and addicts, and 3 million are treated annually, suggesting most should get some care over the course of several years.

Recovered addicts should be wary of joining a sector that often ignores or plays down the very basis of their rehabilitation. Tav Sparks, a former treatment counselor, observed back in 1987 that, "What was originally an adjunct to the grass-roots 12-step movement—a cooperative effort on the part of sympathetic clergy, doctors, and psychiatrists to assist in their limited capacity in the spiritual transformation necessary for recovery—

appears to be becoming a self-serving monolith which has, if not buried, then relegated the spiritual component to only figurehead importance."[62] Some even say recovery groups, by returning to their original practices, could replace the supposedly overtaxed treatment system. Early AA members routinely offered a bed to needy newcomers while others lived together in group homes, much like the Oxford Houses of today. Mutual-aid groups already do much of the work with difficult populations, such as prisoners. In New York State's prisons in 1998, for instance, 10,000 inmates were in full-time treatment and 15,000 in part-time programs, while 20,000 participated in NA or AA meetings (these figures probably overlap).[63]

The power of these support groups—autonomous, disparate, informal—cannot be overestimated. Religion, or spirituality, is a product of a collective consciousness that helps people live. It is sustained in the group's beliefs and practices. Apart from the group, the addicts of whom we speak cannot recover. Recovery groups can fill some of the void left as other intermediate associations have floundered or evaporated. Mutual aid was a primary purpose of the fraternal and other societies that flourished in the late nineteenth and into the mid-twentieth century. These offered the same mix of cooperation and individualism that characterizes Twelve-Step and related recovery groups. Support groups do not provide the financial assistance of fraternal groups, such as life insurance, medical care or short-term loans.[64] But the aid that recovery groups provide has consequences—sobriety, purpose, productivity, life—just as real. And just as fraternal groups were criticized or attacked by professional groups who felt threatened by the aid these rendered, so are recovery groups derided, ignored or, most commonly, treated as a mere adjunct to the serious business of professional treatment.

Religion and Society, God and Humanity

What role are we willing to grant faith in society? Several points are worth mentioning in the context of spiritual solutions to individual and social problems. First, we should acknowledge the ubiquity of belief. Through 50 years of polling and with remarkable consistency, "the overwhelming majority of Americans have said that they believe in God, are involved with religious organizations, use them for voluntary and charitable activities, sound orthodox in respect to biblical beliefs, say that religion matters, and more, and more," Martin E. Marty has written. Not that we always remember this fact. Marty notes that the academics, journalists, entertainers, and others "whose job it is to give an accurate accounting of American life have generally failed to see this consistency and these continuities."[65] Many of these elites subscribe to the decades-old secularization theory, the notion that religion's importance in public and private life will decline. Religion, faith, and spirituality all persist, even thrive in old and new forms. One example of the latter is the growing number of people who are "spiritual but not religious." Though easy to mock, this non-credal creed deserves respect and attention.

In acknowledging faith, we acknowledge its power, present and past. The moral ground upon which we walk—politically and civilly—was created by religion. We can share these common values without subscribing to the faiths that bore them. But we must recognize this foundation of the rights and values by which we live with one another. "Whether its proponents know it or not, the world-affirming work of secularism has always tacitly depended upon the forgiveness and ultimate rightness of an orderly nature, whose scope and majesty are too great to be entirely overcome by the human will," Wilfred M. McClay writes. "Paradoxically, belief in the existence of considerations beyond the world's reach has served to give the world its solidity, to underwrite the possibility of human dignity and to discipline human will."[66]

Next, we can acknowledge differences in faith and belief, in religion and spirituality, in atheism and agnosticism. Tolerance of other religions, fortitude in one's own faith, must be our twin staffs as we walk into a religious territory that is ever more diverse thanks to imported religions as well as new spiritualities. We must neither trivialize the belief of others nor ignore painful differences while also admitting our ignorance, even of our own faith or lack thereof. "If we say we have no ideologies—as my students often do—we deny the truth," Robert Wuthnow writes. "None of us sees with divine wisdom, but only through a glass darkly."[67] Pretending we are all one happy family on the Up With People hayride ignores critical differences, damages religious integrity, and shreds the robust exchange of civil society. As Wuthnow writes, "we may have to withstand the nasty business of tribalism in order to have genuine and health disagreements about the nature of civil society."[68]

The recovery movement, with its far-flung network of self-sustaining groups, has already bridged such divides since small groups function by finding common ground among their members. There is, in AA, NA, and the like, a kinship of hardship, a fraternity of women and men joined by one problem despite all their other differences. Given their longevity and success, recovery fellowships have influenced the entire small group phenomenon. In his research, Wuthnow found that there are three million small groups—half are religious, a quarter AA, and other "self-help"—and that 40 percent of the U.S. population participates in one of these. A majority of members, 55 percent, said they gained greater understanding of people from other religions through their participation.[69] Beyond mere acknowledgement, we must also heed the voices of faith in civil debate and even grant a role to public theology in shaping public policy.[70] We can overcome the current impasse, in which the two camps often talk past one another. Often the secularists refuse to recognize how faith shapes the morals that guide behavior and public policy, while the religious disdain the idea of morals shaped somewhere other than on Mt. Sinai.

A central question in every person's life is "Does God exist?" If no, then the next question is how to live without God; if yes, then how to relate oneself to God. Many struggles within a person involve variations, often in different language, on the question of God. When we ask and answer such questions as "Who am I? Why am I here? How can I live to good purpose? How can I fulfill myself and my goals?" we tackle this primary question. God, of course, means many things. Still, as William James concluded, "We and God have business with each other; and in opening ourselves to his influence our deepest destiny is fulfilled."[71]

From all directions come voices asking that treatment of addictions, illness, and other problems incorporate the spirit. In making public policy, we can acknowledge the role of the spiritual in the lives of citizens, especially those we seek to help, without prescribing its contours. This invisible region of human experience produces visible effects. Ignoring that reality will always yield short-term or incomplete solutions. Hence the wisdom of seeing addiction as a malady that affects body, mind, and spirit. The scientific crowd dismisses this tripartite understanding of addiction only to dress it in new clothes under the term "biopsychosocial." Even from a medical/scientific perspective, treatment must involve more than targeting a faulty gene or neurotransmitter. Genetics, biochemistry, and behavior converge to shape self-perception, according to Roy J. Mathew, a psychiatrist at the Duke University Alcoholism and Addictions Program. When the self is incomplete, as many addicts report, quick fixes will not make it whole. Mathew's goal is to understand the pleasure mechanism physiologically to uncover any flaw in the addict's sensation of pleasure. If there is such a defect, he asks, "What can you do to being about change without taking more chemicals?"[72] Even when science helps, it often will fall short and point toward a spiritual solution in realms where science cannot go. Behavioral scientists increasingly consider how high-order attitudes and values shape action. Their vernacular cannot disguise that they are discussing belief and morality, a central product of the spiritual life.[73] As for encouraging new actions based on those beliefs, counselors talk of volition, self-efficacy, and change-agentry when they are really discussing responsibility, will, and faith.

In a democracy where pragmatism reigns, utility is a good reason for recognizing the role and power of belief. In explaining why New York State prisons accommodate the religious requests of inmates, a spokesman spoke bluntly: "We promote religion because it has been shown to have a positive effect on the rehabilitation of inmates."[74] What else, besides saving money, motivates two presidents from opposing parties to ask religious groups to provide social services? The faith-based initiatives, writes Marvin Olasky, the intellectual architect of Bush's compassionate conservatism, "brings out potentially the most controversial but also the most forward-looking of Bush's social policy ideas: drawing on the reserve of moral strength that exists in America by encouraging religiously motivated volunteers of all faiths to participate fully in the activities that they and other taxpayers fund."[75] A few months after inauguration, Olasky and other conservatives began to worry that funding could hurt religion. From the other side, all citizens should be cautious about funding good works based on faith. Religious conviction can be a powerful and uncontrolled fire that burns best in private.

Belief is at the core of any initiative based in faith. When nonreligious liberals embrace these initiatives, they willfully concentrate on the saccharine. When religious conservatives do so, they sell short their own faith. Nevertheless, we can grant belief a role without promoting religion or even God. Simply to recognize that a person has a spiritual dimension does not breech the freedom to believe or not, to worship or not, or to just be left alone. But there is something inherently troubling about faith-based initiatives, currently conceived as handmaidens of congregations or denominations. With faith, these services violate the Constitution; without faith, these lack their own means to the end. The only broad-based and proven exception is spiritually based addiction treatment, and to even greater extent, the voluntary recovery movement.

A Faith That Works

The approach pioneered by AA and adapted by other treatments and groups consists of a core paradox for the addict: an utmost willingness to live by spiritual principles and complete freedom in finding a path that works. Find God however you define God. Over time, the generally antireligious Bill Wilson became only more convinced of the need, as he proclaimed to a friend, for AA to "stop pussyfooting around about the spiritual."[76] This conviction continues, as does the wariness about religion. From this wariness came the insistence on personal flexibility in finding a higher power. In rejecting religion, Twelve-Step adherents reject the hubris of religion that, so often, claims to have the answers. The spirituality of recovery calls religion to its humbler roots and, most of all, demands of itself an unwavering commitment to humility, to always knowing it knows not much and certainly not all. Spirituality searches, and finds only the truths that are borne out in life.

Stand amid 43 homeless, chronic alcoholics and addicts in the stuffy basement room of an old government building in downtown Washington, D.C. The group has just been admitted to Clean & Sober Streets, one of the city's only free, long-term residential treatment centers. Sweat, body heat, and lived-in clothing make the air humid. It smells. Even though most of the people have leveled out during a week of attending Twelve-Step meetings on their own, most lurk on the far side of recovery. A touch of madness, the potential for violence, plays in their eyes and at the corners of their mouths, jitters their arms and legs. It's hard not to be uneasy.

Come back six weeks later, this time to an open-spaced cafeteria on the second floor with the windows open to a morning breeze. Thirty-seven of the original group sit in two rows of almond-colored plastic chairs facing an audience of families and friends—who would have guessed they had any?—and previous graduates of Clean & Sober Streets. They are at their "step-up" ceremony, having completed the first phase of their treatment. You could not imagine a more changed group of people. Seemingly, some invisible hand has wiped each face and smoothed away the wrinkles, grooves, and tics left by years of anger and despair and thieving and violence and self-imposed suffering. If each person came six weeks ago wearing a face she or he worked hard to deform, so, now, the alchemy of effort and surrender has cast a new visage. A light shines in what had been the dead bulbs of their eye sockets. You peer at some you met last time. Each person's outlines are familiar, but the content is new, like those dreams in which your aged parents appear as newlyweds.

A clinician might say these people are sober thanks to a period of stabilization, housing, counseling, group therapy, regular meals, and sleep. Yes, all that matters. But each person, as he or she walks to the podium to receive a certificate, offers a blunter explanation and prescription.

"God rescued us body, mind, and soul from alcoholism so we could love one another unconditionally the way he loves us," says one woman, Gloria. Most repeat that in different versions, always emphasizing that their addiction battered them down until they reached out for help. When her son was at the podium for his certificate and a few words, a mother—a vibrant muscle of a woman dressed in a dark blue, white-trimmed Sunday dress with a silver broach and a small hat—jumped to her feet. She threw her head and one arm up and down in a single motion and shouted, "Thank you, Lord."

Though her call resembled one heard Sunday mornings in many Christian churches, the setting and the woman's tone allowed it to stand in for the call of hope and thanks that others in that room, and in many other such rooms, would utter. She called out in fierce abandon borne of total faith, in a conviction against the world that might contradict her. She called out in a triumph over the drugs with which her son had enslaved himself, and that had shackled legions of sons and fathers and husbands and brothers, even some sisters and daughters.

As her son paused at the podium, the lady snapped her entire body at the waist—down up!—and punched out the syllables. "Thank you, Lord, thank you Lord, thankyouLord, thankyouLord." She spoke to the Lord she knew. But her cry, in its depth and breadth, could to have been uttered by others who may envision a different God, perhaps Yahweh or Allah or Vishnu. Yes, on Sundays this middle-aged mother might sing of Jesus and of sweet chariots swinging low. But now while thanking her God, her voice seemed to transcend denominational definitions and individual concepts. She called out, in the name of all assembled in this hot cafeteria room, to a power greater than herself or any lesser deity, to a something greater than the earthly powers that give men and women moments of pleasure and pain. She called out to a power that worked, and her call contained more than her thanks. Her call constituted, in some mysterious way, the very power that had changed her son from a drugged man on the street to this smiling, bright-eyed youth at the podium before her with a diploma in his hand. She exercised a power that delivers, the same power called upon daily by perhaps millions of recovered alcoholics and addicts. It is a self-fulfilling gratitude. By giving thanks, she, and they, have something to be thankful for.

Whether God or this higher power exists may forever remain unproven. Despite the dramatic results of belief, the object of belief remains, quite properly, an article of faith. But this mother, and her son, and his peers in Group 41 of Clean & Sober Streets, knew that if they said "thank you," they would receive that for which they gave thanks. They knew, deep in their minds and souls and hearts and guts, that they could bring to life in their lives a higher power that gave its graces without regard to color or creed or money, and who perhaps gave it most to those most in need, even more so to men and women who had sought counterfeit help from the false gods of addictions, and who, when exhausted from being their own god, found for themselves a faith that works.

NOTES

CHAPTER I

1. Green Timothy H. Interview with author. City Rochester, N.Y. 10 October 1997.
2. Roman and Blum, 24. This is quoted as a negative aspect of treatment by Charles Bufe, a compelling critic of AA and mainstream treatment, in his 1998 book, *AA: Cult or Cure?*
3. Clark. Telephone interview with author. 11 December 2000.
4. Tonigan, "Meta-Analysis," 65.
5. AA, *Twelve and Twelve*, 15.
6. Bonniwell, interview, 3 April 1998.
7. AA, *Alcoholics Anonymous*, 12.
8. McGowan, "Finding God", 7 March 1998.
9. Sapir, *Culture*, 125.
10. Ellen. Interviews with author. Albany N.Y., 17 August 1999, and by phone 15 December 2000.
11. AA, *Alcoholics Anonymous*, 30.
12. American Psychiatric Association, DSM-IV, 176.
13. NIAAA, *Alcohol Alert*, October 1995, 2.
14. American Psychiatric Association, DSM-IV, 182.
15. 1999 National Household Survey, 2000.
16. 1999 Analysis of 1997 and 1998 NHSDA figures.
17. Clark, interview by author, Dec. 11, 2000
18. Rouse, Beatrice A. ed., SAMSHA, 1995.
19. McClellan. Interview with author. Washington, D.C., 8 April 1998.
20. McClellan, "Private Treatments," 243.
21. McClellan, "Private Treatments," 252.
22. Marlatt, *Relapse*, 26.
23. McClellan, "Drug Dependence," 1689-95.
24. Hubbard, *Treatment*, 125.

25. SAMHSA, "National Treatment Study," 1.
26. NIDA, "Principles," 21.
27. Clark, interview, 11 December 2000.
28. Bower, Bruce. "Alcoholics Synonymous: Heavy Drinkers of All Stripes May Get Comparable Help From a Variety of Therapies." *Science News*, 25 January 1997.
29. Ibid.
30. Robins, Davis, and Nurco, "Vietnam drug addiction," 38-43.
31. Dawson, "Correlates of Past-Year Status," 771-779.
32. AA, *"Pass It On"* 100-151; Kurtz, *Not-God.* 3-136; White, *Slaying the Dragon,* 1-142. See also Ruden, *Craving Brain,* 74-78.
33. White, *Slaying the Dragon,* 13.
34. White, *Slaying the Dragon,* 12-18.
35. AA, *Alcoholics Anonymous,* and Kurtz, *Not-God.*
36. AA, *Alcoholics Anonymous,* xiii.
37. Ibid., 44.
38. Ibid., 64.
39. Royce, "Effects of Alcoholism," 23.
40. Molea, Joseph. Interviews with author. Tampa, Fl., 19 January 1998, by telephone, 11 August 1999.
41. Royce, "Effects of Alcoholism," 29
42. Kurtz, *Not-God,* 20-21.
43. Ibid., 179.
44. Cited in Kurtz and Ketcham, *Imperfection,* 113.
45. AAGSO, "AA at a Glance."
46. AAGSO, "Estimates of AA Groups and Members."
47. NA Fellowship Services, response to author query; and White and Madara, *Sourcebook,* >>http://mentalhelp.net/selfhelp/<<
48. Cocaine Anonymous website, >>www.ca.org/index.html#home<<
49. Nace, *AA,* 385.
50. AA, *1996 Membership Survey.*
51. AA, *Alcoholics Anonymous,* xxi.
52. Nace, *Alcoholics Anonymous,* 385.
53. White, *Slaying the Dragon,* 198-210.
54. Landry, *Treatment Effectiveness,* 35.
55. Bailey, *Serenity,* 1-35.
56. Leshner, "Conference," April 1998.
57. Hyman, quoted in "Moyers On Addiction," March 1998.
58. Molea, interviews with author, Tampa, Florida and by telephone, 1998-9.
59. Hunsicker. Telephone. Interview with author. City State, 31 July 2000.
60. Kleber. Interview with author. Washington, D.C. 9 April 1998.
61. AA, *Alcoholics Anonymous,* 22-4.
62. Ibid., 45.
63. Ibid., 45.
64. AA, *Twelve and Twelve,* 15.
65. AA, *Alcoholics Anonymous,* 25.
66. Beazley, *AA and Clinical Practice,* 6 March 1998.
67. James, *Varieties,* 205.

68. AA, *Twelve and Twelve*, 15.
69. AA, *Alcoholics Anonymous*, 27.
70. Vaillant, *Natural History*, 367-8.
71. Associated Press, "Study: Alcoholics Need Five Years Sobriety for Safety from Relapse," *Tonawanda News*, 12 March 1996, Main section.
72. Vaillant, *Natural History*, 388.
73. Ibid., 267-9.
74. Miller, "Spiritual Dimensions," 979-984.
75. Miller, "Addictions," 70-72.
76. NIAAA, *Studying Spirituality*, 19.
77. Brown and Peterson, "Values," 63-5.
78. NIAAA, *Studying Spirituality*, 27.
79. Sapir, *Culture*, 122-123.
80. AA, *Alcoholics Anonymous*, 85.
81. Fingarette, *Heavy Drinking*, 117.
82. AA, *Alcoholics Anonymous*, 103.
83. Frank and Frank, *Persuasion and Healing*, 8-9.
84. Miller and Kurtz, *Models of Alcoholism*, 165.
85. James, *Varieties*, 51.
86. Armstrong, *History of God*, 17.
87. Durkheim, *Elementary Forms*, 213.
88. Sapir, *Culture*, 123, 137-8.
89. AA, *Alcoholics Anonymous*, 62.
90. James, *Varieties*, 377-78.
91. Cited in Kazin, *God and The American Writer*, 163.
92. AA, *Alcoholics Anonymous*, xxvi.
93. Kazin, *God and The American Writer*, 168.
94. James, William, cited in Kazin, 172.
95. AA, *Alcoholics Anonymous*, 62.
96. Kurtz, *Not-God*, 35.
97. Kurtz and Ketcham, *Imperfection*, 5.
98. Hunsicker. Telephone interview with author. 31 July 2000.
99. Dennis. Interview by author. Albany, N.Y., 10 September 1997.

CHAPTER II

1. Warner, Brad. Telephone interviews by author. February 1998.
2. AA, *Twelve and Twelve*, 21.
3. James, *Varieties of Religious Experience*, 204 & 208.
4. Molea. Telephone interviews by author. 19 January 1998 and 11 August 1999.
5. Miller, "Increasing Motivation," 95.
6. Miller, "Increasing Motivation," 90.
7. John. Interview by author. Alplaus, N.Y., 13 February 2000.
8. MacDougall and Hazelden staff. Interviews by author. Center City, Minn., 2 April 1998.
9. Stinchfield and Owen, *Hazelden's Twelve-Step Model and its Outcomes*, 3.
10. Samuels, "Annals of Addiction," 49.
11. Stinchfield and Owen, *Hazelden's Twelve-Step Model and its Outcomes*, 12.
12. AA, *Alcoholics Anonymous*, 64.

13. Ibid.
14. Gilliam, *How AA Failed Me*, 84.
15. Ibid., 103.
16. Steigerwald and Stone, "Cognitive Restructuring," 322.
17. Fox, "Changing Violent Minds," 88-89.
18. AA, *Alcoholics Anonymous*, 58.
19. Vaillant, *Natural History*, 247.
20. Steigerwald and Stone, "Cognitive Restructuring," 321-27.
21. George, *Counseling the Chemically Dependent*, 169.
22. AA, *Alcoholics Anonymous*, 570.

CHAPTER III

1. Gantes, Nick. Interview by author. Chicago, Illinois, 11 August 1998.
2. OAS, *National Admissions*, 38.
3. Mäkelä, *AA as Mutual-Help*, 175.
4. Next Step. Interview by author. Albany, N.Y., 11 December 1998.
5. SAMSHA, Statistics Sourcebook, 35.
6. Ibid. 60-61.
7. Wright, Florence. Interview with author. Chicago, Illinois, 19 August 1988.
8. Elias, Marilyn, "Study links sexual abuse, alcoholism among women," *USA Today*, 5 January 1998, final edition.
9. "Treatment Methods for Women," *NIDA Infofax #35*, National Institute on Drug Abuse, 1998.
10. Ibid.
11. Dahlgren and Willander, "Are Special Treatment Facilities for Female Alcoholics Needed?" 499.
12. Griffin, Weiss, and Mirin, "Male and Female Cocaine Abusers," 122-126.
13. OASAS, "Programs for Women and Children, Women, and Youth."
14. Lisa. Telephone interview by author. 7 May 1998.
15. Stephanie Brown. Telephone interview by author. 4 October 1998.
16. Kearney, "Drug Treatment for Women," 464.
17. Mathew, Georgi, Wilson, and Mathew. "Concept of Spirituality," 68.
18. Lightfoot, Julia. Interview with author. Washington, D.C., 19 May 1998.
19. Kearney, 465.
20. Guillory, Sowell, Moneyham, and Seals, "Spirituality Among Women With HIV/AIDS," 59.
21. Garrett, "Recovery from Anorexia Nervosa," 1500.
22. Kearney, "Drug Treatment for Women," 465-466.
23. Nealy, Elinor, *Lesbian AIDS Project Newsletter*, Summer 1995, 5.
24. Kaskutas, "Beliefs on the Source of Sobriety," 639.
25. Kaskutas, "Pathways to Self-help Among Women For Sobriety," 265.
26. Kaskutas, "What Do Women Get Out of Self-help," 185.
27. Hatch. Interview by author. Albany, N.Y., 1 October 1997.
28. Women at Liberty Manor. Interviews by author. Rochester, N.Y., 11 October 14 November and 12 December 1997.
29. Dahlgren and Willander, "Are Special Treatment Facilities for Female Alcoholics Needed?" 502-3.
30. "Success of Programs For Pregnant Substance Abusers is a Matter of Per-

spective," *Brown University Digest of Addiction Theory and Application*, September 1998, 1.

31. Ibid., 6-7.
32. "Specialized Treatment Can Help Pregnant and Parenting Teenagers Who Aubse Drugs," *NIDA Notes* 9:1(February/March 1994).
33. Connors, Maisto, and Zywiak; "Male and Female Alcoholics' Attributions," 30.
34. Annis, Sklar, and Moser, "Gender in Relation to Relapse," 127 & 130.
35. Rubin, Stout, and Longabaugh, "Gender Differences in Relapse," 112.
36. Connors, Maisto, and Zywiak, "Male and Female Alcoholics' Attributions," 38.
37. Schmidt and Weisner, "Emergence of Problem Drinking Women," 321.
38. General Accounting Office, *Drug-Exposed Infants*, 8.
39. Schmidt and Weisner, "Emergence of Problem Drinking Women," 328.
40. Ruether, *Gaia & God*, 3-4.
41. McFague, *Models of God*, 28.
42. Ibid., 101.
43. Ibid., 85.
44. Ruether, *Gaia & God*, 269.
45. Ruether, *Gaia & God*, 269-70.

CHAPTER IV

1. Leland Leonard. Interview by author. Phoenix, Ariz., 6 February 1998.
2. IHS, "Comprehensive Health Care Program for American Indians and Alaska Natives," 1997.
3. May, "Epidemiology of Alcohol Abuse Among American Indians," 121-143.
4. Krech. Interview by author. Phoenix, Ariz., 8 February 1998.
5. Holy Bull. Interview with author by telephone. 3 May 1998.
6. Mitchell, Wayne, and Ken Patch, "Religions, Spiritualism, and Recovery of Native American Alcoholics," *The Provider*, (IHS newsletter) May 1986, 1-2.
7. Tinker, "Religion," 538-539.
8. Mike. Interview with author. Minneapolis, Minn., 30 March 1998.
9. Samuel A. Worcester vs. the State of Georgia, *U.S. Supreme Court Reports*, 6 Peters 559-561 (1832).
10. Vernon, "Religious Rights," 541.
11. Charles H. Burke, U.S. National Archives, File: 10429-22-063 (1923), cited in Kaiser (1997).
12. Leonard, interview with author, Feb. 6, 1998
13. Tafoya and Roeder, "Spiritual Exiles," 184.
14. AHCPR, *Survey of American Indians and Alaska Natives*.
15. Kauffman, Johnson, and Jacobs; "Health Care to American Indians," 48.
16. Sternberg, "Summary," 5.
17. Bill Donovan, "Traditional Navajo Care Gets VA Nod," *The Arizona Republic*, 8 April 1998.
18. Beck, Walters, and Francisco, *The Sacred: Ways of Knowledge, Sources of Life*. 4-5.
19. Isham and Valandra. Interview by author. St. Paul, Minn., 1 March 1998.
20. Yazzie. Interview by author. Phoenix, Ariz., 10 February 1998.

21. Shelton. Interview by author. Phoenix, Ariz., 10 February 1998.
22. Byron and Sam at drumming circle. Interviews by author. Minneapolis, Minn., 1 April 1998.
23. Vermillion. Interview by author. Minneapolis, Minn., 30 March 1998.
24. Archambeault. Interview by author. Minneapolis, Minn., 30 March 1998.
25. Interviews by author. Fond Du Lac Reservation, 31 March 1998.
26. Ibid.
27. Tanner, "Ojibwe," 438-9.
28. Curtis, comments at panel discussion attended by author. Native American Community Health Center, Phoenix, Ariz., 12 February 1998.
29. Malina. Interview by author. Phoenix, Ariz., 12 February 1998.
30. Interviews by author. Gila River Indian Community, Ariz. 12 February 1998.
31. Starr. Interview by author. Gila River Indian Community, Ariz., 12 February 1998.
32. Sando, *Pueblo Nations*.
33. Tinker, "Religion," 540.
34. Hawkins, Day, and Suagee. *American Indian Women's Chemical Health Project*, 1.
35. Turnure. Interview by author. St. Paul, Minn., 1 April 1998.
36. Egan, Timothy, "New Prosperity Brings New Conflict to Indian Country," *The New York Times*, 8 March 1998, Main section.
37. Fenton, *The Great Law*, 117.
38. Montour, "Handsome Lake," 230-231; and Fenton, *Great Law*, 119.
39. Hauptman, letter to author, 1 April 1999.
40. Fenton, *The Great Law*, 117.
41. Kauffman, Johnson, and Jacobs, "Health Care to American Indians," 50.

CHAPTER V

1. "Diagnosis and Treatment of Drug Abuse in Family Practice: Pathophysiology," NIDA, 1997. Found at http://www.nida.nih.gov/Diagnosis-Treatment/Diagnosis4.html
2. Karen Young Kreeger, "Drug Institute Tackles Neurology of Addiction" *The Scientist* 9(16) 21 August 1995. Found at http://www.the-scientist.library.upenn.edu/yr1995/august/drugs=_950821.html
3. " Dopamine May Not Be the Key to Drug Addiction," Associated Press, 3 March 1999. Cited by Join Together Online—Direct, 4 March 1999. Available at http://www.jointogether.org/
4. "More drugs for mental illness are on the horizon," *Manisses Newswire*, 2 July 2000. Available at http://www.manisses.com/
5. Benson, Mitchel, "Governor Supports State Funding For Alcoholism, Addiction Research," *Wall Street Journal*, 3 June 1998.
6. AHCPR, "Pharmacotherapy for Alcohol Dependence."
7. Molea, Joseph. Interviews with author. Tampa, Fl. 19 January 1998, by telephone, 11 August 1999.
8. "Mechanisms of Action," Kramer, Thomas A. M., *Medscape Psychopharmacology Today: Medscape Mental Health* 6(1), 2001. Available at http://www.medscape.com
9. Fingarette, *Heavy Drinking*, 16.

10. Wilson, Bill. Talk to the National Clergy Conference on Alcoholism. New York, N.Y.; 21 April 1960, cited in Kurtz, *Not-God*, 22.

11. Kurtz, *Not-God*, 22.

12. Mäkelä, Klaus, et al. *AA as Mutual-Help*, 190.

13. Leshner, "Addiction Is a Brain Disease," 3.

14. Ibid., 4-6.

15. NIAAA, *10th Special Report*.

16. Ibid., 445-446.

17. "Chronic Alcohol Abuse Profoundly Affects Brain," *Join Together Online—Direct*, 12 December 2000. Available at http://www.jointogether.org/

18. Fingarette, *Heavy Drinking*, 52-53.

19. Wyke, *21st Century Miracle Medicine*, 287.

20. Marlatt, Demming, and Reid, "Loss of Control," 233-241.

21. Fingarette, *Heavy Drinking*, 37, 40.

22. Ibid., 66.

23. Satel, Sally L., "Don't Forget the Addict's Role in Addiction," *New York Times*, 4 April 1998.

24. Office of Juvenile Justice, "Making A Difference For Juveniles," 8.

25. Sara Kershnar. Interview by author. New York, N.Y. 6 June 1998.

26. National Public Radio, *All Things Considered*, 17 March 1999.

27. Samuels, "Annals of Addiction," 55.

28. Owen. Interview by author. Center City, Minnesota. April 2, 1998.

29. Cited in Tymoczko, "The Nitrous Oxide Philosopher," 96.

30. Cited in *DATA: The Brown University Digest of Addiction Theory and Application*, June 1998, 7.

31. Larson, Edward J. and Larry Williams, letter, *Nature*, 5 April 1997.

32. Sonnenstuhl, William. Telephone interview with author, 3 February 1998.

33. Miller, "Spirituality: The Silent Dimension," 259-260.

34. Kendler, Gardner, and Prescott, "Religion and Substance Abuse," 324.

35. Greenfield, Russell. Interview with author. Tucson, Ariz., 11 February 1998.

36. Shaw, Charles J. Interview with author. Phoenix, Ariz., 6 February 1998.

37. Miller, "Spiritual Dimensions," 979-984.

38. Lowinson, *Substance Abuse*, 952.

39. "Clinician Beliefs About Addictions and Treatment," *Bulletin of the Northeastern States Addiction Technology Transfer Center*, October 2000, 2.

40. Daytop Village, "Daytop Spiritual Survey," 10 February 1998.

41. Royce, "Effects on Spirituality," 21.

42. "AA's Changing Role in the New Millenium," *Join Together Online-Direct*, 1 June 1999. Available at http://www.jointogether.com/

43. Durkheim, *Elementary Forms*, 431, 210.

44. Durkheim, *Elementary Forms*, 439.

45. Coppola. Interview with author. Albany, N.Y., 2 October 1997.

46. McClellan, "Moyers on Addiction: Close to Home," March 1998.

47. "Outcomes report may boost ballot initiative in Massachusetts," Manisses Newswire. Available at http://www.manisses.com/. 31 July 2000.

48. Perrin and Koshel, *Assessment of Performance*, 1-4.

49. Owen. Interview with author. Center City, Minn., 2 April 1998.

50. CSAT, The National Treatment Improvement Evaluation Study.

51. Kott, Alan. Telephone interview by author. 2 February 2001.
52. McClellan, "Moyers on Addiction: Close to Home," March 1998.
53. Blazer, Dan. Telephone interview with author. 25 January 2001.
54. Hayden. Interview with author. St. Paul, Minn., 4 April 1998.
55. Puchalski, Christine, "Taking a Spiritual History," *Spirituality and Medicine Connection* Spring 1999, 1.
56. Miller and Bennett, "Research on Spirituality," 3.
57. NIAAA & Fetzer Institute, "Conference Summary: Studying Spirituality and Alcohol," 1-2 February 1999.
58. Gorsuch, "Spiritual Variables," 309-316.
59. Bullock. Interview with author. Washington, DC., April 1998.
60. Bower, Bruce, "Alcoholics Synonymous: Heavy Drinkers of All Stripes May Get Comparable Help From a Variety of Therapies." *Science News*, 25 January 1997.
61. Durkheim, *Elementary Forms*, 420.
62. Ibid., 226.
63. Fenton, interview by author. Bethlehem, New York Sept. 18, 1996.
64. Durkheim, *Elementary Forms*, 423.
65. Ibid. 431, 433, 445.
66. Sapir, *Culture*, 145-146.
67. Kazin, *God and The American Writer*, 171.
68. Tymoczko, "The Nitrous Oxide Philosopher," 101.
69. Ibid., 94.
70. Sternberg, Steve. "Doctors Push Care, Not Prison, For Drug Addicts." *USA Today*, 18 March 1998.
71. Booth, "New Understanding," 6-16.
72. "Spiritual Pleasures Can Replace Drug Addiction," Duke University press release, Durham, N.C., 19 October 1998.
73. Humphreys and Moos, "Reduced Costs," 709.
74. Miller, Martin, "Prayer Aids Healing, HMO Execs Think," *Los Angeles Times*, 15 December 1997.
75. "Survey Shows Bias Against Recovering Alcoholics, Addicts," *Join Together Online-Direct*, 15 December 1999. Available at http://www.jointogether.com/
76. "Managed Care Not Stepping Up to Cover Methadone Treatment," *Manisses Newswire* 15 May 2000. Available at http://www.manisses.com/
77. AA, *Alcoholics Anonymous*, 133.
78. McClellan, A. Thomas. Interview by author. Washington, D.C., 8 April 1998.
79. Joe Molea. Interview with author. Tampa, Fl., 19 January 1998.
80. Eric. Interview with author. Rochester, N.Y., 12 December 1998.

CHAPTER VI

1. Peele, *Diseasing of America*, 202.
2. Muffler, Langrod and Larson; "Religion and Substance Abuse Treatment," 584.
3. Ibid., 585.
4. Albany Challenge, *Albany Challenge: Bringing Deliverance to Those Addicted to Drugs and Alcohol*. Albany, N.Y.: Victory Church. 1997.
5. Ibid.

6. Muller, Charles. Interview with author. Albany, N.Y., 18 May, 1999.
7. Hess, "A Seven-year Follow-up Study," cited in Muffler, Langrod, and Larson; "Religion and Substance Abuse Treatment," 586.
8. Jim. Telephone interview with author. 14 June 1999.
9. Linwood and Nation of Islam members. Interviews by author. Albany, N.Y., 22 & 27 January 1997.
10. Lindner, *Yearbook of American & Canadian Churches*, 14.
11. Bonniwell, Larry. Interviews with author. St. Paul, Minn., 2 & 3 April 1998.
12. Kunz, *Where the Doors Never Close*, 104.
13. SOS, *Sobriety Handbook*, 7.
14. Ibid., 17.
15. Ibid., 8.
16. Flynn, Tom, interview with author by telephone. 5 June 1999
17. SOS, *Sobriety Handbook*, 8-9, 17-18.
18. Connors and Dermen, "Characteristics of Participants in SOS," 281-294.
19. Carol L., "SOS Mailbox," SOS International Newsletter, Winter 1998/1999, 11.
20. "TDCJ Salutes SOS Following Founder's Visit," SOS International Newsletter, Winter 1998/1999, 1.
21. Kirkpatrick, Jean. Telephone interview by author. 26 May 1999.
22. Kirkpatrick, Jean, "New Life Acceptance Program." Available at Women for Sobriety, Inc. website: www.mediapulse.com/wfs/.
23. Rudolf, "Founder of WFS Talks About Self-Help Program."
24. Lisa. Telephone interviews with author. 19 May 1999.
25. Trimpey, Lois and Jack. Telephone interview with author. 2 June 1999.
26. Galanter, Egelko, and Edwards, "RR: Alternatives to AA?" 499-500.
27. Trimpey, Trippel, and Trimpey, "Rational Recovery Society Network," 3.
28. Trimpey, Jack, "Addictive Voice Recognition Technique," June 1999. Available at http://rational.org/recovery
29. Trimpey, Jack, "Alcoholics Anonymous: The Embodiment of The Beast," June 1999. Available at http://rational.org/recovery.
30. Gasbarra, Ron, "Another Road to Recovery," *The Washington Post*, 14 May 1991.
31. Hall, Trish, "New Way to Treat Alcoholism Discards Spirituality of AA," *The New York Times*, 24 December 1990.
32. Shaw, Charles J. Interview with author. Phoenix, Ariz. 6 February 1998.
33. Galanter, Egelko, and Edwards, "Rational Recovery," 499-510.
34. Ibid.
35. Ibid.
36. Miller, "Increasing Motivation," 91.
37. Ibid., 93.
38. Monti, Rohsenow, Colby, and Abrams, "Coping and Social Skills Training", 235, and Hester, "Behavioral Self-control Training," 154.
39. Muffler, Langrod, and Larson, 589.

CHAPTER VII

1. DeBerri, Edward. Interview by author Delmar, NY, July 1997.
2. Kershnar, Sara. Interview by author. New York, N.Y. 6 June, 1998.

3. Stryker, *Dimensions of HIV Prevention: Needle Exchange.*
4. Satel, Sally, "Opiates for the Masses," *The Wall Street Journal,* 8 June 1998.
5. Neuner and Schultz, "Borrow Me A Quarter," 4.
6. DeMaria, Donna. Interviews by author. Albany, N.Y., September 1997.
7. Nadelman, Ethan, "Commonsense Drug Policy," *Foreign Affairs,* January/February 1998, 112.
8. Springer, Edith. Telephone interview by author. 27 May, 1998.
9. Oakley, Deirdre. Telephone interviews by author. 29 October 1997 and 5 May, 1998.
10. McGill Daniel. Interview by author. Albany, N.Y., 10 November, 1997 and by telephone, 21 November, 1997.
11. Archambeault, Philip. Interview by author. Minneapolis, Minn., 30 March, 1998.
12. Grovender, Kelby. Telephone interview by author. 28 May, 1998.
13. Miller, Jean Somers, interview by author, 10 Nov. 1997
14. Oakley and Dennis, "Homeless People with Alcohol, Drug, and/or Mental Disorders," 184.
15. Nadelman, McNeely, and Drucker, "International Perspectives," 25.
16. Summary of data provided by Oakley and Dennis, National Research Center on Homelessness and Mental Illness, various dates, 1997-98.
17. Dennis, Deborah. Interview by author. Delmar, N.Y., May 1997.
18. Feltman, Laurent. Telephone interview by author. 21 October 1997.
19. James, Amos. Telephone interview by author. 21 October 1997.
20. Springer, Edith. Telephone interview by author. 27 May 1998.
21. Kershnar, Sara. Interview by author. New York, N.Y., 6 June 1998.
22. Tsemberis, Sam. Interview by author. New York, N.Y., 4 June 1998.
23. Oakley and Dennis, "Homeless People with Alcohol, Drug, and/or Mental Disorders," 185.
24. Bobby, Dennis Bogen, and Jerry Turner. Interviews with author. St. Paul, Minn., 30 March, 1998.
25. Neuner and Schultz, "Borrow Me A Quarter," 4.
26. Turner. Telephone interview by author. 18 June, 1998.
27. Neitzel, Tracy and Kevin O'Connor. Interview by author. Troy, N.Y., 10 June, 1998.
28. Tsemberis, Sam. Telephone interview by author. 26 May, 1998.
29. Pete, Qamar, and Tsemberis. Interviews by author, New York, N.Y., June 4, 1998.
30. Trebay, Guy, "Change of Focus," *Village Voice,* 19 August, 1997, 33.
31. Chapman, Winston, interview by author, 4 June 1998.
32. Stambul and Polich, "Some Implications of the Rand *Alcoholism and Treatment* Study for Alcoholism Research," 5.
33. Heather, "Application of Harm-Reduction Principles," 171.
34. Marlatt quoted by Timothy Gower, "The Power of Positive Drinking," *Seattle Weekly,* 18 January, 1995, 25.
35. Ibid., 22.
36. Turnure, Cynthia. Interview by author. St. Paul, Minn., 1 April, 1998.
37. DeBerri, Edward. Interviews by author. Delmar, N.Y., May 1997 and (by telephone) June 1998.
38. Dennis, Deborah. Interview by author. Delmar, N.Y., May 1997.

39. Wren, Christopher S., "Drug Policy Official Warns Panel of Effort to Legalize Drugs, *The New York Times*, 18 June 1998, A29.

40. Single, Eric "Harm Reduction as an Alcohol-Prevention Strategy," 243.

41. Armor, Stambul, and Polich, *Alcoholism and Treatment*.

CHAPTER VIII

1. Hospitality House: Mark, Linn Becker, Kim and Dennis. Interviews with author. Albany, N.Y., 5 & 24 March 16 April 1998.

2. Harvard Mental Health Letter, 1 August 1995, 3.

3. Ibid.

4. De Leon, George. Remarks at NIDA Drug Addiction Treatment conference. 8 April 1998.

5. Inciardi, James A. Remarks at NIDA conference on Drug Addiction Treatment. Washington, D.C., 8 April 1998.

6. Landry, *Overview*, 24.

7. Daytop Village:—Anthony Bates, Michael Bosch, Peter Collins, Charles Devlin, and Tony Gelormino. Interviews by author. New York, N.Y., 26 January 1999.

8. Wilson, "Spiritual Therapy," 204.

9. Hinshelwood, *Britain and TCs*, 43-44.

10. Main, Thomas F., "The Hospital as a Therapeutic Institution," *Bulletin of the Menninger Clinic* 10(1946), cited in DeLeon and Ziegenfuss.

11. Casriel, *So Fair A House*, 21.

12. Ibid., 22.

13. Mäkelä, *AA as Mutual-Help*, 214.

14. De Leon, "The Therapeutic Community," 301.

15. Bratter, "Power and Authority Within The TC," 190.

16. Mäkelä, *AA as Mutual-Help*, 21.

17. DeLeon, "Therapeutic Communities," 408.

18. Dunn, *Spirituality, Alcoholism and Drug Addiction*, 37.

19. Ibid.

20. Wilson, "Spiritual Therapy," 204.

21. Rosenthal. Telephone interview by author. 8 August 2000.

22. Dunn, "Relapse: An Analysis," 13.

23. Ibid. 15.

24. O'Brien and Biase, "Therapeutic Communities: Coming of Age," 455.

25. Bratter, "Power and Authority Within The TC," 199.

26. Ibid., 192.

27. Rosenthal. Telephone interview by author. 8 August 2000.

28. Dunn, "Relapse: An Analysis," 33.

29. John. Telephone interviews with author. 11-12 May 1999.

30. Swanson, Carl, "Phoenix House's Hard-*Liner*," *The New York Observer*, 10 August 1998.

31. "Therapeutic Community Leaders Seek Standards for Corrections-based Programs, *Alcoholism & Drug Abuse Week*, 23 February 1998, 1.

32. "Wackenhut Corrections Selected for New Prison Project at Machington, England," *PR Newswire*, 1 December 1998.

33. Miller, Gerald. Interview by author. San Francisco, Calif., 24 September 1997.

34. De Leon, "Therapeutic Communities," 411.
35. Miller, William. Remarks at NIDA conference. Washington, D.C., 8, April 1998.
36. Miller and Tonigan, *Handbook of Alcoholism Treatment Approaches*, 27.
37. Daytop, "Spirituality in a Drug-Free Therapeutic Community," (internal memo) 1998.
38. Wolf Jones, Linda R., *Alcoholism & Drug Abuse Weekly*, 28 September 1998, 5.

CHAPTER IX

1. De Tocqueville, *Democracy II*, 126.
2. De Tocqueville, *Democracy II*, 108-9.
3. Bloom, *The American Religion*, 17.
4. Ibid., 42.
5. Wolfe, Alan, "The Pursuit of Autonomy," *The New York Times Magazine*, 7 May, 2000.
6. AA, *Alcoholics Anonymous*, 93.
7. Nace, "Alcoholics Anonymous," 388.
8. Frank and Frank, *Persuasion and Healing*, 251.
9. Hayden, Peter. Interview with author. St. Paul, Minn., 3 April 1999.
10. James, *Varieties*, 41.
11. Mäkelä, *AA as a Mutual Help Movement*, 157-158.
12. AAWS, *Came to Believe*, 21.
13. Landry, *Treatment Effectiveness*, 67.
14. McIntire, "How Well Does AA Work?" 14.
15. Emrick, et al, "AA: What is Currently Known," 54-59.
16. Kaskutas, "The Role of Religion, Spirituality, and AA Involvement in Sustained Sobriety," 27.
17. Twerski, "Spirituality and Religion," 2.
18. Armstrong, *A History of God*, 4.
19. Armstrong, *A History of God*, 2.
20. Eliade, *Patterns in Comparative Religion*, 52.
21. Kazin, *God and the American Writer*, 175.
22. AA, *Alcoholics Anonymous*, 12.
23. Durkheim, *Elementary Forms*, 43.
24. AA, *Twelve Steps*, 37.
25. Room, *AA as a Social Movement*, 170-182.
26. James, *Varieties*, 51.
27. Whitehead, *Science and the Modern World*.
28. David. Telephone interview with author. 23 September, 1998.
29. Fowler, "AA and Faith Development," 132.
30. Fowler, "AA and Faith Development," 132.
31. Mäkelä, "Cultural Variability of Alcoholics Anonymous," 199-201.
32. Gorsuch, *Spiritual Variables*, 310-311.
33. Ellis, "Rational Emotive Behavior Therapy and Religion," 29.
34. Wilson, Bill. Tape-recorded address to the Kips Bay AA group. 16 November 1950.
35. Egan, Jennifer, "Walking Toward Mindfulness," *The New York Times Magazine*, 7 May 2000.

36. Frankl, *Man's Search For Meaning*, 35 & 67.
37. James, *Varieties*, 193.
38. Landauer, *Briefe I*, 59-60.
39. Kramer, "Abelard," 18-41.
40. Ward, Marsh and residents at Clean & Sober Streets. Interviews by author. Washington, D.C., 20 May 1998.
41. AA, *Alcoholics Anonymous*, 58.
42. Elpenor, "A Drunkard's Progress: AA and the Sobering Strength of Myth," 43-44.
43. Mäkelä, *Alcoholics Anonymous as a Mutual-Help Movement*, 164-65.
44. Stille, Alexander, "Prospecting for Truth in the Ore of Memory," *The New York Times*, 10 March 2001.
45. Durkheim, *Elementary Forms*, 212.
46. Paul M., letter, *AA Grapevine: Our Meeting In Print*, May 2000, 40.
47. Room, *AA as a Social Movement*, 169-170.
48. Ibid., 185.
49. Ibid., 186.
50. Armstrong, *A History of God*, 378.
51. Ibid., xxi.
52. Nouwen, *Ministry and Spirituality*, 165-66.
53. Wuthnow, "How Small Groups are Transforming Our Lives," 21-24.
54. Wuthnow, "Church Realities and Christian Identity," 523.
55. Gorsuch, *Spiritual Variables*, 313.
56. Kazin, *God and The American Writer*, 172.
57. Wuthnow, "How Small Groups are Transforming Our Lives," 21-24.
58. Ibid.
59. Kazin, *God and The American Writer*, 255
60. "Elpenor," "A Drunkard's Progress: AA and the Sobering Strength of Myth," 48.
61. Pareles, Jon, "Many Tongues Extol God in One Voice," *The New York Times*, 4 June 1998.
62. Durkheim, *Elementary Forms*, 432.
63. Carter, *The Culture of Disbelief*, 24 & 26.
64. "Strawberry's Return," *New York Daily News*, 2 September 1999.
65. Room, *AA as a Social Movement*, 186.
66. Wilson, *Apologies to the Iroquois*, 344.
67. Janice. Interviews by author. Rochester, N.Y., 14 November 1997 and by telephone, 10 September 1998.

CHAPTER X

1. "Bush Focuses on Faith Solutions for Alcoholism," *JointTogether Online*, 2 February 2001. Available at http://www.jointogether.org/
2. Wright, Robert, "Alcohol and Free Will," *The New Republic*, 14 December 1987.
3. Lynch, Dan, *Albany Times Union*, 30, July 1988, B-1.
4. Ashley and O'Rourke, *Health Care Ethics*, 385-86.
5. Sonnenstuhl, William. Telephone interview with author. 3 February 1998.
6. White, *Slaying the Dragon*, 41.

7. SAMHSA, *Changing the Conversation*, 17.
8. Peele, "A Moral Vision of Addiction," 187.
9. Peele, "A Moral Vision of Addiction," 215.
10. Lantz, "Socioeconomic Factors," 1705.
11. Bailey, *The Serenity Principle*, 1.
12. Ibid., 124.
13. Stambul & Polich. "Some Implications of the Rand Study," 5.
14. McDonough, "Using and Misusing Anecdote in Policy Making," 210.
15. Ostrow, Ronald J., "Drugs, Alcohol Linked to 80% of Those Behind Bars," *Los Angeles Times*, 9 January 1998.
16. Furillo, Andy, "California Focuses on Treatment, not Drug War," *Sacramento Bee / Scripps Howard News Service*, 8 November 2000.
17. "New York to Offer Treatment to All Non-Violent Offenders," *JointTogether Online*, 27 July 2000. Available at http://www.jointogether.org/
18. "Study Shows Drug Courts Reduce Substance Abuse, Crime," *JointTogether Online*, 11 November 1998. Available at http://www.jointogether.org/
19. "Many Drug Courts Facing Critical Time for Funding," *Manisses Newswire*, 6 March 2001. Available at www.manisses.com/2online/newswire/newswr. html
20. Maruschak, Laura M., "DWI Offenders under Correctional Supervision," *U.S. Bureau of Justice Statistics Special Report*, June 1999.
21. Young, Nancy K., *Alcohol and Other Drug Treatments*, 6.
22. Bower, Bruce. "Alcoholics Synonymous: Heavy Drinkers of All Stripes May Get Comparable Help From a Variety of Therapies." *Science News*, 25 January 1997.
23. Mäkelä, *AA as a Mutual Help Movement*, 185-206.
24. Townsend, Kathleen Kennedy, Lt. Gov. of Maryland, letter to editor, *The Washington Post*, 18 February 1997.
25. Miller and Flaherty, "Effectiveness of Coerced Addiction Treatment," 14.
26. Hubbard, *Evaluation*, 503.
27. Starobin, Paul, "The Daddy State," National Journal, 28 March 1998.
28. "Charitable Choice," *Join Together Online*, 23 May 2000.
29. "Bush Establishes Office for Faith-Based Programs," *Joint Together Online*, 30 January 2001. Available at http://www.jointogether.org/
30. Brown, Jennifer, "Churches Could Get Big Benefits from Federal Support," *Associated Press*, 15 February 2001 International news.
31. Lattin, Don, "Community Services Abound in Churches Study Shows Possibilities of 'Faith-based' Charity," *San Francisco Chronicle*, 14 March 2001.
32. Thomas, Cal, "Smart Compassion for the Homeless," *Albany, Times Union*, 26 December 1997.
33. Cole, David, "Faith Succeeds Where Prison Fails," *The New York Times*, 31 January 2001.
34. Anderson, Brian C. "How Catholic Charities Lost Its Soul," 28 & 38.
35. Milbank, Dana and Thomas B. Edsall, "Faith Initiative May Be Revised, Criticism Surprises Administration," *Washington Post*, 12 March 2001.
36. Rosin, Hanna and Thomas B. Edsall, "Survey Exposes 'Faith-Based' Plan Hurdles," *Washington Post*, 11 April 2001.
37. Hall, remarks at conference sponsored by Trinity College, Greenberg Center

for the Study of Religion in Public Life. Hartford, Conn., 5 February 2001.

38. Morgan, Edward, "God's Place at a Rescue Mission," *The New York Times*, 25 December 1997.

39. Spencer, Gary, "Prison Condition a Religious Violation," *New York Law Journal*, 12 June 1996.

40. Clark. Telephone interview with author. 11 December 2000.

41. Ibid.

42. Reiter, Jendi B., "Mandatory Rehabilitation for Probationers Raises First Amendment Concerns," *New York Law Journal*. 12 January 1998.

43. Clements, "One Church-One Addict," (brochure) Washington, D.C. Available at www.mwbdesign.com/ocoa

44. Brown, Jennifer, "Churches Could Get Big Benefits from Federal Support," *AP*, 15 February 2001.

45. McQueen, Anjetta, "Critics Mounting Challenges to Funds for Religious Groups," *Associated Press*, 3 November 2000.

46. Skillen, James W., "Ashes to Ashcroft," *The Wall Street Journal*, 19 January 2001.

47. Fox, "Changing Violent Minds," 88.

48. Delbanco and Delbanco, "AA at the Crossroads," 51.

49. Ward, telephone interview with author, 1998.

50. Greenfield, Russell. Interview with author. Tucson, Ariz., 11 February 1998.

51. Wolfensberger, *Social Role Valorization*.

52. Miller and C'de Baca, *Quantum Change*.

53. Bufe, *Alcoholics Anonymous: Cult or Cure*, 109.

54. Fingarette, *Heavy Drinking*, 28.

55. Goldhammer, *Under the Influence*, 177.

56. Bailey, *Serenity Principle*, 118-119.

57. Ibid., 73.

58. Humphreys, Moos, and Cohen, "Long-Term Recovery," 237.

59. R.S., "The Spirit of Attraction," *AA Grapevine*, August 2000, 51.

60. *Manissses Newswire*, 27 March 2001. Available at www.manisses.com/2online/newswire/newswr.html

61. "Recovery Movement Needs to Keep Distance from Treatment Field," *Joint Together Online—Direct*, 16 November 2000. Available at http://www.jointogether.org/

62. Sparks, Tav, "Transpersonal Treatment of Addictions," 50.

63. Lapp, Katherine N., "Another Look at the Debate Over Criminal Justice," *Albany Times Union*, 29 July 1998.

64. See Beito, *From Mutual Aid to the Welfare State*.

65. Marty, Martin E., "The Return of the Sociology of Religion," in *Sightings* newsletter, 15 March 2000.

66. McClay, "Two Concepts of Secularism," 71.

67. Wuthnow, *Christianity and Civil Society*, 67.

68. Ibid., 93.

69. Ibid., 35-36, 62.

70. Gilpin, W. Clark, "Possibilities for Public Theology," *Sightings* newsletter, 8 June 2000.

71. James, *Varieties*, 507.

72. Mathew, Roy, "Spiritual Pleasures Can Replace Drug Addiction," *Duke University* press release, 19 October 1998.
73. Miller, *Spirituality: The Silent Dimension*, 261.
74. Benjamin, Elizabeth, "Inmates Extended Religious Amenities," *Albany Times Union*, 27 June 1998.
75. Olasky, Marvin, "A Brand New Game," *Washington Post Outlook*, 17 December 2000.
76. Kurtz, *Not-God*, 41.

BIBLIOGRAPHY

ABBREVIATIONS

AA Alcoholics Anonymous
AAGSO AA General Service Office
AAWS AA World Services Inc.
AHCPR Agency for Health Care Policy and Research
CSAT Center for Substance Abuse Treatment
IHS Indian Health Service
JSA Journal of Studies in Alcoholism
JSAT Journal of Substance Abuse Studies
OAS Office of Applied Studies at SAMSHA
OASAS Office of Alcoholism and Substance Abuse Services, New York State
NHSDA National Household Survey on Drug Abuse
NIAAA National Institute on Alcoholism and Alcohol Abuse
SAMHSA Substance Abuse and Mental Health Services Administration
TEDS Treatment Episode Date Set

AA. *Alcoholics Anonymous.* (1939) New York: AAWS, 1976.
AA. *Twelve Steps and Twelve Traditions.* (1952) New York: AAWS, 1981.
AA. *Came to Believe: The Spiritual Adventure of AA as Experienced by Individual Members.* New York: AAWS, 1973.
AA. "Alcoholics Anonymous 1992 Membership Survey." New York: AAWS, 1993.
AA. "Alcoholics Anonymous 1996 Membership Survey." New York: AAWS, 1997.
AA. "AA At A Glance." New York: AAGSO, May 1997.
AHCPR. *Survey of American Indians and Alaska Natives.* Washington, D.C.: AHCPR, 1987.
AHCPR. "Pharmacotherapy for Alcohol Dependence." Summary, Evidence Report/Technology Assessment: Number 3. AHCPR, Rockville, Md. January 1999. Available at http://www/ahcpr.gov/clinical/alcosumm.htm
American Psychiatric Association. *Diagnostic and Statistical Manual of Mental Disorders* 4th ed. Washington, D.C.: The Association, 1994.
Anderson, Brian C. "How Catholic Charities Lost Its Soul." *City Journal* Winter 2000: 28-39.
Annis, Helen M., Sherril M. Sklar, and Andrea E. Moser. "Gender in Relation to Relapse Crisis Situations, Coping and Outcome Among Treated Alcoholics." *Addictive Behaviors* 23: 1(1998): 127-131.

Armor, D. J., Harriet B. Stambul, and J. Michael Polich. *Alcoholism and Treatment*. Santa Monica, Calif.: Rand Corp., June 1976.

Armstrong, Karen. *A History of God: The 4,000-Year Quest of Judaism, Christianity and Islam*. New York: Ballantine, 1993.

Ashley, Benedict M. and Kevin D. O'Rourke. *Health Care Ethics: A Theological Analysis*. 4th ed. Washington, D.C.: Georgetown University Press, 1997.

Bailey, Joseph V. *The Serenity Principle: Finding Inner Peace in Recovery*. San Francisco: HarperCollins, 1990.

Beazley, Hamilton. "Integration of AA and Clinical Practice." Talk delivered at *Treating the Addictions* conference. Boston: Cambridge Hospital, 7 March 1998.

Beck, Peggy V., Anna. L. Walters, and Nia Francisco. *The Sacred: Ways of Knowledge, Sources of Life*. Tasaile, Arizona: Navajo Community College Press, 1992.

Beito, David T. *From Mutual Aid to the Welfare State: Fraternal Societies and SocialServices, 1890-1967*. Chapel Hill, N.C.: University of North Carolina Press, 2000.

Bloom, Harold. *The American Religion: The Emergence of the Post-Christian Nation*. New York: Simon & Schuster, 1992.

Booth, Leo. "A New Understanding of Spirituality." In *Spirituality and Chemical Dependency*, ed. Robert J. Kus, 5-17. Binghamton, N.Y.: Harrington Park Press, 1995.

Bratter, Thomas E., "Uses and Abuses of Power and Authority Within The American Self-Help Residential Therapeutic Community: A Perversion or a Necessity?" In *Therapeutic Communities for Addictions*, ed. George De Leon and James T. Ziegenfuss Jr. Springfield, Ill.: Thomas, 1986.

Brown, Harold P. and J. H. Peterson Jr. "Values and Recovery from Alcoholism through AA." *Counseling and Values* 35 (June 1990): 63-68.

Bufe, Charles. *Alcoholics Anonymous: Cult or Cure?* Tucson: See Sharp Press, 1998.

Bullitt-Jonas, Margaret. *Holy Hunger: A Memoir of Desire*. New York: Knopf, 1998.

Carroll, Jerome E. "Uncovering Drug Abuse by Alcoholics and Alcohol Abuse by Drug Addicts." *International Journal of Addiction* 15: (1980): 195-595.

Casriel, Daniel. *So Fair A House: The Story of Synanon*. Englewood Cliffs, N.J.: PrenticeHall, 1963.

Christo, George and Christine Franey. "Drug Users' Spiritual Beliefs, Locus of Control and the Disease Concept in Relation to Narcotics Anonymous Attendance and Six Month Outcomes." *Drug and Alcohol Dependence* 38(June 1995): 51-56.

Connors, Gerard J. and Kurt H. Dermen. "Characteristics of Participants in SOS." *The American Journal of Drug and Alcohol Abuse* 22:2(May 1996): 281-295.

Connors, Gerard J., Stephen A. Maisto, and William H. Zywiak. "Male and Female Alcoholics' Attributions Regarding the Onset and Termination of Relapses and the Maintenance of Abstinence." *Journal of Substance Abuse* 10:30(1998): 27-42.

CSAT. *The National Treatment Improvement Evaluation Study*. 1997 Highlights. Available at www.sama.gov/centers/csat/csat.html

Dahlgren, Lena and Anders Willander. "Are Special Treatment Facilities for FemaleAlcoholics Needed? A Controlled 2-year Follow-up Study From a SpecializedFemale Unit (EWA) versus a Mixed Male/Female Treatment Facility." *Alcoholism: Clinical and Experimental Research*. 13:4(August 1989): 499-531.

Dawson, Deborah A. "Correlates of Past-Year Status Among Treated and Untreated Persons with Former Alcohol Dependence: United States, 1992." *Alcoholism: Clinical and Experimental Research* 20/4 (June 1996): 771-779.

Delbanco, Andrew and Thomas Delbanco. "Annals of Addiction: AA at the Crossroads." *The New Yorker* 50-63. 20 March 1995.

De Leon, George. "Therapeutic Communities." In *The American Psychiatric Press Textbook of Substance Abuse Treatment*, ed. Marc Galanter and Herbert D. Kleber, 391-414. Washington, D.C.: American Psychiatric Press, 1994.

———. "The Therapeutic Community for Substance Abuse." In *The American Drug Scene: An Anthology*, ed. James Inciardi and Karen McElrath. Los Angeles: Roxbury, 1995: 301-308.

De Tocqueville, Alexis. *Democracy in America, Vol. I & II*. New York: Knopf, 1994.

Dunn, Richard. *What We Know About Relapse: An Analysis*. New York: DaytopVillage, 1991.

———*Spirituality, Alcoholism and Drug Addiction*. Milford, Penn.: Promethean Institute,1992.

Durkheim, Emile. *The Elementary Forms of Religious Life*. (1912). trans. and intro. Karen E. Fields. New York: Free Press, 1995.

Eliade, Mircea. *Patterns in Comparative Religion*. trans. Rosemary Sheed. (1958)Reprint, New York: Meridian, 1974.

Ellis, Albert. "Can Rational Emotive Behavior Therapy (REBT) Be Effectively Used with People Who have Devout Beliefs in God and Religion?" *Professional Psychology: Research and Practice* 31 No.1 (2000): 29-33.

Elpenor. "A Drunkard's Progress: AA and the Sobering Strength of Myth." *Harper's Magazine*, October 1986. 42-47.

Emrick, Chad D., J. Scott Tonigan, Henry Montgomery, and Laura Little. "AlcoholicsAnonymous: What is Currently Known." In *Research on Alcoholics Anonymous; Opportunities and Alternatives*, ed. Barbara S. McCrady and William R. Miller, 41-76. New Brunswick, N.J.: Rutgers Center of Alcohol Studies, 1993.

Fenton, William N. *The Great Law and the Longhouse: A Political History of the Iroquois Confederacy*. Norman, Okla.: University of Oklahoma Press, 1998.

Fingarette, Herbert. *Heavy Drinking: The Myth of Alcoholism as a Disease*. Berkeley: University of California, 1988.

Fowler, James W. "Alcoholics Anonymous and Faith Development." In *Research on Alcoholics Anonymous: Opportunities and Alternatives*, ed. Barbara S. McCrady and William R. Miller, 113-135. New Brunswick, NJ: Rutgers Center of Alcohol Studies, 1993.

Fox, Kathryn J. "Changing Violent Minds: Discursive Correction and Resistance in theCognitive Treatment of Violent Offenders in Prison." *Social Problems* 46:1(1999): 88-104.

Frank, Jerome D. and Julia Frank. *Persuasion and Healing: A Comparative Study of Psychotherapy*. Baltimore: Johns Hopkins, 1993.

Frank, John W., R. S. Moore and G. M. Ames. "Historical and Cultural Roots of Drinking Problems among American Indians." *American Journal of Public Health* 90 (June 2000): 344-351.

Frankl, Victor E. *Man's Search For Meaning: An Introduction to Logotherapy*. New York: Simon & Schuster, 1984.

Galanter, Marc, Susan Egelko, and Helen Edwards. "Rational Recovery: Alternatives to AA for Addiction?" *American Journal of Drug and Alcohol Abuse* 19: 4 (December 1999) 499-507.

Garrett, C. J. "Recovery from Anorexia Nervosa: A Durkheimian Interpretation." *Social Sciences and Medicine* 43:10 (November 1996): 1489-1506.

George, R. L. *Counseling the Chemically Dependent: Theory and Practice*. Boston:Allyn & Bacon, 1990.

General Accounting Office. *Drug-Exposed Infants: A Generation at Risk*. Washington, D.C.: GAO, 1990.

Goldhammer, John D. *Under the Influence: The Destructive Effects of Group Dynamics*. Amherst, N.Y.: Prometheus Books, 1996.

Gorsuch, Richard L. "Assessing Spiritual Variables in Alcoholics Anonymous Research." In *Research on Alcoholics Anonymous*. ed. McCrady, Barbara S., and William R. Miller, 301-318. New Brunswick, N.J.: Rutgers Center of Alcohol Studies, 1993.

Griffin, Margaret L., R. D. Weiss, and S. M. Mirin. "A Comparison of Male and Female Cocaine Abusers," *Archives of General Psychiatry* 46(1989): 122-126.

Guillory J. A., R. Sowell, L. Moneyham, and B. Seals. "An Exploration of the Meaning and Use of Spirituality Among Women With HIV/AIDS." *Alternative Therapy in Health Medicine* 5 (3 September 1997): 55-60.

Hawkins, Nancy, Sharon Day, and Mary Suagee. *American Indian Women's Chemical Health Project*. Department of Human Services, Chemical Dependency Division, American Indian Section. St. Paul, Minn.: State of Minnesota, June 1993.

Heather, Nick. "Application of Harm-Reduction Principles to the Treatment of Alcohol Problems." In *Psychoactive Drugs and Harm Reduction: From Faith to Science*, ed. Nick Heather, Alex Wodak, Ethan A. Nadelmann, and Pat O'Hare, 168-183. London: Whurr Publishers, 1993.

Hess, Catherine B. "A Seven-year Follow-up Study of 186 Males in a Religious-Therapeutic Community." In *Critical Concerns in the Field of Drug Abuse*," ed. Schechter, Alksne and Kaufman, 289-295. New York: Marcel Dekker, 1977.

Hester, Reid K. "Behavioral Self-Control Training. In *Handbook of Alcoholism Treatment Approaches, Second Edition*, ed. Reid K. Hester and William R. Miller, 148-159. Boston: Allyn & Bacon, 1995.

Hester, Reid K. and William R. Miller, eds. *Handbook of Alcoholism Treatment Approaches, Second Edition*. Boston: Allyn & Bacon, 1995.

Hinshelwood, Robert D., "Britain and the Psychoanalytic Tradition in TCs." In *Therapeutic Communities for Addiction: Readings in Theory, Research, and Practice*, ed. George and J. T. Ziegenfuss, 43-54. Springfield, Ill.: Charles C. Thomas, 1986.

Hubbard, Robert L., "Evaluation and Treatment of Outcome." In *Substance Abuse: A Comprehensive Textbook, Third Edition*. Ed. Lowinson, Joyce H., Pedro Ruiz, Robert Milliman, and John G. Longrod. Baltimore: Williams & Wilkins, 1997, 499-511.

Hubbard, Robert L., Mary Ellen Marsden, et al. *Drug Abuse Treatment: A National Study of Effectiveness*. Chapel Hill: Univ. of North Carolina Press, 1989.

Humphreys, Keith and Rudolf H. Moos. "Reduced Substance Abuse Related Health Care Costs among Voluntary Participants in AA." *Psychiatric Services* 47(1996): 709-713.

Humphreys, Keith, Rudulf H. Moos, and Caryn Cohen. "Social and Community Resources and Long-Term Recovery from Treated and Untreated Alcoholism." *Journal of Studies on Alcoholism* 58 (May 1997): 231-238.

Imani, Zaid. *Millati Islami (The Path of Peace): Islamic Treatment for Addiction.* (1992) Baltimore, Md.: Millati Islami Program, 1997.

James, William. *The Varieties of Religious Experience.* New York: Random House, 1902.

Jung, Carl Gustav. *Psychology and Religion.* New Haven: Yale, 1938.

Kaskutas, Lee A. "Beliefs on the Source of Sobriety: Interactions of Membership in Women for Sobriety and Alcoholics Anonymous." *Contemporary Drug Problems* 19: 4 (April 1992): 631-648.

Kaskutas. "Pathways to Self-help Among Women For Sobriety." *American Journal of Drug and Alcohol Abuse* 22: 2 (May 1996): 265-78.

Kaskutas. "What do women get out of self-help? Their reasons for attending Women for Sobriety and Alcoholics Anonymous." *JSAT* 11:3(March 1994): 185-195.

Kaskutas. "The Role of Religion, Spirituality, and AA Involvement in Sustained Sobriety." *In Conference Summary: Studying Spirituality and Alcohol* 27. Sponsored by NIAAA and the Fetzer Institute. Bethesda, Md.: NIAAA, February 1999.

Kauffman, Jo Ann, Emory Johnson, and Joe Jacobs. "Overview: Current and Evolving Realities of Health Care to Reservations and Urban American Indians." In *A Forum on the Implications of Changes in the Health Care Environment for Native American Health Care.* Menlo Park, Calif.: Kaiser Family Foundation, 1997.

Kazin, Alfred. *God and the American Writer.* New York: Knopf, 1997.

Kearney, Margaret. "Drug Treatment for Women: Traditional Models and New Directions." *Journal of Obstetric, Gynecological and Neonatal Nursing,* 26:4(July/August 1997) 459-468.

Kendler, Kenneth S., Charles O. Gardner, and Carol A. Prescott. "Religion, Psychopathology, and Substance Use and Abuse: A Multimeasure, Genetic-epidemiologic study." *American Journal of Psychiatry* 154 (1 March 1997): 322-329.

Kirkpatrick, Jean. "A Self-Help Program for Women Alcoholics." *Alcohol Health and Research World* Summer 1982.

Kramer, Susan R. " 'We Speak to God With Our Thoughts': Abelard and the Implications of Private Communications with God.' " *Church History* 69:1 (March 2000): 18-41.

Kunz, Virginia Brainard. *Where the Doors Never Close: The Story of St. Paul's Union Gospel Mission.* St. Paul, Minn.: Union Gospel Mission, 1993.

Kurtz, Ernest. *Not-God: A History of Alcoholics Anonymous.* Center City, Minn: Hazelden, 1979.

Kurtz, Ernest and Katherine Ketcham. *The Spirituality of Imperfection: Storytelling and the Journey to Wholeness.* New York: Bantam, 1992.

Landauer, Gustav. *Briefen.* Ed. Martin Buber. 2 vols. Frankfurt: Verlag Rutten & Loening, 1929. In Dennis Sullivan and Larry Tift. *Transformative Justice as a*

Transformative Process: The Application of Restorative Justice Principles to Our Everyday Lives. Voorheesville, N.Y.: Mutual Aid Press, 2000.

Landry, Mim J. *Overview of Addictions Treatment-Effectiveness*. Rockville, Md.: SAMSHA, 1997.

Lantz, Paula M., James S. House, James M. Lepkowski, David R. Williams, Richard P. Mero, and Jieming Chen. "Socioeconomic Factors, Health Behaviors, and Mortality: Results from a Nationally Representative Prospective Study of U.S. adults." *JAMA* 279, no. 21(3 June 1998): 1703-8.

Leshner, Alan I. "Addiction Is a Brain Disease—and It Matters." *National Institute of Justice Journal*. October 1998, 2-6.

Lindner, Eileen W., ed. *Yearbook of American & Canadian Churches 2000*. Nashville, Tenn., 2000.

Lowinson, Joyce H., Pedro Ruiz, Robert Milliman, and John Longrod, eds. *Substance Abuse: A Comprehensive Textbook, Second Edition*. Baltimore: Williams & Wilkins, 1992.

Lowinson, Joyce H., Pedro Ruiz, Robert Milliman, and John G. Longrod, eds. *Substance Abuse: A Comprehensive Textbook, Third Edition*. Baltimore: Williams & Wilkins, 1997.

Mäkelä, Klaus, et al. *Alcoholics Anonymous as a Mutual-Help Movement: A Study in Eight Societies*. Madison, Wis.: University of Wisconsin Press, 1996.

Mäkelä, Klaus. "Implications for Research of the Cultural Variability of Alcoholics Anonymous." In *Research on Alcoholics Anonymous: Opportunities and Alternatives*, ed. McCrady, Barbara S., and William R. Miller, 189-208. New Brunswick, N.J.: Rutgers Center of Alcohol Studies, 1993.

Marlatt, G. Alan and Judith B. Gordon. *Relapse Prevention*. New York: Guilford Press, 1985.

Marlatt, G. Alan, B. Deming, and J. B. Reid. "Loss of Control Drinking in Alcoholics: An Experimental Analogue." *Journal of Abnormal Psychology* 81(1973): 233-241.

Mathew, Roy J., Jeffrey Georgi, William H. Wilson, and V. George Mathew. "A Retrospective Study of the Concept of Spirituality as Understood by Recovering Individuals," *JSAT* 13 (1996), 67-73.

May, Philip A. "The Epidemiology of Alcohol Abuse Among American Indians." *American Indian Culture and Research Journal*, 18:2 (February 1998), 121-143.

McClay, Wilfred M. "Two Concepts of Secularism." *The Wilson Quarterly* 25 (Summer 2000): 54-71.

McClellan, Thomas A., Grant R. Grissom, Peter Brill, Jack Durell, David S. Metzger, and Charles P. O'Brien. "Private Substance Abuse Treatments." *Journal of Substance Abuse Treatment*, 10 (1993), 243-254.

McClellan, Thomas A., David C. Lewis, Charles P. O'Brien, and Herbert D. Kleber. "Drug Dependence, a Chronic Medical Illness: Implications for Treatment, Insurance, and Outcomes Evaluation." *Journal of the American Medical Association*, 284 (4 October 2000): 1689-1695. Earlier version released as: "Compliance and Relapse in Selected Medical Disorders." Physician Leadership on National Drug Policy press release, 3 April 1998.

McCrady, Barbara S. and William R. Miller, eds. *Research on Alcoholics Anonymous; Opportunities and Alternatives*. New Brunswick, N.J.: Rutgers Center of Alcohol Studies, 1993.

McDonough, John E. "Using and Misusing Anecdote in Policy Making." *Health Affairs* 20 No. 1(January/February 2001): 207-212.

McFague, Sally. *Models of God: Theology for an Ecological, Nuclear Age.* Philadelphia: Fortress Press, 1987.

McGowan, Richard. "Finding God in All Things: Ministering to Those With Addictions." (cassette recording) Talk delivered at *Treating the Addictions* conference. Boston: Cambridge Hospital, 7 March 1998.

McIntire, Don. "How Well Does AA Work? An Analyses of Published AA Surveys (1968-1996) and Related Analyses/Comments." *Alcoholism Treatment Quarterly* 18(4), 2000: 1-18.

Miller, Norman S. and Joseph A. Flaherty. "Effectiveness of Coerced Addiction Treatment (Alternative Consequences): A Review of the Literature." *JSAT* 18(2000): 9-16.

Miller, William. R. "Spirituality: The silent dimension in addiction research. The 1990 Leonard Ball oration." *Drug & Alcohol Review,* 9(1990): 259-266.

Miller, William R. "Increasing Motivation for Change," In *Handbook of Alcoholism Treatment Approaches, Second Edition.* ed. Reid K. Hester and William R. Miller. Boston: Allyn & Bacon, 1995.

Miller, William R. "Addictions: Alcohol/Drug Problems." In *Scientific Research on Spirituality and Health: A Consensus Report,* ed. David B. Larson, James P. Swyers, and Michael E. McCullough, 68-82. Rockville, Md.: National Institute for Healthcare Research, 1997.

Miller, William R. "Researching the Spiritual Dimensions of Alcohol and Other Drug Problems," *Addiction* 93(July 1998): 979-990.

Miller, William R. and Melanie E. Bennett. "Toward better research on spirituality and health: The Templeton panels." *Spiritual and Religious Issues in Behavior Change* 10(1997): 3-4.

Miller, William R., and Janet C'de Baca. "Quantum Change: Toward a Psychology of Personality Change." In *Can Personality Change?* ed. T. Heatherton and J. Weinberger, 253-280. Washington, D.C.: American Psychology Association, 1994.

Miller, William R., and Ernest Kurtz. "Models of Alcoholism Used in Treatment: Contrasting AA and Other Perspectives with Which It Is Often Confused." *JAS* 55(March 1994): 159-166.

Monti, Peter M., Damaris J. Rohsenow, Suxanne M. Colby, and David B. Abrams. "Coping and Social Skills Training." In *Handbook of Alcoholism Treatment Approaches, Second Edition,* ed. Reid K. Hester and William R. Miller, 221-241. Boston: Allyn & Bacon, 1995.

Montour, Ted. "Handsome Lake," In *Encyclopedia of North American Indians,* ed. Frederick E. Hoxie, 230-231. New York: Houghton Mifflin, 1996.

Moyers, Bill. "Moyers on Addiction: Close to Home." Public Broadcasting System, March 1998. (Interview transcripts available at www.pbs.org/wnet/closetohome/science/html/)

Muffler, John, John Langrod, and David Larson. "There is a Balm in Gilead: Religion and Substance Abuse Treatment." In *Substance Abuse: A Comprehensive Textbook,* ed. Joyce H. Lowinson, Pedro Ruiz, Robert B. Millman, and John G. Langrod. 440-461. Baltimore: Williams and Wilkins, 1992.

Nace, Edgar P. "Alcoholics Anonymous." In *Substance Abuse: A Comprehensive*

Textbook, Third Edition, ed. Lowinson, Joyce H., Pedro Ruiz, Robert Milliman, and John Longrod, 383-390. Baltimore: Williams & Wilkins, 1997.

Nadelman, Ethan, Jennifer McNeely, and Ernest Drucker. "International Perspectives." In *Substance Abuse: A Comprehensive Textbook Third Edition*, ed. Joyce H. Lowinson, Pedro Ruiz, Robert Milliman, and John Longrod, 22-39. Baltimore: Williams & Wilkins, 1997.

Neuner, Richard P. and David J. Schultz. "Borrow Me A Quarter: A Feasibility Study of Prepaid Case Management for Chronic Recidivist Alcoholics." Anoka, Minn.: Minnesota Institute of Public Health, 1985.

NIAAA and the Fetzer Institute, *Conference Summary: Studying Spirituality and Alcohol*. Bethesda, Md.: NIAAA, February 1999.

NIDA. "Principles of Drug Addiction Treatment." NIH Publication 99-4180. October 1999.

Nouwen, Henri J. M. *Ministry and Spirituality*. New York: Continuum, 1996.

Oakley, Deirdre and Deborah L. Dennis. "Responding to the Needs of Homeless People with Alcohol, Drug, and/or Mental Disorders." In *Homelessness in America*, ed. James Baumohl, 179-186. Phoenix, Ariz.: Oryx Press, 1996.

OASAS Bureau of Treatment Policy & Resource Development, "OASAS-Funded and Certified Discrete Treatment Programs for Women and Children, Women, and Youth," Albany, N.Y.: OASAS, August 1996.

O'Brien, William B. and D. Vincent Biase. "Therapeutic Communities: Coming of Age" In *Substance Abuse: A Comprehensive Textbook*, ed. Joyce H. Lowinson, Pedro Ruiz, Robert B. Millman, and John G. Langrod, 440-461. Baltimore: Williams and Wilkins, 1992.

Office of Applied Studies, SAMHSA, *National Admissions to Substance Abuse Treatment Services: The Treatment Episode Date Set 1992-1996*. Washington, D.C.: U.S. GPO, 1998.

Office of Juvenile Justice and Delinquency Programs. "Making A Difference For Juveniles" report. Washington, D.C.: U.S. Department of Justice, August 1999.

Peele, Stanton. "A Moral Vision of Addiction: How People's Values Determine Whether They Become and Remain Addicts." *Journal of Drug Issues* 17(2)(1987): 187-215.

Peele, Stanton. *The Diseasing of America: How We Allowed Recovery Zealots and the Treatment Industry to Convince Us We Are Out of Control*. San Francisco: Jossey-Bass, 1995.

Perrin, Edward B. and Jeffrey J. Koshel, eds. *Assessment of Performance Measures for Public Health, Substance Abuse and Mental Health*. Washington, D.C.: National Academy Press, 1997.

Project MATCH Research Group. "Matching Alcoholism Treatments to Client Heterogeneity: Project Match Posttreatment Drinking Outcomes." *JSA*. January 1997: 7-29.

Ruether, Rosemary Radford. *Gaia & God: An Ecofeminist Theology of Earth Healing*. New York: Harper Collins, 1992.

Room, Robin. "AA as a Social Movement." In *Research on Alcoholics Anonymous: Opportunities and Alternatives*, ed. McCrady, Barbara S. and William R. Miller, 167-187. New Brunswick, N.J.: Rutgers Center of Alcohol Studies, 1993.

Rouse, Beatrice A., ed. *Substance Abuse and Mental Health Statistics Sourcebook*,

SAMSHA, DHHS. (Washington, D.C.—U.S. Government Printing Office, 1995).

Roman, Paul and Terry Blum. *National Treatment Center Study Six and 12 Month Followup Summary Report.* Athens, Ga.: Institute for Behavioral Research, 1997.

Royce, James. "The Effects of Alcoholism and Recovery on Spirituality." In *Spirituality and Chemical Dependency,* ed. Robert J. Kus, 19-37. Binghamton, N.Y.: Harrington Park Press, 1995.

Rubin, A., R. L. Stout and R. Longabaugh. "Gender Differences in Relapse Situations." *Addiction* December 1996 Supplement: 111-120.

Ruden, Ronald A. with Marcia Baylick. *The Craving Brain: The Biobalance Approach to Controlling Addiction.* New York: Harper Collins, 1997.

Rudolf, J. S. "Jean Kirkpatrick: Founder of WFS Talks about Self-Help Program Basedon '13 Statements.' " *Sober Times.* October 1990.

Sapir, Edward. 1949. *Culture, Language and Personality: Selected Essays,* ed. David G. Mandelbaum, Berkeley: University of California Press, 1949.

SAMHSA. "Preliminary Estimates from the 1993 National Household Survey on Drug Abuse." 1995.

SAMHSA. "National Treatment Improvement Evaluation Study: Preliminary Report." September 1996.

SAMHSA. Treatment Episode Data Set 1993-98: National Admissions to Substance Abuse Treatment. September 2000.

SAMHSA. "1998 National Household Survey on Drug Abuse." 1990.

SAMHSA. "1999 National Household Survey on Drug Abuse." August 2000.

SAMHSA. "Changing the Conversation: Improving Substance Abuse Treatment: The National Treatment Plan Initiative." November 2000.

Samuels, David. "Annals of Addiction: Saying Yes to Drugs." *The New Yorker.* 23 March 1998: 49-62.

Sando, Joe S. *Pueblo Nations: Eight Centuries of Pueblo Indian History.* Santa Fe, N.M.: Clear Light Publishers, 1992.

Satel, Sally L. "The Fallacies of No-Fault Addiction." *The Public Interest* (Winter 1999): 52-67.

Schmidt, Laura and Constance Weisner. "The Emergence of Problem Drinking Women As a Special Population in Need of Treatment," In *Women and Alcoholism,* ed. Marc Galanter. Recent Developments in Alcoholism Series, vol. 12. New York: Plenum Press, 1995.

Secular Organizations for Sobriety. *Sobriety Handbook: The SOS Way: An Introduction to Secular Organizations for Sobriety.* Oakland, Calif.: LifeRing Press, 1997.

Sharkey, Joe. *Bedlam: Greed, Profiteering, and Fraud in a Mental Health System Gone Crazy.* New York: St. Martin's Press, 1994.

Singer, Jefferson A. *Message in a Bottle.* New York: Free Press, 1997.

Single, Eric. "Harm Reduction as an Alcohol-Prevention Strategy." *Alcohol Health & Research World.* 20(4)1996: 239-243.

Sparks, Tav. "Transpersonal Treatment of Addictions: Radical Return to Roots." *ReVISION* 10, no. 2(Fall 1987): 49-64.

Stambul, Harriet B. and J. Michael Polich. "Some Implications of the Rand *Alcoholism and Treatment* Study for Alcoholism Research." Presentation at the 85th

Annual Meeting of the American Psychological Association. San Francisco, August 1977.

Steigerwald, Fran and David Stone. "Cognitive Restructuring and the 12-Step Program of Alcoholics Anonymous." *Journal of Substance Abuse Treatment* 16(June 1999): 321-329.

Sternberg, Steve. "Summary of Proceedings." *A Forum on the Implications of Changes in The Health Care Environment for Native American Health Care.* Menlo Park, Calif.: Henry J. Kaiser Family Foundation, 1997.

Stryker, Jeff. *Dimensions of HIV Prevention: Needle Exchange.* Menlo Park, Calif.: The Henry J. Kaiser Family Foundation, 1993.

Stinchfield, Randy and Patricia Owen. "Hazelden's Twelve-Step Model and its Outcomes." Pre-publication copy. 1997.

Tafoya, Terry and Kevin R. Roeder. "Spiritual Exiles in Their Own Homelands: Gays, Lesbians and Native Americans." In *Spirituality and Chemical Dependency*, ed. Robert J. Kus, 179-197. Binghamton, N.Y.: Harrington Park Press, 1995.

Tanner, Helen Hornbeck. "Ojibwa." In *Encyclopedia of North American Indians*, ed. Frederick E. Hoxie, 438-9. New York: Houghton Mifflin, 1996.

Tinker, George E. "Religion," In *Encyclopedia of North American Indians*, ed. Frederick E. Hoxie, 537-41. New York: Houghton Mifflin, 1996.

Tonigan, J. Scott, Radka Toscova, and William R. Miller. "Meta-Analysis of the Literature on Alcoholics Anonymous." *Journal of Studies on Alcoholism* 57: 1 (January 1996), 65-72.

Trimpey, Jack, David Trippel, and Lois Trimpey. "Rational Recovery Society Network," *The Journal of Rational Recovery.* March-April 1999.

Twerski, Abraham J. "Spirituality and Religion: Are They Identical?" In *The Spiritual Dimension of Mental Health and Substance Abuse* 1-11. Providence, R.I.: Manisses Communications Group, 1996.

Tymoczko, Dimitri. "The Nitrous Oxide Philosopher." *The Atlantic Monthly*, 277: 5 May 1996, 93-101.

Vernon, Irene S. "Religious Rights," *Encyclopedia of North American Indians*, ed. Frederick E. Hoxie, (New York: Houghton Mifflin, 1996), 541.

World Health Organization. *The ICD-10 Classification of Mental and Behavioral Disorders: Clinical Descriptions and Diagnostic Guidelines, Tenth Edition.* Geneva: World Health Organization, 1992.

White, Barbara J. and Edward J. Madara, *American Self-Help Clearinghouse Sourcebook Online*, January 2001.

White, William L. *Slaying the Dragon: The History of Addiction Treatment and Recovery in America.* Bloomington, Ill.: Chestnut Health Systems, 1998.

Whitehead, Alfred North. *Science and the modern world : Lowell lectures, 1925.* New York: Macmillan Co., 1957. Quoted in Alfred Kazin, *God and the American Writer.* New York: Knopf, 1997, 185.

Wilson, Edmund. *Apologies to the Iroquois.* Syracuse, N.Y.: Syracuse University Press, 1992.

Wilson, Frank W., "Spiritual Therapy in the Therapeutic Community." In *Proceedings of the 2nd World Conference of Therapeutic Communities.* ed. Peter Vamos and Janet E. Brown, 204-5. Montreal: Portage Press, 1979.

Wilson, William Julius., *When Work Disappears: The World of the New Urban Poor.* New York: Knopf, 1996.

Wolfensberger, Wolf. *A Brief Introduction to Social Role Valorization: A High Order Concept for Addressing the Plight of Societally Devalued People, and for Structuring Human Services*, 3rd ed. Syracuse, N.Y.: Training Institute for Human Service Planning, Leadership & Change Agentry, 1998.

Wuthnow, Robert. "Church Realities and Christian Identity in the 21st Century," *Christian Century*, 12, May 1993, 520-523.

Wuthrow. "How Small Groups are Transforming Our Lives." *Christianity Today* 38(7 February 1994): 20-24.

Wuthnow. *Christianity and Civil Society: The Contemporary Debate.* Rockwell Lecture Series. Valley Forge, Penn.: Trinity Press International, 1996.

Wyke, Alexandra. *21st Century Miracle Medicine: Robosurgery, Wonder Cures, and the Quest for Immortality.* New York: Plenum, 1997.

Young, Nancy K. *Alcohol and Other Drug Treatment: Policy Choices in Welfare Reform.* Rockville, Md.: SAMSHA, 1996.

INDEX